# GAME ENGINE DESIGN AND IMPLEMENTATION

# THE JONES & BARTLETT LEARNING
## FOUNDATIONS OF GAME DEVELOPMENT SERIES

*Fundamentals of Game Development*
Heather Maxwell Chandler and Rafael Chandler
(978-0-7637-7895-8) © 2011

*Game Engine Design and Implementation*
Alan Thorn
(978-0-7637-8451-5) © 2011

*3D Mathematics for Game Development*
Fletcher Dunn
(978-0-7637-8680-9) © 2012

*Introduction to Game Design*
Jeffrey McConnell
(978-0-7637-8175-0) © 2012

*For more information on any of the titles above, please visit us online at http://www.jblearning.com/. Qualified instructors, contact your Publisher's Representative at 1-800-832-0034 or info@jblearning.com to request review copies for course consideration.*

# GAME ENGINE DESIGN AND IMPLEMENTATION

Alan Thorn

JONES & BARTLETT
LEARNING

*World Headquarters*

Jones & Bartlett Learning
40 Tall Pine Drive
Sudbury, MA 01776
978-443-5000
info@jblearning.com
www.jblearning.com

Jones & Bartlett Learning
Canada
6339 Ormindale Way
Mississauga, Ontario L5V 1J2
Canada

Jones & Bartlett Learning
International
Barb House, Barb Mews
London W6 7PA
United Kingdom

Jones & Bartlett Learning books and products are available through most bookstores and online booksellers. To contact Jones & Bartlett Learning directly, call 800-832-0034, fax 978-443-8000, or visit our website, www.jblearning.com.

Substantial discounts on bulk quantities of Jones & Bartlett Learning publications are available to corporations, professional associations, and other qualified organizations. For details and specific discount information, contact the special sales department at Jones & Bartlett Learning via the above contact information or send an email to specialsales@jblearning.com.

**Production Credits**
Publisher: Dave Pallai
Acquisitions Editor: Tim McEvoy
Editorial Assistant: Molly Whitman
Associate Production Editor: Lisa Lamenzo
Associate Marketing Manager: Lindsay Ruggiero
V.P., Manufacturing and Inventory Control: Therese Connell
Composition: Glyph International
Cover Design: Kristin E. Parker
Cover Image: © St. Nick/ShutterStock, Inc.
Printing and Binding: Malloy, Inc.
Cover Printing: Malloy, Inc.

**Library of Congress Cataloging-in-Publication Data**
Thorn, Alan.
  Game engine design and implementation / Alan Thorn.
    p. cm.
  Includes index.
  ISBN-13: 978-0-7637-8451-5 (pbk.)
  ISBN-10: 0-7637-8451-6 (ibid.)
  1. Computer games—Programming. 2. Computer games—Design. I. Title.
  QA76.76.C672T4963 2010
  794.8'1526—dc22
                        2010017562

6048
Printed in the United States of America
14  13  12  11  10    10 9  8  7  6  5  4  3  2  1

# Credits

*Without these companies and their products, we wouldn't have such a strong and well-rounded game development industry.*

iPhone, iPod, iPod touch, Mac, Mac OS, and Xcode are trademarks of Apple Inc., registered in the U.S. and other countries.

MySpace is a trademark of MySpace, Inc.

Android, Google, Sketchup, and YouTube are trademarks of Google, Inc.

The Bluetooth word mark is a registered trademark and is owned by the Bluetooth SIG, Inc.

Java and JavaScript are trademarks of Sun Microsystems, Inc. or its subsidiaries in the United States and other countries.

Adobe, Director, Flash, Photoshop, and Shockwave are registered trademarks of Adobe Systems Incorporated in the United States and/or other countries.

ActiveX, Direct3D, DirectShow, DirectX, Halo, Internet Explorer, Microsoft, Visual Basic, Visual C++, Visual Studio, Windows, Windows Vista, Xbox, and Xbox 360 are registered trademarks of Microsoft Corporation in the United States and/or other countries.

Lua is copyright © 1994–2008 Lua.org, PUC-Rio.

3ds Max, Maya, Mudbox, and Softimage are registered trademarks of Autodesk, Inc., and/or its subsidiaries and/or affiliates in the USA and/or other countries.

OGRE (www.ogre3d.org) is made available under the MIT License. Copyright © 2000–2009 Torus Knot Software Ltd.

Inno Setup is copyright © 1997–2010 Jordan Russell. All rights reserved. Portions Copyright © 2000–2010 Martijn Laan. All rights reserved.

GameCube, Nintendo DS, and Wii are trademarks and Super Mario Bros. is a registered trademark of Nintendo.

ZBrush is a registered trademark of Pixologic, Inc.

Torchlight and Runic are trademarks/service marks of Runic.

Nokia and Qt are trademarks of Nokia Corporation in Finland and/or other countries worldwide.

Street Fighter is a registered trademark of CAPCOM U.S.A., INC.

LightWave is a trademark of NewTek, Inc., registered in the United States and other countries.

RenderMonkey is a trademark of Advanced Micro Devices, Inc.

nVidia and PhysX and are registered trademarks of NVIDIA Corporation in the U.S. and other countries.

PlayStation and PSP are registered trademarks of Sony Computer Entertainment, Inc.

Call of Juarez, Splinter Cell, Splinter Cell Double Agent, and Ubisoft are trademarks of Ubisoft Entertainment in the U.S. and/or other countries.

Havok Physics is a trademark of Havok.Com, Inc.

Open Dynamics Engine is a trademark of Russell L. Smith.

BloodRayne is a trademark of Majesco Sales, Inc.

Fantastic Contraption is a trademark of inXile Entertainment, Inc.

The IncrediBots name and logo, and other graphics, logos, icons, and service names are trademarks, registered trademarks, or trade dress of Big Fish Games in the United States and/or other countries.

Firefox and Mozilla are registered trademarks of the Mozilla Foundation.

Perspex is a registered trademark of Lucite International.

HawkNL, HawkNLU, and HawkVoice are trademarks of Phil Frisbie.

Crysis is a trademark of Crytek GmbH in the U.S and/or other countries.

Supreme Commander is a registered trademark of Square Enix, Inc.

Palm is a registered trademark of Palm, Inc.

# Contents

# Introduction

There some subjects for which there is an abundance of, and perhaps too much, literature, and there are others for which the literature is disappointingly nonexistent. At first glance, the subject of "game engine development" appears to belong to the former group given the great number of books dedicated to it. However, it is actually closer to the latter group because even with the number of books available, still not enough has been written about it. Even with the addition of this book, the literature will still be comparatively scanty. This indicates both the sheer size and complexity of the field of game engine development and also the importance of the engine's role in game development in general. For this reason, the most that a book on game engines can hope for in the current climate is to provide a clear and accessible introduction that both demystifies much of the subject and offers detailed guidance on where and how to proceed on an independent basis. Thus, one of the main aims of this book is to equip the reader with the tools and knowledge necessary to stand with confidence and greater self-sufficiency in the smoky plains of engine development, a place that appears to change and expand faster than it can be documented.

In short, through 12 chapters and a selection of appendices, this book attempts to explain succinctly and clearly the basics of engine development. Specifically, it seeks to answer the question: "What is involved in making a game engine?" It examines engine development from two perspectives: from a theoretical and *design* perspective and from a practical and *implementation* perspective. Through its design eyes, this book details some of the software design patterns and class-planning issues that pertain to building a game engine. Through its implementation eyes, this book details how to realize both an engine design and coding plan in a working engine programmed in C++. Specifically, this book addresses all of the following issues and more:

- It defines what is generally understood by the term "game engine" and discusses how a game engine is distinguished from other parts of a game.
- It lists and offers introductions to the tools and equipment necessary to build game engines, such as compilers, IDEs, and software development kits.

- It discusses the architecture of a game engine and dissects it into various classes and components. It then details both the design issues underlying these components and offers detailed instruction on how to implement them, providing code samples and commentary.

- Each chapter of this book focuses on a unique aspect of engine development. After all chapters are completed in sequence, the reader will be in a position to create a basic and working game engine.

## ■  Who Should Read This Book?

Books are written with a target audience in mind, and here are some typical readers for whom this book is intended.

- Joe studies computers at school and programs in C++ in his spare time at home; he is hoping to start making computer games. He is computer literate in the sense that he knows his iPod® from his MySpace™ profile, and can distinguish YouTube™ from Bluetooth®, though he doesn't necessarily use them all. He enjoys playing games and has even created some additional game content—such as maps and missions—as part of the fan community for a first-person shooter game.

- Anita is a web designer looking to become an independent game developer and sell her games as online downloads from her website. She has spent almost two years programming in JavaScript™ and PHP, and can also use Adobe® Flash®. She has just started learning C++ and is eager to understand more about developing games and game engines using that language.

- Kurt is already working part-time for an established game development company as a scripter and beta tester, and now he would like to improve his skill set in order to apply for the position of engine developer. He is familiar with Windows®, Mac®, and consoles, and knows C++, Java™, JavaScript, and Lua, but he is not familiar with making games using those languages.

## ■  Who Should Not Read This Book?

There are some to whom this book may not be suited, though I have absolutely no wish to deter anybody who is determined and willing to read along. These classic (perhaps stereotypical) character profiles are intended as guidelines only.

- Alexis is a game enthusiast; she loves playing games on her PC and consoles, though she has never tried her hand at programming. She really hates mathematics and loses interest very quickly.

- Douglas thinks computer games are okay but perhaps a little nerdy. He did some programming at school and knows the basics but doesn't really enjoy it. He sees game development as an easy route to get rich quick.

- Thomas is a veteran engine developer and has been developing engines for over 20 years at one of the largest and most established game development companies in the world. Thomas probably does not need this book.

## ■  Which Game Development Technologies and Techniques Are Considered Throughout This Book?

- Windows
- DirectX® 10
- Simple Directmedia Layer
- Code::Blocks
- Autodesk® 3ds Max®
- TinyXML
- Standard Template Library
- Linked lists and stacks
- JavaScript and scripting integration
- Bullet physics
- Singleton design patterns
- Resource management concepts
- Class hierarchies, polymorphism, and virtual functions
- OIS (Object-Oriented Input System)
- DX Studio™
- BASS audio library
- OGRE 3D
- Inno Setup

# Theory, Design, and Preparation

This book is divided into two distinct parts: the first focusing primarily (though not exclusively) on the theoretical, design, and preparatory issues surrounding engine development, and the second focusing mainly on the implementation of a game engine in the C++ language, along with a selection of other tools and libraries. That is not to say that the first part does not feature implementation work, nor that the second does not feature design work, but simply that each part has a key focus to which other subject matter in that section is subordinate.

The first part of this book lays the foundations for the implementation work that is to follow in Part 2. Specifically, it centers on theory, design, and preparation work. The theory comes in Chapter 1 where questions such as the following are asked and addressed: "What is a game engine?" "How does an engine differ from a video game as a whole?" "Do all games need an engine?" "What is the essence of a game engine, and what are its essential building blocks?" These are all essential questions in that they must be answered in order for engine development to be possible. After all, how can a developer build a solid and reliable engine when they are not entirely sure what an engine is? The first chapter also touches on issues of design, planning, and time management. It enumerates the core components of an engine one by one and plans for their development. Some of these issues might at first seem tedious or boring in comparison to the "real" coding and implementation work, but as I hope these pages (as well as experience) will show, the importance of solid planning cannot be underestimated when developing engines.

The second chapter moves away from the issues of theory and design and into the world of preparation—that is, preparation for engine development. Specifically, that chapter highlights a series of C++ IDEs that can be used for coding engines, and also a series of core and cross-platform libraries common in the world of game development. It examines some important and useful classes from the STL library and explains the purpose and usefulness of the game loop messaging structure for games, game engines, and real-time applications. In short, Chapters 1 and 2 are intended to contain enough of the foundations necessary to get started with game engine development. The design and theory does not end with those chapters, but it is only after those chapters that implementation can begin. Thus, it is now time to turn to the first chapter and to explore the theory behind game engines.

# 1 | Game Engines—Details and Design

"Engine [noun] A machine with moving parts that converts power into motion"— *Oxford English Dictionary*

"Engine [noun] A software system, not a complete program, responsible for a technical task" —Wiktionary

## Overview

After completing this chapter, you should:

- Understand what is meant by the term "game engine"
- Appreciate the distinction between game engine, game content, and development tools
- Recognize the benefits of dividing engines into manager components
- Appreciate the most common managers
- Understand render managers, audio managers, and resource managers
- Understand the benefits of engines to game development

## ■ 1.1 Game Engines

The contemporary video game market is filled with an almost countless number of both free and commercial games, and almost all of these games are powered by an engine: a game engine. To say that a game is "powered" by an engine is not to speak literally, like saying that a computer is powered by electricity or a car by fuel. It is to speak metaphorically; it is to say that a game (any game) *depends* on its engine and that without it the game could neither be developed nor executed. However, it does not mean that a game is equal to its engine, that each are one and the same thing. For this reason, by creating an engine and only an engine a developer does not thereby create a complete game. This is because an engine is only a part of a game, just as the heart is only a part of a body. But like the heart, the engine is an essential part. Thus, a game is greater than its engine, but the engine must be in place before the game can be executed and played on the system of an end user, whether that system be a PC, Mac, Wii™, hand-held device, or some other platform. In addition, the engine must be in place before much of the game development work can occur, since the engine often acts as a pivot around which the team workflow revolves. The engine, for example, often influences the structure and arrangement of the graphics files produced by artist, and the file formats and timing of audio files produced by sound artists and musicians. It follows then that the engine is the heart (or *core*, or *kernel*) of both the game and its development, and thus the building of an engine by the programmers of the team is one of the first steps taken in the development of a game.

It is not enough, however, for a complete understanding of a game engine to say that it is the heart of a game, because this definition is insubstantial and vague insofar as it says nothing specific about the qualities of an engine. Such a definition mentions only how an engine *relates* to a game, and says nothing particular about what an engine *does* or *is*, or *is not*. At this point, however, a problem arises for both the author and the reader. The problem is that there exists no uncontroversial or unchallenged industry standard meaning for the term "game engine." It does not have a precise meaning like "graphics" or "sound," or a mathematical definition. Rather, the term "game engine" is deployed loosely in many contexts by many developers to convey a general sense or idea rather than a precise meaning about which there can be no negotiation. Having said this though, it is not an entirely subjective term either, like the term "beautiful," whose meaning depends almost entirely on individuals with regard to their specific tastes and preferences. "Game engine" then is not simply a catch-all buzzword used to mean whatever any individual chooses at any one moment. True, as a term its meaning is not precise, but still it conveys a sense and idea that is held in common between game developers. This sense and idea is the primary subject of this chapter, along with some general but important guidelines for the design of game engines. To help convey the idea and importance of the game engine, this chapter turns now to explain histori- cally how the concept of an engine developed in order to serve the specific needs of game developers looking to increase their productivity in a competitive market.

## ■ 1.2    Game Engine as an Idea

Let us imagine that during the mid-1980s a small independent video game studio—let's call it Studio X—opened its doors with much celebration as it publicly announced its latest platformer game to be released by the end of that same year. (Platformer games typically are those in which the gamer navigates a character through a level filled with enemies by running and jumping across both static and moving platforms and ledges. Examples of such games include Sonic the Hedgehog™, Super Mario Bros.®, and LittleBigPlanet.™ See Figure 1.1). Once the end of that year arrived, the developer released their game with much success and to the delight of happy gamers worldwide.

**I FIGURE 1.1**   Screenshot from a platformer game. Image from Darwin the Monkey, courtesy of Rock Solid Games.

Their game outsold a rival platformer game developed by competitive Studio Y. In fact, their game became so successful that a sequel was demanded and subsequently planned by Studio X. Studio X, however, began development of the sequel with a time management problem. It was their aim from the outset to capitalize on the success of the first game by releasing the sequel soon after and ahead of another competitive release planned by their rival. But during the development of the first game, Studio X had not considered the possibility that their work back then might help them in the future with the work for their sequels. Instead, they had considered each game a self-contained entity, and their development as separate and distinct processes. For them, each game was to be built from the ground upward, and no work from one game could possibly be of use for the next since each of them were to be released and sold as separate games. Consequently, the developers of Studio X began work for their sequel as they had for their first game. The result was that the second was in development for no less time than the first, and thus it was released into stores later than expected, accompanied by much disappointment for fans of the series and by much loss of sales for Studio X, which had on this occasion been upstaged by their faster rival Studio Y.

Studio Y produced their sequel in half the time it took to make the first. They did not achieve this by cutting corners; each member of the team worked just as hard as they always did. Nor did they achieve this by reducing the length or the content of the sequel; their sequel was bigger and better than the previous game. They achieved this by realizing when developing their first game that many properties and features common to all games and to all platformer games can be extracted from their particular contexts and given an abstract form. An abstract form is one that has lost all reference to concrete circumstances and applies not only to one game but to all. The developers realized, for example, that *all* platformer games featured a player character subject to the laws of physics, who after jumping in the air must eventually fall to the ground because of gravity. This rule would apply just as much to the sequel as to the first game. Similarly, both games would need to play sound and music in connection with events in the game, and though the sounds themselves may vary between games, the mechanisms by which the sounds are played to the speakers need not change since they do not depend on the content of the sounds; a single audio framework plays many sounds. Thinking in this way, Studio Y recognized not only some but almost all the generalizable components of a game and integrated them into a *single system* that could be *reused to produce many different games*. They knew that game content (graphics and sound) would probably need to be created on a game-by-game basis, since games look and sound different, but they realized also that there existed a framework (or infrastructure) supporting this content, and that it was this that was mostly generalizable. This framework or system is known as a game engine.

## ■  1.3    Game Engines and Game Development

The idea that the game engine is the heart or core containing almost all the generalizable components that can be found in a game implies that there are other parts of a game and of game development that do not belong to the engine component on account of their specific, nongeneralizable nature. These parts include at least game content and game development tools.

### 1.3.1    Game Content

Game content refers to all the particulars featured in any one game. Graphics and sound are the most notable members of this category. Any two platformer games, for example, might share many features in common such as enemies that run, jump, and shoot at the player character. Yet these enemies differ between games in both appearance and sound according to the work produced by the art and sound departments of a team, respectively. The graphics and sound, therefore, are specific to a game and are thus part of what makes a game unique. The engine is distinguished from content because it is concerned less

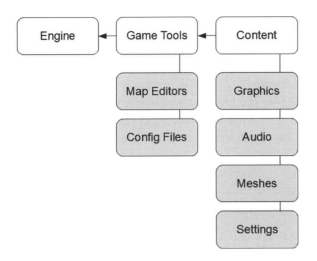

**│ FIGURE 1.2**   The game engine and its relationship to other parts of game development.

with the features unique to any one game than with the features common to all games. For this reason, game content and content creation tools are not the main concern of this book, though they are important for game development generally (see Figure 1.2).

## 1.3.2  Game Development Tools

The distinction between a game engine on the one hand and the game content on the other raises a problem for developers regarding the relationship between the two. The game engine represents everything that is abstract and applicable to all or most games, and the content that is specific to either a single game or a few games. On its own, the engine is only an active collection of rules, forms, and algorithms, and the content is only an inactive collection of images and sounds. Since each of these two parts focuses on a different aspect of the game, a bridge or protocol must be formed between them to allow the engine access to the content so as to form a complete game. It is not enough for a game developer to create the engine and content in isolation from each other, because then the engine has nothing to act upon and the content nothing to bring it to life. For example, an artist might use graphics software to produce some images of weapons and objects for a platformer game, but still the engine is required to direct and move those objects in accordance with gravity or inertia or any other laws appropriate for the game and circumstances. Images and sounds and other content do not act of their own accord; an engine is required to act on them. To build the bridge between game engine and game content during the development process, game development tools are required. These tools take the form of level editors, map generators, mesh exporters, path planners, and others. Their primary purpose is to connect the inactive game content to the active powers of the engine. A level editor, for example, is usually a custom-made GUI tool used by the developer to produce a text or binary file. This file is fed into the engine and defines a specific arrangement of much of the game graphics (trees, walls, doors, and floors, etc.) into an integrated layout of levels and environments with which players will contend as they play the game. Game tools occupy an important place in the relationship between engine and content, and are considered in further detail later in this book. For the purposes of this chapter, it is enough to state that game tools—whatever their form—represent the link between engine and content.

## ■  1.4    Game Engines in Detail

Thus far the game engine has been conceived as a single and enclosed entity representing everything that is generalizable about games and as having a relationship to two other entities—game content and game development tools. However, at present no specific mention has been made of the architecture of an engine, nor of those features of all games that are sufficiently generalizable to warrant their inclusion in an engine. There has been the occasional allusion to formulas, laws, and physics to convey a sense of some of the things that are likely to belong, but no detailed list of features or explanation of their significance. This section considers some of the features of games most likely to be found in a contemporary game engine and how those features are built into the engine so as to work in unison according to an optimal design. However, this examination by no means represents an exhaustive catalog of *all* features found in *all* engines. This is partly because there are too many features and engines to examine in one book and partly because there is no one consensus among all game developers regarding what is and is not an appropriate feature for an engine. One developer might propose an architecture and a set of features almost wholly at odds with those proposed by another, yet neither of them can be said to be entirely wrong in their choices. It is for this reason that any one engine cannot be said to be entirely better or worse than another, but only more or less appropriate for a specific purpose. To some degree, the range and kind of features a developer chooses to put into an engine reflects their professional experience, design preferences, and business intentions. Unsurprisingly, there is great variation among the many engines in circulation today.

### 1.4.1    The Architecture and Features of a Typical Engine

Given what this section has already said about variation among engines in the industry, it might seem something of a contradiction to talk of a typical game engine. Indeed, no engine can strictly be said to be typical where there are no formal or even informal standards governing engine design. However, the term "typical" is used here to refer to a basic engine design that offers enough general components and features to allow the creation of a wide range of games, including platformers, first-person shooters, sports sims, and RPGs (role playing games). These features and components are listed below and explained briefly, and later chapters of this book will tackle the implementation of these items. That is, they will explain how to create these features and components using a range of development tools common in the contemporary games industry.

Architecturally speaking, a typical game engine is divided by a programmer into many components called *managers* or *subsystems*, and each manager is responsible for a range of distinct features related to one another by kind. The physics manager, for example, is responsible for making sure that the laws of physics are applied to the objects of the game, ensuring that gravity pulls airborne objects downward to a ground surface and that collisions between objects are detected to prevent any solid objects from moving through walls or other solids when they are not supposed to. Likewise, an error manager is trusted with the specific duty of catching run-time errors and exceptions when they occur, and with subsequently responding to them appropriately, either by logging their occurrence in a local text file or by cleanly terminating the application. This division of engine work by kind into corresponding manager components, as opposed to sharing the work in one manager, is useful for a programmer because it allows them to segment and sort their source code across many files according to the number of managers supported. By arranging the physics code into one group of files, the error handling code into another, and all other sets of features according to their kind, the programmer can separate and manage vast sections of code according to their functional status. If a run-time error occurs in the game that is related to physics, then the programmer can know without searching the engine source code that debugging is to begin in the physics manager and nowhere else. The remainder of this section details some manager components commonly found in game engines. Before continuing, please see Exercise 1.1, then consider Figure 1.3.

> **NOTE**. In terms of object-oriented programming, a manager is often implemented as a singleton class, and it exposes its features through the class methods and properties. A singleton class is a class that allows one and only one instance of itself to be instantiated at any one time. Thus, by implementing each manager of an engine as a singleton class, the programmer can be certain that there can be no more than one instance of each manager in memory at run time.

### EXERCISE 1.1

List at least three other managers that you think would be suitable for almost any game engine, and why. State at least two reasons for each answer. Answers to this question are to be found throughout subsequent sections of this chapter.

## Resource Manager

The term "resources" (or "assets") is used by developers in the games industry to refer collectively to all the digital materials used by a game. Many nondigital resources may indeed be expended by developers in the production of a game—from blood and sweat to money and tears—but these are not what is meant by a game developer when they speak of resources in a technical sense. Here, "resources" refer more narrowly to two kinds of digital materials essential for games: media data and behavioral data. Media data refers to *all* the graphics, sound, animations, and other digital media that is to be featured in a game. Their purpose ultimately is to define how a game looks and sounds at run time. In contrast, behavioral data defines how a game is to be *behave at run time*, such as whether it should run in full-screen or windowed mode, or run at one resolution rather than another, or use rather than avoid subtitles. Typically, all resources—both media data and behavioral data—are encoded into files that are loaded by the engine at run time as appropriate. Media resources such as graphics are encoded into image files in formats such as PNG, JPG, and TGA, audio into files such as OGG, WAV, and MP3, and animation data into custom-made formats or video formats such as AVI and MPG. Behavioral data usually is in the form of text, sometimes in standard text format, but more often in the format of XML or CFG, and sometimes in the format of a scripting language.

To emphasize the importance of resources generally for video games, it is helpful to consider an imaginary game and the extent of its dependency on resource files. For example, a first-person shooter game, such as Half-Life® or Unreal® Tournament, is one in which the player controls the actions of a character and views the game environment as seen from their eyes. Throughout the game the player is called upon for various reasons to shoot enemies and objects and to avoid dangers. Such a game as this might depend on a wide range of resources for its existence, including all of those mentioned above. For graphics, it will require at least the images necessary to display the environment and characters, from the leaf images used for the trees and shrubbery that are scattered around the game arena to leather images used to texture the clothing of all the characters found there. For sound, it will likely require upbeat background music tracks to be played to enhance the intensity of the atmosphere, and the sound of laser beams or gunfire to be played when weapons are fired, and many others. Finally, for config files it will require a settings file to define the resolution and subtitle modes to be used by the game on execution and a level data file to define the layout of both the game environment and the objects in that environment such as the positions of walls and doors, ceilings and floors, and power-ups and bonuses. In sum, the typical video game and the game engine find themselves dependent for their existence on potentially many megabytes or gigabytes worth of resources of varying kinds. Any particular game will inevitably be dependent on a particular set of resources whose content varies according to the game, but any game is dependent on some set of resources regardless of their content. Thus, as resources apply to games generally they are therefore pertinent to game engines, and the sheer number and variety of resources, compounded with the extent of the dependency of the game on those resources, introduces for the developer a management problem. That is, it signals a *need* for a manager component in the form of a resource manager to govern the relationship between the engine and the resources. It is the duty of the resource manager therefore to: (1) identify and distinguish between all the resources available to the game, (2) both load *and* unload the resources to and from their files and in and out of memory, and (3) ensure that no more than one instance of each resource exists in memory at any one time. Resource managers and their implementation are considered later in this book.

## Render Manager

It is generally accepted that almost all games feature graphics, either 3D, 2D, or a mixture of both. It has been stated already that it is the role of the resource manager to load graphics from files on a storage device and into memory ready for use as appropriate, but this process alone is not enough for the graphics resources themselves to be displayed to the gamer on-screen. For this to occur, a second process must access the loaded graphics resource in memory and then draw it to the screen via the graphics hardware. For example, having loaded a rectangle of pixels from an image file via the resource manager, the engine must then decide how those pixels are plotted to the screen where they will be seen. Should the pixels be drawn as they appear in the file? Or should they be animated? And where on the screen should they appear—at the top left corner, at the bottom right, or elsewhere? Should the image be reversed, tiled, or repeated across the screen? These and many other questions relate to the drawing of pixels to the screen. This process is achieved by way of a graphics rendering library such as OpenGL® or DirectX or SDL, and any one of these in combination with a series of other functions and tools a developer may create from the rendering infrastructure of the game engine, or the render manager. It is the job of the render manager to (1) efficiently communicate between the engine and the graphics hardware installed on the end user system, (2) render image resources from memory to the screen, and (3) set game resolution. Render managers and their implementation are considered later in this book.

## Input Manager

Games in the contemporary market differ almost as much in their support for input devices as they do in their use of resources. The term "input device" is used by developers to signify any unit of hardware the player may use to communicate their intentions to the engine for the purposes of the game. Most PC games expect to receive input via keyboard and mouse devices, console games via remote controllers such as game pads, joysticks, and dance mats, and portable games via the device keypad. The range of input methods accepted by any game and the extent to which each is supported differs between games and platforms. However, across almost all games and platforms there is a *general* need for a mechanism both to receive and to respond to user input, regardless of the specificity of the device or of the input provided and regardless of the particular response appropriate. Thus, in the context of game engines a developmental need arises for an input manager component. The purpose of this component is to: (1) read user input at run time from the entire range of devices accepted by the game and (2) encode that input into a single, device-independent form. That is, to generate from the input a raw interpretation that does not depend for its being understood by the developer or the engine on knowledge of any specifics regarding input hardware. Input managers and their implementation are considered later in this book.

## Audio Manager

What is true for the render manager regarding graphics resources and their rendering to their screen is generally true for the audio manager regarding audio resources and their playback on the system speakers. Though the content of audio differs according to particular games, almost all games demonstrate a generalizable need to play audio. Audio here means both music and sound. The former refers to audio usually longer than 1 minute in duration and intended to be played on a loop, and as the background for any other audio that may play. The latter refers to short sounds (sound effects or SFX) such as door knocks, gunshots, and footsteps that are likely to be played in response to particular events in the game, and are less than 1 minute in duration. It is the role of the resource manager to load audio from files to memory, but it is the role of the audio manager to accept those resources and to play them to the speakers as appropriate for the game. The audio manager is also responsible for: (1) communicating between the game and audio hardware, (2) setting the overall game volume levels, and (3) applying effects to sound such as fade effects, pan effects, and echo effects. Audio managers and their implementation are considered later in this book.

## Error Manager

The esteemed computer scientist Edsger W. Dijkstra once suggested that "Testing shows the presence, not the absence of bugs." This quote often serves to remind developers of the limits of their debugging tools and of their ability to claim certainty regarding the absence of bugs in their software. It serves to emphasize that even when the debugging and testing of an application has uncovered no bugs a developer is still not in a position to claim that their software is bug free. This is because saying, "There are no bugs," is not the same as saying, "No bugs were found." Debugging and testing might uncover no bugs in an application, but that application might not have undergone all possible tests in all possible scenarios, and thus the developer is not in a position to know for certain that all bugs in their software were found and eliminated based on their tests. On this basis, the most a developer is entitled to claim is that no bugs were found in their software, and this limitation applies as much to the engine developer as to any other developer. For this reason, the developer of game engines should accept the possibility that bugs might exist in their engine and in their game no matter how thorough they consider their testing methods to be. If it were possible for a developer to find and eliminate bugs in their software and to know at the same time with complete certainty that no other bugs existed, then perhaps there would be good reason to build game engines that were error free, that is, an engine in which the occurrence of an error was an impossibility. Such an error-free engine would make the developer's life easier insofar as they would have no need to code an error manager to detect and report errors, because errors could not happen. But since the author of this book knows of no such means of achieving certainty regarding the absence of bugs in software, the possibility of error holds for each and every engine developed. Hence, a game engine needs an error manager. The purpose of the error manager is to: (1) detect or "catch" run-time exceptions in a game, (2) handle those exceptions gracefully if and when it encounters them to avoid sudden and shocking crashes to the desktop by displaying a message box before exiting to alert the user to the occurrence of an error, (3) log the occurrence of an error in a human readable text file report that can be sent by the user to the developer to aid the latter in repairing the problem, and (4) identify and mark each error with a unique identification number that can be printed in an error message dialog or in the error log report. This allows the developer to isolate each error and its possible causes. Error managers and their implementation are considered later in this book.

## Scene Manager

In theater or film, a "scene" refers to the stage or place where actors and props come together in action. Much of this meaning applies to the concept of a scene in games. The general outline of a game engine as presented so far in this chapter has conceived of a resource manager for loading resources from disk and into memory, a render manager for drawing graphics resources to the screen via graphics hardware, an audio manager for playing audio resources to the speakers via sound hardware, and an input manager for reading user input from input devices. These components are essential for almost all games to the extent that a game could not exist in a playable form without them, but even together they are not enough to create a complete game. It is not enough, for example, to load a graphics resource from a file only to display it anywhere and anyhow on the screen, without reason; nor is it enough to load an audio resource to likewise play it anyhow and meaninglessly on the speakers. Between the loading of resources from files and their presentation in the game there exists an intervening layer of management, of composition. This layer decides *how* resources are associated to one another and used so as to give them meaning for the player in relation to the actions and events of the game with the passing of time. Consider the famous puzzle game of blocks called Tetris®. In Tetris, the player controls the movement of a series of falling blocks arranged in sequences of four that drop one after another from the top of the screen to the bottom across a game board. The aim is to manipulate each arrangement as it falls by moving it left or right or by rotating it 90 degrees so that as the arrangement reaches the bottom it forms a complete horizontal line of blocks in combination with the other arrangements that fell previously. The line that is formed should contain no gaps if it is to be valid, and valid lines disappear, leaving vacant space for new blocks. As time progresses in the game, the tempo increases, meaning the player encounters every new arrangement of blocks faster than the one before. Consequently, they are forced to think faster as to how to arrange the blocks that fall. The game is lost if a new block falls and finds no vacant space on the board in which it can be held. This game has a precise set of rules governing how the resources of the game relate both to each other and to the input provided by the player. The game does not play sounds arbitrarily or display graphics anywhere on-screen without reason; rather, the graphics resources are used to represent the falling blocks of the board and are positioned and deployed on-screen in combination with the sound according to the rules of the game. In this way, the resources of the game are managed into a meaningful scene, just as a puppet-master deploys his puppets on stage not randomly and meaninglessly according to his fancies, but coherently and sensibly according to the logic of the story to be performed for the audience. The purpose of the scene manager then is to synthesize (or coordinate) the resources of the engine according to the logic of the game, to tie together the work of many managers. Its duty is in part to put on the show for the player. To do this, the scene manager must perform many tasks, some of which include: (1) communicating between many managers such as the render manager, audio manager, resource manager, and others, (2) keeping track of time for the purposes of firing events and coordinating motion on the objects of the game, and (3) enumerating the objects of the scene to allow the developer to iterate and access each of them independently. Scene managers and their implementation are considered later in this book.

## Physics Manager

It was mentioned earlier in this chapter that the physics manager is a component of the engine dedicated to applying the laws of physics to the objects of the game, or more accurately to applying forces and torques to objects of the scene. This physics manager is responsible for, among other things, applying the effects of gravity and inertia to game objects. The former ensures that specified airborne objects—such as chairs, apples, and people but not airplanes, fairies, and dragons—are pulled downward to a ground surface. The latter ensures that moving objects such as cars and runaway mine carts do not come unrealistically to complete and immediate stops whenever they cease to accelerate, but gradually reduce their speed over time toward a stopped state to imitate the real-world resistance of mass to changes in its state of motion. At this point, however, it is important to note a distinction between the physics manager and the scene manager. Given what has been said so far of the duties of both with regard to their role as controllers of the behavior of game objects, it might at first seem that the two managers should be merged into one or that one makes the other redundant. If the purpose of the physics manager is to control at run time the behavior of objects and their relationships in the scene according to the laws of physics, then what place can there be for the scene manager as a controller of behavior? This question draws attention to the distinction between game logic (or game rules) on the one hand and physics on the other, the former being the responsibility of the scene manager. The scene manager, for example, does not apply gravity or inertia to objects, nor does it govern their behavior according to any physical laws; that duty falls to the physics manager. Rather, it governs scene objects according to the rules of the game as they are determined by the developers thinking outside the laws of physics. The rules of the game define the unwritten contract between the gamer and the game, and they are outside the laws of physics in the sense that the laws of physics could alter while the rules of the game remained unchanged. They refer to the terms of play and stipulate the conditions and circumstances that constitute a win for the player and those that constitute a loss, and further stipulate the range and kinds of actions a player may pursue to achieve a win. For example, there might be a set of rules governing a plat-former game that specify that a loss is incurred by the player whenever their health drops below zero as the result of attack from an enemy or of damage from environ-mental hazards, and that a win is incurred whenever they reach the end of a level and defeat in combat the end-of-level boss. Thus, the objects and relationships of a scene in a game are governed by at least two sets of independent laws, those of physics and those of the game. The enforcement of the latter is one of the duties of the scene manager, and the enforcement of the former is the sole duty of the physics manager. Physics managers and physics handling is considered later in this book via a look at the Bullet physics library.

## Scripting Manager

A game engine is typically built by programmers into a standalone executable file or a DLL (dynamic link library) using a compiled language such as C++ or C#. Using a compiled language to build an engine into machine code form often improves its run-time performance but poses a number of challenges to developers seeking to cus-tomize it according to their needs after it is compiled. It has been stated already that one means by which a general engine is customized for a specific game is game tools. These tools are used by developers to produce a variety of text and configuration files detailing the content and behavior specific to a game, and are fed into the engine to customize it accordingly. By accepting many of its instructions through external and independent game files, the compiled engine remains open to the developer in the sense that its behavior can be changed *without having to be recompiled*. This is useful if only because an engine that can be customized without having to be recompiled does not depend on its original creators and their knowledge of its internal mechanics for its use. That is, an open engine can be adapted and customized by any who learn the protocol between the engine and its files. For example, an artist can change the graphics used by the engine simply by substituting a new set of graphics files for the previous set, and a programmer or gamer can change the run-time resolution of the engine by editing the settings of a resolution configuration file before the engine is executed. Thus, the primary reason for an engine's dependency on external files is to produce in it an openness not only to the creators of the engine but also to other developers and even to some gamers; to produce a flexible capacity to be easily customized or *scripted* for specific games without having to be recompiled. Thus, an engine is said to be *scriptable* if it has the general ability to adjust its behavior according to a set of instructions in a file. Those instructions may take many forms, and engines differ in the extent of their support for any specific instruction set. Some engines support instructions written in plain English or in XML, and others support those written in established scripting languages and frameworks such as Lua and Python™ to allow for greater control. The choice of language to be supported by any particular engine often reflects the popularity and currency of the language as well as the professional preferences and intentions of the developers, but whichever language is chosen there is a general need to *manage* the support of that language and its interaction with the engine. This need therefore creates a demand for a scripting manager, and the job of this manager is to: (1) expose a subset of classes and functions of the engine and allow access to them through the scripting language and (2) read and process instructions in a file and respond accordingly. Scripting managers and details surrounding scripting generally are discussed later in this book when considering game tools.

## ■  1.5   Game Engines—Necessary Conditions

Games are said by many developers to be powered by engines, and by this they mean that an engine is a necessary condition for a game, that a game cannot run without an engine. True, any specific game is more than an engine because it contains unique content or dressing such as graphics and sound, but the engine represents the integrated framework on which this dressing hangs. Conceiving of the engine as a framework or a necessary condition for a game is useful for identifying whether or not any library or software is or is not a game engine. Presented with any library or software, such as DirectX or OpenGL, the developer can proceed to ask, "Can I make a game with this and *only* this?"; if the answer to that question is in the affirmative, then it either *is* or *can be used as* a game engine. It is not enough to show that only in combination with other tools could it make games. The software as it is must be capable of producing games on its own merits to be considered a game engine. Thus, OpenGL is a *dedicated* graphics API but not a game engine. Its purpose is to render graphics to the screen via the hardware. No doubt many engines have made use of this library for that specific purpose, but despite this, OpenGL as a library is not responsible for other features of the engine that are equally essential for creating a game—from the playing of game audio to the handling of game logic. In diagram form, the engine exists on a level above dedicated libraries; the engine represents the integrated core of a game that delegates essential duties via manager components to dedicated libraries. Consider Figure 1.3.

It has been established that a game depends on an engine for its existence, and that the essence of an engine (that which makes it what it is) consists of its ability to make games. This ability and its scope are determined in large part by the manager components from which the engine is made, some of which were discussed in the previous section. The render manager determines the feature set for graphics rendering, the audio manager for audio playback, and each other manager for its corresponding duties. Thus, the manager components represent the chief executors of the engine and are the primary means by which engine work is performed. For this reason, the managers are to the engine as the engine is to the game; that is, they are the core. A game depends on its engine and the engine on its managers. Having determined this,

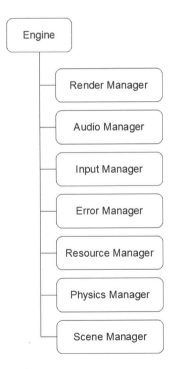

**❘ FIGURE 1.3**   Common set of managers for a game engine.

the question then arises as to where the line is drawn between that which is an engine and that which is not in terms of the number and type of managers supported. Is it possible, for example, to conceive of a minimum collection of managers that together warrant the title of "engine" and from which no manager could be removed without compromising that title? In other words, what is the simplest engine possible? Such an engine might be suitable for creating only the simplest of games, but even so can it be defined? If so, which managers would belong to that group of essential managers?

It is helpful for a developer to think about this question of essential managers because the answer (if there is a definitive one) points to only those managers that are essential for all games and which mark the starting point for the development of almost all engines. Some might be tempted to argue that *all* engine managers listed in this chapter thus far are equally essential for all games. They might argue that many games from platformers to sports sims require a physics manager, render manager, audio manager, and many other managers, and that for this reason these managers are essential in any engine that is intended to create those games. But this response misses the point of the exercise. It is no doubt the case that all managers are important for specific games, but it does not follow from this that all managers are equally important for all games. A physics manager is unquestionably important to a game dependent on physical reactions, such as a flight simulation or a car racing game, but not so important for a card matching game or a game of Tetris or any other game that does not depend on physical laws. Thus, many games exist that do not require an engine with a physics manager. However, it seems unlikely that even the simplest game could exist without an input manager to receive and process user input from a game controller. The task of this section is one of reduction: to create a list of only those managers essential to all games under all circumstances, or essential to the simplest possible game. Having created such a list and confirmed those managers as the foundation of almost all engines, the developer can then recognize the implementation of those managers as the starting point or the first steps on a long road of engine development. In short, with the exception of design, engine development begins with the implementation of its essential managers. So what are the essential managers? Unfortunately, there is no definitive answer to this question, or at least none of which the author is aware. But for the purposes of this book, concerned as it is with the creation of a

### EXERCISE 1.2

List three managers you think should be included in the essential managers group, and state two reasons for each manager to justify your choice. Answers can be found in the following section. Your answers might differ from mine, but it is important to have reasons for your choices and to appreciate the reasons for mine.

general engine suitable for many game genres, it is nonetheless possible to build a rough argument as to which managers ought to be included.

## 1.5.1   Game Engines—Essential Managers

Any manager component may belong to either one of two groups: essential and nonessential. This status relates to its significance for the simplest of games. If the simplest of games cannot exist without a given manager, then that manager is an essential manager. The simplest of engines contains no more than the essential managers, and thus the implementation of these managers represents the starting point of engine development after the stage of design. The following table lists each manager stated earlier in this chapter that is essential, and for each states two reasons why it is an essential manager.

| Essential Manager | Reasons |
|---|---|
| **Render Manager** <br> Status: Essential | 1. Game must *show on-screen* any essential error messages and information. <br> 2. Almost all games feature graphics. |
| **Resource Manager** <br> Status: Essential | 1. The resource manager processes resources, and the render manager depends on resources. The render manager is essential, and therefore the resource manager is essential. <br> 2. The game must keep a list of all resources for the purposes of memory management and tidy resource unloading. |
| **Scene Manager** <br> Status: Essential | 1. The scene manager is required to organize the contents of a scene. Without this manager, resources cannot be placed in meaningful arrangements. <br> 2. Scene managers are essential for monitoring game logic. |
| **Input Manager** <br> Status: Essential | 1. A game depends in part on the input received from the user, and an engine processes user input through the input manager. Therefore, the input manager is an essential manager. <br> 2. User input is necessary to terminate the execution of a game once the gamer has finished playing. |
| **Error Manager** <br> Status: Essential | 1. Developers cannot be sure their engine is free of all errors through standard debugging techniques. Therefore, an error manager is required to handle errors as they occur. <br> 2. The error manager might need to notify users of errors. |

**❙ TABLE 1.1**   Essential Managers

## ■   1.6   Principles of Engine Design—RAMS

The essential managers are the render manager, input manager, scene manager, error manager, and resource manager. Having identified these as the essential managers of an engine, it might appear that there is little else for an engine developer to do but to get started with the implementation of those managers. However, there are a variety of approaches a programmer might take toward coding their implementation. Some might choose to implement each manager as a unique class with its own methods and properties; since the managers must interact with one another, the developer might choose to expose the interface of each manager to every other and to have much *direct* interaction between them. This solution offers the benefit of performance insofar as each manager has a direct channel of communication to every other, but introduces the disadvantage that each manager must have at least some knowledge concerning the implementation of other managers. Another solution might be to choose an indirect route: to hide each manager class from every other and to code an additional messenger class to pass data between the managers as each goes about its work. These two scenarios represent only two possible responses to the one problem of communication between managers, and this design problem is only one among many. The solution to that problem, and those to many others, will influence the form the managers take when implemented. Again, there is no clear-cut right or wrong solution to many, if any, of the design problems an engine developer encounters, but this is not the same as saying that all solutions are equally suitable or that all approaches are just as good. A person might offer 10 different answers to a sum and all of them might be wrong, but some are closer to being right than others. There is simply not enough space in this book or perhaps in any book to address all the possible design problems that might arise and their corresponding solutions, even if all such problems and solutions could be listed. So instead of attempting to list specific design problems and to provide specific solutions, this book details a number of general key design principles or ideas that can be found to underpin the design and implementation of many successful engines used in the contemporary games industry. These ideas detail some sound design advice concerning game engines. Having understood these principles or guidelines, the reader can then proceed to apply them to their specific case and to tailor their solutions accordingly. They can do this by considering all the solutions before them and establishing which of them most coincides with the design principles. The four design principles listed here can be remembered using the acronym RAMS. Many successful engines are designed according to the principles of recyclability, abstractness, modularity, and simplicity. Each of these is now considered in more detail.

## 1.6.1  Recyclability

Materials and processes that can be reused are considered recyclable, and the more frequently and widely they can be reused the more recyclable they are. For game engines, recyclability often relates to efficiency. An engine that consumes half the resources of another engine to perform the same tasks with equal or greater reliability and efficacy is generally considered to be the more efficient of the two. Efficiency refers to the relationship between the resources available and the performance and reliability that result from the processing of those resources. A process is efficient to the extent that it achieves success and reliability from a given set of resources, and efficiency is improved when success and reliability are increased from the same resources or from fewer resources. For this reason, efficiency is improved through recycling whenever a single set of resources can be used and reused for two or more processes successfully and reliably. This is because performance is increased without a corresponding aggregate increase in resources. To illustrate, consider recycling in the context of a resource manager for an engine that is being used to power an imaginary platformer game. The purpose of the resource manager is to load game resources from files on disk or over the Internet and into memory, either system memory or other hardware memory. Resources include graphics, audio, and many other file types. During the playing of the game, the player enters a level and encounters five enemy alien clones, all of which look alike. At this point, the resource manager is called upon to load the graphics resources to be used as a representation of the alien creatures. The resource manager can achieve this using one of at least two solutions: It can either load five copies of the same image, one for each alien, or it can load one copy of the same image and share this among all like aliens. The second solution is the more efficient because it acknowledges the principle of recyclability by using a single resource for many instances. In short, the principle of recyclability advises the developer to consider each and every resource as precious and scarce, and to design the engine so as to extract the greatest use from the fewest resources possible.

## 1.6.2   Abstractness

Abstraction is about producing generalizations from particular instances, and is a matter of degree. A complete abstraction can be identified by its entirely general nature, for it makes no reference to particular cases. The idea of a chair, for example, is an abstraction because it refers to chairs in general and not to any particular chair. Earlier in this chapter, a number of engine managers were identified; these managers represent abstractions also because a general demand for them was identified after having considered particular details. From those particular details, a general and nonparticular idea of a manager was constructed, and from the idea of a manager, various *kinds of managers* were further created. The manager components and even the concept of an engine itself are all abstractions because they are ideas that do not depend on any particular instances but apply to all games as such. The principle of abstraction is useful for engine developers because by designing the components of an engine to be abstract rather than particular, the developer increases their field of use or their versatility. Their versatility is proportional to their degree of abstraction. A render manager, for example, can be used by any and all games, because rendering is an essential process for all games. In contrast, a text render manager is less abstract than a render manager and is consequently more limited in its scope, assuming its purpose is to render text and only text. In short, the principle of abstraction encourages the engine developer to think in the abstract. It encourages them to start by identifying the many particular and contingent needs of one case and then to proceed from this by building abstractions that serve not only the needs of that one particular case but all the like needs of all cases. Thus, the building of abstractions serves to increase the versatility of the engine, and the greater the degree of abstraction, the greater the versatility.

## 1.6.3   Modularity

The idea of a general manager component is the result of abstraction. Having identified this idea, it can be developed further through the principle of modularity. The idea that a manager should be an independent and functional unit responsible for a range of related tasks is often what results when the engine is thought of in terms of modularity. The principle of modularity begins by considering an entity as a working whole (such as a game engine) and then proceeds to subdivide that entity into constituent pieces or modules, each according to their purpose or function as it relates to the whole. In object-oriented programming, each module is likely to correspond to a class. By the principle of modularity, each module is seen as both independent and exchangeable: independent in the sense that it is distinguished from other modules by its function, for no two modules belonging to the same whole should share the same function, and exchangeable in the sense that it could be replaced without damage to the whole only by another module that serves the same function. For example, the principle of modularity when applied to the idea of a game engine will likely subdivide the engine into manager components, each manager satisfying a unique function. The purpose of the render manager is to render, and the audio manager to play audio, and the error manager to log errors. None of these modules can be removed without reducing the whole, and no module can be replaced safely except by another that performs the same function. Two modules that perform the same function need not be entirely identical in every respect; their function and output might be identical, but their working methods might differ for there may be many roads to the same destination. The purpose of the render manager is to draw graphics via the hardware to the screen, and it may achieve this single end via OpenGL, SDL, DirectX, or another graphics library. A render manager that uses the DirectX library, for example, *is not* substitutable for an input manager or a resource manager since their functions differ by kind from that of a render manager, but *is* substitutable for another render manager regardless of which graphics library that manager chooses to use to fulfill its purpose. In this way, modularity allows an engine to be divided into modules, and further allows each module to hide the details and specifics of its implementation while maintain its relationship to the whole. The module does this by focusing on achieving a single purpose. In short, the principle of modularity recommends that an entity is subdivided into smaller functional units. Doing this offers the developer several design and debugging benefits: (1) It allows them to translate complex entities into a collection of simpler ones according to the contribution each makes to the whole, and (2) it allows them to make changes to the implementation of specific modules without affecting the implementation of other modules, or the working of the whole.

## 1.6.4   Simplicity

The 14th-century Franciscan Friar William of Occam stated that "entities should not be multiplied unnecessarily." This principle is now known as Occam's Razor; applied to game engines it might be translated into the mantra "Keep things simple." In this case, keeping things simple refers to a process of reductionism, which refers to the process of reducing the complex into the simple. This works side by side with modularity. The principle of modularity recommends that an engine be subdivided into a range of modules each according to their unique function, and the principle of simplicity is there to remind us that the process of modularity must be performed with simplicity in mind, with the aim of reductionism. Modularity combined with simplicity suggests that an engine should not only be subdivided into modules, but should be subdivided into the *fewest* number of modules possible. This process might proceed as follows: A developer identifies each and every entity or part belonging to an engine, and then for each entity he pauses to ascertain its function. If any two or more parts share the same function or very similar functions, then these parts are candidates for amalgamation. That is, these parts should be merged together into a larger unit. Having performed this process once for each unit, the developer should repeat the procedure for the newly formed larger units, and then repeat it continually on each level upward until the process yields no more amalgamations. At this point, the developer can know that the simplest arrangement of modules has been found. In short, the principle of simplicity, when applied appropriately, ensures that an engine features no entities sharing the same purpose or very similar purposes. This is helpful for a developer because working with the simplest arrangements ensures they not duplicate work across modules and that they work only with the minimum number of modules necessary for the purpose.

### EXERCISE 1.3

Answer the following questions and then compare your answers to those given.

Q1. How does the principle of simplicity differ from the principle of modularity?

A1. Modularity suggests that an entity should be subdivided into smaller functional components. Simplicity suggests that entities should not be multiplied unnecessarily. When the principle of modularity is combined with that of simplicity, the advice is that an entity should be subdivided into the fewest number of functional components possible.

Q2. Does creating a DirectX render manager and an OpenGL render manager for the same engine violate the principle of simplicity?

A2. No. The two modules share the purpose but are implemented differently, and thus are exchangeable modules. The existence of two render managers where one uses OpenGL and another DirectX is useful for creating cross-platform engines. The Windows version might use the DirectX render manager, and the Linux® or Mac version might use the OpenGL render manager.

## ■ 1.7   Engines in Practice

Engines designed according to the four principles of modularity, simplicity, recyclability, and abstractness often benefit the game developer and prove cost effective in many ways, including the following: (1) By their versatility, since they can be used for many games and for many games across many genres, (2) by their increasing the reliability of games, since a bug corrected in the engine potentially represents a fix for all games powered by that engine, and (3) by their saleability, since an engine can be licensed by its creator to one or more other developers for the purpose of powering their games. Having mentioned some of the business and developmental benefits an engine offers to a developer, this section briefly explores some of the commercial and free and open source engines in use in the contemporary games industry.

### EXERCISE 1.4

Select at least two engines from the list below and visit their home pages to read their features and technical information. On the basis of this information, list for each engine chosen all the manager components you can identify.

**Torque 3D and Torque 2D**
*Developer:* GarageGames®
*License:* Commercial
*Website:* http://www.garagegames.com
*Supported Platforms:* PC Windows, Mac, iPhone®, Wii, Xbox® 360

Torque 3D and Torque 2D are two separate commercial game engines created and licensed by GarageGames for the creation of 3D and 2D games, respectively. The engines are not genre specific, meaning that they are intended for the creation of games of various genres and run on several platforms. This engine has been involved in the development of at least the following games: Marble Blast, Wildlife Tycoon, ThinkTanks, and The Destiny of Zorro.

**Unity Engine**
*Developer:* Unity Technologies
*License:* Commercial
*Website:* http://unity3d.com/
*Supported Platforms:* PC Windows, Mac, iPhone, Wii, web deployment

The Unity Engine is a proprietary game engine designed and licensed by Unity Technologies for the creation of 3D games on a variety of platforms, including Windows and Mac. It can also be used to create web browser games. The Unity Engine has been used for the development of several games, including Open Fire and Tiki Magic Mini Golf.

**Crystal Space**
*Developer:* Crystal Space Team
*License:* Open source, free
*Website:* http://www.crystalspace3d.org
*Supported Platforms:* PC Windows, Linux, FreeBSD®

Crystal Space is a free, open source, and cross-platform engine developed by the Crystal Space Team that allows developers to produce 3D games on a variety of platforms. This engine powers many games, both commercial and free, including The Icelands and the free RPG PlaneShift (http://www.planeshift.it).

**Game Blender**
*Developer:* Blender Foundation
*License:* Open source, free
*Website:* http://www.gameblender.org
*Supported Platforms:* PC Windows, Linux, and Mac

Game Blender is a comparative newcomer among the free, open source, and cross-platform game engines designed for producing 3D games. It is associated with the Blender 3D rendering software.

**ClanLib**
*Developer:* ClanLib Team
*License:* Open source, free
*Website:* http://www.clanlib.org/
*Supported Platforms:* PC Windows, Linux, and Mac

ClanLib is a free, open source, and cross-platform game engine developed by the ClanLib team for creating 2D games for Windows, Linux, and Mac.

**Novashell**
*Developer:* Robinson Technologies
*License:* Open source, free
*Website:* http://www.rtsoft.com/novashell/
*Supported Platforms:* PC Windows, Linux, and Mac

Novashell, a free, open source, and cross-platform game engine developed by Robinson Technologies, ships with an integrated level editor for importing game art and defining game maps.

**Multimedia Fusion**
*Developer:* Clickteam
*License:* Commercial
*Website:* http://www.clickteam.com
*Supported Platforms:* PC Windows

Multimedia Fusion is a commercial, proprietary game engine designed and licensed by Clickteam for the creation of 2D games for Windows.

**Leadwerks**
*Developer:* Leadwerks Software
*License:* Commercial
*Website:* http://www.leadwerks.com
*Supported Platforms:* PC Windows

Leadwerks is a proprietary game engine designed and licensed by Leadwerks Software for the creation of 3D games on the Windows platform. It can work with a variety of programming languages including C++, C#, and BlitzMax.

## ■ 1.8   Chapter Summary

This chapter sought to provide some answers to several key questions. These were: (1) what is a game engine? (2) what does a game engine do? (3) how does a game engine differ from other parts of a game and the game development process? and (4) what are the core components of a game engine? Before proceeding to the next chapter, try to provide a one-paragraph answer to each of those questions. Then check your answers by reading the appropriate chapter sections. The next chapter considers the first stage of engine implementation: the configuration of an IDE and a project in preparation for coding.

In short, this chapter has detailed the following:

- A game engine is an integrated framework of managers and components designed for powering games.
- Game engines are often designed according to the four principles of: abstractness, modularity, simplicity, and recyclability.
- Each manager of an engine is an exchangeable unit serving a unique purpose. Managers include but are not limited to render managers, audio managers, input managers, and scene managers.
- There are many third-party managers available in the contemporary games industry, some are commercial and others are free and open source. These can be used to produce games.

# 2

# Configuring a Game Engine Project

## Overview

After completing this chapter, you should:

- Understand what is meant by the term IDE
- Know how to configure a C++ project using either Code::Blocks, Visual Studio® C++, or Visual C++® Express
- Understand how to build an application
- Understand what is meant by the term DLL
- Know how to use an IDE to build a DLL project
- Understand the benefits to game development of building the game engine into a DLL
- Know how to use the STL
- Understand the purpose of the game loop

## ■ 2.1 Engine Development—Getting Started

The first chapter of this book focused in detail on the concept of the game engine and on the core principles of game engine development. From that examination emerged the general but contestable definition of the game engine as an abstract, recyclable, and modular library for programmers that offers at least the basic subset of tools for developing merchantable and functional video games. With this definition in mind, the current chapter moves away from the process of design, with its preoccupation with techniques and principles, to focus on the first steps of engine implementation. Specifically, it examines where and how a programmer might begin the development of an engine. It considers step by step the selection of a programming environment and the stages of its configuration and how the environment can be used by a programmer to build an engine in the form of a Windows DLL (dynamic link library) that can be shared among many unique and separate game applications. It should be noted that the remainder of this chapter and book will focus on the commonly used and popular programming language C++. Though this language is often used for game development, it is certainly not the only language by which games or engines can be created successfully. Other languages such as JavaScript, ActionScript, C#, Visual Basic®, BlitzBasic, and Delphi® have played and continue to play significant roles in game development, and this book will consider some of these languages in superficial detail later. However, it is not the purpose of this book to consider all the available or possible languages in which games and game engines can be made, nor would there be sufficient room to do so even if it was. But in order for the book to be useful, it must present to the reader some examples in code, and thus a decision needed to be made by the author as to the choice of language that was to be used. Given the popularity and availability of C++ editors, tools, and libraries, this book focuses primarily on the C++ language. Thankfully, given the similarities in syntax between C++ and other languages such as C# and JavaScript, the code samples in this book are generally directly portable to those languages.

## ■ 2.2    IDEs (Integrated Development Environments)

> NOTE. Many readers of this book will already be programmers and thus already be familiar with an IDE. These readers may want to skip this section, for it is likely to cover familiar ground. This section is included for completeness and clarity, and for the benefit of those readers who are generally new to programming.

Having settled on the basic principles of game engine design in theory, the issue of implementation still remains; that is, the issue of putting those principles into practice. The question arises as to where engine development begins, for it must begin somewhere: For example, should a developer start by conceiving of a collection of all the necessary manager components (audio manager, render manager, etc.) and then proceed to design and implement a hierarchy of classes based on this collection? Or should he or she instead develop an engine without any direction or foresight whatsoever alongside the development of a game, adding and removing sections of the engine wholesale in accordance with the needs of the game as it develops? Both of these questions, however, put the horse before the cart in that each depends on a number of assumptions that should by no means be foregone conclusions. Each question appears to assume that a programming language has already been chosen for development, and that the IDE for this language has been chosen also. Given that this assumption figures in at least the two questions above related to the starting point of development, it appears reasonable to conclude that development begins with the choice of development tools. This consists of choosing a programming language (C++ for this book) and an appropriate IDE. The term "IDE" is an acronym for integrated development environment and represents a software application used by programmers to build software in their language of choice.

The IDE is to the programmer as the word processor is to the letter writer. As the letter writer must use the word processor to apply their knowledge of a language to write letters, format text, spell check, and print documents, so the IDE offers the programmer the set of tools necessary to apply their knowledge of a programming language to build computer programs. Thus, there is a distinction between knowledge of a language and the application of a language. The learning of a language involves coming to understand the syntax, rules, and specifics regarding that which makes statements valid. The application of a language, however, concerns how a competent user appropriates the language to build valid statements that communicate their intentions and meanings. The IDE then is targeted toward programmers of a specific language, offering them the tools and facilities necessary to build software. There are usually as many IDEs as there are languages, and each IDE is typically devoted to a specific language; thus, there is at least one IDE for C++, one for C#, one for Visual Basic, etc. Each IDE usually features a collection of development tools for building software, including a source code editor, a compiler, and a debugger.

The source code editor allows a programmer to input instructions in their language into the system by typing text into the software; the editor offers the standard text editing tools for this purpose, including copy, paste, and undo features. The compiler validates and processes the instructions entered into the code editor by the programmer, translates valid code into object code, and finally links this as appropriate before outputting the result in an executable form that can be run by the user as a program. To simplify, the purpose of the compilation process is to translate source code into an executable file. Finally, the point of the debugger is to aid the programmer in detecting and eliminating run-time errors (or bugs) in their software. Here, one might raise the issue that if part of the purpose of the compiler is to *validate* the source code, to verify its correctness before translating it into executable form, then how is it possible for the resulting executable to contain errors? Surely all compiled code must necessarily be valid? This question raises the distinction between compile-time errors and run-time errors, and between syntactical correctness and logical correctness. One of the duties of the compiler is to validate each and every statement in the source code for its grammatical correctness, rejecting the compile when even so much as one statement is not grammatically correct and completing the compile when each and every statement is valid. This means that all compiled code is indeed valid code, but unfortunately validity is no assurance against error. Statements that are syntactically correct are valid for that language because they do not infringe on the rules of grammar, but still it is possible for grammatically correct statements to be unintelligible to the reader (e.g., colorless green ideas sleep furiously). For a computer language, it is therefore possible for a valid statement to cause an error at the time of its execution. For example, a Windows GUI program might be written to depend on the existence of a text file elsewhere on the hard disk, whose contents it reads whenever the user clicks a button in the window. Each and every line of code written by the developer for the application might be valid syntactically, but if the text file in question does not exist at run time at the location expected by the application and if the application does not handle the error that will occur when file access fails, then the application fails as a result of a run-time error, so-called because the error occurred while the application was running. Thus, a debugger is used by a programmer to seek not for compile-time errors but for run-time errors.

The following sections of this chapter consider two C++ IDEs, both freely available and ready to use for game development; these are Microsoft® Visual C++ Express and the cross-platform IDE Code::Blocks. Typically, a developer will choose one IDE and use it to develop their entire project.

## ■ 2.3    Microsoft Visual C++ Express

The Microsoft Visual C++ Express IDE is part of the Visual Studio Express product line, available for free by download and which also includes Visual Basic Express and Visual C# Express. This product line is intended to be a "lightweight" (limited) version of the larger and commercial Visual Studio product range. The Microsoft Visual C++ Express IDE contains a code editor, GUI, compiler, and debugger, among other tools. It can be downloaded from the Microsoft official website: http://msdn.microsoft.com/vstudio/express/.

### 2.3.1    Downloading and Installing Microsoft Visual C++ Express

This section features a general set of step-by-step instructions on how to download and install Microsoft Visual C++ Express, and was accurate at the time of writing. Though most of these steps are likely to remain valid for the foreseeable future, version changes and website updates related to this IDE might require the reader to deviate from my instructions at some steps.

> **NOTE.** The full version of Microsoft Visual C++ Express is available free of charge by download. Continued use beyond the initial 30 days requires the user to register their email address with Microsoft. For this reason, Visual C++ Express is said to belong to a group of free applications known as "registerware."

Step 1.   Open a web browser and visit the Microsoft Visual C++ Express website at http://www.microsoft.com/express/windows/. See Figure 2.1.

Step 2.   Click the **Download** button to go to a page offering the selection of products in the Visual Studio Express range. From this menu, scroll down to Visual C++ Express and then click the **Download** button. See Figure 2.2.

**I FIGURE 2.1**    Visit the MSDN website to download Visual C++ Express.

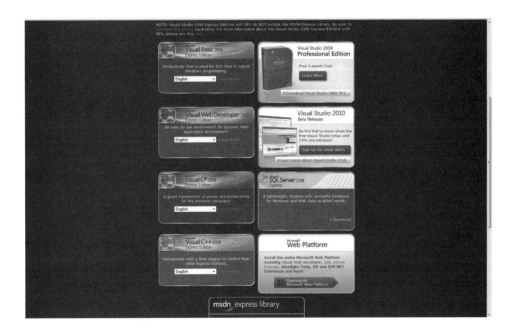

**I FIGURE 2.2**    Select the download appropriate for you.

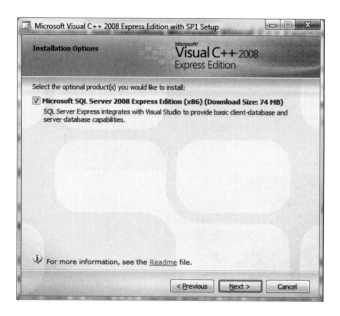

**| FIGURE 2.3**    Run the Visual C++ Express Installer.

Step 3.  Once downloaded, run the installer file. Follow the instructions on the Install Wizard to install Visual C++ Express to your system. See Figure 2.3.

Step 4.  Once installed to the system, Visual C++ Express is ready to use. See Figure 2.4.

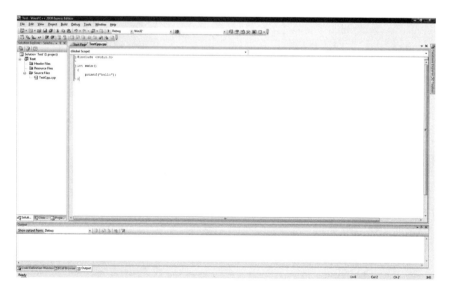

**| FIGURE 2.4**    Visual C++ Express is ready to use.

# ■ 2.4   Code::Blocks

Code::Blocks is a free, cross-platform, and open source C++ IDE. It is free in the sense that it is free of charge, cross-platform in that it can be run on Windows, Linux, and Mac, and open source since its source code is available to the public, though its source code is not needed to use the software. Code::Blocks contains a GUI, source code editor, compiler, and debugger, among other tools. It can be downloaded from http://www.codeblocks.org/.

## 2.4.1   Downloading and Installing Code::Blocks

This section features a general set of step-by-step instructions on how to download and install Code::Blocks, and was accurate at the time of writing. Though most of these steps are likely to remain valid for the foreseeable future, version changes and website updates related to this IDE might require the reader to deviate from my instructions at some steps.

Step 1.   Open a web browser and visit the Code::Blocks website at http://www.
          codeblocks.org/. See Figure 2.5.

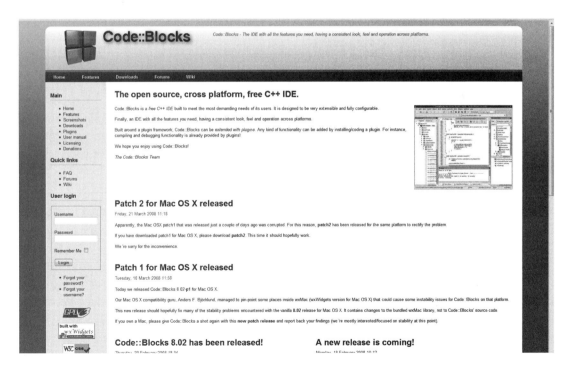

**▎FIGURE 2.5**   Downloading Code::Blocks.

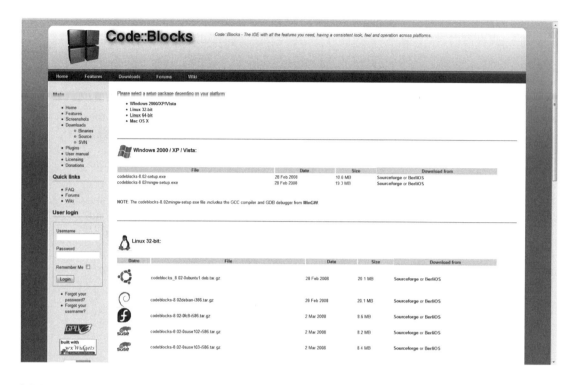

**I FIGURE 2.6**    Selecting a Code::Blocks binary package.

Step 2. Click the **Downloads** button to go to a page offering a binary release, a source release, and a source release via SVN. The binary release features all files needed to use the editor immediately after download. Select **Binary release** to be taken to a platform selection page. See Figure 2.6.

Step 3. From the platform selection page users can choose the version of Code::Blocks to download according to their platform. Options include Windows, Linux, and Mac. This book assumes the user is using Windows. Select the version appropriate for your system to download the file. Before downloading, the website will provide the option of downloading one of two files: Code::Blocks standalone (without a compiler or debugger) or Code::Blocks with a GCC compiler and debugger. Users new to Code::Blocks should select the version with a compiler and debugger.

Step 4. Once downloaded, run the downloaded installer and follow the on-screen instructions of the setup wizard to install Code::Blocks to your system. See Figure 2.7.

Step 5. Once installed to the system, Code::Blocks is ready to use. See Figure 2.8.

**FIGURE 2.7**   Running the Code::Blocks Setup Wizard.

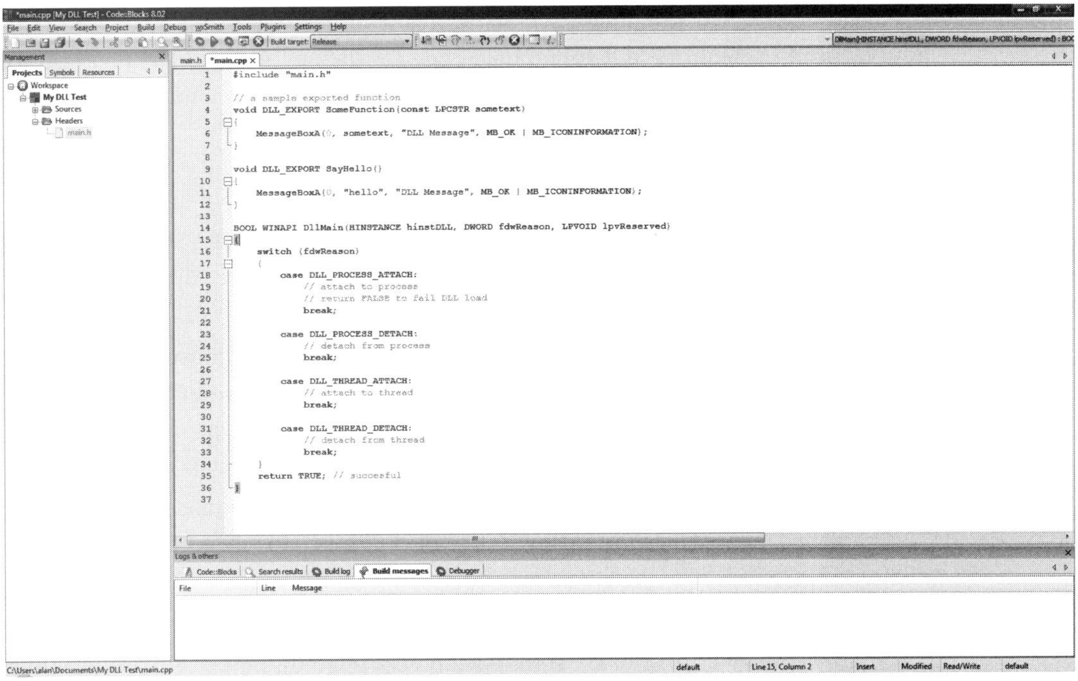

**FIGURE 2.8**   Code::Blocks is ready to use.

## ■ 2.5   Using Visual C++ Express and Code::Blocks

Both Visual C++ and Code::Blocks are C++ IDEs designed to build executable programs from C++ source code. This section considers a selection of tasks programmers often seek to achieve using these IDEs and explains how to achieve them, from compiling software to setting include header directories. However, this section assumes some knowledge of C++ and the usage of C++ IDEs generally. For further information on C++ as a language, the reader can consult either of the following two resources: *Introduction to Game Programming with C++* (ISBN: 1598220322) or *C++ Beginners Guide* (http://msdn.microsoft.com/en-us/beginner/cc305129.aspx). For further details on Visual C++ Express as a C++ IDE, the reader can consult the Microsoft online video tutorials at http://msdn.microsoft.com/en-gb/beginner/bb964629.aspx.

### 2.5.1   Creating a New Application Using Visual C++ Express and Code::Blocks

In both Visual C++ Express and Code::Blocks, a "project" refers to a collection of C++ source and header files that are to be compiled together according to a range of compilation settings into a single unit either to be executed as an application or to be built as a library. Thus, to create an application in either of these IDEs that is to run as a standard standalone Windows executable, a new project must first be created. This project should contain all the appropriate code for the application. The code can be contained in a single file or may be distributed across many files. The following steps indicate how to create and run a sample project in each IDE.

**In Visual C++ Express:**

Step 1.   Launch C++ Express. From the start-up screen of the IDE, select **File | New | Project**. This displays a project template screen from which the user can select a range of project types.

Step 2.   From the project templates dialog, select **Win32 | Win32 Console Application**, and assign the project a name. Click **OK** to create a new standard application project and to initialize the project setup wizard. The project setup wizard helps to configure the compiler for your project. See Figure 2.9.

Step 3.   Click the **Next** button to pass the welcome screen, and arrange the application settings as shown in Figure 2.10. Click **Finish** to create the project. See Figure 2.11.

Step 4.   The new application is now configured and the programmer can input code into the editor to build the application. Consider the sample program featured in Figure 2.11.

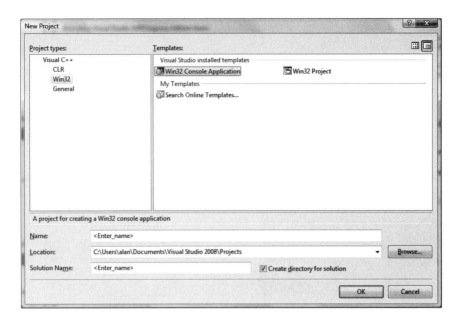

**FIGURE 2.9**   Select a project type to create.

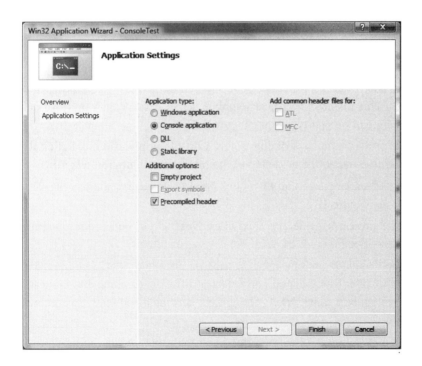

**FIGURE 2.10**   Refine project creation parameters.

**❙ FIGURE 2.11**    New project ready to run.

### In Code::Blocks:

Step 1.    Launch Code::Blocks. From the start-up screen of the IDE, select **File | New | Project**. This displays a project template screen from which the user can select a range of project types. See Figure 2.12.

Step 2.    From the project templates dialog, select **Console application** and click the **Go** button to move to the next step of the project configuration wizard.

Step 3.    Select **C++** as a language and then click **Next** to proceed to the project naming step. See Figure 2.13.

Step 4.    Assign the project a name and then click **Next** to proceed to the compiler options step. See Figure 2.14.

Step 5.    Leave the compiler options intact to use the standard GCC compiler that ships with Code::Blocks. You can select a different compiler by using the drop-down list box. Click **Next**. The project is created and ready to compile. See Figure 2.15.

Step 6.    The new application is now configured and the programmer can input code into the editor to build the application. Consider the sample program featured in Figure 2.15.

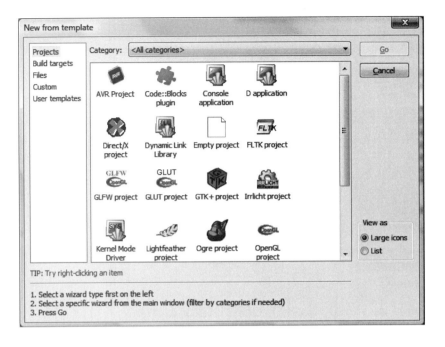

**▌ FIGURE 2.12**   Select a project type to create.

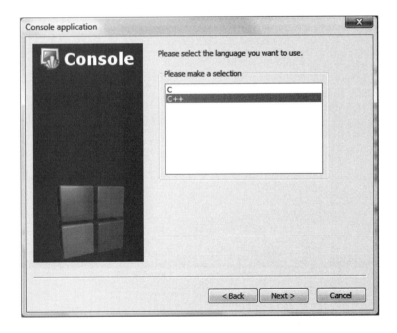

**▌ FIGURE 2.13**   Select the language to use.

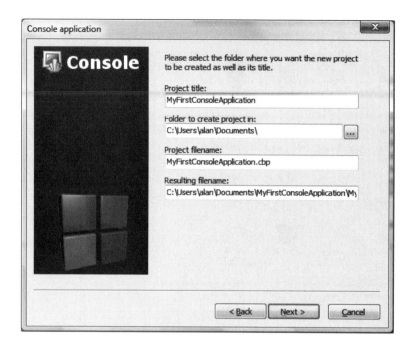

**I FIGURE 2.14**    Assign the project a name.

**I FIGURE 2.15**    New project ready to run.

## 2.5.2  Compiling a Project Using Visual C++ Express and Code::Blocks

For application projects, the process of compilation translates valid source code into an executable file that can be run by a user as a standalone application. Code that is not syntactically correct (that is, invalid C++ code) will invoke a compilation error and the application will not be built. For each and every error the compiler finds, it will print to the debug window both the line number of the erroneous code and a description of the error. A project can be compiled in either debug or release mode. The former encodes extra debugging information into the final EXE file, and the latter omits this data for a reduced file size and encodes the EXE using a variety of optimizations for improved performance. For this reason, debug mode is often used by developers to produce test run applications, and release mode is used to produce the final EXE distributed to end users. The following instructions detail how to compile projects using both Visual C++ Express and Code::Blocks.

**In Visual C++ Express:**

Step 1.  Before compiling a project, a developer typically selects the compilation mode: either debug or release. This can be selected via the drop-down list box on the toolbar of the IDE. For the purposes of this tutorial, select **Release** mode. See Figure 2.16.

Step 2.  To compile the source code into an application EXE without also running the EXE after compilation, select **Build | Build Solution** from the application main menu (or press **F7** on the keyboard). To both compile and run the EXE, click the **Play** button on the toolbar (or press **F5** on the keyboard). See Figure 2.17.

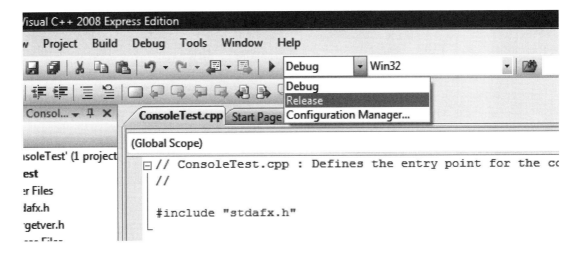

**| FIGURE 2.16**  Setting debug or release mode.

**EXERCISE 2.1**

Search the Internet to find at least three additional C++ IDEs. Compare your list with mine:

- Dev-C++
- C++Builder
- Eclipse

**In Code::Blocks:**

Step 1.   Before compiling a project, a developer typically selects the compilation mode: either debug or release. This can be selected via the drop-down list box on the toolbar of the IDE. For the purposes of this tutorial, select **Release** mode. See Figure 2.18.

Step 2.   To compile the source code into an application EXE without also running the EXE after compilation, select **Build | Build** from the application main menu (or press **Ctrl+F9** on the keyboard or press the blue cog icon on the toolbar). To both compile and run the EXE, click the **Play** button on the toolbar (or press **F9** on the keyboard). See Figure 2.19.

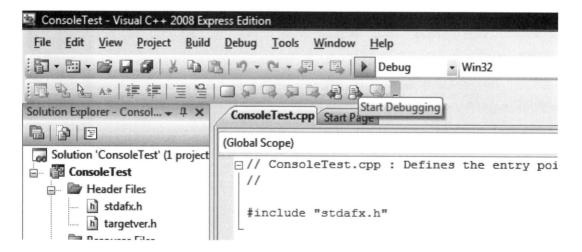

**FIGURE 2.17**   Compile and run project.

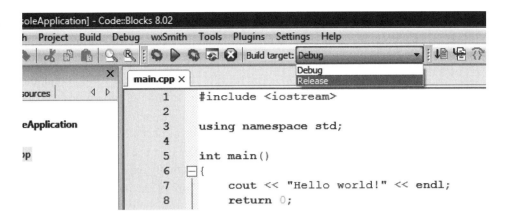

**FIGURE 2.18**  Setting debug or release mode.

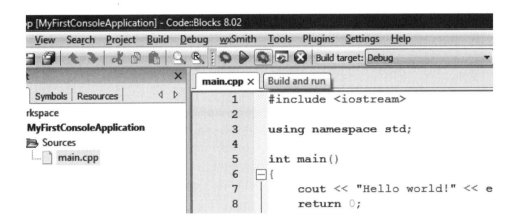

**FIGURE 2.19**  Compile and run project.

### 2.5.3  Setting Include Directories

Until now this chapter has focused on using a C++ IDE to create a sample "Hello World" application—that is, an application that prints the words "hello world" to the standard output (the screen, or more accurately the window). Given that this project requires only a few lines of code, there is little or no reason to spread that code across multiple files. However, as applications grow in size to thousands and even hundreds of thousands of lines, it can be not only convenient but critical to the success of a project to divide the code cleanly across multiple files of the project, linking the files together using the standard C++ #include preprocessor directive. The #include directive when inserted into a C++ source file signals to the compiler that a relationship exists between this file and another, that the code of another file is pertinent to the code of this file. On encountering this directive in a file, the compiler searches all of the include paths on the system for a file whose name was specified in the include directive (e.g., #include<myfile.h>). The list of include paths represents the range of places across which the compiler will search for files. If and when the file is found, the code in the file is included as appropriate by the compiler into the current project and can by accessed by the file featuring the include directive. If the file was not found on any of the include paths, then compilation fails and the project will not be built. It is important to note that the compiler searches for files only on the include paths of the system and not elsewhere. For this reason, a file might actually exist on the system and yet not be found by the compiler because it is not on any of the include paths. Thus, the success of the compilation process depends in part on the compiler's ability to locate and include the files mentioned in the include directives of the C++ files in the current project. Therefore, it is important for successful compilations that a developer can edit the list of include paths used by their compiler. The following set of instructions details for each IDE how to edit the list of include paths.

**In Visual C++ Express:**

Step 1.   Select **Tools | Options** from the IDE main menu. This displays the Options window from which a range of settings can be specified.

Step 2.   In the Options window, select **Projects and Solutions | VC++ Directories** from the tree view list box on the left side of the window. Then use the **Show directories for** drop-down list box on the right side of the window to select the option **Include files**. The list view below is then populated with the list of directories on the current include path. See Figure 2.20.

Step 3.   To add a path to the list, click the folder icon above the list box of included paths. A new line appears in the list box and the user can edit this as appropriate for the newly added path. Paths can be removed by first selecting the path from the list and then clicking the red X icon above the list box. See Figure 2.21.

**In Code::Blocks:**

Step 1.   Select **Project | Build Options** from the IDE main menu. This displays the Project build options window from which a range of settings can be specified.

Step 2.   In the Project build options window, select the **Search Directories** tab. This displays a list view of the directories on the current include path for the current project. See Figure 2.22.

Step 3.   To add a path to the list, click the **Add** button below the list box of included paths. A dialog appears, prompting the user for a path to add. To remove a path, select the path to remove in the list box and then click the **Delete** button at the bottom of the window. See Figure 2.23.

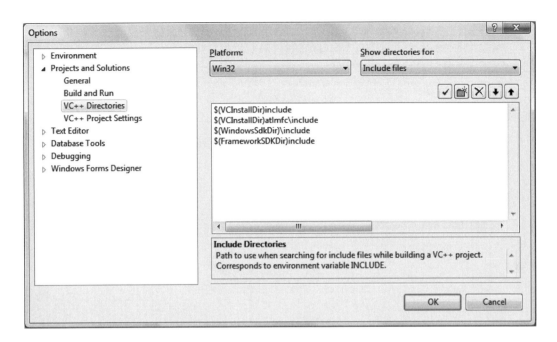

**FIGURE 2.20**   Setting include directories.

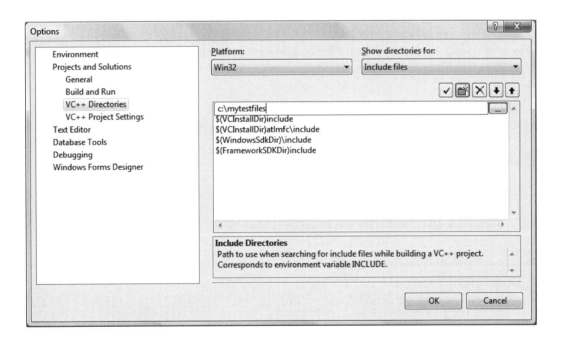

**FIGURE 2.21**   Adding and editing include directories.

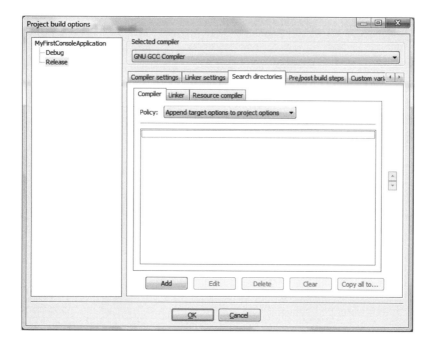

**FIGURE 2.22**   Setting include directories.

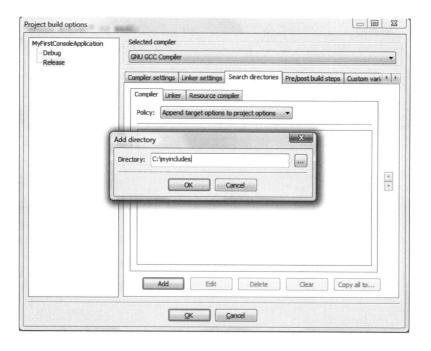

**FIGURE 2.23**   Adding and editing include directories.

## 2.5.4   Linking to Libraries

The standard C++ header and source files (.h, .hpp, .c, and .cpp) are included in a project by way of include directives. For each of those directives found by the compiler in the source files of the project, it will search across the list of include paths for a file with a matching name to incorporate into compilation. However, header and source files are not the only types of files that a project might include. A project can also link to precompiled libraries, and these often take the form of .lib or .a files. A compiler links to these files in a similar but distinct way from the way it links to the standard header and source files. This section offers steps on how to link to library files using Visual Studio Express and Code::Blocks.

**In Visual C++ Express:**

Step 1.   Select **Tools | Options** from the IDE main menu. This displays the Options window from which a range of settings can be specified.

Step 2.   In the Options window, select **Projects and Solutions | VC++ Directories** from the tree view list box on the left side of the window. Then use the **Show directories for** drop-down list box on the right side of the window to select the option **Library files**. The list view below is then populated with the list of directories on; the current library path. See Figure 2.24.

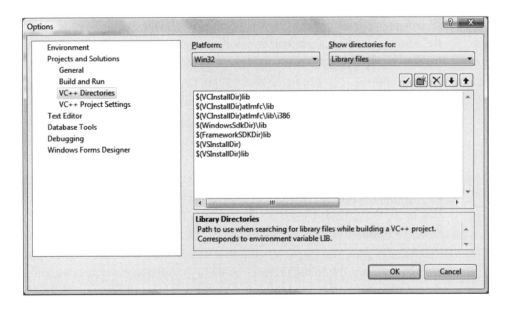

**FIGURE 2.24**   Setting library directories.

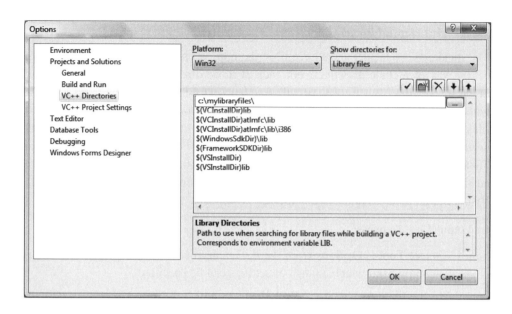

**I FIGURE 2.25**    Adding and editing library directories.

Step 3.  To add a path to the list, click the folder icon above the list box of library paths. A new line appears in the list box and the user can edit this as appropriate for the newly added path. Paths can be removed by first selecting the path from the list and then clicking the red X icon above the list box. See Figure 2.25.

Step 4.  Adding a library path to the list does not link to the project any of the libraries found at that path; it simply indicates that libraries might be found there. To link a specific library to the project, its name must be stated explicitly to the compiler. To do this, first exit the Options screen by clicking the **OK** button at the bottom of the window.

Step 5.  From the main menu of the IDE, select **Project | Properties**. This displays a window from which the user can read and set properties specific not to the IDE but to the project. Then from the tree view on the left side of the window, select **Configuration Properties | Linker | Input**. See Figure 2.26.

Step 6.  The libraries pane now appears to the right side of the tree view menu. To link a specific library file to the project, the library's full name (without the path) should be entered into the **Additional Dependencies** edit box (e.g., Library. lib). This will result in the compiler at compile time searching the library directories for a library of this name; when found, it will link it into the project.

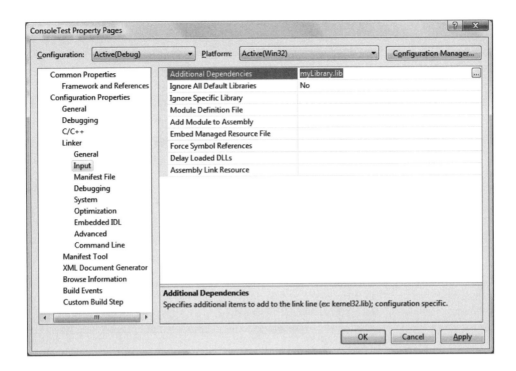

**In Code::Blocks:**

Step 1.  Select **Project | Build Options** from the IDE main menu. This displays the Project build options window from which a range of project settings are specified.

Step 2.  In the Project build options window, select the **Search Directories** tab to show the directories page. From here, click the **Linker** tab. This shows a list of directories; in the current library path. See Figure 2.27.

Step 3.  To add a path to the list, click the **Add** button below the list box of library paths. A window appears, prompting the user to specify a new library path. Paths can be removed by first selecting the path from the list and then clicking the **Delete** button below the list box.

Step 4.  Adding a library path to the list does not link to the project any of the libraries found at that path; it simply indicates that libraries might be found there. To link a specific library to the project, its name must be stated explicitly to the compiler. To do this, proceed by clicking the **Linker settings** tab.

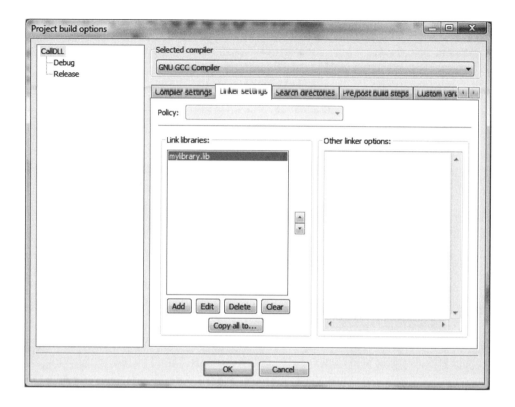

**I FIGURE 2.27**   Linking to libraries.

Step 5. From the Linker Settings page, click the **Add** button beneath the **Link libraries**
list box. To link a specific library file to the project, the library's full name (without
the path) should be entered into the prompt that appears (e.g., Library.lib). This
will result in the compiler at compile time searching the library directories for a
library of this name; when found, it will link it into the project.

## ■   2.6   Engine Architecture and DLLs

The first half of this chapter suggested that the selection of a language and an IDE represent the first steps of implementation on the long road of game engine development.
By choosing a language and an IDE, a developer is able to build libraries and applications, including games and game engines. Having chosen at least one of the two C++
IDEs presented earlier, the developer, now equipped to realize their designs, is faced
with the new issue of exactly how to start realizing their engine using their IDE. Which
is the best way to start? How should the engine be structured? For example, exactly
how should the engine code on the one hand relate to the game code on the other? It

was stated in the previous chapter that a game engine and a game are distinct entities. The game engine represents the foundation on which a game is built, and the more abstract and general an engine is, the greater the number of games for which it can be used. But given that the engine and game are separate units, the question arises as to how each relates to the other and as to whether they should interact (or merge) at compile time or at run time. To merge game and engine at compile time, a developer could code the engine into a series of header and source files and then incorporate them via the include directive into each and every one of their game projects. This method leads to the engine being *compiled into* the final game EXE so that both game and engine ship as one. This has both advantages and disadvantages for the developer. Games that are compiled into one with their engines receive a performance boost, since the engine exists in the same memory space as the game, and they are generally more reliable since the game ships implicitly with the engine and does not depend for its successful execution on the presence of external libraries such as DLLs or ActiveX® controls. The disadvantages, however, are many: First, both the game and engine must be recompiled each time a change is made in either, assuming the developer expects the latest versions of each to continue working together. Second, the developers of the game will typically require some knowledge of the engine code if they are to compile it successfully into their game project. This latter point might not prove problematic if both the game and engine developers are one and the same, but often this is not the case because engine developers frequently capitalize on their work by licensing their engines to third parties who have little or no knowledge of the engine code, as we shall see later in this book.

One alternative to compiling the engine into the game executable is to compile it into an independent DLL that is called and used by the executable as appropriate at run time. A DLL is an independent and precompiled library of functions and classes. This solution represents a run-time rather than a compile-time connection between engine and game. This too has both advantages and disadvantages for the developer. The separation between the engine as a DLL and the game as an executable means that the implementation details of each are generally hidden from the "eyes" of the other since each are separate compiled units. The code of the engine is compiled into a DLL, and the code of the game into an EXE. A common interface or protocol governs the interaction between them; as long as neither deviates from that protocol, the changes made to one typically require no recompilation of the other. This interface usually takes the form of an API (application programming interface) in which the engine DLL exposes a series of documented functions and classes that the application can access and call. Thus, the engine becomes a substitutable component to the extent that it can be replaced by newer versions or even different engines (that is, different DLL files) without raising an exception in the game, provided the newer version continues to observe the original protocol that governs the relations between game and engine. The second advantage of compiling the engine into a DLL is that it offers the engine developer the opportunity to sell and distribute their engine to third parties on a proprietary basis and without releasing its source code. Some engine developers might still choose to release their work on a free and open source basis, but nevertheless the DLL model offers the choice of distribution models. The chief disadvantage of compiling as a DLL is that it produces in the EXE a dependency on the presence of the external engine DLL file. In most circumstances, this does not prove a problem for either the developer or user because games and their dependencies are typically installed to the system by one install process. Unless the engine DLL is corrupted, replaced, or deleted on the end user system, there is little reason to believe it will cause a problem for the successful execution of the game.

In short, the engine as a functional unit can be brought into a relationship with the game either at compile time or at run time; the former involves compiling the engine source code into the game executable and the latter involves compiling the engine into a DLL that the game calls at run time. The next section focuses on implementing the latter strategy. Specifically, it details first how to create a DLL using both Visual C++ Express and Code::Blocks, and then how to create an application in each that accesses the functions and classes of that DLL through an interface. Having practiced and tuned these ideas and skills, they may then be transferred to the implementation of a game engine in the form of a DLL.

## ■ 2.7 Building and Calling a DLL in Visual C++ Express or Visual Studio 2005 and Above

To build a DLL in Visual C++ Express, a developer must use the IDE to create a DLL project, then to code a set of functions and/or classes and reveal their details in a header file, and finally to compile a DLL file and a library file. The DLL file represents the library itself that will be called at run time by game executables, and the header and library files should be compiled into all game projects intended to use the DLL. The following tutorial details step by step the process of building a DLL and of calling the functions and classes of that DLL at run time from a separate application project.

> NOTE. This sample project can be found in the book's associated code package available on the book's web page http://www.jblearning.com/ catalog/9780763784515/.

### 2.7.1    Building a DLL

Step 1.  Launch the Microsoft Visual C++ Express IDE. Create a new project by selecting **File | New | Project** from the main menu. This displays the Project Creation Wizard. See Figure 2.28.

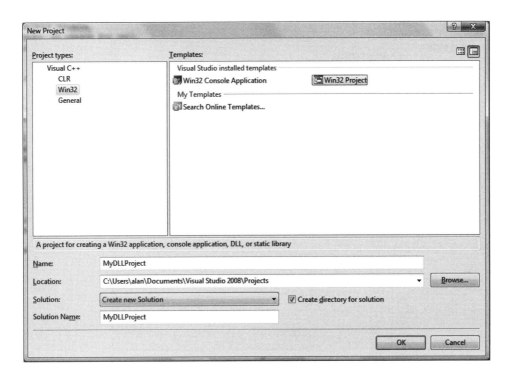

**| FIGURE 2.28**   Create a DLL by starting with a standard Windows project.

Step 2. From the Project Creation Wizard, select **Win32** from the **Project types** list at the left side of the window. Then select **Win32 Project** from the **Templates** list at the right side of the window to define this project as a standard Windows project. After this, assign the project a name using the edit boxes. Once completed, click **OK** to proceed to the next step of the project creation wizard.

Step 3. In the Win32 Application Settings window, select the **DLL** option to create the project as a DLL project. Then click the **Finish** button to close the wizard and prepare to start coding a DLL. See Figure 2.29.

Step 4. The DLL project is created and features the skeleton code of a DLL project. That is, it features the essentials of a DLL file. The job of the developer is to add flesh to this skeleton by coding functions and classes as appropriate. The project will already feature a DllMain. This function represents the entry point or starting point of the DLL and will be called whenever the DLL is first called or initialized by an application. It is also called as the DLL is uninitialized. The skeleton code looks as follows:

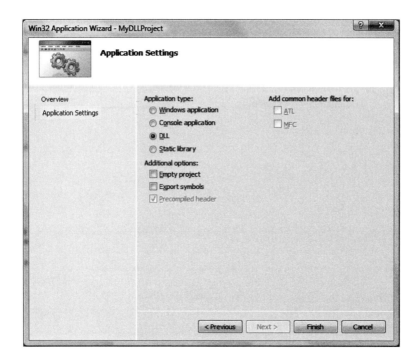

**FIGURE 2.20**    Select DLL project type.

```
// MyDLLTest.cpp : Defines the entry point for the DLL
application.
//

#include "stdafx.h"

#ifdef _MANAGED
#pragma managed(push, off)
#endif

BOOL APIENTRY DllMain( HMODULE hModule,
                       DWORD   ul_reason_for_call,
                       LPVOID lpReserved
                            )
{
    return TRUE;
}

#ifdef _MANAGED
#pragma managed(.pop)
#endif
```

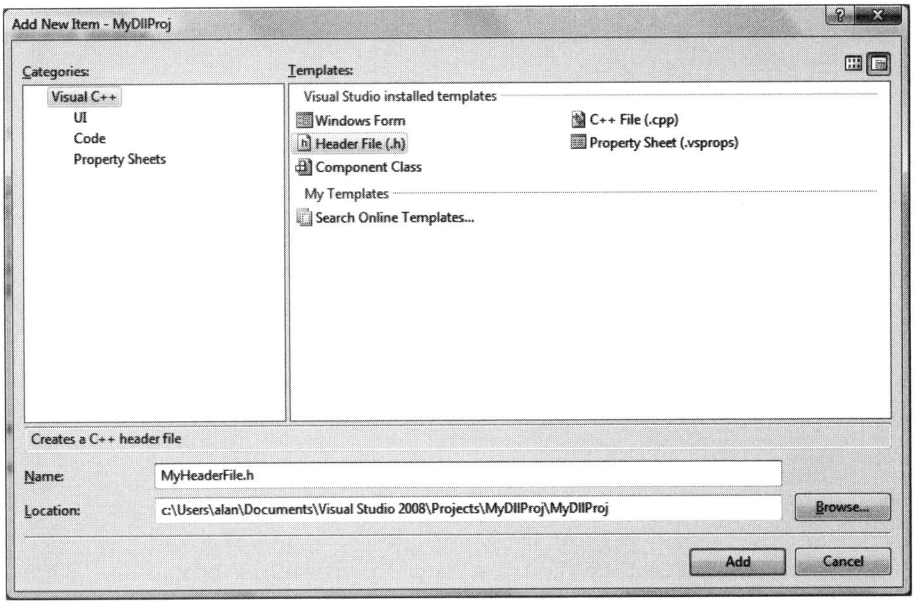

**FIGURE 2.30**    Add header and source files to the created project.

The developer might begin coding the DLL project by creating an additional header file. This file will feature the declarations of all the functions and classes that will appear in the DLL and that can be called by applications. To create a new header file, select **Project | Add New Item** from the IDE main menu. This displays the item creation window. See Figure 2.30.

Step 5.    In the item creation window, select **Header File** to add a new header file to the project. To demonstrate how to export a function from a DLL and to have this function called by an application, this guide will start by creating a simple function in the DLL called sayHello(). This function show a greetings pop-up message when called. To add this function to the DLL, its source and newly added header file must be amended. The header must contain both the function declaration and its export information, and the source must contain the function body in addition to its existing contents. The source and header files should be written as follows:

```
Main.cpp
//source
// MyDLLTest.cpp : Defines the entry point for the DLL
application.
```

```
//

#include "stdafx.h"


#ifdef _MANAGED
#pragma managed(push, off)
#endif

BOOL APIENTRY DllMain( HMODULE hModule,
                       DWORD  ul_reason_for_call,
                       LPVOID lpReserved
                             )
{
    return TRUE;
}

//Shows specified text in a pop-up message box
void DLL_EXPORT SayHello(const LPCSTR Text)
{
    MessageBoxA(NULL,Text,"DLL Text",MB_OK);
}

#ifdef _MANAGED
#pragma managed(pop)
#endif

   DLLHeader.h
   //Header. The header file declaring this function
should look like this:

#ifndef __MAIN_H__
#define __MAIN_H__

#define DLL_EXPORT __declspec(dllexport)

#ifdef __cplusplus
extern "C"
{
void DLL_EXPORT SayHello(const LPCSTR sometext);
}
#endif

#endif // __MAIN_H__
```

**NOTE.** Throughout the code listings in this book, bold formating is used to highlight significant words, statements, and sections.

Step 6. Compiling this DLL project in release mode will produce both a DLL file and a lib file. The DLL file will be required by applications at run time and should be distributed alongside the application executable. The lib file must be included in all projects intending to use the DLL file and will be linked against the project at compile time. It does not need to be distributed with the final executable. It is now time to create a new sample application that will call the (sayHello) function from the DLL. To do that, create a new Windows Console application in Visual Studio. Use the step-by-step guide given earlier in this chapter for information on how to do that.

## 2.7.2 Calling a DLL

Step 7. Once a new application is generated, the DLL lib file should be linked to the application (see section 2.5.4). Once linked, the application should also include the DLL header file that features the declarations for the function and classes exported from the DLL. This file should be exactly the same as the header given in step 5, except the following line:

```
#define DLL_EXPORT __declspec(dllexport)
```

Should be replaced with:

```
#define DLL_EXPORT __declspec(dllimport)
```

Step 8. The main source file for the completed application should look like the following:

```
#include "stdafx.h"
#include "MyDll.h" //Include DLL header

int _tmain(int argc, _TCHAR* argv[])
{
    sayHello("Hello");
    return 0;
}
```

Step 9. This application, which demonstrates how to call a function from a DLL file, can now be compiled and run. Users should remember to include the DLL file in the folder from which the EXE will be launched.

## ■  2.8    Building and Calling a DLL in Code::Blocks

To build a DLL in Code::Blocks, a developer must use the IDE to create a DLL project, then to code a set of functions and/or classes and reveal their details in a header file, and finally to compile a DLL file and a library file. The DLL file represents the library itself that will be called at run time by game executables, and the header and library files should be compiled into all game projects intended to use the DLL. The following tutorial details step by step the process of building a DLL and of calling the functions and classes of that DLL at run time from a separate application project.

> **NOTE.** This sample project can be found in the book's associated code package available on the book's web page http://www.jblearning.com/catalog/9780763784515/.

### 2.8.1    Building a DLL

Step 1.    Launch the Code::Blocks IDE. Create a new project by selecting **File | New | Project** from the main menu. This displays the Project Creation Wizard. See Figure 2.31.

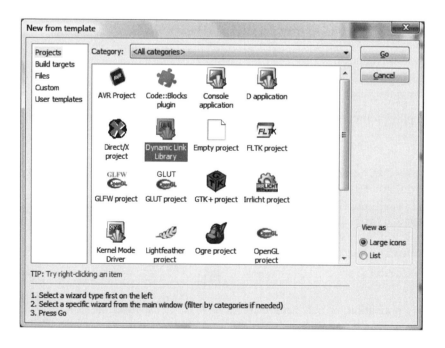

**I FIGURE 2.31**    Create a DLL by selecting the DLL project type.

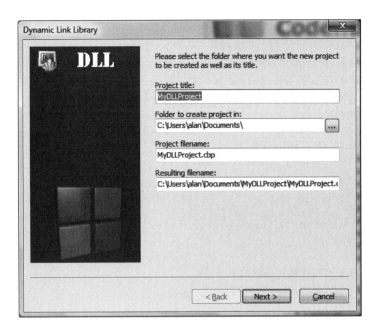

**I FIGURE 2.32**   Name the DLL project.

Step 2. From the Project Creation Wizard, select **Dynamic Link Library** in the list and click **Go**. Then select a destination for the project. Click **Next**. Leave the compiler at the default settings. Click **OK**. A new DLL project is generated and ready to implement. See Figure 2.32.

Step 3. The DLL project is created and features the skeleton code of a DLL. That is, it features the essentials of a DLL file. The job of the developer is to add flesh to this skeleton by coding functions and classes as appropriate. The project will already feature a DllMain. This function represents the entry point or starting point of the DLL, and this function will be called whenever the DLL is first called or initialized by an application. It is also called as the DLL is uninitialized. The skeleton code looks as follows:

```
// MyDLLTest.cpp : Defines the entry point for the DLL
application.
#include "main.h"

BOOL WINAPI DllMain(HINSTANCE hinstDLL, DWORD fdwReason,
LPVOID lpvReserved)
{
```

```
        switch (fdwReason)
        {
            case DLL_PROCESS_ATTACH:
                // attach to process
                // return FALSE to fail DLL load
                break;

            case DLL_PROCESS_DETACH:
                // detach from process
                break;

            case DLL_THREAD_ATTACH:
                // attach to thread
                break;

            case DLL_THREAD_DETACH:
                // detach from thread
                break;
        }
        return TRUE; // successful
    }
```

The developer might begin coding the DLL project by creating an additional header file or by using the header file generated with the project. This file will feature the declarations of all the functions and classes that will appear in the DLL and that can be called by applications. For this sample, the pregenerated header will be edited.

Step 4.   To demonstrate how to export a function from a DLL and to have this function called by an application, this guide will start by creating a simple function in the DLL source file called sayHello(). This function show a greetings pop-up message when called. To add this function to the DLL, its source file and newly added header file must be amended. The header must contain both the function declaration and its export information, and the source must contain the function body in addition to its existing contents. The source and header files should be written as follows:

```
Main.cpp
#include "main.h"

// a sample exported function
void DLL_EXPORT SayHello(const LPCSTR sometext)
{
    MessageBoxA(0, sometext, "DLL Message", MB_OK | MB_
ICONINFORMATION);
```

```
}

BOOL WINAPI DllMain(HINSTANCE hinstDLL, DWORD fdwReason,
LPVOID lpvReserved)
{
    switch (fdwReason)
    {
        case DLL_PROCESS_ATTACH:
            // attach to process
            // return FALSE to fail DLL load
            break;

        case DLL_PROCESS_DETACH:
            // detach from process
            break;

        case DLL_THREAD_ATTACH:
            // attach to thread
            break;

        case DLL_THREAD_DETACH:
            // detach from thread
            break;
    }
    return TRUE; // successful
}

   Main.h
#ifndef __MAIN_H__
#define __MAIN_H__

#include <windows.h>

/*  To use this exported function of dll, include this
header
 *  in your project.
 */

#ifdef BUILD_DLL
    #define DLL_EXPORT __declspec(dllexport)
#else
    #define DLL_EXPORT __declspec(dllimport)
#endif
```

```
#ifdef __cplusplus
extern "C"
{
#endif


void DLL_EXPORT SayHello(const LPCSTR sometext);


#ifdef __cplusplus
}
#endif


#endif // __MAIN_H__
```

Step 5.  Compiling this DLL project in release mode will produce both a DLL file and a .a file. The DLL file will be required by applications at run time and should be distributed alongside the application executable. The .a file must be included in all projects intending to use the DLL file and will be linked against the project at compile time. It does not need to be distributed with the final executable. It is now time to create a new sample application that will call the (sayHello) function from the DLL. To do that, create a new Windows Console application in Code::Blocks. Use the step-by-step guide given earlier in this chapter for information if required.

### 2.8.2   Calling a DLL

Step 6.  Once a new application is generated, the DLL .a file should linked to the application (see section 2.5.4). Once linked, the application should also include the DLL header file that features the declarations for the function and classes exported from the DLL. This file should be exactly the same as the header given in Step 4.

Step 7.  The main source file for the completed application should look like the following:

```
#include <iostream>
#include "main.h" //DLL Header file generated in the DLL
project

using namespace std;

int main()
{
    sayHello("hello");
    return 0;
}
```

Step 8.   This application, which demonstrates how to call a function from a DLL file, can now be compiled and run. Users should remember to include the DLL file in the folder from which the EXE will be launched.

## ■  2.9   **Preparing to Make Games**

The previous sections have demonstrated not only how to get started using a C++ IDE but also how to use them to build a series of basic project types that will prove valuable when creating game engines. Specifically these types are executables and DLLs. This section moves on from exploring IDEs and considers long-established classes, algorithms, and coding conventions that will also prove valuable when coding engines in C++. Before firing up Code::Blocks or Visual Studio to code a game engine according to a design document, any developer who first sits back to carefully consider the basics (the fundamental building blocks) of any games that spring to mind will likely notice a number of common features between them. Some of these features are worth considering further, even though their existence and implementation may *appear* trivial or obvious at first sight.

- First, every game, regardless of genre, must work with data; that is, strings, integers, floats, etc. For example, a game may display text at an (XY) coordinate on the screen, may calculate differences between player scores, may read player input from the keyboard, and may read both numerical and textual data from saved-game files in order to restore sessions saved by the gamer on previous occasions, among many other tasks. In common with most software, therefore, a game is, at its most basic level, a data-handling machine. It accepts incoming data, processes it, and outputs a result. Consequently, developers often find it useful to standardize the data types used throughout their source code for any given game; e.g., use only *one* data type for *all* strings such as the cross-platform STL class std::string, instead of using a variety of string data types for different string variables like char, CString, std::string, etc. Class std::string and the STL are considered in more detail shortly.

- Second, since all games collect and process data at run time whether from files on disk, user input, or the result of additional calculations, it is important for developers to show foresight when making their games by designing algorithms to structure and process data optimally in memory. For example, in a typical RTS (real time strategy) game like StarCraft® or Command & Conquer™, each faction (including the gamer's) must eliminate all rival factions for domination of a given territory. In developing their army, each faction begins by first harvesting nearby resources (such as wood, ore, and gold) in order to fuel the construction of buildings and technology, and from these to ultimately recruit and deploy more creatures and fighters, who are subsequently dispatched across the map to eliminate enemy targets. Here, then, each faction in the course of its in-game development collects at least three kinds of items: resources, buildings, and units. A developer is then faced with the problem of how best to code (create) three separate lists in memory, each designed to keep track of a faction's resources, buildings, and units, respectively, at run time. A developer may initially choose, for example, to create a fixed-sized array for each faction to hold a collection of pointers to its units, where each element in the array is a pointer to a single military unit (a wizard, a goblin, a tank, etc.). However, a problem arises for the developer when they consider that as new units are created by the gamer at run time, those units must be added into the last vacant elements of the units array, and as units are destroyed, by, say, enemy fire, they should then be removed from the array without affecting any other active elements. In short, the developer requires an array class that may dynamically grow or shrink in memory as items are added and removed, respectively, meaning that the array is always sized exactly to hold no more or less than the number of items in memory at any one time. This kind of list arrangement can be achieved using the STL class std::vector, which is discussed in a later section of this chapter.

• Next, most games are driven by a message pump (or lifeline) that is qualitatively different from the event-driven programming used in other nongame software, and consequently it has earned the name "game loop." Almost all nongame software (such as word processors, database applications, or graphics editors) work by listening for and responding to user input (keypresses and mouse movements) as they occur at run time when they are sent to the application window through standard WinAPI messages. For example, a word processor only prints a document when the user clicks the Print button, and it only inserts characters into the active document when the user presses keys on the keyboard; if the user does nothing, then the program does nothing except wait for input from the user. Games, however, work differently; an example illustrates this difference: In a typical first-person-shooter game—like Quake®, Doom®, or Unreal®—the player is armed with a weapon and thrown into an arena with other competitors who each must deploy their aiming skills and stealthy tactics against one another to become the "last man standing." Here, like with nongaming software, the player character shoots when the user presses the fire button, and the player character jumps when the user presses the jump button. But, unlike with event-driven software, the enemy combatants continue to move and other game events occur simultaneously to all other events such that, if the player stood still and the user did nothing, the game wouldn't stop and the opponents wouldn't freeze waiting for the user to press a key. Instead, the game continues, and the NPCs (nonplayer characters) continue to participate as though they were real humans, whether the player is participating or not (unless the user presses a pause button). For this reason, games are usually driven by a message loop mechanism rather than by an event-driven framework since game action occurs in real time and in no way depends on the user's input to continue working. The game loop is considered in more detail in a later section of this chapter.

## ■ 2.10 Using the STL: Strings and Lists

To summarize some of the preceding section on game development basics: Game development for a programmer begins from a library, or a common framework of data structures, algorithms, and functions. The STL (Standard Template Library) offers such a comprehensive set of tools, particularly in the form of classes: std::string (for strings) and std::vector (for lists of objects and lists of pointers to objects). The importance of these two classes for game development is now considered more closely.

### 2.10.1 std::String

A string is a linear array of characters arranged sequentially in memory; the word "hello" is a string of characters, where each character is a letter in the word "hello." Typically, C++ strings are declared literally as an array of chars (e.g., Char mystring[50]), but the STL string class makes this process simpler. The following step-by-step tutorial details how to work with strings using std::string. It considers creating, copying, and editing strings.

> **NOTE.** An exercise in processing strings and characters of strings (like the samples that follow) may prove helpful for any developer who may later choose to use XML for storing data on disk, external to their game. XML files are essentially an organized text file, and so XML strings—like those used for XML properties and tags in the file—may require processing like any other string, meaning using std::string as a class will likely be important, perhaps for processing saved game files and data files.

### Configuring Projects to Use the STL and std::string

1. Beginning from the desktop, start the Visual Studio or Code::Blocks IDE and use the New Project Wizard to create a new Console (shell/command line) project ready to compile. See earlier sections for details on how to do this if needed.

2. Open the main project source file (.cpp) and add the string header to the end of the existing preprocessor directive "include <string>" as shown here. This

directive includes the STL std::string class header, meaning std::string may be used throughout the project:

```
#include <iostream>
#include <string>

using namespace std;

int main()
{
    cout << "Hello world!" << endl;
    return 0;
}
```

3. The project is now configured to use class std::string.

**Declaring, Creating, and Assigning Strings with std::string**

1. Instances of std::string can be created as follows:

```
//Empty
std::string MyString1;

//Set to hello
std::string MyString2 = "hello";

//Set to hello
std::string MyString3 = MyString2;
```

2. Any two or more instances of std::string may be concatenated (combined) together to form a single larger string using the standard addition operator (+):

```
std::string MyString1 = "hello";
std::string MyString2 = "world";

//MyString3 = "hello world"
std::string MyString3 = MyString1 + MyString2;
```

3. The value (contents) of any instance of std::string may be queried or determined by using the C++ equality operator (==):

```
std::string MyString1 = "hello world";

if(MyString1=="hello world")
```

```
{
        //Do something here
}
```

## Looping through Characters of a String with std::string

1. Each character (letter) in a single instance of std::string can be read individually using the standard array subscript operator ([]) along with an array index specifying the character offset into the string, measured rightward from the first character at (0) as follows:

```
std::string MyString1 = "hello world";

cout<<MyString1[3];
```

2. The length method of std::string returns the length of the string (that is, the total number of characters of which the string is composed). This method, in combination with access to individual characters in the string using the array subscript operator, means any std::string can be iterated through (looped through), character by character:

```
std::string MyString1 = "hello world";

for(int i = 0; i < mystring1.length(); i++)
{
   cout<<mystring1[i] << "\n";
}
```

3. Each character in a string may also be iterated through by using STL iterators rather than array indexes, where the begin method returns a pointer to the first character, and the end method returns a pointer to the last character, as follows:

```
std::string MyString1 = "hello world";
string::iterator my_iter;
for(my_iter = MyString1.begin(); my_iter != MyString1.
end(); my_iter++)
{
   cout<<*my_iter;
}
```

## Searching for Characters in a Specified Instance of std::string

1. For situations where the content of a string is unknown or where a string's structure and format must be analyzed closely, the std::string class offers the find method to search through a given string for a specified character or sequence of

characters, returning a pointer to the first character in the string where a match is found. This method may be called as follows:

```
/*Counts all occurrences of the word "hello" in a
specified instance of std::string*/

string input;
int word_count = 0;

cout<<"Please enter a string now:>";
getline(cin, input, '\n');

for(int i = input.find("hello", 0); i != string::npos; i
= input.find("hello", i))
{
    word_count++;
    i++;
}
cout<<word_count;
```

### Extracting and Inserting Substrings from and to a Specified Instance of std::string

1. A string is an array of characters, and a substring is a smaller subset of characters from that array; "ello," "lo," and "o" are all substrings of "hello." To extract a substring (*dest*) from a specified larger string (*source*), the std::string class offers the substr method. This method returns a new string that is the requested substring (*dest*), and it also accepts two integer arguments: one specifying the offset into the source string, marking the first character of the substring (*dest*), and the other specifying the length of the substring (*dest*) in characters as measured rightward from the offset, character by character. An example follows:

```
std::string MyString1 = "hello world";
//string is "o wo"
std::string substr = MyString1.substr(3, 7);
```

2. In addition to substring extraction using the substr method, a string of any length can also be inserted into any instance of std::string using the insert method. Similarly, strings can be removed from any instance of std::string using the erase method. The following code sample illustrates both insert and erase at work:

```
std::string MyString1 = "hello world";
//Now is "helthis is a substringlo world"
```

```
MyString1.insert(3, "this is a substring");
//Now is "hhis is a substringlo world"
MyString1.erase(1, 3);
```

### Converting Instances of std::string to Standard char* Pointers

1. Despite the multitude of benefits afforded by std::string, with features like substring extraction and character insertion, there will undoubtedly be moments when a developer encounters a function from a third-party library (such as a WinAPI call) that requires a string argument of type char*, rather than type std::string. Thus, so that instances of std::string may be type compatible with functions requiring arguments of type char*, the c_str method is offered to convert strings from type std::string to type char*. An example follows:

```
std::string MyString1 = "hello world";
const char* MyString2 = MyString1.c_str();
```

## 2.10.2 std::Vector

Most computer games keep track of lists of items. For example, RTS games (where factions fight one another for domination of a map) maintain at least three lists "under the hood" for each faction that participates in battle: one list for a faction's resources (wood, ore, gold, etc.), one for its buildings (refinery, barracks, etc.), and one for its units (wizard, fighter, goblin, etc.). Similarly, in an adventure game like Monkey Island®, Grim Fandango®, or Syberia™, gamers control a character who solves a mystery by collecting and using objects found around the game world. The objects collected by the player are added to their inventory (pockets) where they remain until they can be used or disposed of to further their progress in the game; here, again, the inventory reveals itself to be a *list* of collected items in the same way a string is a list of collected characters. The primary characteristics of a list are: (1) items can be added or removed from the list at run time, and (2) the list size changes in memory as items are added or removed in order to accommodate exactly the number of items it currently holds, no more or less (it is said to be *dynamic*). Meeting this criteria is the STL std::vector class, which offers game developers a template class for maintaining a dynamic list of items (of any data type) in memory. In short, std::vector is a class for holding a list in memory to which items can be added or removed at run time. The following sections examine how this class is used.

### Creating a List with std::vector

1. Open the main project source file(.cpp) and add the vector header to the end of the existing preprocessor directive "include <vector>" as shown here. This

directive includes the STL std::vector class header so std::vector may be used throughout the project wherever lists are required:

```
#include <iostream>
#include <vector>

using namespace std;

int main()
{
  cout << "Hello world!" << endl;
  return 0;
}
```

### Declaring Instances of std::vector

1. The STL class std::vector is a template class and each instance represents a unique list of objects (of any one data type) in memory; that is, any single instance of std::vector is a list of objects of the same type: a list of integers, a list of strings, a list of pointers, etc. std::vector is said to be a template class because each instance (each list) must be declared as belonging to a specific data type at the time of declaration. Consider the following code:

```
//List of integers
std::vector<int> ListOfIntegers;

//List of strings
std::vector<std::string> ListOfStrings;

//List of pointers
std::vector<CMyClass*> ListOfPointers;
```

### Adding Items to a List Using std::vector

1. std::vector maintains a list of items, and items are added to the list at run time using the push_back method. This method accepts as an argument the template object to be added to the list declared as being a matching type. The following code illustrates the process of adding a list:

```
//List of strings
std::vector<std::string> ListOfStrings;
```

```
//Add strings to vector list
ListOfStrings.push_back("hello");
ListOfStrings.push_back("alan");
ListOfStrings.push_back("list");
```

**Cycling through Items in a List Using std::vector**

1. Like with elements in an array or characters in an instance of std::string, or any other
   data structure where elements are arranged sequentially in memory, the items in an
   instance of std::list can be accessed individually by using the subscript operator ([])
   (e.g., MyList[5]) or by using the standard STL iterators, as follows:

```
//List of strings
std::vector<std::string> ListOfStrings;

//Add strings to vector list
ListOfStrings.push_back("hello");
ListOfStrings.push_back("alan");
ListOfStrings.push_back("list");

for(int i=0; i< ListOfStrings.size(); i++)
        cout<<ListOfStrings[i]<<"\n";
```
Or:

```
//List of strings
std::vector<std::string> ListOfStrings;
std::vector<std::string>::iterator myStringVectorIterator;

//Add strings to vector list
ListOfStrings.push_back("hello");
ListOfStrings.push_back("alan");
ListOfStrings.push_back("list");

for( myStringVectorIterator = ListOfStrings.begin();
     myStringVectorIterator != ListOfStrings.end();
     myStringVectorIterator++)
{
   cout<<(*myStringVectorIterator)<<"\n";
}
```

**Removing Items from a List Using std::vector**

1. The std::vector class supports both the addition of new items to the list and
   the removal of existing items from the list. An item (or a range of items) can

be removed from the list using the erase method of std::vector, a method that accepts two STL iterator arguments specifying the start and end range of items to be deleted; the first argument is an iterator marking the first item in a range to be removed, and the second argument is an iterator marking the final item in a range of items to be removed. The following code illustrates the typical usage of the erase method of std::vector for removing items from a list:

```
//List of strings
std::vector<std::string> ListOfStrings;

//[...] add stuff to the list here

//Remove items 3-5
ListOfStrings.erase(ListOfStrings .begin()+3,
ListOfStrings.begin()+5);
```

## ■ 2.11   The Game Loop

Programmatically, one of the key dividing factors separating games from nongame software is the presence of a game loop; game software is driven by a game loop while nongame software is instead event-driven. The game loop is the heartbeat (or the message pump) unique to games. Traditionally, nongame (event driven) software such as word processors, database applications, or graphics suites work by first waiting for input from the user (such as a keypress or mouse click) before performing an action. That is, a user clicks the Print button in a spreadsheet application, and it responds by printing the active document, or the user press a key on the keyboard and the application responds by adding a character to the active document. The implication is that when the user does nothing, the application does little or nothing except wait for further instructions in the form of WinAPI messages sent to the window whenever user input occurs. Games differ from this event-driven arrangement, however. Certainly, games do respond to events—for example, in a side-scrolling platformer where the gamer must guide a character safely through a level by running and jumping across risk-laden platforms, the gamer may press the jump button and in response the character jumps, or they may press the fire button and consequently the character attacks nearby enemies. But more than this, games also work when the user does nothing— the enemies continue moving, the game world still ticks over even when the player offers no input; in other words, the game does not freeze when user input stops. The game continues working whether or not the user is taking part, and it is this "having a mind of its own" behavior that the game loop is designed to offer. The following code is a sample C++ source file featuring a game loop that is set up and ready for a developer to make a game:

```
MSG mssg;

// prime the message structure
PeekMessage( &mssg, NULL, 0, 0, PM_NOREMOVE);

// run until completed
while (mssg.message!=WM_QUIT) {

  // is there a message to process?
  if (PeekMessage( &mssg, NULL, 0, 0, PM_REMOVE)) {

   // dispatch the message
   TranslateMessage(&mssg);
   DispatchMessage(&mssg);

  } else {

    //FRAME BEGINS HERE
    ReadInput();
    UpdatePhysics();
    UpdateSound();
    DrawFrame();
  }
}
```

As mentioned, the game loop is the heartbeat (or the message pump) unique to games; the loop begins after the game is executed, and exiting from the loop signals a game's termination. In short, the game loop is a C++ while loop where each iteration (each cycle) of the loop corresponds to a single frame; that is, a snapshot moment in the timeline of a game. On each iteration of the loop (on each frame) a game should:

1. **Read user input from the keyboard and mouse** to determine whether the user has moved the game character, clicked a menu item, performed any other action, or requested to exit the game (whereupon the loop should be terminated).

2. **Update game physics** based on user input and the position of other game objects in the world. This may include applying gravity to objects in the air, moving the player character across the screen in the direction corresponding to an arrow keypress, etc.

3. **Update the sound** and play appropriate sounds for that moment of the game such as walking noises corresponding to player movement, etc.

4. **Draw the frame**, which is the final phase of the loop, the moment when all game graphics are refreshed and drawn anew to the window according to the position and perspective of the game camera in the game world. Chapter 5 considers the drawing of game graphics to the application window using a third-party game development library called SDL.

**EXERCISE 2.2**

Search the Internet to find at least three additional STL classes suitable for game programming. List at least one reason for each class. Compare your answers with the following:

1. std::map: This template class is a dynamic two-dimensional array of objects in the form of <key, value> pairs. This class would be useful for creating a lookup table and could be used for an RPG game to maintain a collection of skills/experience attributes such as: <Strength, 50>, <Intelligence, 50>, <Speed, 70>, etc.
   http://www.cplusplus.com/reference/stl/map/

2. std::stringstream: This class represents a collection of strings that can be manipulated as though they were standard output streams. This class would be useful for reading and writing to data files on disk.
   http://www.cplusplus.com/reference/iostream/stringstream/

3. std::queue: This class represents a FIFO list (first-in, first-out). Items pushed first on to the list will be the first items to be removed. This class would be useful for creating a command list for an RTS game. Gamers can queue a series of instructions to their units such as attack, then move, then harvest resources, etc.
   http://www.cplusplus.com/reference/stl/queue/

## ■ 2.12   Chapter Summary

In summary, this chapter has considered the basics of game programming generally in terms of five key developmental issues: (1) selecting an IDE with which to develop game applications, (2) creating two kinds of projects: executables and DLLs, (3) establishing a standard set of data types so that each game made by the same developer handles data (integers, floats, and especially strings) similarly across varied platforms, (4) common framework of classes and functions to provide a cross-platform foundation upon which games can be built, and (5) the game loop to keep a game application alive and running, and to configure games with a frame-based configuration rather than the event-based configuration of most nongames. This will ensure that games continue to operate even when no input is received or processed from the user.

The next part of the book applies the knowledge gained from this chapter and the previous to taking the first steps in engine development. It does this by breaking down engine development into a series of steps, each step being the focus for a unique chapter. The intention is that once the reader has finished the book each chapter will have contributed toward the whole to have left us with a basic but nevertheless complete and workable game engine.

# 2

# Implementing the Engine

The second chapter of this book had a practical focus and prepared the way for development of an engine by introducing a selection of C++ IDEs available in the contemporary games industry and by introducing a core set of classes and concepts that are found in many games. The first chapter, in contrast, was theory focused and sought to define the term "game engine" and to enumerate the core features of an engine—those properties that distinguish it from other aspects of game development. Those other aspects include: the game and its assets and the engine tools. In essence, the engine was found to represent the abstract foundation of subsystems on which a game (the superstructure) is built. The term "subsystem" (or "manager" or "component") refers to a unit of dedicated functionality, and an effective engine is formed when all managers work in unison, each performing their designated role. The purpose of each manager is to achieve a specific end. The render manager is dedicated to rendering graphics to the display, the resource manager to loading and unloading resource data, the input manager to reading and responding to user input, among others. This means the managers are the *constituent pieces* of an engine, and thus engines are built by implementing these pieces and bringing these pieces into a whole. Part 2 of this book then focuses on this implementation work on a chapter-by-chapter basis, each chapter exploring the details of a unique manager component. Once Part 2 is completed, the combination of knowledge gained from all chapters will put the reader in a stronger position to develop a reliable and

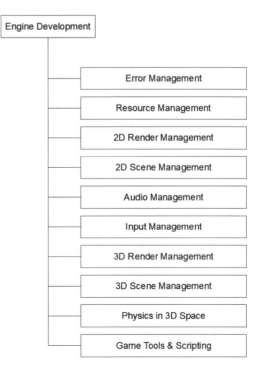

effective game engine. It is now time to begin this development; the previous figure illustrates the order in which each manager will be implemented.

The order in which these components are developed is not entirely a matter of preference. This part of the book begins with the implementation of an error management system to detect and resolve errors as they occur at run time. This component was chosen as the starting point of engine development so that an error-handling framework would already be in place when developing and debugging subsequent components such as the render manager and resource manager. Development of the resource manager follows that of the error manager; this is because most managers depend on the concept of resources to achieve their work. The render manager relies on the concept of "graphics resources" in order to render graphics to the window, and the audio manager depends on the concept of "audio resources" in order to play sound and music to the speakers. The final chapter will consider the issue of engine tools; this subject was placed last because tools such as map editors and scripting windows depend upon a preexisting engine framework. Thus, each chapter can be considered to build on the previous, each extending upon the work of the former. However, the specific focus of each chapter also means that it can be read in isolation, and developers looking for information on only a subset of what is covered in this book can—if required—jump to the appropriate chapter. However, the author recommends the reader read each chapter in sequence.

# 3 | Error and Log Manager

## Overview

After completing this chapter, you should:

- Understand what is meant by an error and log manager
- Appreciate the benefits of logging run-time details
- Understand the singleton design pattern
- Appreciate the benefits of exception handling
- Be able to code an error and log manager in C++
- Have ideas about how to adapt the error and log manager presented here for your own purposes

## ■ 3.1 Introduction

This chapter focuses on the issue of run-time errors and application logs, specifically on how to handle errors as they occur during the execution of a game, and on how and when to log run-time details (not necessarily errors) to a human-readable text file on disk. It does this by detailing both the design and implementation of a log and error manager class for a game engine using the C++ language. The code for this manager can be compiled successfully using either the Microsoft Visual C++ IDE or the Code::Blocks IDE with the MinGW compiler. Details on configuring these IDEs and their respective compilers can be found in Chapter 2.

## ■ 3.2 Errors as Exceptions

Before an error and logging manager can be implemented to serve the purpose of both a game developer and an engine effectively, it is necessary first to consider some underpinning theory and design issues. It is necessary, for example, to state clearly what is meant by the term "error" in the context of programming, even though its meaning might at first seem obvious and uncontroversial. It is important also to distinguish in the next section the process of error handling from that of logging, and to find reasons why logging to a text file both errors and details other than just errors are useful for a game developer.

In common parlance, the term "error" often refers to a mistake. A person can make an error of judgement when they have been wrong in their estimation of someone or something. Similarly, their beliefs can be said to be *in error* whenever those beliefs are demonstrated to be false. But the term "error" in software development takes on a more specific meaning, referring less to mistakes than to failure. Chapter 2 identified at least two kinds of errors in the world of software development: compile-time errors and run-time errors; each signifies a sense of failure. A compile-time error occurs when the compiler fails for one or more reasons to successfully compile the source code of a project, and a run-time error occurs when the application fails in some respect at run time. For example, a word processing application might claim that an error occurred while printing a document; this is intended to mean that printing failed. True, it might have failed due to a bug in the software—a mistake or oversight on the part of the programmer— but it might also have failed due to a lack of ink in the printer cartridge, a faulty cable connecting the printer to the system (if it is not wireless), a power failure, or a conflict between applications running on the system at the time printing was to occur. Under normal or usual circumstances, the document would have printed; the instance of failure resulted from *exceptional circumstances.* That is, printing would have been successful but for one or more *exceptions.* From this point onward this chapter is concerned almost entirely with run-time errors and specifically with run-time errors of the kind known as exceptions. In programming terms, an exception refers to a special condition or circumstance that changes the usual flow of program execution. Thus, an exception is said to have been *raised* or *invoked* whenever an application encounters such a circumstance that prohibits its usual, intended route of execution, a circumstance that demands either that the application respond gracefully and appropriately, or fail entirely.

It might be argued that programmers should code their software so as to respond appropriately in each and every circumstance that might possibly arise, leaving no situation without a suitable reply so that exceptions cannot occur to obstruct execution. But careful reflection shows, if not the impossibility, at least the impracticality of this suggestion. This is because there appears to be no reliable method for being able to know in advance when every possible circumstance has been handled. It is one thing for a programmer to say they have thought of every eventuality that came to mind and handled them as appropriate in code, and another thing for them to say they have handled every possible eventuality and know for certain that there can be no other possibility either now or in the future. It is both conceivable and very frequently the case that many graphics cards and other hardware devices released subsequent to a game cause in it a variety of run-time glitches. Here it is often helpful for a developer to remember the words of computer scientist Edsger W. Dijkstra when he suggested that

"Testing shows the presence, not the absence of bugs." It serves to highlight that even when the debugging and testing of an application has uncovered no bugs a developer is still not in a position to claim that their software is bug free, because there might still exist bugs that their testing did not uncover. For this reason, it is often necessary for a developer to admit to both themselves and their users not only that exceptions might arise in their software when run on some systems and in some circumstances, but also that all the possible reasons for such exceptions cannot be known in advance with certainty. The unlikelihood of detecting all possible exceptions does not of course mean that a developer should code their applications in any way they wish without regard to the bugs and problems that might result from shoddiness. It is true that some bugs and potential exceptions can be foreseen and predicted by developers, that some are more likely than others, and further that some are more general than others. Thus, in striving to make their products as reliable and user friendly as possible, the game developer has not only simply sufficient reason but also good reason to *handle* (that is, to code contingencies and responses to) common exceptions.

In short then: Exceptions are conditions that change the usual flow of program execution and have the *potential* to cause errors if they either *are not handled correctly* or *are not handled at all*. The reasons for some exceptions can be foreseen, while others are likely to remain unknown. With regard to their importance to the execution of an application, exceptions can be divided into two groups: those that can be either handled or ignored without causing the application to exit and those that demand or cause the application to terminate whether handled or not. For example, a game when executed might at startup search the current directory for a configuration file indicating the resolution and color-depth settings at which it is to run. On finding that the file does not exist at the specified location, an exception might be raised in response to indicate that a problem occurred. This exception, however, need not require the application to terminate because the application can resort to default values for the settings that would have been in the file had it existed. Thus, this exception is not *critical*. That is, it can occur without prohibiting a continued and sustained execution of the application. However, now consider the following scenario: A game when executed might at startup test the capabilities of the video hardware installed on the system and find that it lacks support for 3D acceleration, which is necessary for that particular game. Consequently, an exception is raised to signify the problem. In this case, there is little the application can do but exit in reply to remedy the situation, because the hardware limitations prohibit its continued execution. This is an example of a critical exception. The purpose then of the error manager in an engine is to identify exceptions when they occur at run time in an application and to subsequently handle them appropriately, either by directing the flow of execution into contingencies to resolve the problem or by gracefully terminating the application altogether. However, the error and logging manager to be created in this chapter will achieve more than simply detecting and handling errors.

---

## ■ 3.3  Logging Details and Errors

In addition to its ability to detect and handle exceptions as appropriate, the error and log manager will also record specific run-time details in a human-readable text file, called a log, in the application directory. The application will create and maintain only one log file throughout its execution, committing changes as required and overwriting any previous log file that might have been made on a previous run. For this reason, the log file will relate only to the last instance of execution—the last time the game was run.

The purpose of the log file is to list line by line a selection of textual descriptions relating to the execution of the game as it proceeds in order to paint a picture of how execution is performed. Some of the lines might describe errors, if they occur, and others will record successful but important stages of execution such as "File X loaded" or "Texture file X loaded from disk into memory successfully." Since the application writes to the log as instructions are performed, the order in which the lines occur in the log reflects the order in which the instructions were performed by the application. All of these details in the log aid the developer not only in debugging their software but also in offering support to their gamers encountering technical problems. The latter can contact the support team as technical issues arise and send their latest log file. From this, the support team can determine the general execution of the game, and can note obvious omissions in the file or raised exceptions that occurred on the system and thereby identify potential problems and hopefully appropriate solutions. Consider the details in the following sample log file, generated by an application built using the OGRE 3D open source rendering engine. Some of the terms or abbreviations included in the log may not be familiar to the reader, but an understanding of their meaning is not essential for appreciating the utility and importance of a log file generally:

```
20:38:19: Installing plugin: GL RenderSystem
20:38:19: OpenGL Rendering Subsystem created.
20:38:19: Plugin successfully installed
20:38:22: CPU Identifier & Features
20:38:22: -------------------------
20:38:22: *   CPU ID: GenuineIntel: Intel(R) Core(TM)2
CPU        6600  @ 2.40GHz
20:38:22: *      SSE: yes
20:38:22: *     SSE2: yes
20:38:22: *     SSE3: yes
20:38:22: *      MMX: yes
20:38:22: *   MMXEXT: yes
```

```
20:38:22:  *     3DNOW: no
20:38:22:  * 3DNOWEXT: no
20:38:22:  *      CMOV: yes
20:38:22:  *       TSC: yes
20:38:22:  *       FPU: yes
20:38:22:  *       PRO: yes
20:38:22:  *        HT: no
20:38:22: ------------------------
20:38:22: *** Starting Win32GL Subsystem ***
20:38:22: GLRenderSystem::createRenderWindow
"MyTestGame", 1024x768 fullscreen  miscParams: FSAA=0
colourDepth=32 displayFrequency=60 vsync=true
20:38:22: Created Win32Window 'MyTestGame' : 1024x768,
32bpp
20:38:23: GL_VERSION = 2.1.2
20:38:23: GL_VENDOR = NVIDIA Corporation
20:38:23: GL_RENDERER = GeForce 8600 GTS/PCI/SSE2
20:38:23: **************************
20:38:23: *** GL Renderer Started ***
20:38:23: **************************
20:38:23: RenderSystem capabilities
20:38:23: ------------------------
20:38:23:  * Hardware generation of mipmaps: yes
20:38:23:  * Texture blending: yes
20:38:23:  * Anisotropic texture filtering: yes
20:38:23:  * Dot product texture operation: yes
20:38:23:  * Cube mapping: yes
20:38:23:  * Hardware stencil buffer: yes
20:38:23:    - Stencil depth: 8
20:38:23:    - Two sided stencil support: yes
20:38:23:    - Wrap stencil values: yes
20:38:23:  * Hardware vertex/index buffers: yes
20:38:23:  * Vertex programs: yes
20:38:23:    - Max vertex program version: vp40
20:38:23:  * Fragment programs: yes
20:38:23:    - Max fragment program version: fp40
20:38:23:  * Texture Compression: yes
20:38:23:    - DXT: yes
20:38:23:    - VTC: yes
20:38:23:  * Scissor Rectangle: yes
20:38:23:  * Hardware Occlusion Query: yes
20:38:23:  * User clip planes: yes
20:38:23:  * VET_UBYTE4 vertex element type: yes
20:38:23:  * Infinite far plane projection: yes
20:38:23:  * Hardware render-to-texture: yes
```

```
20:38:23:  * Floating point textures: yes
20:38:23:  * Non-power-of-two textures: yes
20:38:23:  * Volume textures: yes
20:38:23:  * Multiple Render Targets: 8
20:38:23:  * Point Sprites: yes
20:38:23:  * Extended point parameters: yes
20:38:23:  * Max Point Size: 63.375
20:38:23:  * Vertex texture fetch: yes
20:38:23:     - Max vertex textures: 32
20:38:23:     - Vertex textures shared: yes
20:38:24: Parsing script OgreLoadingPanel.overlay
20:38:24: Finished parsing scripts for resource group
Bootstrap
20:38:24: Parsing scripts for resource group General
20:38:24: Parsing script cameras.material
20:38:24: Finished parsing scripts for resource group
General
20:38:24: Parsing scripts for resource group Internal
20:38:24: Finished parsing scripts for resource group
Internal
20:41:03: Application terminated cleanly
```

## ■ 3.4  Specifications of the Error and Log Manager

This chapter focuses on both the design and implementation of an error and log manager component for a game engine. This component will be implemented as a single class named cErrorLogManager. Its purpose is both to catch and handle exceptions as appropriate and to log run-time details to a text log file in the application directory. In short, this class:

- Must be able to detect the occurrence of exceptions
- Must handle those exceptions
- Must log exceptions
- Must log run-time details (messages)
- [OPTIONAL] Could have a *filter ability* that allows a developer to limit the messages logged according to a flag or criteria. For example, during debugging a programmer might choose to consult the log and might prefer to see only a subset of related messages as opposed to all messages; perhaps only those messages related to resource loading and unloading (please consult Chapter 1 for a definition of a resource). By assigning each message an integer identifier according to the message content (1=physics messages, 2=audio

messages, 3=resource messages, etc.), a programmer can filter the messages logged. They do this by requesting that the log manager refrain from logging all messages except those carrying the specified integer tag.

The implementation of this class should at least satisfy the above criteria, except for the optional point.

## ■  3.5    Implementing cErrorLogManager—Getting Started

Encapsulating the error and log manager concept into a class requires the developer to translate the idea of an error and log manager and its associated features into a series of properties and methods belonging to a class. In C++, properties correspond to variables and methods to functions. Development of a class usually begins by creating both a header and corresponding source file, and then by declaring the basic skeleton of the class in the header. The error and log manager framework can be divided into two unique classes: the first being an exception class and the second being the error and log manager. The exception class encapsulates any single exception that might occur, and the error and log manager is responsible for handling and logging those exceptions. The following skeleton declarations represent the point from which a developer might begin developing these two classes:

```
#ifndef ERRORLOGMANAGER_H_INCLUDED
#define ERRORLOGMANAGER_H_INCLUDED

#include "EngineObject.h"
//-------------------------------------------------------

class cException : public std::exception
{
    private:
    protected:
    public:

    // Override std::exception::what
    const char* what();
};


//-------------------------------------------------------

//Class inherits from the engine base object type
class cErrorLogManager : public cEngineObject
```

```
{
    private:
    protected:
    public:
};
```

```
#endif
```

> **NOTE**. This class is derived from a base class cEngineObject, as are
> almost all classes in the engine. cEngineObject is an empty class except for
> a few basic properties. It is not essential that classes are derived from here,
> but it can be useful should a programmer later decide it important for them
> all to share common functionality. cEngineObject looks as follows:

```
class cEngineObject
{
    private:
    protected:
    public:
        int m_ID; //Unique ID Value
};
```

Having created the outline for two exception-handling classes, the programmer would
typically proceed by adding methods and properties as appropriate for their design.
However, before implementing these classes further it is important to highlight that
cErrorLogManager will differ in some respects from most standard classes. As it
stands, cErrorLogManager will allow itself to be instantiated many times, if the developer so requires; that is, many particular instances of that class can be created and
used in an application at run time. This approach applies to almost all C++ classes:
A programmer may define one class (or pattern) and then create many particular
instances of that class in their application, just as many china ornaments (instances)
can be cast from the same mold. Though all instances of the class are created according to a single pattern, the actual values of their properties and methods may vary
between instances. cEngineObject, for example, has a public integer ID property.
Though all instances of this class expose this property publicly, its actual value (be
it 5, 10, 15, or any other integer) is specific to each instance and there may be many
instances. All of this is likely to seem so obvious and unremarkable to most readers
familiar with object-oriented programming as to be hardly worth mentioning at all.
However, there is a sense in which the usage of the cErrorLogManager class differs
from that of standard classes. Usually a class is created by a programmer to support
the creation of many instances of that class, as we have been discussing; for example,
a render manager class for an engine defines the pattern for a render manager, and
many instances of it may be created by an application at run time, each instance

representing a unique render manager in system memory, perhaps one DirectX and another OpenGL. By creating many instances of a render manager, a game and its engine can switch between them, perhaps rendering its graphics to the screen using one render system if it is able and falling back on a secondary system if it is not. The usage of the cErrorLogManager class, however, differs in that it will be instantiated *once and only once* as a global object throughout the duration of an application. The class will be instantiated once and only once, and that instance will be used by the engine to handle all exceptions and logging. It will *not* need or want to create a separate instance of this class as a second and competing log or exception-handling system. One system—that is, one instance—is enough for handling *all* exceptions and logging details. Consequently, cErrorLogManager should be *engineered* to limit the number of its instantiations to one and only one. To do this, the cErrorLogManager class should be designed according to the *singleton design pattern*.

Classes designed according to the singleton design pattern are called singleton classes, and the singleton design pattern is an architecture that restricts the number of simultaneous instances of a class to *one* in any single application. This means that *many* separate applications running simultaneously could each have their own singleton class of the same type, and it means also that any *single* application can have *many* singletons of *different* types simultaneously. But no single application may have more than one instance of a singleton class of a given type at any one time. The next section details how to make cErrorLogManager a singleton class.

## ■ 3.6   Making cErrorLogManager a Singleton Class

An exception is raised by an application when an error occurs at run time, and in response an application must either resolve the error or terminate its execution. Exceptions will be encapsulated in the cException class, and it will be the role of the cErrorLogManager class to catch and log those exceptions to a human-readable text file on disk as they occur at run time. An application might raise one or more exceptions of the same or differing types, and therefore the standard C++ class model of "one class to many instances" applies to the exception class, because an application might have need to create one or more instances of cException. However, the same cannot be said for cErrorLogManager. This class is a manager component intended to remain active and globally accessible throughout the lifetime of the engine. For this reason, an application should declare only one instance of cErrorLogManager at any one time, and no more than one instance should be permitted. This is to prevent conflict and confusion between multiple error managers. Thus, cErrorLogManager should be a singleton class because the singleton design pattern allows developers to restrict the number of simultaneous instances of a given class to one and only one.

To implement the cErrorLogManager class according to the single design pattern, the class must be structured as follows:

- There should be no *public* constructor function for a singleton class. All constructors should be implemented as *protected* methods. This prohibits developers from instantiating instances of this class.

- The singleton class should feature a static member of itself. That is, a singleton class (X) should feature one static member of type (X). Variables that are declared *static* are said to have "static duration." This means they are created at application startup and are removed at application termination, and are active throughout the execution of an application even when they are declared within a function or class whose scope is limited. A class member declared as static is shared between all instances of that class. The static member for a singleton class is used to hold the one and only instance of that class. Applications intending to access the properties and methods of the singleton class must do so by accessing this one instance.

- The singleton class should feature a method that returns a pointer to its static member, as above. This provides developers with a means of accessing the single instance of the class.

The following code demonstrates both the header and source files for cErrorLog-Manager implemented as a singleton class. Notice how it meets all three points of the singleton design pattern given above:

**Header File (ErrorLog.h)**

```
class cErrorLogManager : public cEngineObject
{
    public:
        //Returns pointer to single instance
        static cErrorLogManager * GetErrorManager();

    protected:
        //Protected constructor
        cErrorLogManager();

        //Static instance member
        static cErrorLogManager m_ErrorManager;
};
```

**Source File (ErrorLog.cpp)**

```
#include "ErrorLogManager.h"

cErrorLogManager cErrorLogManager::m_ErrorManager;
```

```
cErrorLogManager* cErrorLogManager::GetErrorManager()
{
    return &m_ErrorManager;
}
```

### EXERCISE 3.1

For each of the following statements, answer True or False.

1. A singleton class restricts the number of its instantiations to only one at any one time. It also features a nonpublic constructor function.
2. A singleton class is suitable for all manager components.
3. An application is restricted to only one singleton class.
4. Applications should be terminated when exceptions occur.

**Answers**

1. True.
2. False. A singleton class might be suitable for most or all managers in a single engine, but a singleton class need not necessarily be suitable for all. An application might feature multiple render managers, one for each graphics card on the system or one for each graphics API.
3. False. A singleton object restricts all simultaneous instantiations of that type to one, but an application can feature many singleton objects of different types.
4. False. Applications should terminate only when an exception is critical.

**NOTE**. All other files intending to use the Error Log Manager as a singleton class should include the class header file, and can access a pointer to the singleton instance as follows:

```
cErrorLogManager* ErrorLog = cErrorLogManager::GetError
Manager();
```

## ■ 3.7   Designing cException and cErrorLogManager

It has been stated already that the purpose of the cException class is to encapsulate a runtime error, and the purpose of the cErrorLogManager class is to handle and log all exceptions to a human-readable text log as and when they occur. The cErrorLogManager is implemented as a singleton class to limit its running instances to one, since an application needs only one error log, but an application allows potentially many instances of cException because an application can raise many kinds of errors.

### 3.7.1   cException

Errors come in different kinds, from file access errors to rendering errors, and can be raised anywhere where there is source code, in any source file and at any line number in that file. Given the potentially infinite variety of errors that can occur and the potentially many places where they could be raised in any large project with many source files, developers find it convenient to record some basic properties of errors when they occur. For each error that occurs in an application, developers often invent and record the following properties:

- **Error Number**

  The Error Number is an application-defined unique identifier for an error. Developers assign specific errors a given number in order to simplify the process of identifying the nature of an error when they occur. File access errors might be assigned to Error Number 1, rendering errors to 2, and audio playback errors to 3, and so on. In short, the assigning of numbers (or IDs) to errors is largely a matter of judgment, and developers will typically want to prepare a list of possible errors and their associated IDs.

- **Error Description**

  The Error Description refers to a string of text that describes in human-readable terms the error that occurred. Descriptions should be short, concise, and use as few technical terms as possible. The purpose of the Error Description is to elaborate on the nature of the error and to speculate on its possible cause and solution where possible.

- **Error Source File and Line Number**

  The two properties Error Source File and Line Number define where in the source code the error was raised. Error Source File is a string and Line Number is an integer; together these properties identify both the name of the source file and the line position of the source file in which the error occurred. These properties are especially useful for developers when working on large projects with many files and many lines.

### 3.7.2   cErrorLogManager

The Error Log Manager class is a singleton object that is responsible for logging exceptions that are "thrown" and "caught" in try-catch statements. A *try-catch* statement is divided into two parts: *try* and *catch*. The try section is used to detect when exceptions are thrown, and the catch section is used to handle exceptions when detected. An exception is said to be thrown when an application identifies an error and calls the *throw* statement. When a throw statement is made within the try block of a try-catch statement, the catch section of that statement is initiated to give an application the opportunity to handle the exception. In this section, the ErrorLogManager will be invoked to record the error to a log.

## ■   3.8   Implementing cException and cErrorLogManager

Implementing the Exception class and the Error Log Manager class involves adding flesh to the class skeletons given earlier so that each class is designed to work within the throw-try-catch framework. The following code presents the completed header file with the final declarations of these two classes, and the remainder of this chapter will be spent exploring that implementation under the hood. That is, the completed class declarations will be given first and then the implementation of those classes is detailed further.

```
#ifndef ERRORLOGMANAGER_H_INCLUDED
#define ERRORLOGMANAGER_H_INCLUDED

//-------------------------------------------------------

#include "EngineObject.h"
#include <string>
#include <sstream>
#include <iostream>
#include <time.h>
#include <iomanip>
#include <fstream>
#include <exception>

//Define a throw macro to throw a cException class
//Uses the __FILE__ and __LINE__ constants
#ifndef THROW_EXCEPTION
#define THROW_EXCEPTION(ErrorNum, ErrorDesc) throw
cException(ErrorNum, ErrorDesc, __FILE__, __LINE__ );
#endif

//-------------------------------------------------------

//Custom exception class

class cException : public std::exception
{
```

```
    private:
    protected:
    public:
    int m_ErrorNumber;
    std::string m_ErrorDesc;
    std::string m_SrcFileName;
    int m_LineNumber;
    std::string m_ErrText;

  // Override std::exception::what
  //Returns string featuring: Error Number, Error Desc,
Src File, Line Number
    const char* what();

    cException(int ErrorNumber, std::string ErrorDesc,
std::string SrcFileName, int LineNumber);
    ~cException() throw() {}
};

//-----------------------------------------------------

//Singleton Logging Object

class cErrorLogManager : public cEngineObject
{
    public:
        static cErrorLogManager * GetErrorManager();

    protected:
        cErrorLogManager();
        virtual ~cErrorLogManager(){}
        static cErrorLogManager m_ErrorManager;

    public:
    //Log File Buffer
        std::stringstream m_LogBuffer;

    //Creates a log file
        void create(std::string Filename);

    //Commits contents to file
        void flush();

    //Closes file
        void close();
```

```
    //Logs an exception to the log file
        void logException(cException e);

    //Gets the time as string. Can be used for
    //recording the time of an error in the log
        std::string getTimeString();

    //Handle to log file
        std::ofstream m_LogFile;
};

//------------------------------------------------------

#endif // ERRORLOGMANAGER_H_INCLUDED
```

## Comments

- This header file features class declarations for both cException and cErrorLog-Manager. It also features a THROW_EXCEPTION macro that applications should use to throw exceptions in the form of cException. The THROW_EXCEPTION macro simply calls the throw statement, passing an instance of cException as the raised exception. The constructor for cException requires an Error Number, Error Description, Source File Name, and Line Number.

- The cException class is descended from the STL standard base class for exceptions. That class features only one method: what. This method is overridden in cException and returns a human-readable string that describes the error raised. Specifically, it uses the class members m_ErrorNumber, m_ErrorDesc, m_SrcFileName, and m_LineNumber to build and return a complete string stating the Error Number, Error Description, Source File Name, and Line Number of the error.

- The cErrorLogManager class offers methods for creating a text file, committing changes to that file, and writing exceptions to that file.

---

## ■ 3.9  Implementing the Constructor and What Method of cException

The constructor function of cException requires a total of four arguments that together describe an exception. These are the unique error number, a human-readable description of the error, the name of the source file in which the error occurred, and the line number at which the error occurred. These parameters are provided to cException through a call to the THROW_EXCEPTION macro. Applications that wish to throw exceptions call upon this macro within a try-catch statement. The what method of the class cException is used to retrieve a human-readable string describing all properties of the exception raised. It will be called upon later by the Error Log Manager when seeking to retrieve a description string of an exception to print to the error log. The implementation details of both the class constructor and the what method are given in the following code:

```
//Constructor
cException::cException(int ErrorNumber, std::string
ErrorDesc, std::string SrcFileName, int LineNumber)
{
//Set exception properties
m_ErrorNumber = ErrorNumber;
m_ErrorDesc = ErrorDesc;
m_SrcFileName = SrcFileName;
m_LineNumber = LineNumber;

//Write properties to a human-readable string
std::stringstream ErrStr;

ErrStr << "Error Num: " << m_ErrorNumber << "\nError
Desc: " << m_ErrorDesc << "\nSrc File: " << m_SrcFileName
<< "\nLine Number: " << m_LineNumber << "\n";

m_ErrText = ErrStr.str();
}

//What method will be called by the error log manager to
//Write exception to log file
const char* cException::what()
{
    return m_ErrText.c_str();
}
```

**NOTE.** Applications can throw and catch an exception as follows:

```
try{
THROW_EXCEPTION(1, "this is my error");
}
catch(cException& e)
{
  //print error with:
  //e.what();
}
```

# ■ 3.10   Implementing cErrorLogManager

Exceptions thrown using the THROW_EXCEPTION macro within a try-catch statement will be caught and handled in the catch block. In this block, an application will
need to call upon the methods of the Error Log Manager to record the occurrence of
the exception in a human-readable text log. Because cErrorLogManager is a comparatively small class, its complete implementation is provided, with comments afterward,
as follows:

```
//Creates and opens log file ready for writing
//Should be called at application startup before entering
try-block.
void cErrorLogManager::create(std::string Filename)
{
    m_LogFile.open(Filename.c_str());
}

//--------------------------------------------------------

//Commits information to file and clears text cache
void cErrorLogManager::flush()
{
    m_LogFile << m_LogBuffer.str();
    m_LogFile.flush();
    m_LogBuffer.str("");
}

//--------------------------------------------------------

//Close log file
void cErrorLogManager::close()
{
    m_LogFile.close();
}

//--------------------------------------------------------

//Writes exception to log
void cErrorLogManager::logException(cException e)
{
    m_LogBuffer << getTimeString() << "\n" << e.what();
    flush();
}
```

```
//-----------------------------------------------------------

//Gets current time as string in the form:
hours:mins:secs
std::string cErrorLogManager::getTimeString()
{
    std::stringstream TimeStr;

    struct tm *pTime;
    time_t ctTime; time(&ctTime);
    pTime = localtime( &ctTime );

    TimeStr << std::setw(2) << std::setfill('0') <<pTime-
>tm_hour << «:»;
    TimeStr << std::setw(2) << std::setfill('0') <<pTime-
>tm_min << «:»;
    TimeStr << std::setw(2) << std::setfill('0') <<pTime-
>tm_sec;

    return TimeStr.str();
}

//-----------------------------------------------------------
```

**Comments**

- cErrorLogManager features several methods for working with log files: create, flush, close, logException, and getTimeString.

- The create method creates a new log of a specified name and at the specified path to receive text output from the log when exceptions occur at run time. This method should be called only once at application startup and before an application enters a try-catch statement. The call to the open method should be followed by a corresponding call to the close method at application end to close the opened file. The create method uses the open method of member m_LogFile, which is itself an STL class std::ofstream. std::ofstream represents a file on disk to which data can be sent (flushed).

- The member property m_LogBuffer is of type std::stringstream and is used as a temporary cache of text data in memory that can be committed to the file on disk. Exceptions that are logged by the log manager are first added in string form to m_LogBuffer, and then the contents of m_LogBuffer are dispatched to file through the flush method. The flush method is responsible for committing the contents of m_LogBuffer to the file and clearing the contents of m_LogBuffer.

- The getTimeString method of the cErrorLogManager class retrieves the current system time in terms of hours, minutes, and seconds, and then returns this time in the form of a string. This string will be used by the logException method to log the approximate time an exception occurred.

- The logException method is responsible for writing to the log file both the details of an exception and the time this exception occurred. It does this by calling on the what method of cException to retrieve exception information and on the getTimeString method to express the current time as a string.

## ■ 3.11   Using the Error Logging Framework

The error logging framework considered in this chapter is effective only upon source code contained within the try block of a try-catch statement. Therefore, developers using this framework should strive to contain as much of their application code as possible within a try-catch statement. This is generally not a difficult standard to maintain since the try-catch statement can usually be written within the main or WinMain function of the application. Consider the following sample WinMain function that uses a try-catch block to both catch an exception and log that exception to a log file:

```
int _tmain(int argc, _TCHAR* argv[])
{
    cErrorLogManager* Log = cErrorLogManager::GetErrorMana
ger();
    Log->create("c:\\testlog.txt");

    try{
        //Run application code here

        //Throw test exception
         THROW_EXCEPTION(1, "this is my error");
        }
    catch(cException& e)
    {
        //Handle exception

        //Show error message
        MessageBoxA(NULL, e.what(),"",MB_OK);
```

```
        //log error file
        Log->m_LogBuffer << "*****ERROR*****\n";
            Log->flush();
             Log->logException(e);
        Log->m_LogBuffer << "**************\n";
            Log->flush();
    }

  Log->close();
}
```

**EXERCISE 3.2**

1. How can text be written to the log without calling any of the methods of cErrorLogManager?

2. The catch statement is used to catch exceptions *only* within the try block of a try-catch statement. True or false?

3. The error log manager is used to log *only* errors. True or false?

**Answers**

1. The m_LogBuffer property of cErrorLogManager is an std::string stream. Data can be output to this stream as though it were the standard output, as follows:

```
Log->m_LogBuffer << "*****ERROR*****\n";
```

2. True.

3. False. The error log manager can be used to log any text data.

## ■ 3.12 Chapter Summary

This chapter began the implementation of a game engine by coding an error-handling framework consisting of two separate classes: cException and the singleton class cErrorLogManager. The purpose of cException is to encapsulate a run-time error, recording data such as Error Number, Error Description, Source File Name, and Line Number. The purpose of cErrorLogManager is to handle and log exceptions to a human-readable text file as they occur. These exceptions can be detected via a throw-try-catch series of statements, and the THROW_EXCEPTION macro has been defined to simplify the process of throwing exceptions. Engine development can start in many places, but in this book it begins with an error-handling framework. This is because, with such a framework now in place, a developer can proceed to apply it to all subsequent engine work in order to simplify the process of debugging. The next chapter considers the issue of resource management.

# Resource Management

## Overview

After completing this chapter, you should:

- Understand what is meant by resources and resource management
- Appreciate the importance of managing resources
- Understand XML and how to parse XML files using TinyXML
- Understand caching and resource budgets

## ■ 4.1 Introduction

Resources are the lifeblood of a game in the sense that hardly any game can exist without them, or more accurately without them managed effectively. The term "resource" is typically used by developers to refer to any game-specific asset external to the engine; that is, any game-related data that does not directly influence the architecture of the engine. Resources include but are not limited to: graphics (JPGs, PNGs, BMPs, etc.), audio (WAVs, MP3s, OGGs, etc.), movies (AVIs, MPGs, etc.), and configuration data (.txt, .cfg, .XML, etc.). See Figure 4.1. The concept of a resource is general insofar as nearly all games need and use resources, and thus the resource framework is a part of the engine. But the particular resources themselves—the actual resource files—are context specific, meaning they differ according to the game being made. A platformer game features one set of bitmaps to represent the sprites, scenery, and weapons featured in its scenes, while another game uses a different set of graphics files for its scenes. The responsibility of the engine in relation to resources then is not for the content of the resources themselves, since the content is produced by content creators, but for their management as a unit in either system or hardware memory. Thus, the job of the resource manager is to ensure that resources are available to the game on demand and to ensure that resources are loaded and unloaded efficiently both to and from either system memory or hardware memory when needed by the game. So stated, the task of the resource manager might initially sound simple in comparison to those of other managers. Surely, if the role of the resource manager is limited primarily to loading and unloading

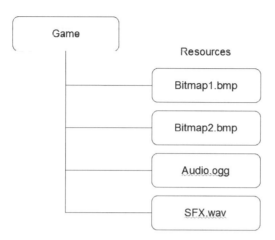

Resources appear as a list in relation to a game

**I FIGURE 4.1**    Resource hierarchies.

files, then few problems can arise? However, the complexities of resources and resource management often become clear when considered in the context of a game that uses many resources of varying kinds and sizes and that has very specific requirements about how and when they are used. The focus of this chapter then is on the issue of resource management and its importance for the efficiency of both games and game engines.

## ■ 4.2   The Problems of Resource Management

Any solid container of a limited size can hold a limited quantity of liquid at any one time: A cup, glass, beaker, or bucket each has a specific capacity and can accept no more liquid than allowed by its capacity. Likewise, a game that is executing on a user's system is allocated a finite memory space in system memory by the operating system, and this space lasts for as long as the game is executing. In this finite region, the game must hold its resources, perform its calculations, and do whatever else needs to be done to operate effectively. If for some reason the game exceeds its quota of memory (perhaps by loading an excess of data or through memory leakage), then unpredictable results can occur: Perhaps the game grinds to a halt or crashes to the desktop. One of the main problems of resource management becomes apparent when one considers the following two points: (1) The system memory space allocated to any running game is *finite*, and (2) the quantity and total size in megabytes of that same game's resources is *potentially infinite*. It is not actually infinite because in practice any one game ships only with the limited set of resources it requires for its purposes: its specific sprites, sounds, and con-figuration data. But it is potentially infinite in the sense that the engine cannot know in advance the total size in megabytes of the resources that will ship with and be used by any game. One game might use 10 MB worth of resources and another 100 MB worth. Furthermore, it is possible for the total size in megabytes of the resources to exceed the total size in megabytes of the system memory allocated to the game. By analogy then, it is both a possibility and a threat that the liquid could exceed the capacity of the cup if the cup is left unmanaged and the liquid allowed to flow limitlessly.

The resource manager of the game engine can respond to this threat of overload in one of at least two ways. First, it could simply set a limit (or *budget*) on the total size in megabytes of the resources allowed to any one game for the entirety of its execution. This method allows the engine to load *all* of the game's resources into memory at any one time without incurring the risk of overloading, provided the engine does not duplicate data. The drawbacks of this solution, however, would be almost fatal for an engine looking to become popular among the developers of large-scale games because the solution limits the total size of the game to the total size of system memory allo-cated for the game's execution. Consequently, it prohibits the creation of *any and all* games that cannot cache (load) the entirety of their resources into system memory at one time. Such an engine would exclude the creation of any game akin to the size of the vast majority of contemporary games, many of which fill one or more DVDs. Hence, though the capping of resource sizes is a possible solution to the problem of overloading, its drawbacks make it largely infeasible for any engine developer seeking to develop a popular engine tailored to the needs of games in the contemporary market. The second solution to the problem of overloading is to design the resource manager to dynamically load *and* unload resources according to a criterion, usually based on the concept of *need*. To load and unload resources according to need means to load and unload them according to whether the game is using those resources. For example, a sprite graphic is loaded from a file on disk and into memory as the game *needs* to show this graphic in a scene. Once that scene has ended and the graphic is no longer needed, it is then unloaded by the resource manager, and the vacant system memory left in its wake can be reused for other needed resources. This solution of loading and unloading resources according to need has at least two key advantages: (1) It does not limit the total size in megabytes of the resources used by the game because the resource manager can both load and unload resources dynamically, and (2) it offloads part of the responsibility of resource memory management to the game developer, since it is they and not the engine who must decide on the number and size of resources used simultaneously. Thus, the second of the two solutions (dynamic loading and unload-ing according to need) is the more promising for a general engine and is the solution chosen for the work in this book. However, accepting it involves tackling a number of design considerations before it can be implemented closer to optimally.

## ■ 4.3   Designing a Resource Manager

A resource manager that loads and unloads resources based on the needs of the game presents the engine developer with some design considerations. For example, what should happen if the game requests the engine to load a resource (say, a JPG) that is loaded already? And also, how should the total collection of loaded and available resources be organized? Should the resource manager maintain the resources in a list? Or should some other data structure be used? The answers to these questions depend largely on the circumstances. However, the workable route taken in this book has the following answers, which many engines share.

**What should happen if the game requests the engine to load a resource that is already loaded?**

This question may be restated as: Should the engine allow resource duplication? If yes, then the engine can load into memory two copies of the same resource. If no, then the engine ensures each resource is unique. The answer taken here is no, because there is usually no reason a resource cannot be shared whenever there are two or more elements in a game that use it. For example, a scene in a platform game might feature many enemies, with each enemy clone based on the same enemy sprite resource. Rather than load multiple instances of the same resource—once for each sprite as necessary—the single sprite resource can be reused for *all* enemies of the same kind. As a result, the resource manager in this chapter requires that all loaded resources be unique, and each resource has a unique ID tag to distinguish it from other resources. The programmer can therefore search for a specific resource item by scanning through the loaded resources for a resource with a given ID.

**How should the total collection of loaded and available resources be organized? In a list array or using some other data structure?**

This question relates to how the resource manager should organize in memory the resources it loads. But here it is important for the engine developer to distinguish between two types of data regarding resources: resource data and resource *metadata* (see Figure 4.2). Resource data refers to the actual data of the resource file: For bitmap resources, it is the pixel data; for audio resources, it is the audio data, etc. Metadata refers to data *about* resources. It includes the file name of the resource and the scenes and times when a resource is used by a game. The engine must load both types of resource data if it is to use resources effectively. It must load the resource data on demand in order to use it for the game; e.g., in order to show a bitmap or play a sound. It must also know the metadata in order to determine, for example, when the data for a specific resource should and should not be loaded, and to determine where on the system that data is to be found. However, it is only the *metadata* of resources

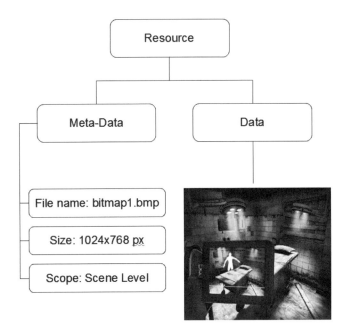

**Resource Data and Meta-Data**

**▌FIGURE 4.2** Data and metadata.

that certainly remains in memory throughout game execution because this data is instructive to the engine on how to use the resources it loads.

The issue of loading and unloading resource data of specific kinds (graphics resources, audio resources, etc.) remains an issue for their respective managers, as we shall see: The render manager will load and unload graphics resources, and the audio manager will load and unload audio resources. The resource manager, however, is responsible for loading and managing the resource metadata and for using this data to coordinate the loading and unloading of resource data in collaboration with other managers. The question then as to whether resources should be stored in arrays or tree structures concerns the arrangement of resource metadata classes, which will contain pointer members to the actual resource data when they are loaded. That is, the resource manager is responsible for maintaining a collection of resource metadata classes, featuring information on file paths, resource file sizes, and when and how resources are to be loaded. The issue of loading actual resource data is considered in subsequent chapters on the render manager and audio manager. For storing metadata there are several possible options: arrays and lists or tree structures such as linked lists. It has been stated already that each game depends on a collection of resources, and that the primary job of the resource manager is to load resource metadata and coordinate the loading and unloading of resources according to the game's needs. If the total collection of resources is considered diagrammatically in relation to the game *as a whole* unit, then a list structure (one-dimensional array) seems the simplest solution for keeping track of the resource metadata. Using a list data structure, a programmer can enumerate through all loaded resources (that is, all resources whose data has been loaded into memory), considering each in turn and coordinating their unloading as and when appropriate. However, what is gained in simplicity by coding resources into a list structure is lost in control over some of the finer details of resources and their relationships. When considered in relation to the game as a whole, resources indeed appear as a list of items. But when considered in relation to the constituent components of a game—the scenes, menus, and characters—resources as a collection appear more hierarchical than linear; that is, more as a tree than as a list (See Figure 4.3). Consider

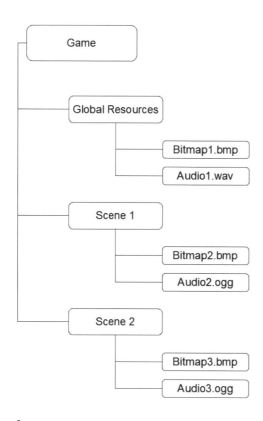

**Resources as hierarchy entities with 'scope'**

**┃ FIGURE 4.3**    Resource hierarchies.

the following tree diagram illustrating the relationship of a group of resources to a specific scene in a platformer game, complete with enemy sprite resources and scenery resources. The diagram demonstrates that resources fall into at least two categories regarding the *scope* of their data, that is, the length of time in which the resource data will be loaded in memory ready for use. These categories are scene-level resources and game-level resources.

Scene-level resources are those with *scene scope*, those whose data (not metadata but raw resource data: pixels or audio) is to be in memory throughout the duration of a *scene*. A single game might feature multiple scenes or stages, and each scene is likely to feature different graphics and sound, and is thereby likely to relate to a specific and unique set of resources not found in other scenes. Hence, each set of scene-level resources together forms a branch on the tree structure, each resource belonging to a single scene being a leaf node on that branch. For example, some scenes might have an arctic theme while others sport a desert theme, cave theme, or forest theme. The themes of each scene influence the graphics and sound to be used for them. In this way, the resources an engine loads at run time is influenced partly by the scene currently being played. For this reason, as one scene ends and another begins (say, when the player completes a mission and moves on to the next), the engine is likely to unload an existing selection of resources and replace them with another selection appropriate for the newly loaded scene.

Scene-level resources refer to those resources on a branch of the tree that are associated with a specific scene in the game and are not used outside of that scene. In contrast, game-level resources occupy the topmost branch of the tree because they have *game scope*; that is, game-level resources remain loaded and available throughout the execution of the game and are shared across all or most scenes, like resource metadata. Such resources include the mouse cursor, health and damage bars, menu screens, the player character that appears in every scene, and many others depending on the game.

In short, this section has recommended a tree structure (a linked list) as an appropriate container for managing resources loaded in memory. The tree structure is appropriate because its branch and leaf node arrangement reflects the hierarchical relationship resources have to elements in the game and to each other. The tree structure and linked list architecture was detailed in an earlier chapter of this book, and readers are advised before proceeding with the rest of this chapter to refresh their memory concerning trees if the concept is not familiar. Having conceptualized game resources in the form of a tree arrangement, and having distinguished between resource data and metadata, resources and their data can be divided into two kinds: scene level and game level. Scene-level resources are those whose data is loaded and active *only* for the duration of the scene being played (the active scene), while game-level resources are loaded and active for the duration of the game. Like game-level resource data, resource metadata remains in memory throughout the duration of the game.

## ■ 4.4   Implementing a Resource Manager

The purpose of the resource manager is to manage resources. Thus, the implementation of the resource manager as a C++ class necessitates the creation of *two* classes: one for the manager (the resource manager) and the other for the managed (the resource). The latter class encapsulates the properties and methods of a single resource, and a game is likely to have many such resources. It has been stated that the resource manager will automatically load and unload resources as appropriate for the game's needs, and it is the scope of a resource (scene or game scope) that determines its life at run time: when it is to be loaded and unloaded. However, for a resource manager to manage resources at all it must be told what those resources are; it must be given a list of resources that will be used by the game during its execution. It must be told at least the path name of the resource file on disk and the scope of the resource in relation to the game. It can be told of these things either at run time in code or via a file that is both loaded and parsed by the resource manager at engine startup. The latter option is chosen for this book and for most engines generally, because by loading resource information from a file the game developer can edit and reedit the resource list without having to recompile the game or engine each time a change is made. The resource manager coded here will parse and read resource information at startup from an XML file on disk, and then use this information to load and unload resources as the game unfolds at run time to ensure that *only* the appropriate resources for the active scene are available in memory. As one scene changes to another, the scene manager will automatically unload the current scene resources and load the new scene resources as appropriate. The XML file will detail the resource tree structure. The XML file then is the starting point for developing the resource manager. This file is considered next.

## ■ 4.5   XML and the Resource Tree

> **NOTE.** Detailed information about XML can be found at http://www. w3schools.com/xml/.

XML, or Extensible Markup Language, has a human-readable form and tree-like structure (its arranging of data into parent and child nodes) that make it a suitable candidate for defining a game resource tree. XML is a declarative language like HTML rather than an imperative language like C++, meaning that it is descriptive rather than instructive. It tells the engine *about* things rather than to *do* things. It can be used to tell the engine about the entire collection of resources available to the game, their relative file paths, and their association to scenes in the game. Specifically, this file is intended to be used by game developers to tell the engine about all the resources necessary for the game. *For each resource* listed in the XML file, the XML data will indicate four core pieces of information that will prove vital if the resource manager of the engine is to manage resources automatically as scenes are loaded and unloaded during game play. The engine will parse and load the data from this file at startup. For each resource there will be:

1. *The UID (unique identifier) of the resource.* This will be an unsigned integer property (nonnegative integer) that uniquely identifies the resource. This identifier will be used by the engine during searches to locate the resource in the resource tree. No two resources may share the same UID.

2. *File path.* This is a string property representing the full or relative path to the resource file on disk associated with the UID (e.g., "C:\my_documents\myfile.jpg"). The resource manager is responsible for maintaining the link between the UID and the file name of a resource. Thus, when the resource manager is requested to load a resource of a given ID, it will know the associated file to load.

3. *Resource type.* This is a string property indicating the resource type: graphic, audio, video, config, mesh, material, or script. When the engine requests a resource to be loaded, the resource manager will delegate the loading process to the appropriate manager, which it will determine by using the resource type property. The render manager will be used to load graphics resources, the audio manager for audio resources, etc.

4. *Resource scope.* This is an integer property indicating the scene of the game to which the resource is to be attached, conceptually speaking. This design assumes that each scene in the game is given a unique ID such as 0=Game-level resources, 1=Scene1, 2=Scene2, etc. Resources loaded with a scope of 0 remain loaded throughout game play because they are game-level resources, and resources loaded with a scope above 0 are scene-level resources and are therefore loaded and available only while the scene with the corresponding ID is active (being played).

Consider the following sample resource XML file using the above convention. It defines three unique resources: one game-scope graphic resource, one scene-scope audio resource, and a final game-scope text file resource:

```
<resources>

<resource UID="1" type="graphic" filename="mygraphic.jpg"
scenescope="0"></resource>

<resource UID="2" type="audio" filename="myaudio.ogg"
scenescope="1"></resource>

<resource UID="3" type="text" filename="gamedata.cfg"
scenescope="0"></resource>

</resources>
```

**EXERCISE 4.1**

1. Explain why a developer might want to load two bitmap resources from the same file.
2. Besides scene scope and game scope, list at least one additional type of scope that a resource manager might feature.

**Answers**

1. A developer might want to load two copies of a single bitmap when they intend to change the pixels of one of the copies, while keeping the other for backup purposes.
2. In addition to scene and game scope, there might be "tmp" scope. Tmp scope resources have a shorter duration than scene-level resources. Such resources might be used for cut-scenes or animation sequences that play only once during a scene, after which they can be removed.

## 4.6    Creating cResourceManager and cResource

The implementation details of reading data from an XML file are considered shortly. Using the resource XML file, game developers can declare a complete list of their game resources to the engine at startup. Using the scope information for each resource, the resource manager of the engine can automatically load and unload resources as required by the game. The XML file list has therefore outlined at least the basic skeleton of a resource that is to be managed by the resource manager. Equipped with this information, both the CResourceManager class and the cResource class can be sketched out in a single header file (ResourceManager.h). This file is as follows.

> **NOTE.** The following code refers to the TinyXML library. This library is used to load and parse XML files, and is considered in the next section of this chapter.

```
#ifndef RESOURCEMANAGER_H_INCLUDED
#define RESOURCEMANAGER_H_INCLUDED

#include "EngineObject.h"
#include <iostream>
#include <list>
#include <map>
```

```
#include <string>

//Tiny XML Header. needs TinyXML library
//Available for free at: http://www.grinninglizard.com/
tinyxml/
#include "TinyXML.h"

//Enum to indicate resource type
typedef enum{
    RESOURCE_NULL = 0,
    RESOURCE_GRAPHIC = 1,
    RESOURCE_MOVIE = 2,
    RESOURCE_AUDIO = 3,
    RESOURCE_TEXT = 4,
}RESOURCE_TYPE;

//---------------------------------------------------------

//Resource class. Represents a resource object.
//To be managed by a resource manager.
//Should be overriden by other classes
//and methods providing specific implementations
//RenderManager, for example, will implement a
//derived graphics resource class
class cResource : public cEngineObject
{
    private:
    protected:
    public:
        unsigned int m_ResourceID;
        unsigned int m_Scope;
        std::string m_FileName;
        RESOURCE_TYPE m_Type;

    //To be overloaded by derived classes
        virtual ~cResource(){};
        virtual void load(){};
        virtual void unload(){};

        inline cResource()
        {
            m_ResourceID = m_Scope = 0;
            m_Type = RESOURCE_NULL;
        }
};
```

```
//-------------------------------------------------------

//Resource Manager. Manages resource objects.
class cResourceManager : public cEngineObject
{
    private:
    protected:

    //Current resource scope
    unsigned int m_CurrentScope;

    //Total number of resources, both loaded and non-
loaded
    unsigned int m_ResourceCount;

    public:

    //STL MAP of form <scope, resource_list>
    //Each scope element contains a list of resources for
that scope
    std::map<unsigned int, std::list<cResource*> > m_
Resources;

    //Finds resource by ID. Returns NULL if specified
resource not found.
    cResource* findResourcebyID(unsigned int UID);

    //Clears all resources and scopes
    void clear();

    //Loads resources from XML file
    bool loadFromXMLFile(std::string Filename);

    //Sets the current scope. Depends on the scene
currently loaded
    //Call this function with a valid scene scope
    //to load and unload appropriate resources
    void setCurrentScope(unsigned int Scope);

    const unsigned int getResourceCount(){return m_
ResourceCount;}

    inline cResourceManager()
```

```
    {
        m_CurrentScope = m_ResourceCount = 0;
    }
};

//-----------------------------------------------------

#endif // RESOURCEMANAGER_H_INCLUDED
```

## Comments

- The ResourceManager.h file contains two classes, cResourceManager and cResource. The former represents the resource manager subsystem, and the latter a resource object. Both classes are derived from the common ancestor class cEngineObject, discussed in an earlier chapter.

- Typically, only one instance will exist of cResourceManager at any one time, there will be as many instances of cResource as there are resources, one instance per resource.

- The resource class is intended to be an abstract base class, a common interface by which the resource manager manages resources. When the XML file is parsed, the resource manager will delegate the finer details of resource initialization to a manager appropriate for the resource kind. Since resources differ in kind, their implementation is likely to vary depending on whether it is an audio, graphic, or other resource. Thus, each manager is expected to create their own customized resource class derived from the common cResource base class where appropriate, and to implement it as suitable for their needs. For example, the render manager should create its own derived resource class CGraphicsResource, and the audio manager should create its own cAudioResource. The resource manager interfaces with them all through the superclass cResource.

- A typedef enum structure is used to enumerate resource types in the form of unsigned integers.

- CResourceManager maintains a complete list of its resources through a combination of the std::map and std::list classes. It uses an std::map class to build a list of pair values. Each element of std::map represents a pair of values in the form: <SceneID, ResourceList>. SceneID is an unsigned integer determining the scope of a collection of resources (0 for resources with game scope and other nonzero values, each value corresponding to a scene with an ID of a matching value). For each SceneID, there is a corresponding std::list class listing all the resources belonging to that group.

- The m_CurrentScope member of cResourceManager corresponds to the UID of the scene currently being played by the engine. This value changes with scene changes. As it changes, the resource manager will both load any resources with a matching SceneID tag and unload any and all nongame-level resources whose SceneID tag does not match.

- The m_CurrentScope member is set by a call to the setCurrentScope method of cResourceManager.

- The cResourceManager loadFromXMLFile method is used to open the resource XML file and to parse the elements of the file to populate the std::map and std::list arrays with a complete list of resources.

## ■ 4.7    Loading Resources from XML Using the TinyXML Library

The resource XML file is used by game developers to list each and every resource used by their game. This file is loaded and parsed by the engine resource manager at startup, and the code in the previous section shows that in the loadFromXMLFile function the same XML file data is cached from the file into a hierarchy in memory, which is built from an std::map and std::list class. This section considers the implementation of this function.

The loadFromXMLFile function uses the TinyXML library to open and parse XML files. This library is free, cross-platform, and open source, covered by the zlib/libpng license. Before implementing and compiling loadFromXMLFile then, the developer must first download, install, and configure this library for their C++ project.

> NOTE. Though this chapter includes a demonstration of how TinyXML is used to parse data from an XML file for the purposes of loading game resources, a more detailed tutorial detailing its use can be found at the following URL: http://www.grinninglizard.com/tinyxmldocs/tutorial0.html.

### 4.7.1    Downloading and Configuring TinyXML

This section details step by step both where and how to download TinyXML from its homepage and how to configure this library for both the Code::Blocks and Visual C++ IDEs.

Step 1.  Open a web browser and navigate to the TinyXML homepage at http://www.grinninglizard.com/tinyxml/. Once there, select the **latest source release** hyperlink. This automatically redirects the user to a SourceForge download page. From there, click the **Download Now** button to download the TinyXML zip source package to the local system. See Figure 4.4.

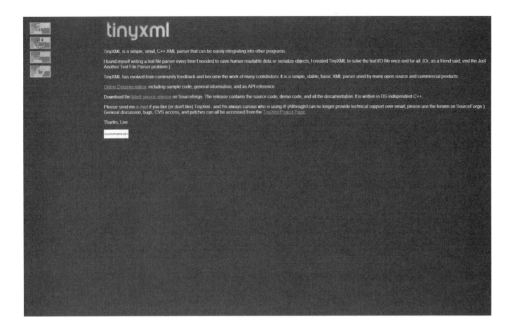

**I FIGURE 4.4**   Downloading TinyXML.

Step 2.   Once downloaded, unzip the contents of the zip file to an identifiable local directory.

Step 3.   Both Visual C++ and Code::Blocks users should add the folder location of the newly installed TinyXML to the standard include path. Instructions on how to do this for each IDE are provided in Chapter 2. In addition, users should add both the source and header files of TinyXML to the current project. Finally, the TinyXML.h file should be included in all files intending to use the library.

## 4.7.2   Implementing the loadFromXMLFile Method

The purpose of the loadFromXMLFile method of cResourceManager is to read and parse *metadata* regarding the total set of resources for any given game. It reads this metadata from an XML file on a local disk into a combination of data structures in system memory, specifically into a combination of stl::map and stl:list classes. Once the resource metadata is cached into memory, the resource manager will subsequently reference the *cached* version and not the XML file for all of its work on resources. It is important to note that loadFromXMLFile loads only information *about* the resources to be used (metadata: UID, file path, scope, etc.) and not the actual resources themselves such as the actual pixel data of a bitmap resource. This is because the scope of a resource (game or scene level) and the ID of the active scene will determine when the data of a resource is loaded or unloaded. It should be remembered that a key function of the resource manager, after the metadata is cached, is to reduce the number of loaded resources to the minimum necessary for the purposes of the active scene—the scene currently being played. The loadFromXMLFile function returns true if it is successful and false if it fails. In the event of an error, the engine developer might want to make use of the exception-handling system, as coded in an earlier chapter. For brevity and clarity, however, the code of this chapter concentrates exclusively on the issues of resource management and does not depend on the implementation of any particular exception-handling system. The full C++ source code of the loadFromXMLFile follows, with comments afterward:

```cpp
bool cResourceManager::loadFromXMLFile(std::string
Filename)
{

TiXmlDocument doc(Filename.c_str());

   if(doc.LoadFile())
   {
        //Find topmost resources node in XML file
        TiXmlNode* ResourceTree = doc.
FirstChild("resources");

        if(ResourceTree)
        {
           //Enumerate resource objects
           for(TiXmlNode* child = ResourceTree->
FirstChild(); child; child = child->NextSibling())
           {
                TiXmlElement *Element = child-
>ToElement();

                if(Element)
                {
                    cResource *Resource = NULL;

                    for(TiXmlAttribute* ElementAttrib =
Element->FirstAttribute(); ElementAttrib; ElementAttrib =
ElementAttrib->Next())
```

```
                              {
                              //Examine resource object
                              std::string AttribName =
ElementAttrib->Name();
                              std::string AttribValue =
ElementAttrib->Value();

                              //Detect resource type. Graphic?
Audio? Text?
                              if(AttribName=="type")
                              {
   //Allow managers to implement their own derived
versions of //cResource. Appropriate manager creates
resources and
//passes back a cResource pointer to be added to the
//resource list. Specific implementations for each
manager
//are considered later in this book.

                                  if(AttribValue=="graphic")
                                  {
                                      //Resource = g_
RenderManager->loadResourceFromXML(Element);
                                  }

                                  if(AttribValue=="audio")
                                  {
                                      //Resource = g_
AudioManager->loadResourceFromXML(Element);
                                  }

                                  if(AttribValue=="text")
                                  {
                                      Resource = g_
ConfigManager->loadResourceFromXML(Element);
                                  }
                              }

                              if(Resource)
                              {
                                  if(AttribName=="UID")
                                  {
                                      Resource->m_ResourceID =
atoi(AttribValue.c_str());
```

```
                                        }

                                        if(AttribName=="filename")
                                        {
                                            Resource->m_FileName =
            AttribValue;
                                        }

                                        if(AttribName=="scenescope")
                                        {
                                            Resource->m_Scope =
            atoi(AttribValue.c_str());
                                        }
                                    }
                            }

                                if(Resource)
                                {
                                    //Resources Added Here
                            m_Resources[Resource->m_Scope].push_
            back(Resource);
                                    m_ResourceCount++;
                                }
                            }
                        }

                    return true;
                }
            }

        return false;
    }
```

## Comments

- The loadFromXMLFile function begins by declaring an instance of the TinyXML object TiXmlDocument, the document-level object representing the entirety of the XML file: a collection of XML nodes. The following line calls the loadFile method of this object to ready the contents of the XML file for reading. This method returns false if an error occurred during the loading process.

- TiXmlNode* ResourceTree = doc.FirstChild("resources");
  This line calls the firstChild method of TiXmlDocument to retrieve a pointer to the first XML node object of the specified name "resources" in the collection. As mentioned earlier in this chapter, the name "resources" is the name of the top-level

node in the resource XML document, of which many resource nodes are children. Each resource node represents a unique resource in the collection.

- Having accessed the first and topmost node of the XML document, the function then iterates through all child resource nodes; that is, it cycles through each and every unique resource belonging to the resources node. For each node, it retrieves a TiXmlElement pointer from the ToElement method of TiXmlNode. This method converts a standard XML node to an XMLElement. An XML node represents a branch within the XML hierarchy, and it may or may not contain child nodes. An XMLElement represents all of this information and more. An element might contain additional properties in the form of attributes, and an XMLElement pointer allows a programmer to access these attributes and their values. Consider the following XML resource element:

```
<resource UID="3" type="text" filename="gamedata.cfg"
scenescope="0"></resource>
```

The name of this node is "resource." However, this node is also an element. The four attributes of this element are: UID="3", type="text", filename="gamedata.cfg", and scenescope="0". Each attribute consists of two parts: a name and a value. The name appears before the equality operator (=), and the value appears after.

- After retrieving a pointer to an XML element through TiXmlElement, the loop reads the value of the type attribute of the element to determine its type and how it should be handled for loading. The type element indicates whether a resource is a graphics resource, an audio resource, or another type of resource, and the loading of a resource will be delegated to the appropriate manager for its kind. Graphics resources will be loaded by the render manager, audio resources by the audio manager, etc. Here, the function calls the appropriate loading methods of these managers. These managers and their loading implementations are discussed in later chapters of this book. Each method, however, accepts a pointer to the current XML element, in case the manager needs to read additional, custom data, and returns a pointer to a cResource class representing the loaded metadata of the resource. In short, the loadResource-FromXML method of the manager classes accepts as input an XML element describing a resource and returns as output a valid pointer to a cResource object representing the resource metadata. If the method fails, a null pointer is returned.

- Once the function has a pointer to a loaded cResource object, it proceeds to add it to the cached collection of resources maintained by the combination of std::map and std::list. The m_Resources property of the class cResourceManager is an std::map array of std::list objects. Each element in the std::map array is a std::list of resource objects appropriate for a specific game scope.

### 4.7.3    Searching and Clearing Resources

The loadFromXMLFile method of cResourceManager is intended to cache resource metadata from an XML file to the system. Once there, it will be used during game play to load and unload the data of resources according to the ID of the active scene. Before implementing the loading and unloading process, it will be useful to code two complementary methods of cResourceManager: one to search through the collection of cResources for a given ID and the other to clear the total collection of cResources from memory; that is, to reset the resource collection to its default, empty state. The searching method may be coded as follows:

```
cResource* cResourceManager::findResourcebyID(unsigned
int UID)
{
    std::map<unsigned int, std::list<cResource*>
>::iterator it;

    //Search through scopes
    for(it=m_Resources.begin();it!=m_Resources.end();it++)
    {
        if(!(*it).second.empty())
        {
            std::list<cResource*>::iterator list_it;

            //Search through resources of scope
            for(list_it=(*it).second.begin();list_
it!=(*it).second.end();list_it++)
            {
                //If matches ID
                if((*list_it)->m_ResourceID == UID)
                    return (*list_it);
            }
        }
    }

    return NULL;
}
```

**Comments**

- The findResourcebyID method searches the cResource collection for a resource of a given ID and returns a pointer to this resource if found or a null pointer.

- The function begins by retrieving an element iterator for std::map and cycling through each element in the map. Each element corresponds to a resource scope: One element is 0 (game-level scope), and other integers represent the scope for a scene of a corresponding ID.

- For each scope element, the function retrieves a second iterator for std::list, and uses it to cycle through all the cResource objects belonging to the list. For each resource, the function tests for a match between the resource ID and the specified ID passed as an argument of the function. If a match is found, a pointer to the current cResource of the loop is returned. If the total collection of cResources is exhausted and no match is found, a null pointer is returned to indicate that no resource could be found matching the given ID.

The clear method removes all cResources from the collection in system memory maintained by the resource manager. It can be coded as follows:

```
void cResourceManager::clear()
{
    std::map<unsigned int, std::list<cResource*>
>::iterator it;

    //Search through scopes
    for(it=m_Resources.begin();it!=m_Resources.end();it++)
    {
        if(!(*it).second.empty())
        {
            std::list<cResource*>::iterator list_it;

            //Search through resources of scope
            for(list_it=(*it).second.begin();list_
it!=(*it).second.end();list_it++)
            {
                //Delete resource object
                (*list_it)->unload();
                SAFE_DELETE(*list_it);
            }

            (*it).second.clear();
        }
    }
}
```

```
        }

        m_Resources.clear();
    }
```

**Comments**

- The clear method clears the cResource collection of cResourceManager. It makes use of the SAFE_DELETE macro to delete from system memory cResource objects created earlier with the new keyword. This macro can be defined as:

```
#define SAFE_DELETE(a) { delete (a); (a) = NULL; }
```

- The function begins like findResourcebyID by retrieving an element iterator for std::map and cycling through each element in the map. For each scope element, the function retrieves a second iterator for std::list and uses it to cycle through all the cResource objects belonging to the list. For each resource, the function calls the resource unload method and then deletes the object. The call to the unload method of cResource appeals to the idea of polymorphism in the sense that its call will invoke an overloaded unload method implemented in a descendent class of cResource. The exact details of the descendent class and the details of unloading will vary depending on the kind of resource. It is important to note that cResource is an abstract base class from which derived resource classes are to be made. Each derived class will implement their own unload method, and the resource manager invokes this function by calling the unload method declared in the cResource base class.

## 4.7.4  Loading and Unloading Resource Data

The resource manager maintains a cached collection of resource metadata in system memory throughout the execution of a game. The metadata for any resource describes at least: (1) the path name to the resource object, (2) the unique integer identifier of the resource, (3) the resource type (graphics, audio, etc.), and (4) the resource scope, in terms of scene ID (the ID of the scene during which the resource data should be loaded and available). It has been mentioned already that a resource can have either one of at least two scopes: *game level* for resources that should be available throughout the execution of the game and *scene level* for resources that are scene specific. The data of scene-level resources should be loaded and available throughout the duration of a specified scene and should be unloaded and out of memory whenever that scene is not the active scene. To ensure the resource manager automatically loads and unloads resources on the basis of their scope, a game should notify the resource manager whenever a scene change occurs, e.g., a change of level or a transition from a game scene to a menu screen. On being notified of the change, the resource manager should unload the data for those resources attached to the previous scene, and then load the resource data for those attached to the new scene. The resource loading and unloading processes can be implemented in a method called setCurrentScope, which is detailed in the following code with comments afterward:

```
void cResourceManager::setCurrentScope(unsigned int
Scope)
{
    //Unload old scope, if not global scope.
    if(m_CurrentScope!=0)
    {
        std::list<cResource*>::iterator list_it;

        for(list_it=m_Resources[m_CurrentScope].
begin();list_it!=m_Resources[m_CurrentScope].end();list_
it++)
            (*list_it)->unload();
    }

    m_CurrentScope = Scope;

    //Load new scope.
    std::list<cResource*>::iterator list_it;

    for(list_it=m_Resources[m_CurrentScope].begin();list_
it!=m_Resources[m_CurrentScope].end();list_it++)
        (*list_it)->load();
}
```

## Comments

- The method setCurrentScope should be called for each and every scene change in a game. It accepts one unsigned integer parameter indicating the unique ID of the new scene for which resources are to be loaded. The method sets and reads the m_CurrentScope property. This member indicates the ID of the currently active scene.

- The method proceeds by first cycling through all resources belonging to the previous scene (provided the ID is not 0, as 0=game scope). For each resource, it calls the unload method but not the delete method. The unload method unloads the *data* of the resource, but delete would also erase the metadata: the cResource object. The metadata of the resource in system memory must remain because it might again be used to reload the resource data should the appropriate scene become active again.

- Once the data of resources in the previous scene have been removed, the m_ CurrentScope property is updated to reflect the new scene ID. The data of the resources attached to the new scene are then loaded as appropriate.

## ◾ 4.8  Improving the Resource Manager

The resource manager coded in this chapter in the form of a C++ class cResourceManager is able to load resource metadata from XML files into a cached collection in system memory, to search and clear that collection, and to delegate and coordinate the loading and unloading of the actual data of resources on the basis of their relationship to the active scene. These features of the resource manager tackle a number of key problems related to resource management already detailed. Specifically, the hierarchical structure of the resources and the distinction drawn between metadata and data allows the resource manager to maintain a collection of resource metadata and to use that collection to coordinate the loading and unloading of resources. Furthermore, the concept of resource scope ensures that unused resources are unloaded to make room in both system and hardware memory for newly loaded and used resources, according to the scene changes of the game. However, this resource manager is not without room for improvement.

Some programmers would argue that loading and unloading resources according to a concept of scene scope as presented here introduces unnecessary performance penalties for a game, since there are times when the engine could be made to unload resources on scene changes when those resources might very shortly be loaded again. To consider a simple example: A game might feature two scenes between which it alternates, loading one and then the other, and vice versa (Scene A and Scene B). Neither scene shares resources, and Scene A features over 80 MB worth of unique resources and Scene B features only 2 MB worth of unique resources. According to the current scope model, the resource manager will load and unload all appropriate resources when the scene change between A and B occurs, meaning the larger Scene A would take longer to load than Scene B, and this will occur for each and every scene change. This is a problem because if the host computer can load 80 MB worth of resources without impairment for Scene A, there appears no reason why the processor should waste time and power unloading all of it simply to present the much smaller Scene B, and then load it back again to re-present Scene A when the next change occurs. A potential solution to this problem is to extend the scene scope concept to include the concept of a *memory budget*, a maximum quota of system memory allowed for game resource data. Using this system, the resource manager is permitted to load resources without any corresponding unloading until the budget is reached—until that quota of memory has been consumed. Once reached, the resource manager may then unload unused resources (resources not in the active scene) until either all unused resources are unloaded or a specific minimum memory budget is reached if possible. Implementing these improvements is not considered in this book, and is left as an exercise for the reader.

## ■ 4.9   Chapter Summary

This chapter focused on the design of a resource manager and its implementation in object-oriented form using the C++ language. It considered the problems that center on resource management and proposed some solutions to them. The next chapter moves away from the issues of resource management and considers those of rendering and graphics, focusing on the design and implementation of a render manager component of a game engine. It considers first a render manager coded with SDL and then a render manager coded with DirectX.

# 5

# 2D Render Manager
# with SDL

## Overview

After completing this chapter, you should:

- Know how to download, install, and configure the SDL graphics library
- Be able to build and run SDL-powered applications
- Know how to wrap SDL functions into a 2D render manager class
- Be able to implement features such as sprite animation and color keying
- Know how to extend SDL functionality by installing add-ons

## ■ 5.1 Introduction

This chapter is the first of two in this book to focus on creating a render manager. This chapter focuses on the creation of a 2D render manager and Chapter 9 on the creation of a 3D render manager. As mentioned previously, the render manager component is responsible for almost all graphical tasks performed by a game engine, and these tasks vary greatly depending on circumstances. It is worth noting that a 2D render manager differs in some important respects from its 3D counterpart. Not only does the purview of the 2D render manager encompass only two rather than three dimensions, but this lack of a third dimension has important implications for how a programmer is likely to implement the 2D manager. In 3D, graphical entities—such as meshes, textures, and effects—are positioned and oriented in 3D world space in terms of (XYZ) coordinate values, and this distance along any and all of the three axes means that some of these entities can be farther or nearer to the camera at any one time. In 2D, however, graphical entities are positioned in screen space rather than world space, in terms of XY rather than XYZ. The result is that all entities in the scene are an equal distance from the camera and are oriented directly toward it. The origin (0,0) of 2D screen space is usually at the top left corner of the screen, and this is also the case with the SDL library. As we shall see, the SDL library is an open source and freely available programming toolkit for rendering graphics to the screen via the graphical hardware.

Before considering the SDL in more detail, it is worth considering the primary functions of the 2D render manager. These functions—with the exception of one—shall be implemented as this chapter proceeds; the other is left for a later chapter for reasons that will be stated soon.

The 2D render manager should:

• Create the main application window at a specified size, switch to full-screen mode if required, and initialize the hardware as appropriate for displaying graphics to the user.

• Be able to create and initialize 2D graphics resources on demand (loading and unloading pixel data to and from memory) in conjunction with the resource manager. The resource manager was created in an earlier chapter.

• Position, render (draw), and animate graphical elements to the window as required. This should include transparency and color-keying effects where appropriate.

• Work in conjunction with the 2D scene manager to render and composite complete 2D scenes. This feature will be reserved for a later chapter when considering the 2D scene manager in more detail.

## ■  5.2   2D Graphics with the SDL Library

The previous section mentioned that one of the chief purposes of the 2D render manager is to utilize the graphics hardware for drawing graphical entities to the application window in 2D screen space (2D coordinates). In other words, the developer wants simply to specify any graphical entity and some appropriate render parameters (such as position and rotation values), and for the render manager to draw that entity according to those values. That is the chief appeal of the render manager. The engine developer seeks to implement the render manager as an API-independent mechanism to handle the tedium of rendering. The term "API-independent" is used here to emphasize how the render manager, though created using an API on the "inside," should be so designed (as a C++ class) that any developer working with the manager from the "outside" (as a caller of its functions and methods) should not need familiarity with that API in order to use it successfully. Designing the render manager class in this way—to have an API-independent interface—has at least two key advantages: First, such a manager does not demand of its user knowledge of a specific API, and second, the internal details of the class can be adjusted without breaking or adjusting the class interface; that is, without needing to change the details of its public properties or methods. It is therefore entirely possible—theoretically—for a developer at a later time to overhaul the implementation of the render manager class, changing from one API

**❙ FIGURE 5.1**    Example of a 2D game. From Loonyland 2, courtesy of Mike Hommel, Hamumu Software.

to another, without breaking the original interface of that class and without requiring a change in any other dependent component of the engine.

Hence, the 2D render manager will be implemented as an API-independent component for rendering 2D graphics to the window in 2D screen space. The class will be built using an API, but will not require users of the class to be familiar with it. Many APIs could have been chosen to implement this render manager, including ClanLib and PTK, but eventually SDL was selected. SDL is an acronym for Simple Directmedia Layer, and it is a free, cross-platform, and open source library that is often used for rendering 2D graphics. It is open source in the strictest sense of the term in that its source code is publicly available and can be downloaded, inspected, and amended if a developer so chooses, though working with the SDL source code is not required to build SDL applications since precompiled binary libraries are also available with documentation. It is cross-platform in that it can support the development of applications that run on Linux, Windows, Windows CE, BeOS, Mac OS®, Mac OS X, FreeBSD, NetBSD®, OpenBSD, BSD/OS, Solaris, IRIX®, and QNX®. Furthermore, version 1.3, in development, also boasts support for iPhone, iPod touch®, and Nintendo DS™. Finally, it is free in the sense that developers can use the SDL to produce commercial applications without having to pay for a license, under certain conditions. The SDL is covered by the GNU LGPL version 2 license, a copy of which can be found at: http://www.gnu.org/licenses/gpl-2.0.html.

> **NOTE.** It should be noted that the SDL library can be used for more than just rendering graphics. SDL contains components for reading input from joysticks and other devices, functions for other game-related tasks, and add-ons to extend its feature set to include sound, animation, networking, and more. This book, however, concentrates on its rendering feature set.

The SDL, then, is selected for our work in this chapter on creating a render manager to: (1) create an application window, (2) set up a rendering device (initialize graphics hardware), (3) load and process pixel data from graphics files such as JPG and PNG, and (4) render those graphics to the screen at application run time. The next section considers the details of downloading, installing, and configuring the SDL library for use in either the Visual C++ or the Code::Blocks IDE.

### EXERCISE 5.1

Before implementing an engine manager component using a third-party library, a developer should research the market, trying to find as many libraries as possible to serve their purpose. Having identified all options, a developer is in a position to make a choice of the library most suited for their project. Search the Internet and find at least three alternative graphics libraries to the SDL that could be used for the render manager.

**Answers**
- ClanLib: http://www.clanlib.org/
- PTK: http://www.phelios.com/ptk/
- Love2D: http://love2d.org/

### ■  5.3   Configuring SDL for Visual C++ and Code::Blocks

The SDL library can be used for rendering 2D graphics to the application window in 2D screen space. This library is free, open source, and cross-platform and can be downloaded from the official homepage at: http://www.libsdl.org/. The instructions for downloading and installing the SDL library differ depending on the IDE for which it is being configured. This chapter considers configuration for two IDES, Visual C++ and Code::Blocks.

## 5.3.1   Configuring SDL for Visual C++

Step 1.   Visit the SDL homepage at http://www.libsdl.org/ and select **SDL 1.2** from the Download section to download the 1.2 API (the latest version at the time of writing is 1.2.14). For Visual C++ 2005 or Visual C++ Express Edition, download the package named SDL-devel-1.2.14-VC8.zip (Visual C++ 2005 Service Pack 1), as shown in Figure 5.2.

Step 2.   Unzip the contents of the newly downloaded SDL API package to a folder on the local hard disk. Once completed, start Visual C++ Express and add the header and lib folders of the SDL package to the include and library paths of the C++ project, the details of which were mentioned in an earlier chapter.

Step 3.   To configure a C++ project for use with SDL, some further steps must be applied in the configuration of the compiler. To do this, access the Project Properties menu by selecting **Project | Properties** from the main application menu. A window appears, displaying options for the current project. From this window, select **Configuration Properties | C/C++ | General** from the list view. Find the option for Detect 64-bit Portability Issues and set this to **No** if it is not set to No already.

Step 4.   From the Project Properties menu, select **Configuration Properties | C/C++ | Code Generation** from the list view. Find the option Runtime Library and set this to **Multi-Threaded DLL (/MD)**.

**Development Libraries:**

**Linux:**
SDL-devel-1.2.14-1.i586.rpm
SDL-debuginfo-1.2.14-1.i586.rpm
SDL-devel-1.2.14-1.x86_64.rpm
SDL-debuginfo-1.2.14-1.x86_64.rpm
http://packages.debian.org/stable/libdevel/

**Win32:**
SDL-devel-1.2.14-VC6.zip (Visual C++ 6.0)
SDL-devel-1.2.14-VC8.zip (Visual C++ 2005 Service Pack 1)
SDL-devel-1.2.14-mingw32.tar.gz (Mingw32)

**Mac OS X:**
SDL-devel-1.2.14-extras.dmg (templates and documentation)

**I FIGURE 5.2**   Downloading the SDL for Visual C++.

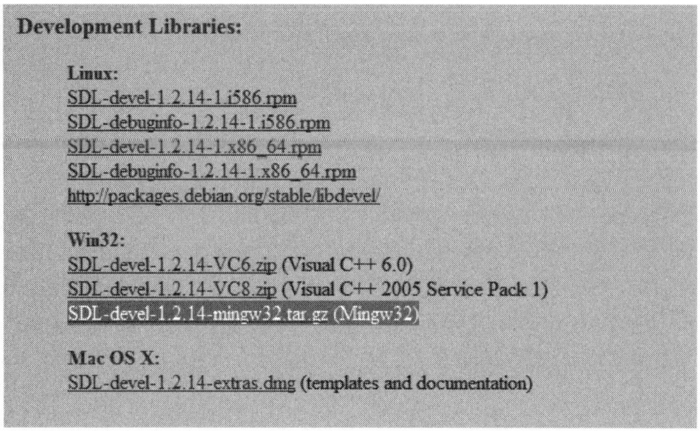

**Development Libraries:**

**Linux:**
SDL-devel-1.2.14-1.i586.rpm
SDL-debuginfo-1.2.14-1.i586.rpm
SDL-devel-1.2.14-1.x86_64.rpm
SDL-debuginfo-1.2.14-1.x86_64.rpm
http://packages.debian.org/stable/libdevel/

**Win32:**
SDL-devel-1.2.14-VC6.zip (Visual C++ 6.0)
SDL-devel-1.2.14-VC8.zip (Visual C++ 2005 Service Pack 1)
SDL-devel-1.2.14-mingw32.tar.gz (Mingw32)

**Mac OS X:**
SDL-devel-1.2.14-extras.dmg (templates and documentation)

**FIGURE 5.3**    Downloading the SDL for Code::Blocks.

Step 5. Having performed the steps above, the SDL application should compile by including the appropriate #include directive in project source files: #include<SDL.h>.

## 5.3.2    Configuring SDL for Code::Blocks

Step 1. Visit the SDL homepage at http://www.libsdl.org/ and select **SDL 1.2** from the Download section to download the 1.2 API (the latest version at the time of writing is 1.2.14). For Code::Blocks, download the package named SDL-devel-1.2.14-mingw32.tar.gz (MingW32), as shown in Figure 5.3.

Step 2. Unzip the contents of the newly downloaded SDL API package to a folder on the local hard disk. Once completed, start Code::Blocks and create a new SDL application using the Application Wizard, following each step as required.

## ■ 5.4    Using SDL to Create a Render Manager

Before proceeding with this chapter, it is recommended, though not required, that the reader examine the SDL documentation and at least one sample SDL application to get a feel for the library and for the overall structure of an SDL application. However, this chapter will detail the SDL library and explain many of its key functions, including those for window creation and graphics rendering, alongside the development of the render manager class. The introduction to this chapter listed the core features of the render manager, and all of these besides the one exception mentioned can be encapsulated into that class using the SDL library. There are many places in which the development of the render manager as a class could begin, and the place that is chosen often reflects the design patterns being used by the developers and the specific requirements of the engine. A developer might, for example, start by coding the resource loading mechanism for loading graphics resources and pixel data into memory. But the course development we will take in this chapter reflects roughly the typical order in which the render manager and its functions are called upon by a game engine as it executes at run time. One of the first tasks an engine must perform before it can proceed is to create a main application window and to initialize the graphics hardware, readying it for work. This, then, is where development of the render manager shall begin for the purposes of this chapter. Before considering the implementation details of hardware initialization and window creation, however, it is useful for reference to present here the class declaration of the render manager in full, as it will appear in its .h (C++ header) file, outlining the methods and classes that must be created for a complete, working 2D render manager in SDL. This code, however, is likely to include some functions and classes whose purpose might not at first sight be clear or obvious to the reader at this point. But by the end of the chapter, all functions, classes, and other features listed here will be explained in detail.

```
#ifndef SDL2DRENDERMANAGER_H_INCLUDED
#define SDL2DRENDERMANAGER_H_INCLUDED

#include "2DRenderManager.h"
#include "ResourceManager.h"
#include <SDL.h>
#include <SDL_Image.h>
#include <string>
#include <sstream>
#include <iostream>
#include <time.h>
#include <iomanip>
#include <windows.h>
#include <math.h>

//Tiny XML Header. Needs TinyXML library
//Available for free at: http://www.grinninglizard.com/
tinyxml/
#include "TinyXML.h"


//-----------------------------------------------------
```

```
//Render Resource Definition
//Derived from cResource. Represents a graphics resource.
//Pointers to instances of this class are maintained by
the
//Resource Manager.
class cRenderResource : public cResource
{
    private:
    protected:
    public:
        SDL_Surface *m_Surface;

        ~cRenderResource();
        void load();
        void unload();
        cRenderResource();
};


//------------------------------------------------------

//2D Render Object
//Each instance of this class represents a unique
renderable item in a 2D scene.
//It is a reference to a graphics resource, and position,
scale, and rotation values.
//This combination of values allows the render manager to
determine
//Which graphics resource should be rendered, and where
and how.
//There may be many render objects referencing only one
graphics resource.
//e.g., where a scene contains many identical enemy
characters.
class cSDLRenderObject : public cEngineObject
{
    private:
    protected:
    public:

    cRenderResource *m_RenderResource;
    SDL_Rect m_RenderRect;
    float m_PosX;
    float m_PosY;
    bool m_bVisible;
    SDL_Color m_ColorKey;
```

```
    bool m_bColorKeyEnabled;

    cSDLRenderObject();
    void setResourceObject(cRenderResource
*RenderResource);
    virtual void update(){};
};

//------------------------------------------------------

//2D Sprite Object
//Derived from render object. This class features extra
properties
//for creating animated tile sets. By including all
frames in a single image,
//and by specifying the dimensions of each frame, this
class can
//animate through the frames at a specified speed

class cSpriteObject : public cSDLRenderObject
{
    private:
    protected:
    DWORD m_TimeLastFrame;

    public:
    unsigned int m_TotalFrames;
    unsigned int m_FramsPerRow;
    unsigned int m_FramsPerColumn;
    unsigned int m_CurrentFrame;
    unsigned int m_StartFrame;
    float m_Speed;
    unsigned int m_FrameWidth;
    unsigned int m_FrameHeight;

    void update();
    void play();
    void stop();
    void setFrameRect(unsigned int FrameNumber);
    cSpriteObject();
};

//------------------------------------------------------

//2D Render Manager class
```

```
//This is the 2D SDL render manager component, and it
works with all
//classes listed above.
//Its purpose is to create a window, initialize hardware,
//create, load, and unload graphics resources, and render
graphics

class cSDL2DRenderManager : public c2DRenderManager
{
    private:
    protected:
    cSDL2DRenderManager();
    static cSDL2DRenderManager m_SDL2DRenderManager;
    public:
    static cSDL2DRenderManager* GetSDL2DRenderManager();
    SDL_Surface* m_RenderWindow; //Standard window for
render context
    std::stringstream m_VideoInfo;
    bool init(unsigned int Width=800, unsigned int
Height=600, bool fullScreen=false, char* WindowTitle=0);
    void free();
    bool update();
    void toggleFullScreen();
    cResource* loadResourceFromXML(TiXmlElement
*Element);
    void renderAllObjects();

    std::list<cSDLRenderObject*> m_RenderObjects;
};

//-----------------------------------------------------

#endif // SDL2DRENDERMANAGER_H_INCLUDED
```

**Comments**

- This header file includes declarations for four individual but related classes: cRenderResource, cSDLRenderObject, cSpriteObject, and cSDL2DRenderManager.

- cRenderResource is derived from the base class cResource (defined in an earlier chapter) and represents a graphics resource in system or hardware memory. For the 2D render manager created here, a graphics resource refers to a standard 2D image (.BMP, .JPG, .PNG, and others). By way of its base class, the cRenderResource is intended to work with the resource manager as well as the render manager. The resource manager is responsible for maintaining a pointer to the resource in a list and for scheduling loads and unloads as required, according to resource scope. The render manager is responsible for the actual creation, destroying, loading, and unloading of the resource, as well as rendering it to the display as necessary.

- cSDLRenderObject is allied to the cRenderResource class. cRenderResource represents the raw data of a graphics resource in memory, and cSDLRender-Object tells the render manager *how* that resource is to be used in a scene. A scene will contain as many instances of cSDLRenderObject as there are entities in the scene, one instance per entity. For example, one instance for the player character, another for an enemy, another for a scenery unit or prop, and so on. Each instance of cSDLRenderObject indicates the position (XY), scale (XY), and orientation (degrees) at which the associated graphics resource must be drawn at render time.

- cSpriteObject is derived from cSDLRenderObject, and is a tilemap-based animation class. cSDLRenderObject is responsible for drawing the entirety of a graphics resource at a specified position, scale, and orientation, and this resource is drawn in an inanimate (motionless) form. This class is appropriate for drawing graphics that do not animate: trees, backgrounds, statues, etc. However, for animated graphics, the cSpriteObject has been created. This class features extra values in addition to those of its ancestors for setting the time, frame, and speed settings of animation playback.

- cSDL2DRenderManager represents the render manager component that ties together all of the above classes into a coherent functional whole that renders scenes. This class is responsible for creating an application window, initializing hardware, maintaining a list of render objects, and rendering those objects on each frame according to their visibility in a scene.

## ■ 5.5  Encapsulating Window Creation into the Render Manager with SDL

For the purposes of this book, development of the 2D SDL render manager begins with window creation and hardware initialization; that is, graphics hardware initialization. Other hardware, such as audio hardware, remains unaffected by the render manager. The initialization process performed in init uses the SDL library initialization functions. This method should be called once at application startup. The SDL functions it calls

are: SDL_Init, SDL_SetVideoMode, SDL_WM_SetCaption, and SDL_GetVideoInfo.
More details are given shortly on these SDL functions and their arguments. First, the
full definition of the init method of the render manager is provided:

```
//Function requires window width and height (default:
800x600), a bool to
//determine whether the resolution should be changed to
match the
//window, and a string for the window title.

bool cSDL2DRenderManager::init(unsigned int Width,
unsigned int Height, bool fullScreen, char* WindowTitle)
{
    if ( SDL_Init( SDL_INIT_VIDEO ) < 0 )
    {
        //Error: could not initialize SDL renderer
        return false;
    }

    if(fullScreen)
        m_RenderWindow = SDL_SetVideoMode(Width, Height,
16, SDL_HWSURFACE|SDL_DOUBLEBUF|SDL_FULLSCREEN);
    else
        m_RenderWindow = SDL_SetVideoMode(Width, Height,
16, SDL_HWSURFACE|SDL_DOUBLEBUF);

    if(!m_RenderWindow)
    {
        //Error: could not create window
        return false;
    }

    SDL_WM_SetCaption(WindowTitle,NULL);

    //Populate video info

    const SDL_VideoInfo *VidInfo = SDL_GetVideoInfo();

    m_VideoInfo << "Video Info\nCan Create Hardware
Surfaces: " << VidInfo->hw_available <<
        "\nWindow Manager Available: " << VidInfo->wm_
available << "\nHardware to hardware blits accelerated:
" << VidInfo->blit_hw
            << "\nHardware to hardware colorkey blits
```

```
accelerated: " << VidInfo->blit_hw_CC
        << "\nHardware to hardware alpha blits
accelerated: " << VidInfo->blit_hw_A
        << "\nSoftware to hardware blits accelerated:
" << VidInfo->blit_sw
        << "\nSoftware to hardware colorkey blits
accelerated: " << VidInfo->blit_sw_CC
        << "\nSoftware to hardware alpha blits
accelerated: " << VidInfo->blit_sw_A
        << "\nColor fills accelerated: " << VidInfo-
>blit_fill
        << "\nTotal amount of video memory in Kilobytes:
" << VidInfo->video_mem;

    return true;
}
```

## Comments

- The method starts by calling SDL_Init to initialize the graphics rendering components of the SDL library. If successful, the method proceeds. If it fails, an application should resort to its error-handling facilities (coded in an earlier chapter).

- Next, the init method calls the SDL function SDL_SetVideoMode to initialize the graphics hardware and create an application window according to the specified width, height, and full-screen settings. A valid pointer to this window is returned in the variable m_RenderWindow if the call is successful. Otherwise, null is returned. The render manager maintains a pointer to this window throughout the execution of the engine.

- The window created by SDL in the previous step carries the default title "SDL Application," which is displayed both in the window title region at the top and in its associated button on the Windows task bar, assuming the developer is working on the Windows platform. A developer will likely want to change this title to something suited to their application. This can be changed using the SDL_WM_SetCaption function.

- The last step of the render manager init method uses the SDL function SDL_GetVideoInfo to populate an STL string object with diagnostic information relating to the video hardware being used to power the application. This stage is not essential to the successful initialization of an SDL application, but the information returned can be useful for troubleshooting purposes.

## ■ SDL Initialization Functions

### SDL_Init

The general form of this function is:

```
int SDL_Init(Uint32 flags);
```

*Description*

This function initializes a specified subsystem (component) of the SDL library. SDL features a range of subsystems, each dedicated to a particular task. These are specified by the flags argument, and can be any one or more of the following: SDL_INIT_TIMER, SDL_INIT_AUDIO, SDL_INIT_VIDEO, SDL_INIT_CDROM, SDL_INIT_JOYSTICK, and SDL_INIT_EVERYTHING. Of these, SDL_INIT_VIDEO refers to the graphics hardware and is therefore especially pertinent to the render manager.

*Returns*

The function returns either 0 on success, or –1 on failure.

### SDL_SetVideoMode

The general form of this function is:

```
SDL_Surface *SDL_SetVideoMode(int width, int height,
int bpp, Uint32 flags);
```

*Description*

This function is intended both to initialize the graphics hardware and to create an associated window. It accepts four arguments: the width and height of the window to be created, the bits-per-pixel of the window (usually 16, 24, or 32), and a series of qualifying flags detailing more about the window to be created and the device to be initialized. The flags argument can be one or more of the following values:

- SDL_SWSURFACE|SDL_HWSURFACE

  Mutually exclusive options. Determines whether rendering should be powered by a software or hardware renderer. SDL_HWSURFACE almost always offers better performance and is therefore preferred by developers. SDL_SWSURFACE is often used as a fallback option of last resort.

- SDL_ASYNCBLIT

  Determines whether rendering (blitting) should be performed asynchronously. Specifying this flag often results in performance penalties on single-processor machines. Typically, this option is disabled.

- SDL_ANYFORMAT

  Determines how SDL reacts if a device cannot be initialized at the specified bits-per-pixel setting. If this flag is not specified and the specified bits-per-pixel depth (bpp) is not available, the function fails. If this flag is specified and the specified bits-per-pixel depth (bpp) is not available, the function chooses the next available setting.

- SDL_DOUBLEBUF

  This flag works only in combination with SDL_HWSURFACE and specifies whether double buffering should be used. The finer details of double buffering are beyond the scope of this book, but in short it involves two video surfaces that are flipped on every frame. The user sees only the front surface, and the back surface is hidden. All rendering for the next frame occurs on the back surface, and the surfaces are flipped only after all drawing to the back surface is completed. After being flipped, the back surface comes to the front and is visible, and the old front surface is moved to the back and is hidden. The result of this process is smoother-looking animations and frame refreshes. Therefore, most developers specify this flag where it is supported.

- SDL_FULLSCREEN

  When specified, full-screen mode is used. SDL will attempt to change the screen resolution to match the size of the window, and the title bar and icons associated with the window will not be shown. If the screen cannot be switched to the specified resolution, SDL will switch to the next highest resolution and show the application window centered in the screen surrounded by a black border.

- SDL_OPENGL

  This can be specified if a developer plans to work with SDL in combination with OpenGL functions.

- SDL_RESIZABLE

  Determines whether the created window should be resizable.

- SDL_NOFRAME

  Determines whether the created window should have a border with title frame, application buttons, and border decoration.

*Returns*

If successful, this function returns a valid pointer to an SDL_Surface object representing the graphics context (the canvas) of the window onto which graphics will be rendered on each frame. If the function fails, null is returned.

*Note*

This function should be accompanied by a closing call to SDL_Quit at application termination.

**SDL_WM_SetCaption**

The general form of this function is:

```
void SDL_WM_SetCaption(const char *title, const char
*icon);
```

*Description*

This function sets the text of the window title in its title region (title) and in its associated task bar button (icon).

**SDL_GetVideoInfo**

The general form of this function is:

```
SDL VideoInfo *SDL GetVideoInfo(void);
```

*Description*

This function populates an SDL_VideoInfo data structure with information regarding the graphics device being used to power the application. SDL_VideoInfo is as follows:

```
typedef struct{
  Uint32 hw_available:1; //Can create hardware
surfaces?
  Uint32 wm_available:1; //Is window manager
available?
  Uint32 blit_hw:1; //Hardware to hardware blits
supported?
  Uint32 blit_hw_CC:1; //Hardware to hardware color
key blits supported?
  Uint32 blit_hw_A:1; //Hardware to hardware alpha
blits supported?
  Uint32 blit_sw:1; //Software to hardware blits
accelerated?
  Uint32 blit_sw_CC:1; //Software to hardware color
key blits supported?
  Uint32 blit_sw_A:1; //Software to hardware alpha
```

```
blits accelerated?
  Uint32 blit_fill; //Color fills accelerated?
  Uint32 video_mem; //Total video memory in
kilobytes
  SDL_PixelFormat *vfmt; //Pixel format of the video
device
} SDL_VideoInfo;
```

## ■  5.6   Render Resource Objects and the Render Manager

The primary purpose of the init method of the render manager is to initialize the graphics hardware and create an associated window of specified dimensions onto which the render manager can draw the contents of a scene on each and every frame until application exit. The frame drawing method of the render manager will be called by update, and this will be called once on each and every frame—in a game loop, as mentioned earlier. The details of the update method are considered later in this chapter. Having considered the implementation of the init method, it is necessary now to turn our attention to the resource loading features of the render manager.

The resource manager is distinct from the render manager, and was coded in an earlier chapter. Its chief responsibility is to manage resources (graphics, sound, meshes, text), particularly resource metadata in memory. The work on the resource manager involved drawing a distinction between resource raw data and resource metadata. The former refers to the actual data of a resource (say, the pixels of a bitmap or the audio information of a WAV file), and the latter refers to information *about* the resource such as the fully qualified path to the resource file on disk or the scope index of a resource determining when its raw data should be loaded and unloaded at run time. The duty of the resource manager is to maintain a list of the resource metadata pertaining to all the resources used throughout the game, and furthermore to delegate and coordinate the loading and unloading of the resource raw data according to its scope. The simplest resource object is encapsulated in the class cResource, and the resource manager uses this class to interface with all resource objects. But the resource manager must also delegate some of the resource work to other classes because resources differ in their details and implementation. Graphics resources differ from audio resources, and SDL graphics resources differ from DirectX graphics resources. Thus, to make the resource manager as extensible and versatile as possible, it should make as few assumptions as possible about the implementation of any particular resource beyond the details encoded into cResource. For this reason, the resource manager depends on the render manager for at least two core functions: first, the ability to create a cResource-derived class encoding all the metadata necessary for a graphics resource, and second, the ability to load and unload the raw data of a graphics resource as required. Loading the metadata for a resource typically occurs only once in an application, as the resource manager processes the resource XML file at initialization. Loading and unloading the raw data of a resource occurs on demand, according to the scope of a resource. The render manager and the cResource-derived cRenderResource class must together expose at least three methods to achieve these functions for working successfully with the resource manager. These methods are cRenderManager::loadResourceFromXML, cRenderResource::load, and cRenderResource::unload. These methods are detailed further in the next few sections.

## 5.6.1   Creating Render Resource Objects from XML Elements

The loadResourceFromXML method of the render manager is intended to be called by the resource manager (in the loadFromXMLFile method) for each graphics resource it finds as it parses the resource.xml file at application startup. When called, loadResourceFromXML accepts a pointer to a valid XML element representing the resource *metadata* in an XML file, then it parses this data and encodes it into a graphics resource object; an instance of the class cRenderResource. The method returns a pointer to the newly created instance of cRenderResource by way of a pointer to its base class cResource—the common currency used by the resource manager. It should be noted that this function creates a graphics resource populated only with resource metadata. It does not load or unload the raw data of the resource. This loading and unloading is implemented in the cRenderResource class, and will be called upon by the resource manager as required. The implementation of loadResourceFromXML is as follows:

```
cResource* cSDL2DRenderManager::loadResourceFromXML(TiXml
Element *Element)
{
    if(Element)
    {
        //Create instance of render resource
    cResource* Resource = new cRenderResource();

    //Cycle through XML element properties and populate
class properties
        for(TiXmlAttribute* ElementAttrib = Element->
FirstAttribute(); ElementAttrib; ElementAttrib =
```

```
ElementAttrib->Next())
        {
            std::string AttribName = ElementAttrib->
Name();
            std::string AttribValue = ElementAttrib->
Value();

            if(AttribName=="UID")
            {
                Resource->m_ResourceID =
atoi(AttribValue.c_str());
            }

            if(AttribName=="filename")
            {
                Resource->m_FileName = AttribValue;
            }

            if(AttribName=="scenescope")
            {
                Resource->m_Scope = atoi(AttribValue.c_
str());
            }
        }

        return Resource;
    }

    return NULL;
}
```

## 5.6.2   Loading and Unloading Graphics Resource Raw Data

The scope of a resource is an integer property that corresponds to the ID of a scene, and it determines the lifetime of the raw data of a resource at run time. When the ID of the current scene and the scope of a resource match, the raw data of the resource must be loaded for that scene if it is not loaded already. When the ID of the current scene and the scope of a resource differ, the resource can be safely unloaded if the application considers it necessary for the purposes of memory efficiency, unless the resource has an ID of 0, meaning that its raw data should always remain loaded because it is a global resource. When the resource manager decides that a resource must be either loaded or unloaded as appropriate, it is responsible for initiating that process. The process itself, however—its implementation—is delegated to the related manager component because the resource manager—being a general manager of resources—cannot know in advance the specific implementation details of any particular type of resource. In the case of the SDL render manager, the process of loading and unloading an SDL graphics resource is delegated to the respective load and unload methods of class cRenderResource, derived from cResource. The load method of that class is responsible for caching the raw data of a resource into system or hardware memory, and the unload method for unloading (or removing) the data from this cache. The reader is here advised to refresh their memory of the cRenderResource class declaration listed in the previous section before considering the implementation of the load method. Comments on this method follow the code.

```
void cRenderResource::load()
{

    //Unload resource if already loaded
    unload();

    //Load image into temp buffer
    //Uses IMG_Load function of SDL plug-in SDL Image.
    //SDL Image supports image formats:
    //BMP, GIF, JPEG, LBM, PCX, PNG, PNM, TGA, TIFF, XCF,
XPM, XV

  SDL_Surface *TmpSurface = IMG_Load(m_FileName.c_str());

    if(TmpSurface)
    {
    //Create optimized image buffer
        m_Surface = SDL_DisplayFormat(TmpSurface);

    //Free old buffer
        SDL_FreeSurface(TmpSurface);

        if(m_Surface)
            m_bLoaded = true;
    }
}
```

NOTE. The code sample above uses the function IMG_Load from the header file SDL_Image.h. The IMG_Load function is not native to the SDL library and is provided by a free and open source SDL add-on called SDL Image, downloaded separately. The SDL library offers the function SDL_LoadBMP to load a Windows bitmap from a file on disk into video memory or system memory.

The SDL_LoadBMP function, however, does not support image file types other than BMP. For this reason, if a programmer requires their application to load image files such as JPG, PNG, and others, they require an SDL add-on, such as SDL Image, whose IMG_Load function supports the following image formats: BMP, GIF, JPEG, LBM, PCX, PNG, PNM, TGA, TIFF, XCF, XPM, and XV. SDL Image can be downloaded at the following URL: http://www.libsdl.org/projects/SDL_image/.

SDL Image can be installed by unpacking the contents of the downloaded package to the SDL library directory already installed and unpacking the header files to the header subfolder and the binary object files to the lib subfolder. Projects intending to use SDL Image in both Visual C++ and Code::Blocks should include the relevant SDL_Image.h header and link to the corresponding SDL_image.lib.

## Comments

- The load method begins by calling the unload method to prevent duplicate loading of the same resource and to release any currently loaded resource of the same name, if any. The implementation of the unload method is provided at the end of this section.

- Next, the method calls the SDL Image function IMG_Load to load the raw data of a valid image file, as specified by the fileName parameter, into system or video memory. The pointer to this block of memory and its associated metadata is returned by the IMG_Load function in the form of an SDL Surface object. This object represents the raw data of an image in memory, and at least one copy of this pointer should be retained by an application for the purposes of referencing and releasing the SDL library. The SDL_Surface structure is listed here, and details regarding each member follow:

### ■ SDL Surface Structure

```
typedef struct SDL_Surface {
    Uint32 flags;                   /* Read-only */
    SDL_PixelFormat *format;        /* Read-only */
    int w, h;                       /* Read-only */
    Uint16 pitch;                   /* Read-only */
    void *pixels;                   /* Read-write */

                            /* clipping information */
    SDL_Rect clip_rect;             /* Read-only */
```

```
            /* Reference count -- used when freeing
surface */
            int refcount;                    /* Read-mostly */

   /* This structure also contains private fields
not shown here */
      } SDL_Surface;
```

**flags**

Properties of the SDL surface. Can be a combination of one or more of the flags listed for the SDL_SetVideoMode function listed in section 5.5 of this chapter.

**format**

The pixel format of the surface (SDL_PixelFormat).

**w, h**

The total width (w) and height (h) of the surface in pixels

**pitch**

Length of the surface in scan-line bytes; this varies according to hardware and pixel format.

**clip_rect**

A RECT structure (x,y, width, height) that defines a rectangular clipping region on the image surface. If specified (if not null or zero), SDL treats the surface as though it had been trimmed to include only the pixels that fall within the boundaries of the clipping rectangle. The clipping rectangle of a given surface can be set with a call to the SDL_SetClipRect function.

**void *pixels**

Pointer to a buffer in memory containing all pixels of the SDL surface.

- Notice that the IMG_Load function populates an SDL_Surface variable named TmpSurface (that is, *temporary* surface). In subsequent lines of the function, the TmpSurface variable is passed through the SDL_DisplayFormat function, from which a more permanent surface is returned. After this, the temporary surface is released. The reason for this is that the IMG_Load function can load an image whose pixel formatting is different from that of the video display surface on which the image pixels will ultimately be transferred on each frame. For pixels to be transferred between two surfaces of different formats, a conversion process must occur—a process that converts the pixel format of the source surface to that of the destination surface. If an image is not preconverted at load time (when it is loaded from a file), then it must be converted on-the-fly at render time (for each frame in which it is shown). The former solution is generally optimal because it requires SDL to perform the conversion process only once per image loaded, and it does not burden the render loop with unnecessary overheads. The SDL_DisplayFormat function performs this conversion process by accepting as an argument a given surface and returning a pointer to the resultant surface converted to the pixel format of the main video surface. Once the converted and optimized surface has been returned, the original surface can be released.

Class cRenderResource also supports the unload method to complement its load method. The unload method is used to release the raw pixel data of a surface from memory. Its implementation is as follows:

```
void cRenderResource::unload()
{
    if(m_Surface)
    {
        SDL_FreeSurface(m_Surface);
        m_Surface = NULL;
    }

    m_bLoaded = false;
}
```

## ■  5.7   Drawing Image Data Using Render Objects

Class cRenderResource is derived from cResource and is intended to work with the resource manager to represent a graphics resource in memory. The resource manager is responsible for managing a collection of generic resources, insofar as it tells them when to load and unload their data, and each particular resource class is responsible for itself in responding appropriately to the resource manager and handling the implementation of its loading and unloading when requested. However, nothing in this procedure touches on the process of drawing the graphics resource to the display during the render loop; it focuses primarily on the loading and unloading of resource raw data. To draw the graphical data to the display, an additional class or component must be added to the engine architecture, and the details of this component will also extend into the next chapter where we consider the design and implementation of a 2D scene manager and accompanying scene graph. For the purposes of this chapter, however, it is enough to demonstrate a straightforward and direct procedure for displaying a graphics resource to the display; that is, for showing the loaded graphic on-screen. This will be achieved using a cSDLRenderObject class. The declaration for this class is provided in the header definition in section 5.4, but it is reproduced here in isolation for convenience with comments afterward:

```
class cSDLRenderObject : public cEngineObject
{
    private:
    protected:
    public:

    cRenderResource *m_RenderResource;
    SDL_Rect m_RenderRect;
    float m_PosX;
    float m_PosY;
    bool m_bVisible;
    SDL_Color m_ColorKey;
    bool m_bColorKeyEnabled;

    cSDLRenderObject();
    void setResourceObject(cRenderResource
*RenderResource);
    virtual void update(){};
};
```

## Comments

• Each instance of cSDLRenderObject represents a unique and renderable item or object in a scene, and may range from the player character and enemies to pow-er-ups and trees. Furthermore, each instance of cSDLRenderObject references an instance of cRenderResource (a graphics resource), and this represents the graph-ics resource to be used for this item when rendering occurs. The cSDLRenderOb-ject is responsible for maintaining the transformation data necessary for rendering the graphics resource correctly in a scene. It maintains the on-screen position of a resource in terms of a pixel (XY offset) and could be extended to maintain rota-tion and scaling information. It is important to note that one or more instances of cSDLRenderObject can reference the same graphics resource, because a scene might contain many identical-looking items such as identical-looking zombie clones or many identical-looking trees. In these cases, what differs between these clones is not their appearance, because they look identical, but their position and transformation data since each might appear at different locations on the screen.

In short, the cSDLRenderObject is responsible for drawing a specified graphics resource on-screen according to a given range of settings.

## 5.7.1   The Render Manager and Render Objects

It has been stated that a render object couples a graphics resource to positional and transformation data, and that the responsibility of the render manager is to render all the visible render objects of the scene on each frame. The class declaration of cRenderManager given earlier in this chapter features a public std::list member called m_RenderObjects, and this member represents the complete list of render objects in the scene. The engine can have a graphics resource rendered to the display by adding an instance of cSDLRenderObject to this list. Likewise, removing an object from this list ensures it no longer appears in the scene. On each and every frame, the render manager will cycle through the list of render objects, rendering each in turn; that is, in the order in which they appear in the list. The render manager does this in the renderAllObjects method, called from the update method, which should be called on each frame during the main application loop. The implementation of the renderAllObjects method is provided here and comments follow:

```
void cSDL2DRenderManager::renderAllObjects()
{
    std::list<cSDLRenderObject*>::iterator list_it;

    //Render all associated render objects
    for(list_it=m_RenderObjects.begin();list_it!=m_
RenderObjects.end();list_it++)
    {
        if((*list_it)->m_bVisible)
        {
            (*list_it)->update();
            SDL_Rect Pos;
            Pos.x = int((*list_it)->m_PosX);
            Pos.y = int((*list_it)->m_PosY);
            SDL_BlitSurface((*list_it)->m_RenderResource-
>m_Surface, &(*list_it)->m_RenderRect, m_RenderWindow,
&Pos);
        }
    }
}
```

## Comments

- The renderAllObjects method iterates through an std::list of render objects, rendering each in turn.

- For each render object in the list, the function checks its visibility status, rendering only visible objects. Then it calls the object's update method—should this be overloaded in derived classes—sets its XY position on-screen, and finally calls the SDL function SDL_BlitSurface to copy the pixel data from the graphics resource to the video surface where it becomes visible at the end of the frame.

The renderAllObjects method of cRenderManager is called from its update method, which in turn is called once every frame in the main application loop. The update method is responsible for using the SDL to prepare the video hardware for rendering, for rendering each render object (via renderAllObjects), and for flipping the video surfaces to mark the end of the frame and to update the display with the latest renderings. Consider the following definition of the update method:

```cpp
bool cSDL2DRenderManager::update()
{
    SDL_Event event;
    while (SDL_PollEvent(&event))
    {
        // check for messages
        switch (event.type)
        {
            // exit if the window is closed
            case SDL_QUIT:
                return false;

            // check for keypresses
            case SDL_KEYDOWN:
            {
                // exit if ESCAPE is pressed
                if (event.key.keysym.sym == SDLK_ESCAPE)
                    return false;
            }
        } // end switch
    } // end of message processing

    // clear screen
    SDL_FillRect(m_RenderWindow, 0, SDL_MapRGB(m_
RenderWindow->format, 0, 0, 0));

    renderAllObjects();

    SDL_Flip(m_RenderWindow);

    return true;
}
```

**Comments**

- The update method begins by calling the SDL function SDL_PollEvent to populate an SDL_Event structure with information regarding any SDL events that
  might have occurred since SDL_PollEvent was called in the previous frame.
  This function watches for two events: SDL_QUIT and SDL_KEYDOWN.
  The former is invoked when the SDL library is closed at application exit or
  when a fatal error occurs, and the latter is invoked when a key is pressed on the
  keyboard. In relation to the keypress event, the application watches for an
  ESCAPE keypress and exits the application when this occurs.

- When all SDL events have been processed or when there are no SDL events in
  the queue, the update method proceeds to prepare the back buffer (or off-screen
  surface) for rendering. The off-screen surface is a hidden surface in memory and
  receives all renderings for the *next* frame. When the current frame ends, the off-
  screen surface is exchanged for the on-screen surface (flipped), and thus the
  off-screen surface now becomes visible (on-screen) and the former on-screen
  surface becomes the new off-screen surface. The update method begins the process of rendering by clearing the contents of the off-screen surface by calling
  the SDL function SDL_FillRect. This function flood fills a given surface with a
  specified color, in this case black.

- Next, the renderAllObjects method is called to render all the objects in the
  scene. This is followed by a call to the SDL function SDL_Flip, which ends
  the frame and swaps the on- and off-screen surfaces. At this point, all rendered
  objects should be shown on the screen at the appropriate positions.

## ■ 5.8    Color Keying Effects

The previous section demonstrated how to render the render objects of a scene at a specified position measured as a pixel XY offset from the top left corner of the screen. This
section extends the ability of the render object class by using the SDL color key feature to
add transparent effects to graphics resources when rendered. This is useful for an engine
because many game graphics are intended to be shown apart from their background. For
example, in a 2D platformer game, the player character and enemies are not surrounded
by the square border and background of the image from which they were taken but are
presented in the scene without the background being visible. These transparency effects
can be achieved by color blending, opacity mapping, alpha transparency, and color keying.
Each has their advantages and disadvantages, but this section focuses on color keying.

The color of pixels shown by the majority of contemporary video hardware on the
majority of monitors is represented in an RGB structure (as an additive combination of
red, green, and blue). Each color component is an integer (nonfractional number) that

can range from 0 to 255 and represents the strength of that component in the overall blend of RGB. If the red component of an RGB structure is set to 0, the resultant color contains no red, and if the same component is set to 255, the resultant color contains bold red, mixed with the G and B components. When all components of the color (RGB) are 255, the resultant color is white, and when all are 0, the resultant color is black. The total number of colors that can be represented by RGB is 16,581,375.

The SDL color key feature allows a developer to achieve transparency effects by accepting any specified RGB color value and treating it as transparent for any given surface. This means that whenever the pixels of that surface are copied to another, such as the main video surface, the color key determines which color is to be ignored during the copying. Typically, the key color corresponds to the background color of the image, and the artist endeavors to keep the background color unique in the image to ensure only the background is removed when blitting (copying pixels) using color keys in the engine. Consider the following image of a face on a black background. In this instance, the background can be removed by specifying a color key of RGB (0,0,0), which is black. (See Figure 5.4)

Based on the class declaration of cSDLRenderObject in the previous section, it should be noted that this class is already equipped with a color key property (m_ColorKey), and this property is of type SDL_Color. The SDL_Color structure is as follows:

```
typedef struct{
   Uint8 r; //Red
   Uint8 g; //Green
   Uint8 b; //Blue
   Uint8 unused;
} SDL_Color;
```

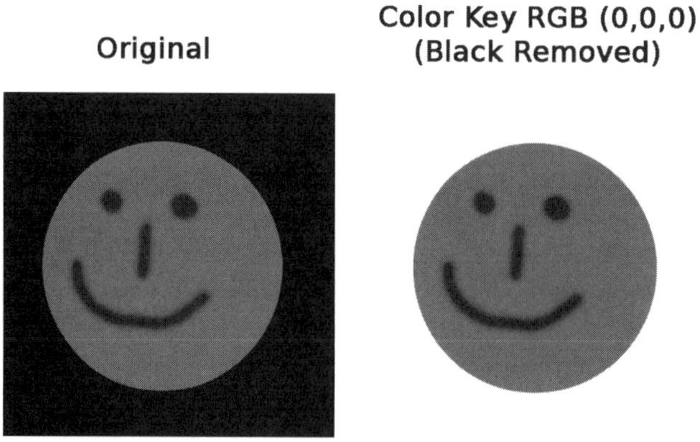

**FIGURE 5.4**   Color keying at work.

Using the color key property, a developer can specify the color key for any render object in the scene. The setResourceObject method has been added to class cSDL-RenderObject and allows the developer to set the associated graphics resource and its color key in one step, as follows:

```
void cSDLRenderObject::setResourceObject(cRenderResource
*RenderResource)
{
    if(RenderResource)
    {
        m_RenderResource = RenderResource;
        m_RenderRect.w=m_RenderResource->m_Surface->w;
        m_RenderRect.h=m_RenderResource->m_Surface->h;

        if(m_bColorKeyEnabled)
        {
            Uint32 colorkey = SDL_MapRGB
(m_RenderResource->m_Surface->format, m_ColorKey.r,
m_ColorKey.g, m_ColorKey.b);

            SDL_SetColorKey(m_RenderResource->m_Surface,
SDL_SRCCOLORKEY, colorkey);
        }
    }
}
```

**Comments**

- The function begins by checking the validity of the passed pointer, and if valid proceeds to assign that as the resource associated with the current render object.

- If color keying is enabled for this render object, it then proceeds to process color keying information. To do this, it first calls the SDL function SDL_MapRGB. This function accepts R, G, and B values for the color key, and a pixel format. It then returns a valid SDL RGB color value for the *specified* pixel format, since the actual implementation details of color vary between formats. With the returned RGB value—representing the color key—the setResourceObject function then continues by setting the color key of the specified surface using the SDL function SDL_SetColorKey. If successful, the color key remains applied to the surface; it will render with the color key as transparent until it is either changed to a new color key or disabled entirely. Color keying can be disabled by passing 0 for the second parameter (flags). The form of the SDL_ SetColorKey function is as follows:

```
        int SDL_SetColorKey(SDL_Surface *surface, Uint32
    flag, Uint32 key);
```

**SDL_Surface *surface**

Pointer to the SDL surface to which the specified color key (*key*) should be applied.

**Uint32 flag**

This is normally SDL_SRCCOLORKEY.

**Uint32 key**

An SDL_Color value specifying the color key; that is, the color on the surface to be considered transparent.

## ■ 5.9   Sprites and Animation

This chapter considers one final issue related to the render manager, render objects, and render resources: the issue of animated graphics, or sprites. A *sprite* is a graphic that plays a set of frames one by one in sequence according to a specified speed or time. They are useful for any graphic that must animate at run time such as the player character, enemies, some scenery objects such as rustling trees, waving flags, and explosions, among others. There are primarily two methods for encoding these animations in graphics files: One is to create each and every frame of the animation in a separate file and then have the engine load them all onto separate surfaces, playing back the animation by showing and hiding those surfaces in sequence. The other is to align all the frames of the animation side by side into a grid of equally sized rows and columns in a single image (a tile set). With this latter method, the engine loads the single image into a surface and plays back the animation frame by frame by adjusting the clipping RECT of the surface to reflect the current frame. This chapter focuses on latter, tile set, method of sprite animation. For the purposes of demonstration, it will work with the following tile set image shown in Figure 5.5, available in the book's companion code.

The image contains a total of 16 frames arranged in equally sized rows and columns of the order 4×4. Each frame is also called a tile. Each tile is 64×64 pixels, and the total width and height of the image is 256×256 pixels.

To show and play this animation, a new class is created by deriving from the cSDLRenderObject class. It will be called cSpriteObject. Its class declaration was shown earlier in this chapter but is reproduced here for convenience.

**FIGURE 5.5**  Tile set; frames are arranged in rows and columns within one image.

```
class cSpriteObject : public cSDLRenderObject
{
    private:
    protected:
    DWORD m_TimeLastFrame;

    public:
    unsigned int m_TotalFrames;
    unsigned int m_FramsPerRow;
    unsigned int m_FramsPerColumn;
    unsigned int m_CurrentFrame;
    unsigned int m_StartFrame;
    float m_Speed;
    unsigned int m_FrameWidth;
    unsigned int m_FrameHeight;

    void update();
    void play();
    void stop();
    void setFrameRect(unsigned int FrameNumber);
    cSpriteObject();
};
```

## 5.9.1  Sprite Tile Set and Seeking to Frames

The purpose of the sprite animation object as featured here is to play a loop-able sequence of frames loaded from a tile set, one after the other at a specified speed. Before the object can play such a sequence, it must know a minimum set of details and have the ability to locate any isolated frame in the tile set. It must know the total number of frames in the tile set, the number of tiles per row, the width and height of each tile in pixels (assuming all tiles in the set are equal in width and height), and the total speed or time at which the animation should play. Assuming the class has been provided with this information, and assuming it has loaded the complete tile set on to an SDL surface in a graphics resource, and assuming a pointer to that resource has been assigned to the parent class (cSDLRenderObject), then the sprite class can successfully locate and display any single frame in the tile set using the following method:

```
void cSpriteObject::setFrameRect(unsigned int
FrameNumber)
{
    unsigned int RowNumber = floor(FrameNumber/m_
FramsPerRow);
    unsigned int ColumnNumber = FrameNumber;

    if(RowNumber>0)
        ColumnNumber = FrameNumber - (RowNumber * m_
FramsPerRow);

    m_RenderRect.x = ColumnNumber * m_FrameWidth;
    m_RenderRect.y = RowNumber * m_FrameHeight;
    m_RenderRect.w = m_FrameWidth;
    m_RenderRect.h = m_FrameHeight;
}
```

**Comments**

- The FrameNumber argument represents the number of the frame to show (where 0 is the first frame in the sequence, $n-1$ is the last frame in the sequence, and $n$ is the total number of frames).

- The function then calculates the XY pixel offset of the top left corner for the current frame. Then using the frame width and height values, it can also determine the total RECT of the frame.

- Then it sets the RenderRect property of its base class cSDLRenderObject to match the RECT settings of the specified tile in the tile set. Setting this value affects which region of the graphics resource is drawn during the render loop. See the call to the SDL function SDL_BlitSurface in the renderAllObjects method of cRenderManager.

### 5.9.2    Playing the Animation

Being able to isolate and show a single frame in the tile set is the first step to being able to play them all in a sequence. The job of the sprite class as an animator is to play the complete sequence of frames in a tile set at a specified speed in terms of milliseconds per frame. Consider the play and update methods of the sprite class for playing all the frames in the tile set at a speed of 500 milliseconds (0.5 seconds) per frame:

```
//Called to start animation playback
void cSpriteObject::play()
{
    //calculate frame dimensions

    SDL_Surface *TmpSurface = m_RenderResource->m_
Surface;
    m_FrameWidth = TmpSurface->w/m_FramsPerRow;
    m_FrameHeight = TmpSurface->h/m_FramsPerColumn;
    m_CurrentFrame = m_StartFrame;
    setFrameRect(m_CurrentFrame);
    m_TimeLastFrame = timeGetTime();
}

//----------------------------------------------------------

//Called once per frame
void cSpriteObject::update()
{
    DWORD timeSinceLastFrame = timeGetTime() - m_
TimeLastFrame;

    if(timeSinceLastFrame >= m_Speed)
    {
        //Increment current frame
        m_CurrentFrame++;

        if(m_CurrentFrame>=m_TotalFrames)
            m_CurrentFrame = m_StartFrame;

        setFrameRect(m_CurrentFrame);

        m_TimeLastFrame = timeGetTime();
    }
}
```

**Comments**

- The play function initiates playback of the tile set animation from the beginning. It resets the animation timer and the frame count, resetting the animation back to the first frame.

- The update method should be called once per frame and represents the main loop, or pump, of the sprite animation framework. On each frame, the method calculates the total time in milliseconds that has elapsed since the last frame increment and uses this in comparison with the animation speed to determine whether the frame counter should be incremented to show the next frame.

  **NOTE**. Consult the companion code at the book's website, http://www.jblearning.com/catalog/9780763784515/ to see a complete working example featuring the source code in this chapter.

**EXERCISE 5.2**

For each of the following statements, answer True or False.

1. The SDL library is a 2D game engine.
2. The 2D render manager is also responsible for managing 2D scenes.
3. The 2D render manager is also responsible for loading and unloading graphics resources.

**Answers**

1. Probably not, but debatable. The SDL library defines itself as a *library* and not an *engine*, though it features components such as graphics, audio, and input, which together with error and resource managers could be used to make a complete game.
2. False. Scene managers are used for managing scenes. Render managers are used for presenting those scenes to the window.
3. True.

## ■ 5.10   Chapter Summary

This chapter has examined in some depth the creation of at least four unique but related classes for ultimately drawing graphics to the display: cSDL2DRenderManager, cRenderResource, cSDLRenderObject, and cSpriteObject. The render resource class encapsulates the raw data of a graphics resource in system or video memory. The render object class associates itself with a specific instance of a render resource and represents an object in a scene; it provides positional, rotational, and scaling information for rendering its associated resource in particular configurations. In addition, the render object can also apply a color key to its associated resource and thereby render specified colors as transparent. The sprite object is used for showing tile set animations. Finally, the render manager is responsible for holding these classes together in a complete 2D render framework. The next chapter extends this feature set by considering the design and implementation of a 2D scene manager for enhancing the management of the objects in a scene.

# 6

# 2D Scene Manager

## Overview

After completing this chapter, you should:

- Understand the purpose of a 2D scene manager
- Appreciate the complexity of scenes
- Be able to work with combined, or inherited, transformations
- Understand the painter's algorithm
- Be able to encapsulate a 2D scene manager into a C++ class

The previous chapter considered both the design and implementation of a 2D render manager using the Simple Directmedia Layer (SDL) library. The render manager works closely with the resource manager, and together they are used for loading raw pixel data from images in files and rendering them to the screen at specified positions, scales, and rotations. This chapter focuses on the design and implementation of a scene manager component, and it begins by examining exactly why a scene manager is necessary at all. The term "scene" refers to a substantial section of a game that features sound, graphics, and logic such as a complete level in a platformer game that includes platforms, physics, background objects, the player character, artificially intelligent enemies, sounds, and music. Another example is a complete race track in a racing game—including the audience, weather effects, cars, and more—or a complete dungeon (or room) in an RPG game. The exact details of a scene, and its size and extent, differ from game to game and from developer to developer, and even from scene to scene. But the essential property of a scene, no matter how large or small, is that it is self-contained insofar as it contains every asset necessary to present a coherent and playable scenario to the player. Therefore, the scene often determines which set of resources is loaded into memory at any one time (refer to the concept of scope in Chapter 4). Furthermore, the scene not only determines which resources are loaded and unloaded but also must consolidate them into a playable whole, to ensure they "hang together"; that is, are used appropriately in game. In short then, the scene is responsible for presenting to the player a specified set of resources in a configuration that constitutes a game, or a part of a game, and the scene manager will be the component (or C++ class) that encapsulates this behavior.

**NOTE.** Much of what is said in this chapter about 2D scenes applies also to 3D scenes, though specific chapters have been reserved for each in order to examine their specifics and the points at which they differ from each other.

## ■ 6.1    The Domain of the 2D Scene Manager

Before implementing a 2D scene manager in C++ or any other language, it is first necessary for the developer to establish a design that states each of the functions the scene manager is expected to perform and why they are necessary for the scene. There are many functions a developer could list (many of which would be game specific), and for that reason this chapter cannot consider them all. Instead, it will focus on a selection of common but important scene management functions likely to be featured in almost all 2D scene managers, and for each function this chapter will state why it is necessary. The rest of this chapter will then be concerned with implementing these functions in sequence according to the design to create a working 2D scene manager component.

This chapter identifies in a 2D scene manager at least three core features for creating complete and playable 2D scenes. These are: (1) a scene graph for expressing object positions and relations, (2) depth sorting to determine occlusion of scene objects and to emphasize their distance from the camera, and (3) time keeping; that is, the ability to maintain a scenewide concept of time to synchronize events in the scene and to trigger events as and when required. These three functions are now considered in more detail.

### 6.1.1    Scene Graph

The render manager, as developed in an earlier chapter, allows a developer to draw any loaded graphical item (image) at any valid XY position on-screen. This fundamental ability to position items on-screen might at first glance seem powerful enough in itself to allow a developer to create any number of game scenes without having to perform any further scene management work, and because of this it can be tempting to think of any additional scene management features as merely a luxury at best or

### EXERCISE 6.1

List at least three functions you think a 2D scene manager *should* perform and give at least one reason for each answer. Then compare your answers with what follows in this section.

unnecessary at worst. This is because each graphical item of a scene can already be positioned where required, and objects in motion are simply items whose position changes at a specified speed. However, this attitude and its dismissal of further scene management work are usually unveiled as simplification when the motion and position of objects in a scene are considered in more detail.

The complexities of scene management usually first emerge when one realizes that objects in a scene do not exist in isolation but in a relationship, each in relation to every other. Certainly, each unique item in a scene (the player character, each enemy, trees, and walls) has its own position, scale, and orientation, but these values are not entirely independent of those of other objects in the scene. This means that the movement of one object may or may not directly affect the position of another. For example, consider a game with a scene that features a road, and driving on the road is a car, and inside the car is seated one driver and one passenger. All three items listed here—road, car, and passengers—exist in a relationship in terms of their position in the scene, and this relationship involves a certain degree of dependency and interdependency. As the car drives along the road, the passengers seated inside are expected to follow the movement of the car, not to remain motionless in the air as the car moves away, leaving them behind. This is because the passengers and their position inside the car are to some extent dependent on the position of the car. The passengers can move around inside the car without affecting the position of the car, but the movement of the car along the road affects the position of the passengers in the scene. Similarly, if a giant hand were to reach down from the clouds and tear the road from its surroundings, the position of both the car and its occupants would be affected: The position of the car is dependent on the road, and the position of the passengers is dependent on the car.

The graph in Figure 6.1 helps demonstrate how the position, rotation, and scaling (transformations) of objects in the scene can be expressed hierarchically in a graph (*scene graph*), with the transformations of high-order objects cascading downward additively to lower-order objects. In other words, each item in the graph can move independently of its parent and ancestors, but the movement of parent items affects (cascades downward to) all child items because children depend on parents. To summarize then, the purpose of the scene graph as a hierarchy is to efficiently record the position of objects and their interrelationships in the scene.

## 6.1.2   Depth Sorting

The scene graph represents the network of relations that exist between scene objects and which affect their position, rotation, and scale in the scene (see Figure 6.1). Depth sorting, in contrast, refers to the actual order in which scene objects are drawn to the display—the order in which they are rendered to the back buffer on each frame of the game loop. This order is significant because when any two objects overlap on the

**Scene Graph and Inherited Transformations**

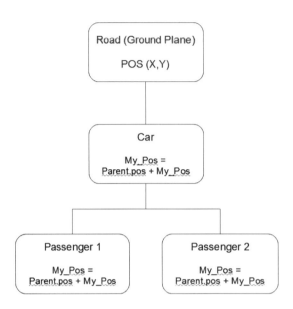

**▌FIGURE 6.1**   Scene object relationships.

screen, the object rendered last will appear *on top of* all previously rendered objects, obscuring the objects below or behind. This has implications for creating depth in a scene because objects nearer to the camera should appear in front of those farther away. To allow developers to manage the order in which objects are drawn in a scene, the concept of layers can be introduced to the scene manager.

For the purposes of the scene manager developed here, the concept of a layer corresponds almost identically to the layer object found in many popular photo-editing programs such as Adobe® Photoshop® or GIMP. In these applications, the layer is a transparent cell or film on to which pixels can be drawn. Any layer can accept the pixels of any number of images, just as an SDLsurface can accept any number of blits in a single frame. Layers can be stacked one atop the other, and wherever a layer is transparent it will show the pixels of the layers beneath. The topmost layer appears in front of the others and has the lowest Z-order (0), and the bottommost layer appears at the back and has the highest Z-order of $n-1$ (where $n$ represents the total number of layers). Changing the Z-order integer of a layer will adjust the order in which the layers of a scene are drawn, thus determining which objects appear in front of others (see Figure 6.2).

Layer 1        Layer 2

**| FIGURE 6.2**   Layers and depth sorting.

### 6.1.3   Timing

The importance of timing is often overlooked by many newcomers to game programming as well as some established veterans. The main purpose of timekeeping in regard to scene management is to establish a scenewide concept of time and an ability to measure its passing. This is useful both for synchronizing and cueing events correctly in a scene, and for ensuring that animations play back at consistent speeds across systems. In the world of animation, it can sometimes be tempting to measure time in terms of frames, but this can be problematic because frame rates (the speed at which frames play) can differ from one computer to another according to the power of the hardware. For example, an animation of 100 frames may feature several key events—perhaps one that occurs at frame 30 and another at frame 50. But if this animation were played at full speed on two separate computers with differing power (each frame of the animation corresponding to one frame of the rendering loop), it would play back at different speeds, and the user of one system would not have the same experience as the user on the other. This is because the timing of the animation is hardware dependent (system specific). The speed at which it plays will vary from system to system.

In order to counter this problem and ensure consistency between systems, the scene manager could maintain a scenewide time that relies on the time elapsed according to the system clock, in terms of milliseconds and seconds. The scene manager does this by updating a fractional value on each frame to reflect the number of seconds that have elapsed since the previous frame (1 refers to 1 second, 0.5 to half a second, and 2 to two seconds, etc.). Typically this value will be a fractional value (e.g., 0.0321). Using this, the scene manager can pace and cue events in the scene correctly and consistently. More on this will be shown throughout the chapter.

## ■ 6.2    Implementing the 2D Scene Manager

The previous sections have highlighted at least three core functions of a scene manager: (1) encoding and updating the transformations and relations between scene objects via a scene graph, (2) adjusting the render order of objects to control the depth of a 2D scene via depth sorting and layers, and (3) timing and cueing events and motion in a scene consistently across hardware using a "time elapsed" property that is calculated on each frame. To implement and encapsulate these features into a C++ class framework, several classes should be created to distribute the work according to its kind. These are as follows:

- **c2DLayer**

  This class represents a single layer object in a scene; that is, a transparent cell or film that can display one or more graphical entities. Layers in this implementation have position (XY) on-screen but no width or height—they stretch infinitely.

- **cSceneObject**

  This class is descended from cSDLRenderObject (see Chapter 5) and represents any renderable entity in a scene (the player object, an enemy, a gun, etc.). A scene object has position, width, and height, and can be added as *children* to layers. cSceneObjects will not be rendered themselves directly but will be added to layers in the scene from which they will be rendered.

- **cTimer and cSceneListener**

  These two allied classes are timing and event classes responsible for executing customizable events at specified times or intervals.

- **cCSDL2DSceneManager**

  This is the overarching scene manager class responsible for tying together instances of the above classes into a unified scene management framework.

The following code represents the entirety of the SceneManager.h file and includes the above-mentioned classes and their declarations as they appear in their final form once the work of this chapter is completed. In short, it represents the whole set of scene manager classes for 2D scenes. Previewing these class declarations here before proceeding helps outline the work ahead and the course that work will take.

> **NOTE.** The purpose of some properties or classes listed in the following code sample might not at first glance be obvious, but they will be explained in detail in subsequent sections of this chapter.

```
#ifndef SDL2DSCENEMANAGER_H_INCLUDED
#define SDL2DSCENEMANAGER_H_INCLUDED

#include <string>
#include <sstream>
#include <iostream>
#include <time.h>
#include <iomanip>
#include <windows.h>
#include <math.h>
#include "ResourceManager.h"
#include "TinyXML.h"
#include "RenderData.h"


//---------------------------------------------------
//Typedef structure, used for timing events
typedef enum {SE_TIMER_EXPIRED=0}SCENE_EVENT_TYPE;

//Forward declaration of scene manager class
class cSDL2DSceneManager;

//---------------------------------------------------

//Scene listener class is an abstract base class whose
Event method is
//intended to be overridden and redefined as a callback
function.
//Developers override this method with their own custom
functionality
//and then have it called back at specific times and/or
intervals.

class cSceneListener : public cEngineObject
{
    public:
        SCENE_EVENT_TYPE m_ListenFor;
```

```
        virtual void Event(cSDL2DSceneManager* Manager,
void* customData) const = 0;
};


//-----------------------------------------------------

//Timer class is fully defined in the header. The purpose
of this class
//is to measure the elapsed time and to initiate events
if and where
//appropriate. Works in combination with class
cSceneListener.

class cTimer : public cEngineObject
{
    private:
    protected:
    public:

        unsigned int m_ID;
        DWORD m_StartTime;
        DWORD m_Interval;
        bool m_Expired;

        cTimer()
        {
            m_ID = 0;
            m_StartTime = 0;
            m_Interval = 0;
            m_Expired = false;
        }

        void start()
        {
            m_StartTime = timeGetTime();
            m_Expired = false;
        }

        void update()
        {
            if(m_Expired)
                return;

            DWORD ElapsedTime = timeGetTime() - m_
StartTime;
```

```
            if(ElapsedTime>=m_Interval)
            {
                m_Expired = true;
            }
        }
};


//-------------------------------------------------------

//This class is the basic currency of a scene. All items
intended to belong
//to the scene should be derived from this class.
Instances of this class should
//be assigned to a layer.

class cSceneObject : public cSDLRenderObject
{
    private:
    protected:
    public:
};


//-------------------------------------------------------

//This class represents a layer object. Each instance may
have a
//specified Z-order, and the scene manager class will
sort the layers
//according to that order.

class c2DLayer : public cEngineObject
{
    private:
    protected:
    public:
        //Render objects for the layer
        c2DLayer();
        bool m_bVisible;
        unsigned int m_ZOrder;
        float m_PosX;
        float m_PosY;
        std::string m_Name;
```

```
    //Objects of the layer
        std::list<cSceneObject*> m_SceneObjects;

        void update();
};

//------------------------------------------------------

//The main scene manager object. Contains a list of
layers, timers, and
//listener objects.

class cSDL2DSceneManager : public cEngineObject
{
    private:
    protected:
        void addLayerObjects(c2DLayer *Layer,
TiXmlElement *Element);
        void checkTimerExpired();
    public:

    //Layer list
        std::list<c2DLayer*> m_Layers;

    //Timer list
    std::list<cTimer*> m_Timers;

    //Listener list
    std::list<cSceneListener*> m_Listeners;

        c2DLayer* addLayer(std::string Name);
        c2DLayer* findLayer(std::string Name);
        void removeLayer(std::string Name);
        void sortLayers();

    //Loads a scene from an XML file
        bool loadFromXMLFile(std::string Filename);

        void addTimer(unsigned int ID, DWORD Interval);
        void addListener(cSceneListener* Object);

        void update();
};
```

```
//-----------------------------------------------------

#endif // 2DSDLSCENEMANAGER_H_INCLUDED
```

## ■ 6.3   Implementing the Layer Class

As stated earlier in this chapter, the layer class (c2DLayer) encapsulates a transparent film or cell onto which pixels are drawn, similar to the layer object found in Photoshop or GIMP or other popular photo-editing applications. Each scene is intended to contain one or more layers, which can in turn contain one or more scene objects. The Z-ordering of layers corresponds to the rendering order of scene objects (2D images), and thus it determines how depth is conveyed in the scene; higher-order layers are rendered first and lower-order layers on top. This means that scene objects belonging to a layer with a Z-order of 3 appear behind those objects on a layer with an order of 1, and those on a layer with an order of 2 appear between layers 1 and 3. With reference to the c2DLayer class in the code sample above, a layer can be seen to have several properties, most of which determine how and if a layer will be drawn on screen:

- **bool m_bVisible**

  A boolean value determining whether or not the contents of a layer (its member scene objects) are visible. If true, then all scene objects belonging to this layer will be drawn on each frame according to their own visibility status. If false, then none of the scene objects on this layer will be drawn, whatever their own visibility status.

- **unsigned int m_ZOrder**

  An unsigned integer value (nonnegative integer) indicating the Z-order of the layer. Setting this value adjusts the Z-order of the layer, and the scene manager class is responsible for sorting the layers in order of this property, lowest to highest, before rendering them to the display.

- **float m_PosX, float m_PosY**

  Represent the X and Y positions in the pixels of the top left corner of the layer when drawn to the display.

- **std::string m_Name**

  Unique identifying name of the layer, if applicable. Developers should assign the layer a name if they intend to search for and reference the layer at run time.

- **std::list<cSceneObject*> m_SceneObjects**

  STL list of instances of cSceneObject, each instance representing a unique, renderable SceneObject belonging to this layer.

**NOTE.** The only method of c2DLayer is the constructor, which initializes its member properties to appropriate starting values. It is defined as follows:

```
c2DLayer::c2DLayer() : cEngineObject()
{
    m_bVisible=true;
    m_PosX = m_PosY = 0.0f;
    m_ZOrder = 0;
}
```

## ■ 6.4    Implementing the Scene Object Class

The scene object class represents a renderable object on a layer in the scene, and it derives from class cSDLRenderObject, as developed in Chapter 5. A single layer can contain one or more scene objects, and all objects belonging to that layer share the same Z-order. Though the cSceneObject class implemented in this chapter derives from cSDLRenderObject, it does not expose any additional methods or properties. One might then wonder why a derived class was created when the base class could have been used since no additional functionality was implemented. The separation between these two classes is made here, however, for at least two reasons: (1) to emphasize the modular design of the engine by ensuring the scene management framework is distinct from the render manager classes, and (2) because developers tailoring their engine toward a specific game or a specific genre of game are likely, at some point, to customize their scene object classes by adding their own properties and methods.

## ■ 6.5    Implementing the Timer and Scene Listener Classes

Timekeeping across the scene and the ability to cue custom functions at specified times or intervals is managed by the timer and scene listener classes. The ability to call functions at specified times or intervals is useful for games in a wide range of circumstances, including timed sequences in which the player must complete a challenge within a time limit before an explosive is detonated or in which the player must defeat an enemy before their reinforcements arrive after a specified time.

The cTimer class should be updated on each frame and measures the amount of time that has elapsed in milliseconds since it was first started or last reset. In addition to measuring elapsed time, the timer supports an interval property. This can be set to a specific time in terms of milliseconds. When the elapsed time of the timer matches or exceeds the specified interval, the timer can call the Event method of any instance of a class derived from cSceneListener as a notification of this event. Thus, by deriving classes from cSceneListener and overriding the Event method with customized behavior, developers can initiate a whole slew of application-specific events at specified times or intervals. The entirety of the cTimer class is given in the header file source code presented previously, and readers are advised to read or reread that section of code before proceeding. The cTimer class features the following properties:

- **unsigned int m_ID**

  The unique unsigned integer ID of the timer. Any single scene can have one or more timers, but each timer must have a unique ID for identification purposes.

- **DWORD m_StartTime**

  Represents either the time at which the timer began (was first started) or the time at which it was last reset. On each update or frame, the timer measures the elapsed time as an offset in milliseconds from the start time. See the Update method of cTimer. This class calculates time using the timeGetTime function of the Windows API. The general form of this function is as follows:

  ```
  DWORD timeGetTime(void);
  ```

  Returns the system time in milliseconds. Developers should note that the value returned from this function wraps around (resets) after every 49.71 days of consecutive execution. For this reason, developers are advised to use only the difference between two timeGetTime return values in their calculations.

- **DWORD m_Interval**

  This value is the user-specified timer interval value in milliseconds, and it indicates the total period of time that must elapse from the start time before the timer is satisfied and calls the event method of an associated SceneListener class if there is one. As we shall see later in this chapter, it is the duty of the scene manager and not the timer to actually call the event method of any listener classes when the timer interval expires.

- **bool m_Expired**

  A boolean value indicating whether the timer interval has expired.

The cSceneListener class is an abstract base class allied to the cTimer class, and its event method is intended to be overridden by developers with application-specific functionality in a derived class. The listener works by being added to a list of listeners maintained by the scene manager, and then by declaring itself to be listening for a specific event or group of events in the scene such as a "Timer Expired" event. Then whenever such an event is triggered, the scene manager is responsible for calling the Event methods of all listeners in the list that are listening for that event. At present, only one event type is defined; this is SE_TIMER_EXPIRED, which is a member of the following typedef enum given at the start of the "SDLSceneManager.h" header file:

```
typedef enum {SE_TIMER_EXPIRED=0}SCENE_EVENT_TYPE;
```

Here is an example of a listener class derived from cSceneListener, and which listens for a timer expired event. When added to the scene manager's list of listeners, this class's event method will be called when the timer interval expires:

```
class cTestListener : public cSceneListener
{
    private:
    protected:
    public:

        cTestListener()
        {
      //Declare the event for which to listen
            m_ListenFor = SE_TIMER_EXPIRED;
        }

        void Event(cSDL2DSceneManager* Manager, void*
customData) const
        {
      //On every timer interval

            //Search scene for layer of matching name
            c2DLayer* Layer = Manager->
findLayer("layer2");

            //Toggle visibility status. That is, make layer
flash on and off.
            Layer->m_bVisible = !Layer->m_bVisible;
        }
};
```

## ■ 6.6  Implementing the Scene Manager Class

The set of scene management classes developed thus far in this chapter include c2DLayer, cSceneObject, cTimer, and cSceneListener. Each of these classes is to some extent ancillary to the scene manager class, an overarching component whose primary duty is to create a synthesis, or a whole from the simpler pieces. Therefore, the scene manager is ultimately responsible for organizing and synchronizing the workings of a scene, and when a developer wants to add a layer and object to a scene, remove a layer and object from a scene, or cue an event at a specified time, it is to the scene manager class that they turn. The scene manager is the main interface between a developer and a scene. The class declaration for the cSceneManager class is given in the header code listed at the start of this chapter, but is reproduced below in isolation for convenience:

```
class cSDL2DSceneManager : public cEngineObject
{
    private:
    protected:
        void addLayerObjects(c2DLayer *Layer,
TiXmlElement *Element);
        void checkTimerExpired();
    public:

    //Layer list
        std::list<c2DLayer*> m_Layers;

    //Timer list
    std::list<cTimer*> m_Timers;

    //Listener list
    std::list<cSceneListener*> m_Listeners;

        c2DLayer* addLayer(std::string Name);
        c2DLayer* findLayer(std::string Name);
        void removeLayer(std::string Name);
        void sortLayers();

    //Loads a scene from an XML file
        bool loadFromXMLFile(std::string Filename);

        void addTimer(unsigned int ID, DWORD Interval);
        void addListener(cSceneListener* Object);

        void update();
};
```

In short, the scene manager will be able to:

- Add layers to, find layers in, and remove layers from a scene.
- Sort and render layers according to their Z-order.
- Apply hierarchical transformations to scene objects; that is, ensure the positions of scene objects inherit the positions of their owning layer.

- Add timers and scene listeners to a scene.
- Initiate the event method of all appropriate scene listeners whenever an associated event occurs in the scene.
- Load and configure a scene from an XML file on disk.

This section of the chapter considers the properties of this class, and subsequent sections detail the implementation and appropriate usage of each of its methods in managing the specifics of a scene.

- **std::list<c2DLayer*> m_Layers**

  STL list of layers in the scene. The scene manager will sort this list of layers according to Z-order, lowest at the front and highest at the back, and then render each and every layer in sequence.

- **std::list<cTimer*> m_Timers**

  STL list of timers in the scene. On each frame of the render loop, the scene manager will update each and every time through the list and check for timer expired events.

- **std::list<cSceneListener*> m_Listeners**

  STL list of listener objects in the scene. When an event is triggered in the scene, the scene manager will cycle through the list of all listeners and call their Event method wherever a listener is found to be waiting for a notification of that event.

## 6.6.1    Adding, Finding, and Removing Layers in a 2D Scene

The scene manager class maintains a linear list of all layers in the scene, both visible and nonvisible, through its STL list member m_Layers, and this list is sorted in order of Z-order. Those layers with a lower Z-order appear at the end of the list and are rendered last, and those with a higher Z-order appear at the front of the list and are rendered first. The scene manager features three separate methods for managing layers in a scene with regard to adding, finding and removing them: addLayer, findLayer, and removeLayer. Their definitions are given, and then comments follow:

```
c2DLayer* cSDL2DSceneManager::addLayer(std::string Name)
{
    c2DLayer *Layer = findLayer(Name);

    if(!Layer)
    {
        Layer = new c2DLayer();
        Layer->m_Name=Name;
```

```
        m_Layers.push_back(Layer);
    }

    return Layer;
}
```

## Comments

- The addLayer function accepts a string argument as the unique identifier of a new layer. It then calls the findLayer function to search the existing list of layers for a layer with a matching name.

- If no layer is found in the search, then a new layer of the specified name is created and added to the list, and a pointer to this layer is returned.

- If a layer with a matching name is found in the search, then a pointer to this layer is returned, as follows:

```
//Searches the list of layers for a layer with a matching
name and returns a pointer
 //to this layer if found
c2DLayer* cSDL2DSceneManager::findLayer(std::string Name)
{
    std::list<c2DLayer*>::iterator list_it;

    //Render all associated render objects
    for(list_it=m_Layers.begin();list_it!=m_Layers.
end();list_it++)
    {
        if((*list_it)->m_Name==Name)
            return (*list_it);
    }

    return NULL;
}
```

## Comments

- The findLayer function accepts a string argument as the unique identifier of an existing layer.

- It then iterates through each and every layer in the list to find a layer with a matching name. If found, the function returns a pointer to the matching layer; otherwise, null is returned.

```
//Removes a layer with a specified name from the scene
void cSDL2DSceneManager::removeLayer(std::string Name)
{
    std::list<c2DLayer*>::iterator list_it;

    //Render all associated render objects
    for(list_it=m_Layers.begin();list_it!=m_Layers.
end();list_it++)
    {
        if((*list_it)->m_Name==Name)
            m_Layers.remove(*list_it);
    }
}
```

**Comments**

- The removeLayer function accepts a string argument as the unique identifier of an existing layer to remove.

- It then iterates through each and every layer in the list to find a layer with a matching name. If found, the function removes the layer.

## 6.6.2   Adding Listeners and Timers to a 2D Scene

Adding listeners and timers to a scene is much like adding layers, since layers, timers, and listeners are held by the scene manager in STL list structures. For this reason, the following methods for adding listeners and timers speak for themselves:

```
//----------------------------------------------------
//Add a timer to a 2D Scene
void cSDL2DSceneManager::addTimer(unsigned int ID, DWORD
Interval)
{
    cTimer *Timer = new cTimer();
    Timer->m_ID=ID;
    Timer->m_Interval=Interval;
    m_Timers.push_back(Timer);

    //Start the timer
    Timer->start();
}

//----------------------------------------------------

//Add a listener to the scene
```

```
void cSDL2DSceneManager::addListener(cSceneListener*
Object)
{
    m_Listeners.push_back(Object);
}
```

```
//----------------------------------------------------------
```

### 6.6.3    Sorting Layers by Z-Order

It was mentioned earlier that the order in which the objects of a scene are rendered to the display in any one frame influences the depth of a scene. This is because any rendered object appears in front of the objects rendered previously. The result is that objects rendered first will appear in the background and objects rendered last will appear in the foreground. Since objects in a 2D scene are grouped and rendered according to their layers, it follows that the order in which layers are rendered on each frame affects the appearance of depth concerning the objects of the scene. Thus, each layer has its own Z-order property indicating where along the Z (depth) axis it should appear in relation to the other layers. A Z-order of 0 should be assigned to the front layer, and $n-1$ to the back layer (where $n$ is the total number of layers in the scene); all other layers are some value in between as is appropriate for any particular scene.

The layers of the cSceneManager class are stored in a linear STL list member (m_Layers), and at render time the scene manager will cycle through this list from left to right and render each layer in sequence. Since the list is rendered in sequence, it should be sorted by Z-order so that higher-order layers appear to the front of the list and lower-order layers appear to the back; the list must be sorted every time the Z-order changes to ensure the order is maintained. To sort the STL list, the List::Sort method will be used. This method expects a callback function as an argument, which will be called whenever the method must compare any two items in the list in order to determine which of them is the greater. For this reason, sorting the STL list involves the creation of two functions: one is a method of the cSceneManager class, which should be called to initiate the sort process, and the other is the callback function that will be called by the STL sort method when sorting the list. The former is called cSDL2DSceneManager::sortLayers, and the latter is a global function called compareLayerOrder. The code for these sorting functions is as follows:

```
bool compareLayerOrder(const c2DLayer *lhs, const
c2DLayer *rhs)
{
    return lhs->m_ZOrder < rhs->m_ZOrder;
}
```

```
//-----------------------------------------------------

//Sorts the list of layers by Z-order
//Should be called once for every Z-order change
//e.g., On: myLayer->m_ZOrder=5;
void cSDL2DSceneManager::sortLayers()
{
    m_Layers.sort(compareLayerOrder);
}
```

### 6.6.4   Rendering Scenes with the Render Manager

Rendering a scene involves iterating through each layer in sequence and rendering each and every one of its scene objects to the display, taking into account the visibility status of both the layer and the scene object. The actual task of rendering the scene, however, rests with the render manager and not the scene manager, for it is the duty of the render manager to send pixels to the display. Consequently, the render manager must be amended to include an additional property and method: Its new property should be a pointer to a valid scene manager, and its new method should be for rendering a scene. The new class declaration for the render manager follows, with additions highlighted in bold:

```
class cSDL2DRenderManager : public c2DRenderManager
{
    private:
    protected:
    cSDL2DRenderManager();
    static cSDL2DRenderManager m_SDL2DRenderManager;
    void renderScene();
    public:
    static cSDL2DRenderManager* GetSDL2DRenderManager();
    SDL_Surface* m_RenderWindow; //Standard window for
render context
    std::stringstream m_VideoInfo;
    bool init(unsigned int Width=800, unsigned int
Height=600, bool fullScreen=false, char* WindowTitle=0);
    void free();
    bool update();
    void toggleFullScreen();
    cResource* loadResourceFromXML(TiXmlElement
*Element);
    void renderAllObjects();
```

```
        std::list<cSDLRenderObject*> m_RenderObjects;
        cSDL2DSceneManager *m_SceneManager;
};
```

Based on this class declaration, the member m_SceneManager is a valid pointer to the active scene manager, and the protected method renderScene is called on each frame to render the scene represented by the scene manager. The definition of renderScene is as follows, with comments afterward:

```
void cSDL2DRenderManager::renderScene()
{
    if(m_SceneManager)
    {
        std::list<c2DLayer*>::iterator list_it;

        //Render all associated render objects
        for(list_it=m_SceneManager->m_Layers.
begin();list_it!=m_SceneManager->m_Layers.end();list_
it++)
        {
            c2DLayer *Layer = *list_it;

            if(Layer->m_bVisible)
            {
                std::list<cSceneObject*>::iterator
object_it;

                for(object_it=Layer->m_SceneObjects.
begin();object_it!=Layer->m_SceneObjects.end();object_
it++)
                {
                    cSceneObject* Object = *object_it;

                    if(Object->m_bVisible)
                    {
                        Object->update();
                        SDL_Rect Pos;

                        //Render object X Y as offset
from layer X Y
                        Pos.x = int(Layer->m_PosX) +
int(Object->m_PosX);
                        Pos.y = int(Layer->m_PosY) +
int(Object->m_PosY);
```

```
                              SDL_BlitSurface(Object->m_
RenderResource->m_Surface, &Object->m_RenderRect,
m_RenderWindow, &Pos);
                          }
                      }
                  }
              }
          }
      }
```

## Comments

- The renderScene function begins by iterating through each and every layer of the active scene manager.

- For each layer, the function checks to see whether the current layer is visible. If so, further processing ensues as described in the following comments. If not, the next layer, if any, is considered.

- If the layer is visible, the function cycles through each and every scene object attached to the layer. For each object, the function checks its visibility status.

- If the object is visible, its update method is called to prepare the object for rendering. Then the function calculates the object's inherited position on-screen by summing the XY position of the layer to the XY position of the scene object. Finally, the scene object is blitted (rendered) to the display using the SDL library.

- In short, this function renders a complete scene to the display.

### EXERCISE 6.2

List at least three improvements that could be made to the 2D scene manager class. Do this and then compare your list with mine:

1. Scene objects could support a rotation property in addition to position and scale values. This property would allow scene objects to be drawn at specified angles and orientations.

2. Layer objects could support an opacity property that affects the transparency of all scene objects belonging to that layer.

3. The scene manager could support an "Export to XML" method that exports the positions and arrangements of all objects and layers in the scene to an XML file.

## 6.6.5    Checking for Expired Timers and Invoking Events

The cTimer class measures the time elapsed in milliseconds since a starting time, and when the elapsed time matches or exceeds a given interval, the timer is said to expire (its m_Expired property is set to true). On expiration, a timer_elapsed event is detected by the scene manager. And when an event occurs, the scene manager iterates through a list of listener instances to see whether one or more of them are listening for the generated event. If so, the scene manager then calls the Event method for that listener, which is a method overridden with customized behavior in a derived class. In this way, application-specific functionality can be invoked at a specified time or on a specified interval. The scene manager checks for timer expiration on each frame in the method checkTimerExpired. Its definition is as follows:

```
void cSDL2DSceneManager::checkTimerExpired()
{
    std::list<cTimer*>::iterator list_it;

    //Check all timers
    for(list_it=m_Timers.begin();list_it!=m_Timers.
end();list_it++)
    {
        (*list_it)->update();

    //If expired
        if((*list_it)->m_Expired)
        {
            std::list<cSceneListener*>::iterator
listener_it;

            for(listener_it=m_Listeners.begin();listener_
it!=m_Listeners.end();listener_it++)
            {
        //If event handled
                if((*listener_it)->m_ListenFor == SE_
TIMER_EXPIRED)
                {
        //Raise event
                    (*listener_it)->Event(this, NULL);

        //Restart timer
                    (*list_it)->start();
                }
            }
        }
    }
```

```
            }
    }
```

**Comments**

- This function begins by iterating through all timers in the scene and checking each for their expiration status.

- If expired, a timer expired event is generated by the scene manager.

- The function then iterates through all listener objects and calls the Event method for each listener associated with this event.

- In sum, this method equips the scene manager with a basic ability to invoke custom behavior at a specified time or interval.

## 6.6.6    Loading Scenes from XML Files

In an earlier chapter, the resource manager was given the ability to load the resource metadata for a game at application startup from the settings in an XML file. This section codes similar functionality into the scene manager for loading scenes. At present, the only means of constructing a scene with layers and scene objects is by manually building the scene in code through the methods and properties of the scene manager class. While this method works and is effective, it is likely to become tiresome for the majority of scenes given the volume of objects and layers they can potentially contain. Furthermore, hard coding a scene requires a developer to recompile the code whenever a change is made. Thus, there is a strong argument in favor of "opening up" the scene framework by allowing the scene manager to build a scene from the settings in an XML file. The text of a sample scene XML file might look like this:

```
<scene>
    <layer name="layer1" posx="0" posy="0" visible="true">
        <objects>
            <object posx="0" posy="0" resourceID="1"
visible="true" colorkey="false"></object>
        </objects>
    </layer>
    <layer name="layer2" posx="0" posy="0" visible="true">
        <objects>
            <object posx="150" posy="0" resourceID="2"
visible="true" colorkey="true" r="0" g="0" b="0">
</object>
        </objects>
    </layer>
</scene>
```

**Comments**

- The root node of a scene is <scene></scene>. This node contains layer child nodes, and each layer contains a list of objects.

- Each layer has a unique name, an X and Y position on-screen, and a visible status. Each object has an X and Y position, a visible status, and a resource ID reference. This ID corresponds to the graphical resource ID of one of the resources loaded by the resource manager, and it will be used as the graphical representation of the scene object.

- Notice the colorkey property for an object, which enables transparency, e.g., colorkey="true" r="0" g="0" b="0".

Having established a general XML structure for the scene file, it remains to implement the XML loading functionality into the scene manager class using the free and open source TinyXML library, as considered in an earlier chapter. The XML loading is achieved by way of two methods: loadFromXMLFile and addLayerObjects. The former is called to initiate the XML loading process and to populate the scene with objects and layers, and the latter method is called internally by loadFromXMLFile to add layers one by one. The definitions of these methods are given here, and then comments follow:

```
bool cSDL2DSceneManager::loadFromXMLFile(std::string
Filename)
{
    TiXmlDocument doc(Filename.c_str());

    std::list<c2DLayer*> List;

     if(doc.LoadFile())
     {
         //Find scene node
         TiXmlNode* ResourceTree = doc.
FirstChild("scene");

         if(ResourceTree)
         {
             //Enumerate layer objects
             for(TiXmlNode* child = ResourceTree-
>FirstChild(); child; child = child->NextSibling())
             {
                 TiXmlElement *Element = child-
>ToElement();

                 if(Element)
```

```
                {
                    c2DLayer *Layer = new c2DLayer();
                    Layer->m_ZOrder = m_Layers.size();

                    for(TiXmlAttribute* ElementAttrib =
Element->FirstAttribute(); ElementAttrib; ElementAttrib =
ElementAttrib->Next())
                        {
                        //Examine layers
                        std::string AttribName =
ElementAttrib->Name();
                        std::string AttribValue =
ElementAttrib->Value();

                        if(AttribName=="name")
                        {
                            Layer->m_Name=AttribValue;
                            continue;
                        }

                        if(AttribName=="posx")
                        {
                            Layer->m_PosX =
atof(AttribValue.c_str());
                        }

                        if(AttribName=="posy")
                        {
                            Layer->m_PosY =
atof(AttribValue.c_str());
                        }

                        if(AttribName=="visible")
                        {
                            if(AttribValue=="true")
                                Layer->m_bVisible=true;
                            else
                                Layer->m_bVisible=false;
                        }
                        }

                        m_Layers.push_back(Layer);

                        //Cycle through layer objects
                        for(TiXmlNode* objs = child-
```

```
>FirstChild(); objs; objs = objs->NextSibling())
                    {
                            if(std::string
(objs->Value())=="objects")
                    {
                            for(TiXmlNode* obj =
objs->FirstChild(); obj; obj = obj->NextSibling())
                            {
                            TiXmlElement *ObjElement
= obj->ToElement();

                    //Add object to current layer

                            addLayerObjects(Layer,
ObjElement);
                            }
                }
                }
            }
        }

        sortLayers();
        return true;
        }
    }
    return false;
}
```

## Comments

- This method begins by calling the TinyXML loadFile method of the Document object to parse and load the scene XML file into memory for processing. Once loaded, it searches for the "Scene" root node and, if found, proceeds to iterate through all child layer nodes.

- For each layer, it cycles through all child objects. For each object, it calls the addLayerObjects method (considered next). This method accepts a pointer to the current layer, and the current XML Element represents the current object. After calling this function, the current object is added as a member of the current layer.

- Finally, this method calls sortLayers to sort the loaded layers according to their Z-order:

```
void cSDL2DSceneManager::addLayerObjects(c2DLayer *Layer,
TiXmlElement *Element)
```

```cpp
{
    cSceneObject* Object = new cSceneObject();
    unsigned int r=0;
    unsigned int g=0;
    unsigned int b=0;

    for(TiXmlAttribute* ElementAttrib = Element->
    FirstAttribute(); ElementAttrib; ElementAttrib =
    ElementAttrib->Next())
    {
        std::string AttribName = ElementAttrib->Name();
        std::string AttribValue = ElementAttrib->Value();

        if(AttribName=="resourceID")
        {
            cResourceManager* ResourceManager = cResource
    Manager::GetResourceManager();

            Object->setResourceObject((cRenderResource*)
    ResourceManager->findResourcebyID(atoi(AttribValue.c_
    str())));
        }

        if(AttribName=="posx")
        {
            Object->m_PosX = atof(AttribValue.c_str());
        }

        if(AttribName=="posy")
        {
            Object->m_PosY = atof(AttribValue.c_str());
        }

        if(AttribName=="colorkey")
        {
            if(AttribValue=="true")
                Object->m_bColorKeyEnabled=true;
            else
                Object->m_bColorKeyEnabled=false;
        }

        if(AttribName=="r")
        {
            r = atoi(AttribValue.c_str());
        }
```

```
        if(AttribName=="g")
        {
            g = atoi(AttribValue.c_str());
        }

        if(AttribName=="b")
        {
            b = atoi(AttribValue.c_str());
        }
    }

    if(Object->m_bColorKeyEnabled)
        Object->setColorKey(r,g,b);

    Layer->m_SceneObjects.push_back(Object);
}
```

**Comments**

- The addLayerObjects method accepts two arguments: a pointer to a valid layer and a Tiny XML Element object representing the object details in XML format. The addLayerObjects method begins by creating a blank, default scene object and then proceeds to populate this class from the settings it reads from the XML.

- Once the scene object is loaded from the XML, the function proceeds to set a color key, if appropriate, and then adds the object to the current layer (passed as an argument of the method).

- In short, this method in combination with loadFromXMLFile allows a scene manager to build a scene from an XML file. To load a scene from an XML file, a developer uses the scene manager as follows:

```
g_MySceneManager->loadFromXMLFile("My_Scene_Xml.xml");
```

## ■ 6.7   Chapter Summary

This chapter detailed some of the most common design and implementation work involved in creating generic 2D scene managers for game engines, though the scene manager presented here certainly has room for improvement. The chapter considered issues relating to scene object positions and interrelationships, hierarchical transformations, layers and Z-ordering, timing and synchronization, and loading scene data from XML files. One area in which this scene manager can be improved substantially in combination with the render manager is in the area of rendering optimization. At present, it is possible for a scene to contain hundreds of layers with hundreds of objects, and for every layer and object to be visible at one time. This raises a problem regarding performance because currently the render manager will try to render all visible items, even when such an item has scrolled off the edge of the screen and is technically not visible even though its visible property is still set to true. Thus, the first optimization a developer might like to add to this scene manager would be off-screen culling, the ability of the scene manager to test each layer to see whether it falls out of the boundaries of the screen and has become invisible, and therefore need not be rendered. This chapter concludes our 2D engine work, and now we move into the world of audio.

# 7

# Music and Sound with the Audio Manager

## Overview

After completing this chapter, you should:

- Understand the difference between music and sound
- Be able to use the BASS audio library to play audio
- Know how to refine the resource manager to accommodate audio resources
- Appreciate the nuances and importance of audio management

The chief concern of this chapter is with all things audible in games, and just as the graphics resources of an engine require careful management if the engine is not to buckle under an overwhelming weight of data, so also must the audio resources be managed and contained. This chapter starts by considering audio as a concept in more detail, and this consideration will lead us to distinguish between sound and music. This distinction and its implications has a bearing on appropriate methods for implementing audio in games and on designing the audio manager component that will play back audio files. After considering some of the crucial design issues pertaining to game audio, the chapter then proceeds to implement an audio manager; its implementation will require some amendments to be made to the resource manager in order to accommodate audio resources.

## ■ 7.1 Audio, Sound, and Music—Designing Audible Games

The terms "audio," "sound," and "music" are often used loosely and interchangeably by developers working in the games industry, especially the terms "audio" and "sound." Although this habit does not usually cause developmental problems in practice (since most developers already know the difference), it is nevertheless important for clarity to recognize that the three terms have distinct and specific meanings. The term "audio" is an umbrella term referring to anything audible, both music and sound. These latter two terms ("music" and "sound") together emphasize that any unit of audio can be divided into one of two groups depending on both its intrinsic properties and its uses in a game. To simplify a little: Music typically refers to any piece of audio played continuously for the purpose of enhancing mood or atmosphere such as background tracks played on a loop or a track that makes a sudden interruption to convey an appropriate atmosphere of, say, fear or action. In contrast, sound (or sound effect) is a usually short audio sample (such as a footstep, a gunshot, or a door creak) played once or many times repeatedly in response to activity in the game. Sound effects often impart life, adding depth and a sense of motion to a scene. For this reason, they can (to some extent and in some cases) even be used to stand in for the absence of graphical animation. For example, consider a scenario where a player character standing in the street descends the ladder of a man-hole into the dark recesses of a sewer beneath. The scene of their descent is likely to be a scene of contrasts: the change from a naturally lit street to a barely illuminated sewer, from airy sounds to claustrophobic sounds, from comfort and tranquility to fear and the unknown. These contrasts can be communicated by the developer to the gamer in many ways: through graphical cues and animation, camera work and lighting, and sound and music. Some developers might choose to combine all elements and take an extravagant approach, while other developers might take a minimalist approach. This minimalist approach might involve only sound: As the player descends the ladder, the view fades to black. Amid the blackness (absence of graphics), the player hears the sounds of steps on a ladder and notices the changes in atmosphere, from light steps in an open space fading toward heavier steps in a space of echoes, punctuated now and then by the sound of water droplets reverberating through the tunnel as they fall from the ceiling and strike puddles of water on the ground. In short, music and sound, and their timing, enhance the setting of a game.

How then does a developer go about deciding whether any piece of audio for their game should be classified as sound or music, and what difference does it make for a game and engine? Initially, the first part of this question might seem silly since most developers and nondevelopers can distinguish music from sound based on our current definitions by simply listening to the audio track itself. However, in making a decision about whether a given piece of audio should be classified as sound or music, a developer is motivated not only by intuition and common sense but also by technical considerations. In particular, a developer will likely be very much alert to the following:

- Music and sound differ in the sense that the former refers to a longer, continuous piece of audio while the latter is typically shorter in terms of duration. For this reason, music files on a computer are likely to be larger in file size than are sound effect files.

- Music and sound are likely to differ in terms of the regularity at which they are repeated, if they are repeated at all. For example: Gunshot sounds are repeated each time a gun fires, and in shooter games this is likely to be many times per minute. In contrast, the title theme song for a game might be activated only for the menu screen, which is accessed whenever the player starts, exits, loads, or saves the game (perhaps once or twice per hour or half hour on average).

The combination of these two factors—the size of the data and the regularity of its playback—have a bearing on how a developer is likely to see an audio track in terms of sound and music when developing a game and a game engine. Since a sound is short in duration, small in file size, and likely to be repeated more often than music, a developer typically loads the entirety of the sound file into memory before playback to facilitate rapid and frequent playback on demand later. In contrast, since music files are longer in duration (perhaps very long), larger in file size (perhaps very large), and are either not repeated or repeated infrequently, a developer streams the file in chunks as it is played rather than loading the complete file into memory before playback. *Streaming* refers to the process of loading and unloading a media file in segments or blocks as it is played back. A small block of data, corresponding to the current position of play, is loaded from the media file and into memory for decoding. As playback proceeds linearly from left to right, it pushes the horizon of data forward, bringing as much new data into memory as it removes of the old data, which has fallen outside. In this way, mammoth-sized files can be played back with greater consistency and efficiency. Specific implementations of streaming may differ from this model in theory, but almost all follow this basic idea. For our purposes, it is necessary to know only that a file loaded and played through streaming is not loaded into memory

### EXERCISE 7.1

For each of the following files, list whether it should be loaded into an engine as either a sample or a stream.

1. A 100 K MP3 gunshot sound lasting 2 seconds, played frequently.
2. A 300 K OGG page turn sound lasting 11 seconds, played infrequently.
3. A 3.5 MB OGG musical score, played very infrequently.
4. A 900 MB OGG voice-over track, played throughout the game.

**Answers**

1. A sample. The audio is small in file size and played frequently.
2. A sample. Though played infrequently, the sound is small and will be expected to play immediately on demand.
3. A stream. The audio is comparatively large in file size.
4. A stream. Though used throughout the game, the file is comparatively enormous and prohibitive to load entirely.

in its entirety, is sometimes prone to stalling depending on hardware circumstances and codecs, and often takes longer to start than a file loaded completely in memory because the system must read data from the hard disk rather than from RAM or hardware memory. Thus, streaming is usually not suitable for a sound effect file that is intended to be played quickly and frequently. But it is suitable for music, and especially for files whose size makes it prohibitive to load them in their entirety. Throughout the rest of this chapter, the common terms "music" and "'sound" will be replaced by the more specific terms "stream" and "sample," respectively, where stream refers to audio that is streamed, and sample to audio that is loaded entirely into memory for faster playback.

## ■  7.2    Designing the Audio Playback Framework

The previous section stated that game audio can be divided into music and sound and that both of the latter terms generally map to the terms stream and sample, respectively. Like graphics resources, audio resources consume memory and their loading and unloading must therefore be managed by the resource manager, but unlike graphics resources some audio resources can be "streamed'"; that is, loaded on-the-fly as they are played back on the audio hardware at run time. Thus, it will be the job of the audio manager to coordinate both the playback of loaded samples and the streaming and playback of streams as required by the engine and game. This section sketches out the main features of the audio manager and thereby outlines the implementation work of subsequent sections. Specifically, the audio playback framework will consist of three separate classes:

### cAudioResource

The audio resource class works in conjunction with the resource manager, and is derived from base class cResource, created in an earlier chapter. It represents an audio resource in memory, and like graphics resources the audio resource will have scope, which determines when the raw data of the resource—audio data in this case—is and is not loaded and ready for use in the active scene of the game. However, since audio data can be either a stream or a sample, the loading and unloading features apply only to samples because streams can never be cached entirely.

### cAudioPlayer

For each and every instance of an audio resource, there may be one or more associated instances of cAudioPlayer. Each instance of cAudioPlayer maintains a pointer to a single instance of cAudioResource and encodes preferences about the playback of that resource. In other words, a cAudioPlayer class will be dispatched to the audio manager whenever a sound should be played at run time. The class will tell the audio manager which audio resource is to be played and whether or not it is to be played once or repeatedly for a specified number of plays. Furthermore, it features an OnMediaComplete event callback function, which will be invoked by the audio manager when it detects that the playback of an associated audio resource has completed, including any repeats. This class is intended to be an abstract base class that is overridden and whose OnMediaComplete event is redefined in descendant classes to allow for custom functionality when audio playback completes.

**cAudioManager**

The audio manager is the chief instigator in the audio playback process, and all calls to play a sample or stream must be made through the audio manager. Furthermore, like all the other managers listed in this book, the interface of the class (its public methods and properties) must be API independent. That is, callers of this class should not be required to understand any of the class's implementation details in order to use it successfully. The audio manager must allow the developer to: (1) initialize and collect diagnostic information about the audio hardware installed on the user's system, (2) set the global volume level, (3) start, stop, and pause sound at a global level, meaning that such commands should affect *all* audio in the game, and (4) play a specified audio resource.

## ◼ 7.3   Audio Playback and BASS

The audio playing framework of the engine coded in this book will consist of three core classes: cAudioResource, cAudioPlayer, and cAudioManager; together these classes allow an engine to play audio on demand, both samples and streams. To do its work of playing audio via the hardware, these classes will make use of the BASS audio library developed by Un4seen Developments. BASS is a cross-platform audio library designed to simplify the process of playing audio files in compiled applications. It supports Windows and Mac, and several languages including Delphi, C++, and Visual Basic. It supports playback of the following audio file formats:

- WAV
- AIFF
- MP3
- MP2
- MP1
- OGG

BASS is free to try and free for noncommercial use, and at the time of writing it offers three licenses for commercial projects. More information about BASS and its licenses can be found at http://www.un4seen.com/. The next section details how to download and configure BASS for a C++ project.

> NOTE. Readers not wishing to use BASS might like to try SDL_mixer, a free sound library. This can be found at http://www.libsdl.org/projects/SDL_mixer/. However, the remainder of this chapter considers the use of BASS.

## 7.3.1   Downloading, Installing, and Configuring BASS

The BASS audio library is a software kit used by developers to play audio in their application via the sound hardware. Before it can be used to create an application, it must first be downloaded, installed, and configured. *Users* of applications made with BASS will *not* need to download and install the library; it is intended only for *developers* of software using BASS. However, applications that use the BASS audio library depend at run time on an external bass.dll file, which should be located either in the application folder alongside the main application EXE file or in the Windows system folder. This file should be installed to the user's system along with all other game files. The following step-by-step instructions detail how to download and prepare BASS for use in development:

Step 1.   Navigate a web browser to the BASS homepage at http://www.un4seen.com/. (The current version at the time of writing is version 2.4.5.)

Step 2.   BASS is available for both Windows and Mac, although this book considers development with BASS only in the context of Windows. Click the download button to download the BASS library to the local computer. The library is packaged in a ZIP file. Once downloaded, use Winzip or other archive software to extract the contents of this package to a folder.

Step 3.   The root BASS folder contains the following files and directories; a description of each accompanies their names:

**c**

Contains all source, header, example, and library files necessary to use the BASS audio library with C or C++ applications. Almost all of the files necessary for the purposes of this book will be found in this folder.

**delphi**

Contains all source, header, example, and library files necessary to use the BASS audio library with applications built in Embarcadero Delphi.

**masm**

Contains all source, header, example, and library files necessary to use the BASS audio library with applications developed with Microsoft Assembler.

**mp3-free**

Contains a precompiled BASS library DLL with MP3 support removed. This version still plays all other BASS supported formats, including OGG and WAV. One might wonder why a separate build of BASS without MP3 support should be necessary. This is probably due to MP3 patenting issues, on which more information can be found at the MP3 entry at Wikipedia should the reader be interested: http://en.wikipedia.org/wiki/MP3.

**vb**

Contains all source, header, example, and library files necessary to use the BASS audio library with applications developed with Microsoft Visual Basic.

**bass.chm, bass.dll, bass.txt**

The bass.chm file is a standard Windows help file and reference for the BASS audio library listing all functions and variables available in the BASS library. The bass.dll file is the precompiled binary library (with MP3 support) that should be distributed alongside any BASS-powered application. The smaller bass.dll file (without MP3 support) can be distributed in its place, provided an application does not play MP3 files. Finally, the bass.txt file contains detailed library and release information that newcomers to BASS should examine.

Step 4.  Once downloaded and extracted in place, the BASS audio library should be configured in the C++ IDE for each and every C++ project in which it will be used. Specifically, each project must include the bass.h header file and link to the bass.lib compiled library file. These files can be found in the c folder of the bass library root folder. Instructions on how to include header files and how to add header and library file directories can be found in an earlier chapter of this book.

---

## ■ 7.4  Implementing the Audio Playback Framework with BASS Audio

Together, the previous sections of this chapter have established a three-part design for the audio playback framework in terms of manager components and discussed how to appropriately install and configure the BASS audio library for use in Windows-based C++ applications. Having achieved this, the developer is now in a position to implement their design, and the following sections of this chapter consider the stages of this implementation. To outline the work that is to come, this section lists the completed audio playback header file containing three core audio playback classes: cAudioResource, cAudioPlayer, and cAudioManager. The job of the remainder of this chapter will be to implement these classes to work successfully alongside the existing engine framework pieced together thus far in this book. Since the complete class declarations are given in advance in the following code, there might be some properties, methods, or design quirks in the code that are not immediately self-explanatory. However, subsequent sections of this chapter explain the implementation of these classes in detail. Furthermore, the accompanying code comments summarize the purpose of each class.

```
#ifndef AUDIOMANAGER_H_INCLUDED
#define AUDIOMANAGER_H_INCLUDED

#include "EngineObject.h"
#include "ResourceManager.h"
#include "Bass.h"
#include <string>
#include <sstream>
#include <list>


//------------------------------------------------------------

typedef enum {AUDIO_TYPE_SAMPLE=0, AUDIO_TYPE_STREAM=1}
AUDIO_TYPE;

//Class cAudioResource encapsulates an audio resource as
loaded by the BASS
//audio library
class cAudioResource : public cResource
{
   private:
   protected:
   public:

        HSAMPLE m_SampleData;
        HSTREAM m_StreamData;
        HCHANNEL m_ChannelData;

        AUDIO_TYPE m_AudioType;

        void load();
        void unload();
```

```
};

//-----------------------------------------------------------

//class cAudioPlayer corresponds to an audio object in a
scene.
//Abstract base class intended to be overridden with a
handled
//onMediaComplete method. This class is passed to the
audio manager
//and specifies how a file is to be played (Num of
repeats, etc).
// onMediaComplete is called by the audio manager to
notify the class
//When media playback has completed.

class cAudioPlayer : public cEngineObject
{
   private:
   protected:
   public:
        cAudioResource* m_AudioResource;
        int m_NumRepeats;
        int m_RepeatCount;

        cAudioPlayer()
        {
              m_AudioResource = NULL;
              m_NumRepeats = m_RepeatCount = 0;
        }

        virtual void onMediaComplete()=0;
};

//-----------------------------------------------------------

class cAudioManager :  public cEngineObject
{
private:
protected:
   cAudioManager();
   static cAudioManager m_AudioManager;

   std::list<cAudioPlayer*> m_Players;
```

```
public:
   BASS_DEVICEINFO m_DeviceInfo;
   std::string m_DeviceInfoString;
   static cAudioManager* GetAudioManager();
   bool init(int Device=-1, DWORD SampleRate-44100, DWORD
flags=0, HWND win=0);
   void free();
   void setVolume(float Volume) {BASS_SetVolume(Volume);}
   void pause() {BASS_Pause();}
   void start() {BASS_Start();}
   cResource* loadResourceFromXML(TiXmlElement *Element);

   //Plays audio resource once
   void playFromResource(cAudioResource* AudioResource);
   void addAudioPlayer(cAudioPlayer *Player);

   void update();
};


//----------------------------------------------------

#endif //AUDIOMANAGER_II_INCLUDED
```

NOTE. Notice the inclusion of the BASS library header file: #include Bass.h.

## ■ 7.5   Implementing the Audio Resource Class

The audio playback framework consists of three core classes: cAudioResource, cAudio-Player, and cAudioManager. The cAudioPlayer class defines how any specified segment of audio—an MP3 file, a WAV sound, etc.—*should* be played, and the cAudioManager is responsible for initiating the playback of audio according to the requirements of the player class, for keeping track of all playing samples, and for notifying event callbacks when playback completes. Both of these classes, however, must at some time during their operation work with the raw materials—or rather, the common currency—of audio playback: namely, audio resources. Audio resources are encapsulated in the cAudioResource class and bear some similarity to their graphics resource counterparts, insofar as any single audio resource may be readied and uninitialized according to changes in the active scene of a game. Each scene of a game differs in its requirements and is likely to depend both on a common set of audio segments shared throughout the game such as a jump sound or gunshot sound, and on a specific set of audio segments played only during that scene such as the spoken words of a nonplayer character (NPC). For this reason, some audio segments will be loaded throughout game execution and others will be loaded and unloaded as and when the active scene demands. At this functional level, the audio resource bears resemblance to the graphics resource, but the audio resource differs in that it may be either one of two kinds—a sample or a stream. Its kind determines whether the audio data, when called to be loaded for a scene, should be loaded entirely into memory as a sample for fast and immediate playback or should only be initialized and ready for streaming. It has been stated already that frequently played audio that is short in duration is suitable for samples, and longer segments are suitable for streams. Developers are required to use their judgment when choosing whether a given segment of audio should be either a sample or a stream.

Thus, audio resources come in two kinds, and the cAudioResource class has been designed to reflect this requirement. It features two mutually exclusive properties—HSAMPLE m_SampleData and HSTREAM m_StreamData, which represent a sample and stream, respectively—of which only one property will be valid for any single instance of a resource. If a resource is a sample, then m_SampleData represents a pointer to the raw audio data and m_StreamData will be null. If a resource is a stream, then m_StreamData represents a pointer to the stream data and m_SampleData will be null. The HSAMPLE and HSTREAM data types are provided by the BASS audio library to represent samples and streams, respectively; they are to be used as handles to the library functions. In addition to these two properties, a further property has been added to the cAudioResource class to indicate which of the two types of resources it is. AUDIO_TYPE m_AudioType indicates the resource type and is an instance of the enum type AUDIO_TYPE; this property can be either AUDIO_TYPE_SAMPLE or AUDIO_TYPE_STREAM. The following code demonstrates how to create a new audio resource of a specified type:

```
cAudioResource* Resource = new cAudioResource();
Resource->m_ResourceID=MyID;
Resource->m_FileName = "test.mp3";
Resource->m_Scope=0;
Resource->m_AudioType = AUDIO_TYPE_STREAM;
```

**NOTE.** Please note that cAudioResource is a class derived from cResource. Therefore, it inherits the properties of this latter class, including properties such as m_FileName and m_Scope. cResource was defined in an earlier chapter, but for convenience the class declaration is reproduced here:

```
class cResource : public cEngineObject
{
```

```
        private:
        protected:
        public:
            unsigned int m_ResourceID;
            unsigned int m_Scope;
            std::string m_FileName;
            RESOURCE_TYPE m_Type;
            bool m_bLoaded;

            //To be overloaded by derived classes
            virtual ~cResource(){};
            virtual void load(){};
            virtual void unload(){};

            inline cResource()
            {
                m_ResourceID = m_Scope = 0;
                m_Type = RESOURCE_NULL;
                m_bLoaded = false;
            }
    };
```

## 7.5.1   Loading Audio Resources

The load and unload methods of cAudioResource are intended to be called whenever an active scene change demands, to either prepare or unload an audio resource as necessary. Resources with a scope of 0 remain active throughout execution because they are global resources, and those with a nonzero scope can be trusted to be active only when required by the active scene. In short, the load and unload methods of a resource are called as scene changes occur during the execution of a game. The load method of class cAudioResource is given here, with comments following:

```
void cAudioResource::load()
{
    if(m_AudioType == AUDIO_TYPE_SAMPLE)
    {
        m_SampleData = BASS_SampleLoad(FALSE, m_
FileName.c_str(),0,0,1,0);
        m_ChannelData = BASS_SampleGetChannel(m_
SampleData,false);
    }
    else
    {
        m_StreamData = BASS_StreamCreateFile(FALSE,
m_FileName.c_str(),0,0,0);
```

```
        m_ChannelData = m_StreamData;
    }
}
```

## Comments

- This function begins by testing the m_AudioType property to determine the type of the audio resource. This is necessary because the BASS audio library offers distinct functions for loading samples and streams.

- If the resource is a sample, execution falls into the sample branch of the code. This section calls the BASS_SampleLoad function to cache the audio data from a specified audio file into memory. If successful, the function returns the loaded data in the HSAMPLE handle. If unsuccessful, the function returns 0. It is important to note that calling this function does not play the specified audio file; it simply caches the file into memory and readies it for playback. The BASS_ SampleLoad function has the following form:

```
HSAMPLE BASS_SampleLoad(
    BOOL mem,
    void *file,
    QWORD offset,
    DWORD length,
    DWORD max,
    DWORD flags
);
```

- If the audio file is successfully loaded into memory as a sample using the BASS_ SampleLoad function, then class member m_SampleData is filled with valid audio information loaded by the BASS audio library. That is, the actual audio data, either all or part, is loaded from the file and into memory; once loaded the data is represented by an HSAMPLE handle. This handle is maintained by the audio resource class in its member m_SampleData and is used in subsequent calls to BASS functions. Once the audio is loaded as a sample, an application should retrieve a *channel* for that sample if it expects the sample to play successfully to the speakers in later calls. The channel represents the *track* on which the sample will be played. For a sample to be played, it must be loaded into a channel, and by controlling properties of the channel a developer can control the playback of a sample. Channels can be paused, stopped, and played. Furthermore, BASS offers developers the ability to set and get channel volume, apply special effects, set panning and 3D position for cards supporting these features, and change the channel frequency. The load method given above, however, simply retrieves the default (or first) channel associated with a given sample using the BASS_ SampleGetChannel function. If successful, this channel returns a valid pointer to a

## ■ BASS_SampleLoad Details

**BOOL mem**

Species whether the function is to load the audio data from a valid audio file on disk or from a file already loaded into memory. True specifies the former, and false the latter. Often, game developers avoid distributing games with their audio available in separate files that can be opened and played by the user using Windows Explorer. Instead, the total audio data for a game is often compressed and packed into one or two archive files, which at run time are then extracted and sometimes loaded into memory for processing. Thus, the BASS_SampleLoad function allows audio to be loaded from memory locations. However, given that the packing and archiving mechanisms differ from developer to developer and from engine to engine, this chapter considers only the loading of audio data from files on disk.

**void *file**

Either the fully qualified file name of the audio file to load (if mem=false) or the memory address of the audio file in memory (if mem=true).

**QWORD offset**

File offset in bytes from which file loading should begin (if mem=false). This should be 0 if the file to be loaded is not packed in an archive and is simply open in a standard MP3 or OGG file.

**DWORD length**

Length of the file to load in bytes (if mem=false). Specifying 0 instructs BASS to load the entirety of the file.

**DWORD max**

Specifies the maximum number of simultaneous playbacks allowed for the loaded sample stream from 1 (MIN) to 65535 (MAX). It might at first glance be tempting to simply pass MAX for all loaded samples, but for performance reasons and completeness a developer should seek to pass values appropriate for their needs.

**DWORD flags**

Can be 0 or any of the constants in the following list. The code in this chapter will typically pass 0, but the other values are listed for reference. Readers should consult the BASS documentation for more detailed descriptions of these values.

```
BASS_SAMPLE_FLOAT
BASS_SAMPLE_LOOP
```

```
BASS_SAMPLE_MONO
BASS_SAMPLE_SOFTWARE
BASS_SAMPLE_VAM
BASS_SAMPLE_3D
BASS_SAMPLE_MUTEMAX
BASS_SAMPLE_OVER_VOL
BASS_SAMPLE_OVER_POS
BASS_SAMPLE_OVER_DIST
BASS_UNICODE
```

channel configured to play the specified sample. Again, this function does not play the sample, but only prepares a channel for playback at a later time. The channel pointer is maintained in the class member HCHANNEL m_ChannelData. The BASS_SampleGetChannel function of the BASS library has the following form:

```
HCHANNEL BASS_SampleGetChannel(
HSAMPLE handle,
        BOOL onlynew
);
```

- If the load method identifies the current audio resource as a stream and not a sample, then it enters the stream loading branch. In this branch, the BASS_ StreamCreateFile function is called to create a stream object from a valid audio file such as an MP3 or OGG file. If the function is successful, it returns a pointer to the loaded stream object, and the cAudioResource keeps a copy of this pointer in member m_StreamData. The m_StreamData member is derived from a channel

---

### ■ BASS_SampleGetChannel Details

**HSAMPLE handle**

Handle of the sample for which a channel should be retrieved.

**BOOL onlynew**

Specifies whether BASS should return any available channel, existing or new, or whether it should always create a new channel to return. Typically, this will be FALSE.

object (HCHANNEL) and can therefore work also as a channel. For this reason, the load method assigns m_StreamData to m_ChannelData. It is important to note that the BASS_StreamCreateFile function does not play the stream; it only creates a stream object that is ready to play. The form of this function is as follows:

```
HSTREAM BASS_StreamCreateFile(
    BOOL mem,
    void *file,
    QWORD offset,
    QWORD length,
    DWORD flags
);
```

NOTE. The BASS_StreamCreateFile function supports the following audio formats: MP3, MP2, MP1, OGG, WAV, and AIFF.

---

### ■ BASS_StreamCreateFile Details

**BOOL mem**

Specifies whether the stream should be created directly from a file on disk (mem=false) or from a file loaded in memory (mem=true). Please see the mem argument description given earlier for BASS_SampleLoad for more details regarding files in memory.

**void *file**

Fully qualified file name of the file to load as a stream if the file is being loaded from disk (mem=false). Otherwise (mem=true), the memory address of the audio data from which the stream should be created.

**QWORD offset**

File offset in bytes from which the file loading should begin (if mem=false). This should be 0 if the file to be loaded is not packed in an archive and is simply open in a standard MP3 or OGG file.

**QWORD length**

Refers to the total length of the file in bytes.

**DWORD flags**

Can be 0 or any combination of a selection of flags. More information concerning these flags can be found in the description of the flags parameter for the BASS_SampleLoad function given earlier.

## 7.5.2   Unloading Audio Resources

The load method of cAudioResource is responsible for loading audio resources on demand, and its complementary unload method is used for "reversing"' that process; that is, for unloading an audio resource, either a sample or a stream. The implementation of the unload method is given here, with comments following:

```
void cAudioResource::unload()
{
    if(m_Type == AUDIO_TYPE_SAMPLE)
        BASS_SampleFree(m_SampleData);
    else
        BASS_StreamFree(m_StreamData);

    m_SampleData = m_StreamData = NULL;
}
```

This short function first determines the type of the audio resource by verifying the value of the m_Type class member. If set to AUDIO_TYPE_SAMPLE (if it is a sample), it calls the BASS function BASS_SampleFree to unload the audio resource from memory. The BASS_SampleFree function requires only a handle to the sample to unload. If the resource is a stream (AUDIO_TYPE_STREAM), the function BASS_StreamFree function is called to free the stream. Like the BASS_SampleFree function, BASS_StreamFree requires the handle of a stream to free. Once free, both members are set to null to confirm the unload process.

## ■  7.6   Building the Audio Resource Player Component

The audio resource class encapsulates an audio resource but does not feature any methods for playing audio files, just as the graphics resource does not feature any methods for displaying graphics. The division of work between the various components of the engine ensures their *modularity* and *recylability* (see Chapter 1). The component responsible for initiating the playback process for audio resources is the audio manager component; as playback must occur, this component receives its instructions through the cAudioPlayer class, whose purpose is to instruct the audio manager on *how* to play a specified file. It is to this class that our attention now turns. The audio player given here is simple in the sense that it offers only the ability to repeat the playback of an audio file for a specified number of times, if repetition is required at all. The intention of this section is to construct the foundations of a player class from which the reader can build and expand using other functions in the BASS library such as adding the ability to set volume, panning, and other special effects through the BASS function BASS_ChannelSetAttribute. It could further support a time delay method that allows

playback to start after a specified interval has elapsed. Before detailing the player class
further, the entire class declaration is reproduced here for convenience. Furthermore,
the class declaration represents the *entirety* of the class.

```
class cAudioPlayer : public cEngineObject
{
    private:
    protected:
    public:
            cAudioResource* m_AudioResource;
            int m_NumRepeats;
            int m_RepeatCount;

            cAudioPlayer()
            {
                    m_AudioResource = NULL;
                    m_NumRepeats = m_RepeatCount = 0;
            }

            virtual void onMediaComplete()=0;
};
```

cAudioPlayer is an abstract base class that describes how a given sound is to be
played. The m_AudioResource member is a pointer to a valid audio resource, specifying the audio sample or stream to be played. The m_NumRepeats member defines the
number of repetitions for which the sound should be played (0= play once, 1=repeat
once, etc.). The m_RepeatCount member is a counter used to keep track of the total
number of repeats for which the sound has already been played, if it is currently
playing. Finally, the class features the virtual method onMediaComplete. It should
be noted that cAudioPlayer is considered an abstract base class *because* it features
a virtual method (onMediaComplete) with a null definition. This method is intended
to be overridden and redefined with custom functionality in descendant classes. The
onMediaComplete method is an event callback that is called implicitly by the audio
manager class whenever the associated audio resource (m_AudioResource) has completed playback (all repetitions). It might be the case that an engine wishes to play an
audio resource once and cares little or nothing for event callbacks or repetitions. For
these cases, the audio manager will support a play method that does not require the
cAudioPlayer class. Before moving on to the implementation of the audio manager, it
will be useful here to provide an example of a derived cAudioPlayer class:

```
class cMySoundEffect: public cAudioPlayer
{
    private:
```

```
    protected:
    public:

        cMySoundEffect()
        {
            //Set playback repeats
            m_NumRepeats = 2;

            //Set audio resource
            m_AudioResource = (cAudioResource*)
ResourceManager->findResourcebyID(5);
        }

        //Will be called when playback completes
        void onMediaComplete()
        {
            //Handle completed event
            MessageBoxA(NULL,"media completed","", MB_
OK);
        }
};
```

NOTE. It should be mentioned that the cAudioPlayer class is not in any way affiliated with audio playback. The audio manager class will initiate playback and is the topic of the next section.

## ■ 7.7   Implementing the Audio Manager Class

Overseeing the workings of both cAudioResource and cAudioPlayer is the audio manager component, which ensures that playing audio runs smoothly for the engine. Its purpose is to act as the chief interface of the audio playback framework, offering developers the ability to start, stop, and pause audio playback at run time. Furthermore, the audio manager is responsible for initializing and uninitializing the audio hardware installed on the local machine. The general order in which the audio manager performs its work is as follows:

1. Initialize audio hardware at application startup, before other BASS functions are called. This is a one-off process; that is, it must be performed once per application.

2. Play and manage audio resources as required. This is a repeated and continuous process throughout game execution.

3. Uninitialize audio hardware at application end, after all BASS calls are made. Like initialization, this is a one-off process.

This chapter now considers the complete implementation of the audio manager class in the context of these three duties sequentially.

## 7.7.1   Initializing Audio Hardware with the Audio Manager

The audio manager is the overarching manager component for audio playback encapsulated in the class cAudioManager, managing the process of which audio files are played, and when and how. With the exception of its class constructor, the audio manager begins its work of initializing audio hardware in the init method, called at application startup. The implementation of this method is given here with comments following:

```
bool cAudioManager::init(int Device, DWORD SampleRate,
DWORD flags, HWND win)
{
    BOOL bassActive = BASS_Init(Device, SampleRate, flags,
win, NULL);

    if(bassActive)
    {
        //Get Device Info
        std::stringstream DeviceStringStream;

        if(BASS_GetDeviceInfo(Device, &m_DeviceInfo))
        {
            DeviceStringStream << "Audio Device
Info. Name: " << m_DeviceInfo.name << " Driver: " << m_
DeviceInfo.driver;
            m_DeviceInfoString = DeviceStringStream.
str();
        }
    }

    return bassActive;
}
```

**Comments**

- This method accepts a total of four optional arguments, all of which have default values if they are not specified explicitly by the developer in making the call. These are: int Device, DWORD SampleRate, DWORD flags, and HWND win. Device specifies the ID of the audio hardware to be initialized; this is useful in cases where a system is supporting more than one audio device. In most cases, an application will initialize the default audio hardware (1). The SampleRate and flags parameters are specific to the BASS library and are considered shortly. The win argument is a valid window handle. Often this will be null for the current window.

- The init method begins by calling the BASS function BASS_Init to initialize the audio hardware. This function should be called once for each execution of an application and called before any other BASS function is called. Here it is simply passed many of the parameters included as arguments of the init function.

---

### ■ BASS_GetDeviceInfo Details

**int device**
Device ID of the audio hardware used to play sound throughout application execution. 1= Default Device; 0 = No Sound. Values greater than 1 refer to additional devices.

**DWORD freq**
The output sample rate at which audio on the selected device will play. A typical value is 44100 for 44 kHz stereo.

**DWORD flags**
Can be 0 or a combination of any of the following values:

  BASS_DEVICE_8BITS

  The default setting is 16-bit. This flag can be used to adjust the sound resolution to 8-bit.

  BASS_DEVICE_MONO

  The default setting is stereo. This flag can be used to adjust playback to mono.

  BASS_DEVICE_3D

  Turns on 3D sound if supported by the sound hardware. That is, it allows audio to be positioned in 3D space and adjusts volume and speaker orientation accordingly.

  BASS_DEVICE_LATENCY

  BASS_DEVICE_CPSPEAKERS

  BASS_DEVICE_SPEAKERS

  BASS_DEVICE_NOSPEAKER

  For detailed information on these additional values, please consult the BASS library documentation.

If the function call is successful, the audio hardware is initialized and ready for loading and playing audio. If unsuccessful, the audio hardware could not be initialized. In cases of failure, a developer might not choose to terminate the application altogether. They might instead allow the application to continue without sound support. The form of BASS_Init is as follows:

```
BOOL BASS_Init(
    int device,
    DWORD freq,
    DWORD flags,
    HWND win,
    GUID *clsid
);
```

- Once the audio hardware is initialized, the init method then proceeds to print human-readable information into a string detailing the hardware information of the currently selected audio device. This function collects device information using the BASS_GetDeviceInfo function. The audio manager stores this data in string member m_DeviceInfoString, which can be printed to a message box or an application log for diagnostic and debugging purposes if required.

   **NOTE.** On application exit, the audio manager uninitializes BASS with a call to BASS_Free, in the free method.

```
void cAudioManager::free()
{
    BASS_Free();
}
```

## 7.7.2   Playing Audio with the Audio Manager

The audio manager coded in this chapter offers two methods for playing active audio resources. "Active audio resources" means those audio resources—either sample or stream—that are currently loaded either because they are global resources or because the active scene demands their being loaded. The audio manager cannot play unloaded audio resources. These two methods are playFromResource, for playing an audio resource once without requiring repetition or without concern for when playback completes, and addAudioPlayer, for playing an audio resource according to the requirements of a derived instance of cAudioPlayer, which should also be notified when playback of the file completes. These two methods are now considered in turn, starting with playFromResource. Comments on the methods follow.

```
void cAudioManager::playFromResource(cAudioResource*
AudioResource)
{
    if(!AudioResource)
        return;

    BASS_ChannelPlay(AudioResource->m_ChannelData, false);
}
```

**NOTE**. The resource manager coded in an earlier chapter supported a findResourcebyID method for returning a pointer to the first resource matching the specified ID. This method can be used to retrieve a cAudioResource pointer to a specified audio resource.

The playFromResource method of cAudioManager plays the audio resource specified by the argument AudioResource. It plays the resource once, at the default volume and standard position and offers no notification when audio playback is completed. This argument calls the BASS_ChannelPlay function of the BASS library to start the playback of an audio resource. This function accepts a pointer to a valid BASS channel to play. It takes the following form:

```
BOOL BASS_ChannelPlay(
    DWORD handle,
    BOOL restart
);
```

The second function to initiate audio playback is the addAudioPlayer method of cAudioManager. This method accepts a pointer to a cAudioPlayer object and plays the specified resource according to the settings provided by the class. Its definition is given here, with comments following:

---

### ■ BASS_ChannelPlay Details

**DWORD handle**
Handle of the channel to play.

**BOOL restart**
True specifies that playback should restart if the channel is not already at the beginning. False does not restart the channel if the channel is already playing or if the channel is otherwise not at the beginning.

```
void cAudioManager::addAudioPlayer(cAudioPlayer *Player)
{
   m_Players.push_back(Player);
   BASS_ChannelPlay(Player->m_AudioResource->m_
ChannelData, false);
   Player->m_RepeatCount = 0;
}
```

## Comments

- The addAudioPlayer method accepts an argument, cAudioPlayer *Player. This argument will not actually *be* the cAudioPlayer abstract base class but a class derived from it and which therefore implements the cAudioPlayer interface. This instance will specify the audio resource to play and the number of repeats, and will also implement an event handler, which must be called when playback completes.

- This method begins by pushing a pointer to the player class onto its existing list of audio players, representing a list of all the audio resources currently being played. New audio players are added to the list and completed players will be removed on completion.

- This method resets the repeat count of the audio player, since a new playback has been initiated, and it also calls the BASS ChannelPlay function to begin playback.

## 7.7.3   Calling the Media Event on Audio Playback Completion

Developers call the addAudioPlayer method of cAudioManager when they require an audio resource to be played according to specific settings and to be notified when playback has completed, perhaps because a subsequent event trigger depends on the audio completing first. To detect when audio playback has completed and to notify any added audio player of this event, the audio manager uses the update method, which should be called once per frame of the game loop. This method is shown here, and comments follow:

```
void cAudioManager::update()
{
   std::list<cAudioPlayer*>::iterator list_it;

   for(list_it=m_Players.begin();list_it!=m_Players.
end();list_it++)
      {
            if(BASS_ChannelIsActive((*list_it)-
>m_AudioResource->m_ChannelData)==BASS_ACTIVE_STOPPED)
            {
```

```
                    if((*list_it)->m_RepeatCount>=(*list_it)-
>m_NumRepeats)
                    {
                            (*list_it)->onMediaComplete();
                            m_Players.erase(list_it);
                            return;
                    }
                    else
                    {
                            (*list_it)->m_RepeatCount++;
                            BASS_ChannelPlay((*list_it)-
>m_AudioResource->m_ChannelData, false);
                    }
            }
    }
}
```

## Comments

- The update method should be called once per frame of the game loop. On each call the function cycles through its list of added audio player instances. For each instance it calls the BASS function BASS_ChannelIsActive to determine whether the channel is currently playing. This function can return the following values:

BASS_ACTIVE_STOPPED

Playback has stopped or has not begun.

BASS_ACTIVE_PLAYING

The channel is currently playing.

BASS_ACTIVE_PAUSED

The channel is currently paused.

BASS_ACTIVE_STALLED

The channel is stalled. This can happen when a stream stalls.

- If the channel is stopped, the function then proceeds to determine whether the repeat count (the number of times the audio has repeated) exceeds or matches the number of repeats intended. If the file has played its specified number of repeats, then playback has completed. When this occurs, the onMediaComplete event is raised and the audio manager removes the current audio player from its list of audio players. If the current audio has not completed its repeat cycle, then the audio manager repeats the audio resource and increments the repeat count accordingly.

## ■ 7.8   Loading Audio Resources from XML Files

It was shown in an earlier chapter how the resource manager uses the loadFromXML-File method to load resources from an XML file on disk, and further how this method was amended when implementing the 2D render manager in order to load 2D graphics resources from XML definitions. This section picks up that thread of work. It does this by coding a loadResourceFromXML method in the audio manager class. This method is intended to be called by the resource manager loadFromXMLFile method, called at application startup to parse the resources used by a game. For each and every resource found, the resource manager determines the type of resource from its type property. When an audio resource is found in the XML file, the resource manager should call the loadResourceFromXML method of the audio manager, passing as an argument the TinyXML XML element representing the audio resource. From this element, the audio manager creates an audio resource object from the parsed XML data, and then returns a pointer to this newly created resource by way of the cResource pointer. In this way, the resource manager can be certain to maintain a list of all loaded resources and their metadata. The following sample XML lists two audio resources:

```
<resources>
<resource UID="4" type="audio" filename="Track1.mp3"
scenescope="0" audio type="stream"></resource>

<resource UID="5" type="audio" filename="SFX.ogg"
scenescope="0" audio_type="sample"></resource>
</resources>
```

The above structure of an XML audio resource governs how the loadResource-FromXML method of cAudioManager reads its data. The implementation of this method is shown here, and comments follow:

```
cResource* cAudioManager::loadResourceFromXML(TiXmlElemen
t *Element)
{
    if(Element)
    {
        cAudioResource* Resource = new cAudioResource();

        for(TiXmlAttribute* ElementAttrib = Element-
>FirstAttribute(); ElementAttrib; ElementAttrib =
ElementAttrib->Next())
        {
            std::string AttribName = ElementAttrib-
>Name();
            std::string AttribValue = ElementAttrib-
```

```
>Value();

            if(AttribName=="UID")
            {
                Resource->m_ResourceID =
atoi(AttribValue.c_str());
            }

            if(AttribName=="filename")
            {
                Resource->m_FileName = AttribValue;
            }

            if(AttribName=="scenescope")
            {
                Resource->m_Scope = atoi(AttribValue.c_
str());
            }

            if(AttribName=="audio_type")
            {
                    if(AttribValue=="sample")
                        Resource->m_AudioType = AUDIO_
TYPE_SAMPLE;
                    else
                        Resource->m_AudioType = AUDIO_
TYPE_STREAM;
            }
        }

        return Resource;
    }

    return NULL;
}
```

## Comments

- The loadResourceFromXML method accepts as an argument a valid TinyXML XML element representing an audio resource, passed by the resource manager at application startup during its loop phase while parsing all the resources in the resource XML.

- For the passed audio resource, the function reads its essential metadata. It reads in the resource UID, the file name of the audio resource, the scene scope, and the audio type (sample or stream). It populates a created audio resource class with this data and then returns a pointer to an instance of that class. The resource manager then adds this instance to its list of resources.

**EXERCISE 7.2**

List at least three other audio libraries that can be used as an alternative to BASS. Search the Internet, and then compare your answers with mine:

- SDL_mixer: http://www.libsdl.org/projects/SDL_mixer/
- FMOD®: http://www.fmod.org/
- OpenAL™: http://connect.creativelabs.com/openal/default.aspx

## ■ 7.9  Chapter Summary

Though the focus of this chapter has been narrowly on designing and implementing a basic audio playing framework for a game engine using the BASS audio library, it has nevertheless covered much ground. In addition to the 2D render manager created earlier, it demonstrates how an independent third-party software development kit such as BASS can be integrated into a class framework, and further how that framework exposes an interface that is not library dependent and thereby could continue to operate as before were the underlying software kit changed. This perhaps is one of the key points of this chapter. To summarize, this chapter began by designing an audio framework, which it divided into three core classes: cAudioResource, cAudioPlayer, and cAudioManager. The resource class represents the raw data of an audio resource—whether sample or stream—and the abstract base class audio player both stipulates how a specified resource is to be played and listens for playback to complete via the onMediaComplete method. Finally, the audio manager class cAudioManager is responsible for mediating between the two aforementioned classes, in addition to initializing audio hardware at application startup, and for listening to determine when media completes. The next chapter moves away from the world of audio and audio programming and into the realms of 3D and 3D programming.

# 8 Reading and Processing User Input

## Overview

After completing this chapter, you should:

- Understand the difference between polled and buffered input
- Be able to handle input from the PC keyboard, mouse, and joystick
- Know how to detect the number of input devices attached to the computer
- Understand how to use the OIS library to encapsulate input functionality into an input manager component

User input is a subject that has historically been much overlooked by developers when creating their engines. There exist a slew of game engines that do not support nearly as many input peripherals as they could if only the developers had made some simple adjustments to the implementation of their input system. Thus, the main focus of this chapter is user input, or more specifically, the handling and parsing of user input as received from a common input device, including the keyboard and mouse (the joystick will be left as an exercise for the reader). The term "input" or "user input" refers to the data a user provides at run time to a game engine by way of an input device, and the nature of that data—its structure—varies from device to device, as we shall see. In summary, the purpose of this chapter is to *encapsulate* a user input framework into a game engine input manager; that is, this chapter seeks to create a manager class that allows an engine to receive input information from input devices and to parse and process the information once received.

## ■ 8.1 Input Basics

Perhaps the simplest input system for an engine is one that handles input events directly. By the term "directly" it is meant that the engine queries (or *polls*) an input device for an input event such as checking to see whether a keyboard button is currently being pressed, and then—if the check returns positive—immediately triggers the appropriate in-game action without troubling itself any further. Such an engine for a platformer game might, for example, check for a spacebar press, and on finding that it is pressed will then cause the player character to jump into the air. However, this style of checking for input has two significant drawbacks for the programmer that typically makes it an unpopular choice for all but the simplest of games. First, as long as the engine has no layer of mediation between the input device (such as the keyboard) and the game action (such as jumping), the engine remains *device dependent*. That is, so long as the engine continually checks the keyboard for its current status and so long as it links that device directly to a specific action, it remains locked to that device. If the user unplugs the keyboard and replaces it with a joystick, the game will not receive input data unless it has handled for this in a fashion similar to that of the keyboard. Second, since a hard-coded query for the depressed status of a specific key on the keyboard is associated with a specific in-game action, the programmer must edit the source code and recompile the engine if the controls change. That is, they must change how the engine responds to a particular keypress. Furthermore, if the developer later decides that a mouse left-click should be handled the same as a keyboard spacebar press, then they must duplicate code to ensure the same set of instructions are run for each of the unique input events: the left-button click for the mouse and the button press for the keyboard. Handling input in this way can and frequently does become messy and inefficient for the programmer; thus, the need for an input manager. The input manager in this chapter will be specifically targeted to avoid the two principal pitfalls mentioned above. Before proceeding further with the design of the input manager, it will be useful to consider input generally as it pertains to both games and game engines.

The input workflow of a game typically passes through four stages, and in so doing avoids the problems posed by handling input directly: (1) The user provides input via an input device such as a button press on a keyboard or a button press on a mouse; (2) the engine detects that input has occurred and determines whether the input should be processed at all, for there might be times when input should be ignored such as during a loading screen; (3) if the passed input *is* to be processed, the engine should decode the data from the device and then immediately proceed to the next step; and (4) after decoding the data from the device, the game should then encode it into a proprietary, abstract, and device-independent form suitable for the engine and game. This means extracting the essential input data from the device and stripping it of its device-specific flavor. A game does this by using an *input map*. By using an input map, a game exposes its complete function set available to input (all available game actions) and then proceeds to define which input events correspond to which actions; more than one input event can correspond to the same action. For example, a first-person shooter game might expose the following action set to input for the player character: walk forward, walk backward, turn left, turn right, change weapon, and shoot the currently selected weapon. Each and every one of these game actions can be triggered by user input, and in order to determine which input event maps to which action, the game uses its input map. The input map for such a game might appear as follows:

| Walk forward | Keypress w, or Keypress Up, or Mouse Wheel Up |
| Walk backward | Keypress s, or Keypress Dn, or Mouse Wheel Dn |
| Turn left | Keypress a, or Keypress Lf, or Mouse Scroll Left |
| Turn right | Keypress d, or Keypress Rt, or Mouse Scroll Right |
| Change weapon | Keypress c or Mouse Right-Click |
| Shoot | Keypress SPACE or Mouse Left-Click |

**▌TABLE 8.1**   Sample Keyboard Map

By using the input map, a game can receive an input event, look up in its table whether the event is handled, and trigger the action if it is. By abstracting the input system into a map, a game allows the user the ability to redefine the control system on-the-fly by changing the input map. The issue of the input map, however, is not strictly speaking an engine issue since the handling of input events and their mapping to specific actions via an input map will vary from game to game, depending on the controls of that game. However, the concept of the input map and the benefits to be secured by abstracting input with mapping in mind will influence much of the design and implementation of the input framework of this chapter. The next section considers in more detail the design of the input manager that will be implemented in later sections of this chapter.

# ■  8.2    Designing the Input Manager

The input manager in its simplest form is responsible for receiving user input from peripheral input devices, including the mouse, keyboard, and joystick. A developer might add complexity to this manager by increasing the number of supported devices and by extending its feature set to fit with their design plan; this varies from game to game. The input manager implemented in this chapter, like the rest of the components in this book, will be general in its design so as to be suitable for the greatest number of games. The following points detail the core features to be created:

- The input manager will receive and parse input from three main gaming devices on the PC: keyboard, mouse, and joystick. The following table details the input events that can be triggered by each device.

- It is not enough for a game that the input manager should *only* read input from input devices, because input without response cannot lead to action. For this reason, the input manager must notify the game about the input it receives, as and when it receives it. It must notify a game when mouse moves, button presses, and joystick events occur so that it may react appropriately by mapping them to action in the

| Device | Events |
|--------|--------|
| **Keyboard** | OnKeyDown(key) |
| | The OnKeyDown event is triggered on each and every occasion a keyboard button (key) is pressed. |
| | OnKeyUp(key) |
| | The OnKeyUp event is triggered on each and every occasion a keyboard button (key) is released. |
| **Mouse** | OnMouseMove(PosX, PosY) |
| | OnMouseMove is triggered once for every movement of the mouse ball; that is, whenever the user moves the mouse. Thus, this event is likely to be triggered many times per second for every second of mouse movement. The PosX and PosY parameters of this event will refer either to the current *absolute* position of the mouse cursor in screen coordinates or to the *relative* X and Y movement of the mouse in screen coordinates since the last mouse move event was triggered. |
| | OnMousePressed(Button) |
| | A typical PC mouse has three buttons: left mouse button, right mouse button, and the mouse wheel at the center. The OnMousePressed event is raised on each and every occasion any one of these three buttons is pressed. The Button parameter is an integer ID referring to the button that was pressed at the time the event was raised; this might be: 1=Left, 2=Right, 3=Middle. The implementation details of handling mouse input will be discussed later in this chapter. |
| | OnMouseReleased(Button) |
| | OnMouseReleased is the complement to OnMousePressed. It is raised on each and every occasion any one of the three mouse buttons is released after a button press. The Button parameter is an integer ID referring to the button that was released at the time the event was raised; this might be: 1=Left, 2=Right, 3=Middle. |
| **Joystick** | ButtonPressed and ButtonReleased |
| | As with the keyboard and mouse pressed and released events, the joystick pressed and released events correspond to the pressing and releasing of buttons on the joystick device. The ID of the button refers to the exact button that was pressed, and the number of buttons supported by a joystick differs from joystick to joystick, usually ranging from two to six. |
| | axisMoved and POVMoved |
| | The axis and POV moved events are triggered when the joystick stick is moved. The stick can be pushed forward, pulled backward, moved from side to side, and rotated in circles. |

**❚ TABLE 8.2** Input Devices and Events

EXERCISE 8.1

Many input peripherals can map on to the standard keyboard and mouse input events. That is, many peripherals can transparently substitute for the keyboard and mouse. List two devices that map to keyboard input and two that map to mouse input.

**Answers**

**Keyboard:**

- Dance mats
- Mouth keyboards

**Mouse:**

- Pen and graphics tablets
- Touch screen displays

game. The input manager will notify the game by way of invoking the methods of custom-defined callback classes, which wait to receive notifications from the input manager. These classes will handle functions (such as onMouseDown), and these functions will be invoked appropriately by the input manager when input occurs.

## ■ 8.3   Preparing to Implement the Input Manager with OIS

An engine developer may set about implementing input in an engine in many ways and by using any one of the many libraries available for reading input from devices. There are no clear-cut right or wrong, black or white answers as to how such a manager ought to be implemented, and the decision a developer makes will typically reflect their experience, preference, and intentions as well as the needs of the game and the platform on which it will be released. As mentioned, this book limits itself to the PC platform with a keyboard, mouse, and joystick, but by *encapsulating* the input system into an input manager that provides the interface to all attached input devices, the developer is in no way limited to these three devices. The developer could choose to develop for the Wii console or the iPhone, and they can add support to their engine for their additional input devices by expanding the existing input manager.

This section begins the process of implementing the input manager for a Windows PC game engine. It will do this by first choosing an input library to use for reading input data from input devices. There are a range of input libraries available; for reading input from the keyboard and mouse a developer could choose to use the Windows API, but this choice would limit the developer to the Windows platform, at least for *that* implementation of the input manager. Instead, a developer could choose a third-party open source library that supports mouse, keyboard, and joystick input on a variety of platforms, including Windows, Mac, and the many—alas, often incompatible—flavors of Linux such as Ubuntu®, Mandriva, and Xandros™ to name but a few of the flavors gaining popularity in Linux gaming at the time of writing.

This chapter chooses the latter route of *not* relying on the Windows API for reading input from input devices, and opting to use a third-party library. It chooses the free library called OIS (Object-Oriented Input System), released under the zlib/libpng license and developed by Wrecked Games using C++ and Python.

> **NOTE.** More information on OIS, including community help and support, can be found at the Wrecked Games forum website at http://www.wreckedgames.com/forum/.

---

### ■ zlib/libpng License

The license is provided in the Appendices section at the back of this book, but given its shortness it is reproduced here for convenience.

The zlib/libpng License
Copyright © <year> <copyright holders>

This software is provided 'as-is', without any express or implied warranty. In no event will the authors be held liable for any damages arising from the use of this software.

Permission is granted to anyone to use this software for any purpose, including commercial applications, and to alter it and redistribute it freely, subject to the following restrictions:

1. The origin of this software must not be misrepresented; you must not claim that you wrote the original software. If you use this software in a product, an acknowledgment in the product documentation would be appreciated but is not required.

2. Altered source versions must be plainly marked as such, and must not be misrepresented as being the original software.

3. This notice may not be removed or altered from any source distribution.

## ■ 8.4   Downloading, Installing, and Configuring OIS

OIS-powered applications can support most versions of Microsoft Windows, including 95/98/NT/2000/XP/Vista/Windows 7, as well as many flavors of Linux. OIS applications can be *built* using many C++ compilers and IDEs, including Visual Studio and Code::Blocks with the GNU compiler. Unfortunately, the OIS documentation for developers is arguably limited and far from as comprehensive as some would like it to be, but this book aims to compensate for that by offering clear and concise instruction in the configuration and use of this library for the Windows PC. The following steps detail the process for downloading, installing, and configuring the OIS library:

Step 1.   Navigate a web browser to the OIS homepage at SourceForge at http://sourceforge.net/projects/wgois/. Click the **Download Now** button to download the latest installer. Once downloaded, run the installer to install the OIS SDK to the local computer. See Figure 8.1.

Step 2.   OIS installs the following folders, each containing a set of related files (see Figure 8.2):

**Docs**

Contains the SDK reference documentation.

**FIGURE 8.1**   Downloading OIS.

**┃ FIGURE 8.2**    Foldoro inotallod by OIS.

**extras**

Features the OIS SDK and examples for use with the *Python* language.

**includes**

Features the C++ include files for the OIS library. It should contain the following files:

- OIS.h
- OISConfig.h
- OISEffect.h
- OISEvents.h
- OISException.h
- OISForceFeedback.h
- OISInputManager.h
- OISInterface.h
- OISJoyStick.h

- OISKeyboard.h
- OISMouse.h
- OISObject.h
- OISPrereqs.h

**Libs**

Features the precompiled binaries of OIS for use with C++ application; used in combination with the C++ headers.

**License.rtf**

A rich text format version of the zlib/libpng license governing the use of the OIS SDK.

Step 3.   The OIS SDK for C++ and Windows consists of a collection of header and lib files; the exact version of the lib file to be used depends on the C++ IDE and compiler of the developer. Developers using Microsoft Visual Studio or Visual C++ Express should ensure their applications are built with the OIS.lib file in either the VC7 or VC8 subfolders of the lib folder. Visual C++ 2005 or above should use the file from VC8. Developers using Code::Blocks with the MinGW C++ compiler (its default compiler on Windows) should build their applications with the OIS.a file found in the MinGW_stlport subfolder of the lib folder. All C++ applications should include the OIS.h file found in the include folder, and all OIS-powered applications require at run time the presence of the OIS.dll file in either the application directory or the Windows system folder.

NOTE. The instructions for configuring headers and lib files in specific C++ IDEs can be found in an earlier chapter of this book, which considered both the Code::Blocks C++ IDE and the Microsoft Visual Studio IDE.

NOTE. Some libraries and DLL file names end in "_d" (e.g., OIS_d.dll). These files are debug versions and are intended to be used by programmers when debugging their applications. For the final release versions of their software, developers should use the alternative libraries and DLLs that omit the "_d" in their file names (e.g., OIS.dll).

## ■ 8.5   Building the Input Manager with the OIS Library

As with other chapters in this book, the implementation of the input manager can be considered either in isolation *or* as an extension of the work completed in previous chapters. The first stage of implementing an input manager as a C++ class (cInput-Manager) involves fleshing out a class declaration that will be defined throughout the remainder of this chapter. The following code provides the complete header file for the input manager class and its related components. As such, the purpose of some properties, methods, and features in this code might not be immediately clear to the reader at first glance, but its details are explained in what follows.

```
//Header file for input manager
#ifndef INPUTMANAGER_H_INCLUDED
#define INPUTMANAGER_H_INCLUDED

#include <OIS.h> //Include OIS library
#include <list>
#include "SDL2DRenderManager.h"
#include "EngineObject.h"
#include <map>

//-------------------------------------------------------


//Input Listener class to be used as a callback class for
cInputManager.
//Abstract base class.
//Handles input events.
class cInputListener : public cEngineObject
{
private:
protected:
public:
    //Input events
    virtual bool keyPressed( const OIS::KeyEvent &e )
{return true;};
    virtual bool keyReleased( const OIS::KeyEvent &e )
{return true;};

    //Mouse events
    virtual bool mouseMoved( const OIS::MouseEvent &e )
{return true;};
     virtual bool mousePressed( const OIS::MouseEvent &e,
OIS::MouseButtonID id ){return true;};
     virtual bool mouseReleased( const OIS::MouseEvent &e,
OIS::MouseButtonID id ){return true;};

    //Joystick events
    virtual bool povMoved( const OIS::JoyStickEvent &e,
int pov ){return true;};
```

```
   virtual bool axisMoved( const OIS::JoyStickEvent &e,
int axis ){return true;};
   virtual bool sliderMoved( const OIS::JoyStickEvent
&e, int sliderID ){return true;};
   virtual bool buttonPressed( const OIS::JoyStickEvent
&e, int button ){return true;};
   virtual bool buttonReleased( const OIS::JoyStickEvent
&e, int button ){return true;};
};

//---------------------------------------------------------

//Main input manager class
//Derives from three OIS classes and receives input
//from keyboard, mouse, and joystick
//Calls the listener class when events are received

class cInputManager : public OIS::KeyListener, public
OIS::MouseListener, public OIS::JoyStickListener,
public cEngineObject
{
private:
protected:
public:

   //Pointers of OIS input objects
   OIS::InputManager* m_OISInputManager;
   OIS::Keyboard* m_Keyboard;
   OIS::Mouse* m_Mouse;

   //List of input listeners
   std::list<cInputListener*> m_InputListeners;

   cInputManager();

   //Should be called at application startup to
initialize OIS library
   void init();

   //Should be called at application end to free OIS
library
   void free();

   //Input events
   bool keyPressed( const OIS::KeyEvent &e );
```

```
      bool keyReleased( const OIS::KeyEvent &e );

   //Mouse events
   bool mouseMoved( const OIS::MouseEvent &e );
    bool mousePressed( const OIS::MouseEvent &e,
OIS::MouseButtonID id );
    bool mouseReleased( const OIS::MouseEvent &e,
OIS::MouseButtonID id );

   //Joystick events
   bool povMoved( const OIS::JoyStickEvent &e, int pov );
    bool axisMoved( const OIS::JoyStickEvent &e, int axis
);
    bool sliderMoved( const OIS::JoyStickEvent &e, int
sliderID );
    bool buttonPressed( const OIS::JoyStickEvent &e, int
button );
    bool buttonReleased( const OIS::JoyStickEvent &e, int
button );

   //Should be called once per frame to update status of
input devices
   void update();

   void addListener(cInputListener* Listener);
};

#endif // INPUTMANAGER_H_INCLUDED

//----------------------------------------------------
```

## Comments

- Notice that the input manager header file includes the OIS header file: #include<OIS.h> with the #include preprocessor directive. It also includes the STL list header file for creating standard STL linked lists, used later.

- The header file includes two classes, as follows:

### cInputManager

cInputManager derives from several ancestor classes and encapsulates the engine input manager. It derives not only from base class cEngineObject, as do most other classes in the engine framework, but also from three OIS-specific classes, each dedicated to working with a unique input device: one with the keyboard, one with the mouse, and another with the joystick. As detailed in the design, the input manager is responsible both for reading input from input devices and for notifying a game when input occurs. The latter it achieves by maintaining a list of instances of the callback class cInputListener, whose methods it calls appropriately when input is received.

**CInputListener**

CInputListener is an *abstract base class* that works in collaboration with the input manager. Developers are not expected to instantiate this class directly, but are expected to use it as a base class from which to derive their own, overriding its methods with customized functionality suited to the needs of their game. Instances of this class are designed to be used as callback classes for the input manager, which maintains a list of them in its member m_InputListeners. Their methods— such as OnMouseDown, OnKeyPress, and OnMouseMove—are invoked by the input manager at run time, as the corresponding input event occurs. In this way, an application can handle each and every input event according to its own requirements and the input manager need not have knowledge of the implementation details of the game.

---

## ■ 8.6   Initializing OIS with the Input Manager

At application startup, a typical game expects the input manager to initialize the input library and devices, preparing them for use when necessary, just as it expects the graphics and audio managers to initialize all devices in their domain—the video card and the sound hardware, respectively. This initialization stage is a prerequisite for the successful continuation of application execution. This means that if initialization fails, the engine must either resort to secondary courses of action, such as resorting to an alternative library if one is available or trying to initialize the same library under different settings to see if success can be had, or else exit to the desktop with an error message describing the nature of the error encountered using the error manager. This is especially true in the case of input, because without the ability to input instructions into the game, the user cannot play.

The input manager initializes the OIS library and attached input devices in the init method. This method is intended to be called once at application startup. Its implementation is as follows, with comments afterward:

> **NOTE.** The input manager actually begins in its constructor. However, this function simply initializes its member properties to starting values and does not call upon the functions of the OIS library.

```
cInputManager::cInputManager()
{
    m_OISInputManager = NULL;
    m_Keyboard = NULL;
    m_Mouse = NULL;
}
```

```
void cInputManager::init()
{
   //Use try-catch block. OIS uses its own exceptions.
   try{

   //Get render manager. For this example, 2D render
manager.
   cSDL2DRenderManager* g_RenderManager = cSDL2DRenderMan
ager::GetSDL2DRenderManager();

   OIS::ParamList pl;
   std::ostringstream windowHndStr;
   size_t handle = (size_t)g_RenderManager->m_
WindowHandle;
   windowHndStr << handle;
   pl.insert(std::make_pair(std::string("WINDOW"),
windowHndStr.str()));

   m_OISInputManager = OIS::InputManager::createInputSyst
em( pl );

   //If there is a keyboard
   if(m_OISInputManager->numKeyBoards() > 0)
   {
       m_Keyboard = static_cast<OIS::Keyboard*>(m_
OISInputManager->createInputObject(OIS::OISKeyboard,
true));
       m_Keyboard->setEventCallback(this);
   }

   //If there is a mouse
   if(m_OISInputManager->numMice() > 0)
   {
       m_Mouse = static_cast<OIS::Mouse*>(m_
OISInputManager->createInputObject(OIS::OISMouse, true));
       m_Mouse->setEventCallback(this);
   }

   }catch(...){;}
}
```

## Comments

- The init method of class cInputManager begins by retrieving a pointer to a 2D
  SDL render manager, created in an earlier chapter, for the purposes of accessing

the window handle of the application. In short, the window handle is the object Windows uses to uniquely identify each application window on the desktop. It is not essential that an engine use its 2D render manager to retrieve this handle: It could have used its 3D manager or it could instead have striven to be more cross-platform by encapsulating the window handle object into a generic application handle. For example, they could have created a class to wrap the window handle, ensuring the implementation of that class differs between platforms. The point, however, is that OIS, as we shall see, requires a unique handle to identify the application, and this sample code has chosen to use the 2D SDL render manager to retrieve that handle. It is one of the many methods that could have been chosen.

- Once a pointer to the render manager is retrieved, the init method creates an OIS ParamList object (abbreviation of parameter list). This object represents a list of creation parameters that OIS will use when initializing input devices. Declaring this object creates an empty parameter list. Each element in the list takes the following form: <string, value>. The string is the name of the element and the value is the value associated with the name. The list in this method is used to store only one property—that of the window handle retrieved from the 2D render manager; in the form, <"WINDOW", Value>.

- The input system is initialized with the call to the OIS function OIS::InputM-anager::createInputSystem. This function accepts a parameter list as an argument and returns a pointer to an OIS::InputManager object, which represents a successfully initialized input system. Here we reach a point of unfortunate nomenclature. It should be noted that the OIS InputManager class *is distinct* from cInputManager. OIS::InputManager is an *OIS API-specific* object representing an input system, and cInputManager is the *engine-specific* input manager created in this chapter. cInputManager will maintain a pointer to the OIS::InputManager object, as it is returned from the function createInputSystem. In short, OIS::InputManager is an object returned by OIS representing the lifeline of the input system and is used *internally* by cInputManager; as long as the OIS::InputManager is initialized, an application can use input devices. cInputManager frees this object either as the application closes or as it is called to uninitialize. cInputManager *is* the input manager for the engine; when an engine component requires access to input, it interfaces with cInputManager and not OIS::InputManager.

- Once an input system is successfully initialized, the init method of cInputManager proceeds to determine the number of attached devices, checking to make sure there is at least one keyboard and one mouse connected to the system at the time of the function call. It does this with a call to the numKeyBoards and num-Mice methods of OIS::InputManager, respectively, each method returning the number of devices of the specified kind that are attached to the computer.

- For each device where there is at least *one* connected to the computer, the function creates an OIS:InputObject to represent the default device of that type such as the default keyboard or default mouse. In each case—keyboard, mouse, joystick, or other—the OIS::InputManager method of createInputObject is called to create an object representing the default specified device. The form of this method is as follows:

```
Object* createInputObject( Type iType, bool bufferMode
)
```

- As mentioned, the purpose of the createInputObject method of OIS::InputManager is to create an OIS object encapsulating the specified input device, either in buffered or nonbuffered mode according to the bufferMode parameter. Using this object and its properties and methods, a developer can manually retrieve input and diagnostic information from the input device. However, in buffered mode it should not be necessary to query a device manually. Instead, OIS will notify an application as input occurs for the

| Parameters | |
|---|---|
| Type iType | Indicates the device type for which an object should be created in order to receive input. This parameter can be one of the following for each call:<br><br>OISKeyboard<br>OISMouse<br>OISJoyStick<br>OISTablet |
| bool bufferMode | Specifies whether the input from the specified device should be received in buffered mode. If false (nonbuffered), the developer is expected to query the specified input device for its current status on each frame or whenever necessary. For keyboards, for example, the developer is expected to query the object for its input status to check whether a specified key is currently down or up. Likewise, for mice, a developer is expected to check—when appropriate—whether the mouse buttons are down or released, and to check the current position of the mouse cursor. If true (buffered), the developer does not need to manually check the input status of devices. Instead, OIS is requested to notify an application on each and every input event for the specified device. It is possible to configure one device as being in buffered mode and another as being in nonbuffered mode, but this book and chapter will use buffered mode only (true). |

**I TABLE 8.3**   OIS Device Parameters

buffered device. It does this through the OIS:MouseListener, OIS:KeyboardListener, and OIS:JoystickListener objects, from all of which the cInputManager object is derived. For this reason, the cInputManager object will be notified by OIS when input events occur. Notice that a "this" pointer to cInputManager is passed to the method setEventCallback of each device. This method requires a pointer to a valid callback class appropriate for the device, and cInputManager implements the required interfaces to receive notifications from all devices. Thus, the following methods of cInputManager will be called when input occurs:

**Keyboard Input:**

bool keyPressed( const OIS::KeyEvent &e );

bool keyReleased( const OIS::KeyEvent &e );

**Mouse Input:**

bool mouseMoved( const OIS::MouseEvent &e );

bool mousePressed( const OIS::MouseEvent &e, OIS::MouseButtonID id );

bool mouseReleased( const OIS::MouseEvent &e, OIS::MouseButtonID id );

**Joystick Input:**

bool povMoved( const OIS::JoyStickEvent &e, int pov );

bool axisMoved( const OIS::JoyStickEvent &e, int axis );

bool sliderMoved( const OIS::JoyStickEvent &e, int sliderID );

bool buttonPressed( const OIS::JoyStickEvent &e, int button );

bool buttonReleased( const OIS::JoyStickEvent &e, int button );

---

### ■ OIS Input Devices

The OIS library will notify applications when input events occur to any input device created in buffered mode but not to those in nonbuffered mode. In the latter case, an application should query the device manually for its input status as and when required. It can do this using any of the properties and methods of the device object returned from the createInputObject method. The returned object varies depending on the device created. OIS:Keyboard objects are returned for keyboard devices, OIS:Mouse objects for mouse devices, and OIS:Joystick objects for joystick devices. All of these classes derive from class OIS:Object. The class interface for both the keyboard and mouse are provided here since they are the most common input peripherals on a PC, together with a brief description of each of the core functions for that device and with any related enums and constants.

> **NOTE.** The following code for both the keyboard and mouse is part of the OIS library. It is not code from the engine created in this book.

## OIS Keyboard Device

The keyboard device is encapsulated by OIS in the OIS:Keyboard class. Its class declaration looks as follows, featuring methods with companion code comments:

```
class Keyboard : public Object
{
public:

    //------------------------------------------------
    //Enum structure. This data is passed to some of the
    functions
    //of the class and is used to specify a keyboard
    mode- unicode or ascii.
        enum TextTranslationMode
        {
            Off,
            Unicode,
            Ascii
        };

    //------------------------------------------------
    //An enum used to specify the shift, ctrl, or alt
    key.
        enum Modifier
        {
            Shift = 0x0000001,
            Ctrl  = 0x0000010,
            Alt   = 0x0000100
        };

    //------------------------------------------------
        //returns true if the specified key is pressed;
    else returns false.
```

```
    //The list of OIS key codes passed in the key
parameter can be found in
    //the Appendices section of this book.
    bool isKeyDown( KeyCode key );

    //Sets the event callback class to receive
keyboard input
    //notifications, if the device is in buffered mode.
    void setEventCallback( KeyListener *keyListener
);

    //Returns the associated key listener callback
class, if any
    KeyListener* getEventCallback();

    //Sets and gets the keyboard text translation mode
    //Can be any value from the TextTranslationMode
enum above
    void setTextTranslation( TextTranslationMode mode
);
    TextTranslationMode getTextTranslation();

    //Converts a key code to its string
representation.
    //e.g., KC_SEMICOLON converts to ';'
    const std::string& getAsString( KeyCode kc );

    //Returns true if the specified modifier key is
pressed.
    //The mod argument can be any value from the
Modifier enum above.
    bool isModifierDown( Modifier mod );
};
```

## OIS Mouse Device

The mouse device is encapsulated by OIS in the OIS:Mouse class. Its class declaration looks as follows, featuring methods with companion code comments:

```
//-----------------------------------------------
//Enum used by OIS to refer to mouse buttons.
```

```
enum MouseButtonID
{
   MB_Left = 0, MB_Right, MB_Middle,
   MB_Button3, MB_Button4, MB_Button5, MB_Button6,
MB_Button7
};

//OIS structure representing a snapshot of the mouse
status at any one time.
struct _OISExport MouseState : public Axis
{
//Returns true if the specified mouse button is
being held down
bool buttonDown( MouseButtonID button );

//The absolute cursor coordinates of the mouse
measured
//in pixels from the top left corner of the screen.
int abX, abY;

//The cursor coordinates relative to the last time
the mouse was queried.
//Measured in pixels from the last mouse position.
int relX, relY,;

//Clears the info structure.
void clear();
};

//---------------------------------------------
class Mouse : public Object
{
   //Sets the event callback class to be notified of
mouse events,
   //if the mouse is in buffered mode.
   void setEventCallback( MouseListener
*mouseListener );

   //Gets the current input status of the mouse.
   //This object represents a snapshot of the mouse
status for any given frame.
//When update is called, this object is populated
with information regarding
```

```
//the current status of the mouse, such as which
button is pressed and the
//position of the mouse cursor.
   //Object returned is an instance of MouseState,
defined above.
   const MouseState& getMouseState();
};
```

**NOTE.** The init method initializes the OIS input library and is intended to be called once at application startup. This method has a complementary method, free, which is intended to be called once at application close and uninitializes the OIS library when completed. Its implementation is as follows:

```
void cInputManager::free()
{
   if(m_OISInputManager)
   {
         m_OISInputManager->destroyInputSystem();
   }
}
```

## ■  8.7   Managing Input with the Input Manager

The work thus far on the input manager centers on reading data from input peripherals whenever user input occurs. It has been stated that with the OIS library, any given input device can be in either buffered or nonbuffered mode, and this mode determines how input is read from a device. In nonbuffered mode, a developer must manually query the state of an input device whenever input must be known, while in buffered mode an application can simply wait to be notified of input events as they happen. The input manager created here opts for the latter buffered mode and thus it exposes a series of callback functions that are invoked by OIS when input occurs. In these callback functions, the input manager will have the responsibility of passing on the notification and its data to all its registered listener classes to ensure the game is notified of input. However, if a developer were to compile and run this input manager class as it stands at present, they would likely be disappointed to find that OIS does not appear to send notifications of input events as promised. Instead, a press of the keys on the keyboard or a click of the mouse will seem to have no appreciable effect on OIS and the input manager; at least for the moment. This is because it is necessary to call the update method of an OIS device for *each* device on each and every frame; that is, on each and every iteration of the game loop in a single-threaded application. Calling update for each device on each frame helps keep the OIS input system "ticking over" so to speak, keeping OIS alive and updated with the latest input information for each active input device. Only when update is called to end a frame and when input occurs will OIS send input notifications to event listeners, such as cInputManager. The OIS update process is handled in the update method of cInputManager, which is intended to be called once per frame. The code for this method is provided here:

```
void cInputManager::update()
{
    //Updates mouse input status
     if(m_Mouse)
         m_Mouse->capture();

    //Updates keyboard input status
     if(m_Keyboard)
         m_Keyboard->capture();
}
```

**NOTE.** Compiling and running an application using this input manager (with the update method) will ensure OIS responds as intended, notifying the input manager of input events as they happen.

## ■ 8.8    Calling Input Listeners with cInputManager

The cInputManager class is updated once per frame with a call to its update method, which is responsible for capturing the latest snapshot of the input devices of OIS. When input events occur, the input manager class is notified by way of its input event handlers, of which there are several for a total of three unique devices: keyboard, mouse, and joystick. Once the input manager receives an input notification from OIS, it has a duty to pass on that notification to all the instances of cInputListener in its list of registered listeners. This list is maintained using an STL linked list class (member: m_InputListeners), and listeners can be added to this list by calling the addListener method of cInputManager. It is a short method, as shown here:

```
void cInputManager::addListener(cInputListener* Listener)
{
```

```
        m_InputListeners.push_back(Listener);
    }
```

As mentioned earlier, the cInputListener class is intended to be not instantiated directly but used as a base class from which derived classes can be made. These derived classes *override* the common input event handlers with custom functionality, just as cInputManager overrides those of the OIS classes from which it derives, and cInputManager notifies these classes of input events by calling those event handlers. The following methods of cInputManager are called by OIS when input events occur, and the input manager passes on these notifications to the listeners, as follows:

```
    //---------------------------------------------------------

    //Received when keys are pressed on the keyboard
    //KeyEvent param refers to the OIS key code of the
    pressed key
    bool cInputManager::keyPressed( const OIS::KeyEvent &e )
    {
        std::list<cInputListener*>::iterator list_it;

        for(list_it=m_InputListeners.begin();list_it!=m_
    InputListeners.end();list_it++)
                (*list_it)->keyPressed(e);

        return true;
    }

    //---------------------------------------------------------
    //Received when keys are released on the keyboard
    //KeyEvent param refers to the OIS key code of the
    released key

    bool cInputManager::keyReleased( const OIS::KeyEvent &e )
    {
        std::list<cInputListener*>::iterator list_it;

        for(list_it=m_InputListeners.begin();list_it!=m_
    InputListeners.end();list_it++)
                (*list_it)->keyReleased(e);

        return true;
    }

    //---------------------------------------------------------
```

```
//Received when the mouse is moved
//The MouseEvent parameter features the latest mouse
state information

bool cInputManager::mouseMoved( const OIS::MouseEvent &e )
{
    std::list<cInputListener*>::iterator list_it;

    for(list_it=m_InputListeners.begin();list_it!=m_
InputListeners.end();list_it++)
            (*list_it)->mouseMoved(e);

    return true;
}

//-------------------------------------------------------

//Received when a mouse button is pressed
//The MouseEvent parameter features the latest mouse
state information
bool cInputManager::mousePressed( const OIS::MouseEvent
&e, OIS::MouseButtonID id )
{
    std::list<cInputListener*>::iterator list_it;

    for(list_it=m_InputListeners.begin();list_it!=m_
InputListeners.end();list_it++)
            (*list_it)->mousePressed(e, id);

    return true;
}

//-------------------------------------------------------

//Received when a mouse button is released
//The MouseEvent parameter features the latest mouse
state information
bool cInputManager::mouseReleased( const OIS::MouseEvent
&e, OIS::MouseButtonID id )
{
    std::list<cInputListener*>::iterator list_it;

    for(list_it=m_InputListeners.begin();list_it!=m_
InputListeners.end();list_it++)
```

```
        (*list_it)->mouseReleased(e, id);

    return true;
}

//----------------------------------------------------
```

At this point, the reader might observe that the OIS key codes and OIS structures specific to the API are passed as function parameters in the preceding event functions, directly on to the input listeners used by the engine. This, they will likely say, is certainly contrary to the practice of abstraction, which seeks to remove the specifics of the API in a general and seamless engine framework. If, for example, the OIS library and its data types and structures are allowed to leak onto the engine components outside of the input manager, such as the render manager or the audio manager, then the engine is in danger of becoming dependent on the OIS library. Such a dependency as this would mean that sections of the engine outside the input manager must be adjusted and perhaps recoded if a decision were made to abandon OIS support or to change to an alternative input library.

This is true, and indeed is generally to be avoided. Typically, an engine will wrap an API into its own framework to avoid these dependencies. In so doing, they will develop their own engine-specific key codes and their own constants and enums, and these will map onto those of the API. While this book recommends the engine developer follow that practice in their own work, it has not been followed here in the preceding code samples, since doing so would have been neither informative nor useful. It would have been both tedious and unnecessary to have provided a list of custom-made constants and key codes that mapped on to those of OIS when it is most likely that the reader will have ignored these to develop their own values tailored to their projects and needs.

Having completed the implementation of the input manager, the next section will examine its usage in further detail.

## ■ 8.9   Using the Input Manager

Once development of the input manager is completed, it will become one part among the collection of other manager parts whose interaction together constitute the engine. The use of the input manager involves instantiating it, initializing it, and then using it to receive input before freeing it at application close. The full engine source code, including the input manager, can be found in the book's companion code at the book's website. What follows is a sample section of code that uses the input manager to receive keyboard input and displays a message box when a key is pressed:

```
//----------------------------------------------------

//Input listener class derived from cInputListener
class MyInputListener : public cInputListener
{
   private:
   protected:
   public:
         //Handle keypress event
         bool keyPressed(const OIS::KeyEvent &e)
         {
               //Show message box
               MessageBoxA(NULL,"Pressed a key","",MB_
OK);
               return true;
         }
};

//----------------------------------------------------

int _tmain(int argc, _TCHAR* argv[])
{
//Application start here

//(...) Create and initialize other managers: scene
managers and
//audio managers and render managers

//Create input manager
cInputManager Input;
Input.init();

//Create input listener
MyInputListener List;

//Add input listener
m_Input.addListener(&List);

//create game loop

   while (g_RenderManager->update())
   {
//On each frame, perform necessary work (...)
//Call input update
m_Input.update();
```

```
        }
    }
```

**Comments**

- This code sample begins by deriving an input listener from the engine standard cInputListener abstract base class. It overrides one event, a key pressed event, and will display a message box when that is called. An instance of this class will be added to the list of input listeners maintained by the input manager, which will call its events as input is received from OIS.

- Application execution begins in the main function. This function creates instances of the input manager and the input listener and uses the addListener function to pass a pointer of the instantiated listener to the input manager.

- The game loop is the main message pump of the application. On each frame, the input manager update method is called to instruct OIS to log the latest snapshot of the buffered input devices and to call event handlers if required.

## ■ 8.10   Chapter Summary

This chapter considered both the design and implementation of an input framework for the engine, an often overlooked aspect of game development. It encapsulated the free and cross-platform input SDK OIS into an input manager class that can read input from devices such as keyboards, mice, and joysticks, as well as call back event handlers when input occurs. In doing this, this chapter was able to lay the foundation for an input framework a little more sophisticated than one that just involves the checking of input devices for keypresses when necessary.

# 3D Render Manager with DirectX 10

## Overview

After completing this chapter, you should:

- Appreciate the intricacies of a 3D render manager in DirectX 10
- Understand how to configure DirectX and 3D graphics hardware
- Understand the DirectX rendering pipeline
- Be able to load textures and meshes
- Be able to create basic vertex and pixel shaders
- Appreciate the challenges a 3D render manager poses to the engine

This book has distinguished between 2D and 3D graphics by creating separate 2D and 3D render managers, the former implemented earlier in this book using the open source library SDL (Simple Directmedia Layer) and the latter to be implemented in this chapter with Microsoft DirectX 10 (August 2009 SDK). Before proceeding with this chapter, it would be wise to venture a definition of the term "3D graphics" because, while undefined, it remains undefended against the criticism some people might make in suggesting that there is no such thing as 3D graphics, since all graphics are projected onto the flat 2D surface of the monitor. Thus, they argue, all graphics must by definition be 2D. This is no doubt a valid point when one considers only the *medium* (the hardware) by which graphics are presented to the user at run time, for the monitor surface is indeed flat and two-dimensional. However, the distinction between 2D and 3D graphics has its basis *not* on the hardware by which such graphics are presented but on how the graphics behave and react at run time and on the different techniques developers must use when choosing to work with one or the other style. 2D and 3D graphics involve differing programming patterns for programmers and differing workflows for artists. A classic example of a 2D graphic is a rasterized image such as a Windows bitmap, composed from a grid of variegated pixels. Such an image can be cropped, recolored, stretched, and shrunk, but it cannot be rotated in all directions for the viewer to observe every side and angle because the image contains no detail concerning the areas not directly in view. It is not possible, for example, for a photographer to photograph a car and then to use Photoshop to rotate that same car about its local Y axis in order to see its other side hidden from view. True, the photographer could photograph the other side or could edit the original so as to appear like it was the other side. but in these cases the photographer is creating a separate image for the purpose and is not actually rotating the original image. These images—that is, images that cannot be rotated and explored as though they were 3D—therefore are *two* dimensional. This is because they exist in 2D space and contain no data on the third dimension. It should be noted that it is in no way part of my purpose to suggest that 2D images are in any way deficient or inferior to those of 3D, nor that 2D games are anything less than their 3D counterparts; it is simply to state that 2D images are so distinguished from those of 3D by the absence of data for the third dimension. 3D graphics, in contrast, can be rotated and *can* be viewed from all sides as though they were a real 3D object. Such 3D graphics are typically created by artists using 3D modeling software such as 3ds Max, Maya®, Softimage® XSI, Mudbox™, ZBrush®, and Blender. Once created, those 3D assets are typically imported by programmers into 3D game engines as *meshes* (or models) and are transformed (moved, rotated, scaled) according to the requirements of the game, using a 3D graphics library such as DirectX.

2D graphics are concerned with pixels, points, and motions in 2D Euclidean space (or screen space), such space being measured and defined by way of two axes—X (horizontal) and Y (vertical). Points in this space can be expressed mathematically as XY offsets from an *origin* point at (0,0). Using the (XY) coordinate notation, a coordinate of (5,5) would refer to a *point* that can be reached by starting at the origin, traveling by 5 along the horizontal X axis, and then traveling upward by 5 on the vertical Y axis. The exact location of the origin in 2D space as well as the scale and the units by which distance is measured have varied throughout the history of game development, and even now these details can and do vary from engine to engine. Some engines situate the 2D origin at the *top left* corner of the screen where positive X refers to rightward movement and positive Y refers to downward movement. Others put the origin at the bottom left where positive Y refers to upward movement. Some have measured distance in absolute pixels where an X value of 200 refers to 200 pixels, and thus a sprite positioned at (200,400) would appear at 200 pixels from the origin on the X axis and 400 pixels from the origin on the Y axis. And still others have used *relative* and *resolution-independent* screen coordinates. Here, the extents of the screen on each axis (XY) range from 0 to 1; for example, a value 0 on the X axis refers to the leftmost side of the screen, and a value of 1 refers to the rightmost side. 0.5 refers to the center of the screen. See Figures 9.1 and 9.2 for illustrations of relative and absolute coordinate systems. 3D coordinate systems in games, as we shall see, also have their variations, being divided generally between left-handed and right-handed coordinate systems. In 3D coordinate systems, the additional Z axis refers to depth. In left-handed coordinate systems, positive Z points away from the viewer into the distance. In right-handed coordinate systems, positive Z stretches backward, behind the viewer. Consider Figure 9.3, which illustrates the two forms of 3D coordinates. The remainder of this chapter focuses on 3D graphics and 3D coordinate systems, which situate the origin at (0,0,0) and have three axes: XYZ.

> **NOTE.** The main focus of this book is on game engines and not 3D mathematics for games. For this reason, it does not provide much in the way of explanation of the concepts of 3D mathematics but rather assumes the reader has some familiarity with them. However, in offering explanations and in providing code examples, every effort has been made to ensure as few assumptions as possible have been made regarding the reader and their background. It will, however, be helpful to have some familiarity with vectors, matrices, and transformations. If the reader is looking for guidance in this area, the author recommends the following book dedicated to this subject: *3D Math Primer for Graphics and Game Development* by Fletcher Dunn and Ian Parberry (ISBN: 1556229119).

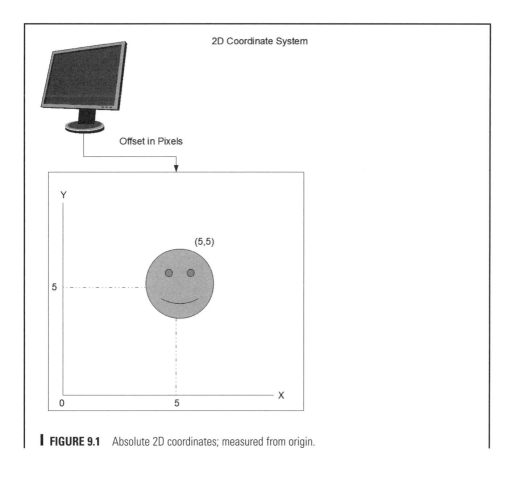

**FIGURE 9.1**   Absolute 2D coordinates; measured from origin.

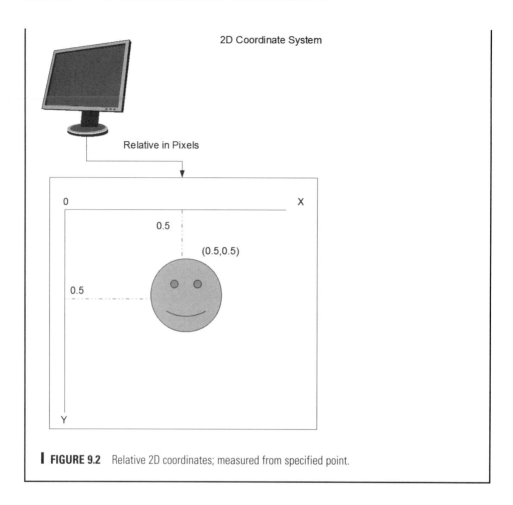

**FIGURE 9.2**  Relative 2D coordinates; measured from specified point.

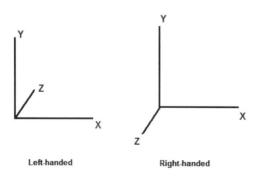

**FIGURE 9.3**  3D coordinate systems.

## ■ 9.1   Scenes, Objects, and Space in 3D

3D engines are intended to power 3D games—that is, games featuring real-time 3D graphics. Such engines are common in the contemporary games industry and include names such as the Unreal Engine™, the Jupiter Extended engine, and the Torque 3D engine. The key feature of a 3D engine with regard to the graphics it produces is that it works by producing 3D *scenes* from 3D *objects* arranged in 3D *space*. This introduces us to three related terms—scenes, objects, and space—each of which will now be considered, starting with the 3D object.

### 9.1.1   3D Objects

The 2D render manager chapter demonstrated that in 2D a graphical entity in a game is most often a rectangle of pixels (or a *surface*): a player character, background object, weapon, or sprite. Though the appearance of these entities differs as much from game to game as they do from one another, each has the quality of being a collection of pixels both in memory and on-screen. It has been stated that 3D objects differ from this in that they can be rotated and viewed from many sides and angles and under many perspectives and fields of view. A cube object can at one time be viewed from one side and then later, at the user's convenience, can be rotated and viewed from another. The fundamental difference between the 2D and 3D entity is that the former exists in 2D space while the latter exists in 3D space, and thus the addition of a third dimension requires the 3D object to be structured differently and parametrically.

The standard 3D object consists of vertices, edges, and faces. The vertex (plural: vertices) refers to a point in 3D space, and a vertex in isolation is nothing but a point, just as vertices in isolation are nothing but points. See Figure 9.4.

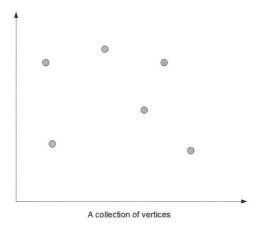

A collection of vertices

**| FIGURE 9.4**   Vertices.

Two vertices connected by a line form a line segment. Each of the two vertices is referred to as an end point, and the line is called an *edge*. See Figure 9.5.

Three vertices that are connected by edges forming an enclosed space create a *face* (or *polygon*). See Figure 9.6.

Faces can be arranged together adjacently in specific configurations, each face angling this way or that, to build more complex objects with real-world likenesses such as cars, people, buildings, dragons, etc. These complex models are called *topologies*, or *meshes* (or *3D objects*). See Figure 9.7.

Initially, it might seem improbable to some that organic-looking objects with smooth curvature (like balls, rocks, eggs, and faces) could be modeled from hard-edged polygons

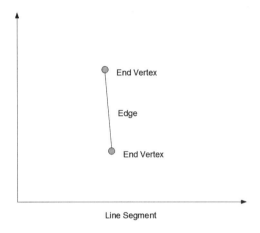

**| FIGURE 9.5**    Line segment.

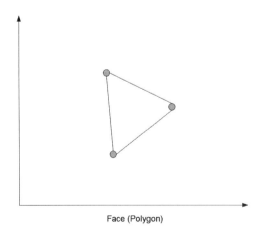

**| FIGURE 9.6**    Faces.

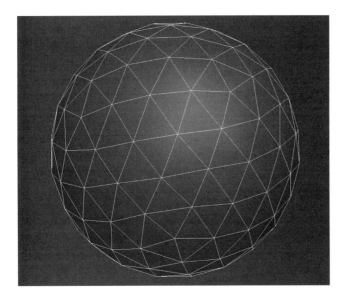

**FIGURE 9.7**   A sphere mesh object.

composed from vertices and edges. However, it is possible to approximate the curvature found in the natural world in a video game by increasing the density of the polygons of the mesh. Detail can be added to a mesh by increasing the number of polygons used to define its curves. Increasing the number of polygons in this way is referred to as "increasing the resolution (res) of a mesh." The greater its resolution, the greater its realism but the heavier is the performance penalty incurred by the computer for having to process so many polygons. Thus, the developer of 3D games must seek to find an acceptable balance between *detail* and *performance*; one often comes at the expense of the other.

However, though the *form* or *substance* of a 3D object is composed of vertices, edges, and faces, there is more to a 3D object than simply its form. A set of vertices might be arranged into the configuration of a ball so as to produce a ball mesh, but this ball has a "skin" whose appearance is independent of the structure of the object. The skin could be dull or shiny, reflective or nonreflective, and could appear to be of leather or of wood. All of these properties could change and yet the structure of the object remain intact. Thus, in addition to structure as defined by vertices, edges, and faces, an object has a skin, referred to as its *material*. The material defines how the skin of an object reacts under light and whether it should appear smooth or bumpy. Furthermore, it defines how the surface of an object appears, and it does this by using a *texture*. A texture is a 2D image (bitmap) that is wrapped around the 3D object in order to stylize it with an appearance. For example, a brick image could be used to make the ball appear as though it were made from brick, or a wood image could make it appear as though it were made from wood. The exact technique by which a 2D texture is wrapped onto a 3D object is typically determined by a graphics artist using *mapping coordinates*. These are often specified using 3D rendering software, which defines them on a per vertex basis. That is, an artist can bind a section of a 2D image to a specific vertex or group of vertices on a mesh to ensure the texture is stretched and pulled appropriately across the mesh surface.

In short, a 3D object is built from vertices, edges, and faces, and has a skin whose appearance can be customized using a material.

## 9.1.2   3D Coordinate Systems

The 3D objects of a game are situated in a 3D Euclidean coordinate system, composed from three axes XYZ, which intersect at one point to form the origin at (0,0,0). The positions of objects in a coordinate system are measured as offsets from the origin. These are the fundamental features of a 3D coordinate system, and 3D games make use of this system for creating and measuring several kinds of independent but related spaces: object (local) space, world space, view space, and projection space and screen space.

### Object Space

Object space is also known as local space and refers to a self-contained 3D coordinate system that holds only for a single object. Thus, there are as many object spaces as there are objects in a single 3D scene, one object space per object. It is assumed that the pivot center or center of mass of an object represents the origin of object space, and all other parts of the object (its vertices, edges, and faces) have a position relative to that origin. For example, the center of mass of a person might be around the hip region of their body, and thus their hands, arms, eyes, nose, and other body parts each have their own position and orientation relative to that origin. Furthermore, their relative positions in object space remain intact no matter where in the *world* the person is standing at any time, so long as their body parts maintain the same relation to each other. See Figure 9.8.

### World Space

Object space refers to a 3D coordinate system used for measuring and expressing the relationship of an object's parts to all other parts of the same object. World space, in contrast, is a unified coordinate system that throws all objects of the scene into one commensurable space, allowing the positions of all objects to be measured relative to a single origin and to each other. If a room were considered to represent the entirety of a world space (that of a room) whose origin was at its center, then all objects and people in that room would inherit a position relative to that origin. This would allow distances between objects to be measured and orientations to be compared. See Figure 9.9.

**▮ FIGURE 9.8**   Object space.

**▮ FIGURE 9.9**   World space.

## View and Projection Space

If none of the objects in a 3D coordinate system had the power of vision and if it were not necessary to show 3D scenes to a camera or an eye, then neither view space nor projection space would be necessary to a game developer. But it is *because* 3D scenes are *seen* from a specific vantage point and because this involves issues of depth and perspective that such spaces are required for presenting 3D scenes to the screen in ways that look both believable and meaningful. It is the duty of view space to translate the objects of a world space coordinate system into a new 3D coordinate system that relates the objective positions of world space to a camera point (vantage point) that is viewing that world. In view space, the Z axis is always defined as the direction in which the camera is pointing, the Y axis is always pointing upward and outward from the top of the camera, and the X axis always stretches outward from the right-hand side of the camera. Thus, the position and orientation of the camera as it points into world space transforms that space according to what it sees, and the result is view space. View space, however, is a 3D coordinate system and the screen is a flat 2D surface onto which 3D space is projected. Thus it is the role of projection space to transform view space into a space that maps correctly to the screen. Once transformed by the projection space to the monitor, the 3D scene takes on many of the characteristics of a standard 2D image in that it exists in screen space. See Figure 9.10.

### 9.1.3   3D Scenes

A 3D object is composed of vertices, edges, polygons, and materials, and can exist in several kinds of 3D spaces. However, all objects existing together in a single world space constitute a *3D scene*. A 3D scene therefore refers to a single unified coordinate space containing objects, lights, effects, sounds, and other objects that are part of that space.

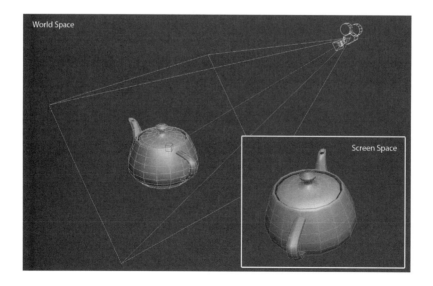

**FIGURE 9.10**   View and projection space.

## ■ 9.2   Designing the 3D Render Manager

The main focus of this chapter is on both the design and implementation of a DirectX 3D render manager component for a game engine, and this component is the 3D counterpart of the 2D render manager coded earlier in this book using the SDL library. As such, it shares a similar role to the 2D render manager, although its 3D nature requires some additional responsibilities. The following subsections outline the design considerations pertaining to the 3D render manager:

- First, the 3D render manager will be implemented using the Microsoft DirectX 10 SDK. Such a choice was not a foregone conclusion, as some might be tempted to think. Popular alternatives are available. OpenGL (Open Graphics Library) is a widely used and well-established open source and cross-platform graphics library intended for rendering 3D graphics. OpenGL applications can support Windows, Mac, Linux, and other operating systems, and the OpenGL SDK itself offers its own high-level shader language for creating pixel and vertex shaders and can be called from C++ applications. However, given the wider prevalence of DirectX in the established development houses making games for the PC, the OpenGL library was dropped in favor of DirectX. However, even when the choice to use DirectX has been made by a developer, it does not necessarily follow that they would want to use DirectX 10 or 11, the latest versions. Though versions 10 and 11 offer the game developer an exciting set of features for achieving some spectacular real-time 3D effects, both fail to officially support the Windows XP platform whose user base includes a sizable population of gamers. For compatibility reasons therefore, many developers (particularly independent developers) continue to opt for DirectX 9 in order to expose their games to the widest PC audience possible with DirectX. However, given that many books and tutorials detail the specifics of DirectX 9, this book has chosen DirectX 10 for implementing the render manager. It should be noted that this chapter cannot be considered a complete guide to DirectX 10. Far from it: DirectX and its feature set is considered only insofar as it pertains to the 3D render manager of an engine. However, enough DirectX material is covered here to make this chapter a short and concise springboard to getting started with DirectX for those readers not already familiar with it.

- The 3D render manager for the game engine will assume the following duties and responsibilities:

  1. The render manager is responsible for initializing and freeing the graphics hardware (video card) attached to the local computer. That is, it is responsible for creating an application window, for setting the video mode to the specified resolution, and for cleanly freeing the hardware when required by releasing any data in

graphics memory. The SDL library was instrumental for achieving this with the 2D render manager, and DirectX 10 will be instrumental in achieving this with the 3D manager.

2. The render manager will also support the loading, processing, and unloading of three distinct graphics resources: textures, sprites, and meshes. Textures refer to 2D rasterized images loaded from files such as BMPs, JPGs, and PNGs. Sprites refer to 2D images rendered to the display at run time; these are often used for information panels, health bars, GUI elements, and effects. Finally, meshes refer to the 3D geometry—vertices, edges, and faces—loaded from files into graphics memory for inclusion into 3D scenes during game execution. Please recall that a 3D scene consists of one or more 3D objects existing together in a unified 3D world space where each object has its own position, scale, and orientation.

3. The render manager is further responsible for performing all coordinate system transformations necessary for presenting 3D scenes correctly to the display: transforming *object space* into *world space*, then world space into *view space*, view space into *projection space*, and projection space into *screen space*. The render manager will seek wherever possible to manage this process transparently so as to allow callers of the manager to pass only measurements in world space, after which it will perform the necessary transformations. This is to ensure both that the manager component does not become dependent on the specifics of DirectX and that the user of the manager class as an engine component does not need knowledge of either the DirectX API or of the methods and processes governing the transformations of 3D space.

4. The render manager has the duty of maintaining the application render pump, which keeps the application ticking over frame by frame. This involves the render manager updating both itself and any other renderable objects once per frame.

5. The render manager component will be encapsulated into a class cDirectXRender-Manager. However, this design has stated the necessity for the render manager to handle textures, sprites, and meshes, and the positing of these entities requires the creation of classes to encapsulate them. These classes will work alongside the render manager and are, respectively: cDirectXTexture, cSprites, and cDirectXMesh.

## ■  9.3   Downloading, Installing, and Configuring the DirectX SDK

The outline of the work to come when implementing the render manager has been stated in the previous section. To summarize, the render manager must: (1) create an application window and both initialize and free the video hardware, (2) load, unload, and process graphics resources including textures, sprites, and meshes, (3) perform all 3D space transformations necessary for presenting scenes to the display, (4) update all graphics resources once per frame for each and every frame. And (5): All of the aforementioned functionality must be encapsulated in a total of no more than four C++ classes: cDirectXRenderManager, cDirectXTexture, cSprites, and cDirectXMesh. These classes will be implemented using the Microsoft DirectX 10 SDK. The following steps detail how to download, install, and configure this SDK for use in Microsoft Visual Studio.

## 9.3.1 Downloading and Installing DirectX 10

Step 1. Navigate a web browser to the following Microsoft DirectX download URL:

http://www.microsoft.com/downloads/details.aspx?FamilyID=24A541D6-0486-4453-8641-1EEE9E21B282&displaylang=en.

Step 2. Once there, click the **Download** button to download the DirectX SDK to the local computer. Then run the downloaded installer. See Figure 9.11.

Step 3. Once installed, the DirectX installer will have created the following files and folders at the installation path, and almost all folders contain additional subfolders: Developer Runtime, Documentation, Extras, Include, Lib, Redist,

**FIGURE 9.11** Downloading DirectX.

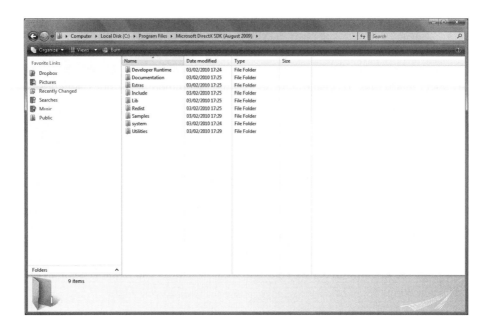

**I FIGURE 9.12**    Folders installed by DirectX.

Samples, System, and Utilities. Descriptions of these folders follow. See Figure 9.12.

**Developer Runtime**

The DirectX Developer Runtime refers to a set of DLL files representing the entirety of the DirectX library on which all DirectX applications depend at *run time* on any system in order to run as intended. The Developer Runtime folders contain these files, and developers should ensure they, and specifically those versions of the files, are present on each and every system on which their DirectX application runs. The files should be in either the application folder or the Windows\System folder while the application is running to ensure it executes successfully. Most developers, however, usually ship their product with the appropriate Microsoft DirectX Runtime installer, which automatically installs only the necessary runtime files (not the development libraries) to a user's computer. The end user run-time files can be found at the following URL:

http://www.microsoft.com/downloads/details.aspx?FamilyID=04ac064b-00d1-474e-b7b1-442d8712d553&displaylang=en.

The Runtime DLLs are:

d3d9d.dll
D3D10Ref.DLL

D3D10SDKLayers.DLL
D3D11Ref.dll
D3D11SDKLayers.dll
D3DCSXd_42.dll
d3dref9.dll
d3dx9d_33.dll
D3dx9d_42.dll
D3DX10d_42.dll
D3DX11d_42.dll
X3DAudioD1_6.dll
XactEngineA3_5.dll
XactEngineD3_5.dll
XAPOFXD1_3.dll
XaudioD2_5.dll

**Documentation**
The Documentation folder features all of the latest and official DirectX documentation and programmer reference material. This documentation details
not only all DirectX functions, classes, and methods but also offers both guidance in getting started with DirectX and explanations of some of the tutorial
C++ projects provided with the SDK.

**Extras**
This folder features only the DirectSound run-time DLL (dsound.dll), an
essential run-time library for all DirectSound-powered projects. This book uses
BASS audio for audio playback rather than DirectSound, and for this reason,
this file should not be required when developing or distributing any of the components coded in this book.

**Include**
This folder contains all the C++ header files necessary for building DirectX
projects in C++. Developers intending to create DirectX applications in this
language (as we will be in this book) should ensure the DirectX Include
folder is added to their list of include paths, as specified using a C++ IDE
(in this case, Visual Studio). Typically, however, the DirectX SDK installer
will automatically configure Visual Studio for building DirectX applications
during installation.

**Lib**
The Lib folder contains all the C++ binary libraries necessary for compiling
DirectX projects against the header files. As with the header file folder, developers
should ensure the Lib folder of the SDK is added to the Lib path in their C++

IDE. However, the DirectX SDK installer should automatically configure any existing installations of Visual Studio for building DirectX applications.

### Redist

The Redist folder contains the installation file for the DirectX Runtime Install, which installs the requisite DirectX run-time files to the computer to allow for the execution of DirectX-powered applications. Developers looking to distribute their DirectX applications to end users should ship them with this installer.

### Samples

Once the DirectX SDK has been installed, the Samples folder is likely to be one of the first places a developer new to DirectX will want to visit, since a collection of DirectX sample applications complete with C++ source code and Visual Studio project files, open for examination can be found here. Alongside the DirectX documentation, the sample files offer detailed guidance and instruction in the use of DirectX. See Figure 9.13 and 9.14.

**I FIGURE 9.13**   Sample application.

**FIGURE 9.14**   DirectX sample browser.

### System
The system folder contains a DirectX uninstall application to remove this version of the SDK from the computer.

### Utilities
The Utilities folder contains a wealth of helpful tools, applications, and libraries to enhance the integration of DirectX with third-party applications. One notable plug-in for third-party software is the DirectX Texture file format plug-in for Adobe Photoshop. Photoshop is an image-editing application for images in common and popular formats such as JPEG, TGA, PNG, and more. Though DirectX supports the loading of those files, it also offers support for its own proprietary image formats (such as DDS); formats which Photoshop does not natively support. However, the DirectX Photoshop plug-in can be installed to Photoshop to extend its support to those DirectX image files, allowing Photoshop users the ability to edit DirectX proprietary images using the standard File | Open command and standard Photoshop tools, as though the DirectX files were any other image file. To install this plug-in, Photoshop users should copy the plug-in file from the DirectX SDK path Utilities\bin\plugins\Photoshop\x86 and then paste this into the Photoshop plug-in folder: Photoshop\Plug-ins\File Formats. Once copied, restart Photoshop for the new plug-in to take effect.

## 9.3.2    Configuring DirectX and Building DirectX Applications

The DirectX SDK installer should automatically configure any existing installation of Visual Studio as appropriate on the local computer for building C++ DirectX applications. For this reason, it should not be necessary for a developer to manually add the DirectX Include and Lib folders to the Include and Lib paths in the IDE. Instead, developers should simply be able to open a valid and correct DirectX project and then compile and run. This can be tested by opening one of the tutorial DirectX projects provided by the SDK in the Samples folder. The tutorial projects can be found in the folder Samples\C++\Direct3D10\Tutorials. The first of these tutorial projects to use the DirectX library is Tutorial01 (not tutorial00). It is recommended but not essential that readers compile and run all of the tutorials and then glance through their source code to get a feel for the library before proceeding.

> NOTE. Most DirectX applications include the header files d3d10.h and d3dx10.h and link to the libraries d3d10.lib and d3dx10.lib.

## ■    9.4    Starting to Build the 3D Render Manager with DirectX 10

The DirectX render manager is responsible for initializing the graphics hardware, rendering graphics to the display, and loading and unloading graphics resources such as textures, sprites, and meshes. The 3D render manager component will be encapsulated into a C++ standard class named cDirectXRenderManager. It has been stated that this class necessitates the creation of three other classes, each representing a unique resource type: cDirectXTexture for representing texture resources, cSprites for representing a collection of sprite resources, and cDirectXMesh for representing a mesh resource—complete with vertices, edges, faces, and textures. It should be remembered that a *3D* scene is composed of a collection of mesh objects existing in a unified world space, and it will be the duty of the render manager to render these 3D scenes from a specified camera position and according to a specified camera lens (FOV). To begin, the complete header file and declarations for the classes to be created are provided. It will be the work of this chapter to put flesh on this skeleton by implementing the methods and functions contained in the header. Providing the header declaration ahead of time in this way can be useful for outlining the work to come and for structuring both how that work ought to proceed and the order in which each task is to be completed. However, it can mean that some properties and features of the code will not be immediately obvious to the reader viewing the code for first time, but all functions and methods contained in the header will be implemented and explained in turn as the chapter proceeds.

```
//Define safe release macro. Used to cleanly release
valid COM interfaces.
```

```
//DirectX uses COM to provide interfaces to its internal
classes.
//For this reason it will be essential to both create and
release COM interfaces.
#ifndef SAFE_RELEASE
#define SAFE_RELEASE(x) \
    if(x != NULL)         \
    {                     \
       x->Release();    \
       x = NULL;          \
    }
#endif

#ifndef DIRECTXRENDERMANAGER_H_INCLUDED
#define DIRECTXRENDERMANAGER_H_INCLUDED

#define MAX_SPRITES 4096

//Include engine base classes and requisites
#include "3DRenderManager.h"
#include "EngineObject.h"

//Include DirectX headers
#include <d3d10.h>
#include <d3dx10.h>

//Include STL string and list classes
#include <string>
#include <list>

//------------------------------------------------------

//Define a structure representing a single vertex on a
mesh.
//This mesh contains position (XYZ) and a color.
//A mesh will therefore represent a collection of
connected vertices
//This class will be used by cDirectXMesh for rendering
meshes

struct vertex
{
    D3DXVECTOR3 Pos;
    D3DXVECTOR4 Color;
};
```

```
//----------------------------------------------------------

//cDirectXTexture represents a 2D texture resource in
graphics memory
//Such a 2D image can be drawn to the screen in 2D screen
space as a spritc
//Or mapped onto a 3D object as a texture via texture
coordinates

class cDirectXTexture : public cEngineObject
{
private:
protected:
public:
   ID3D10Resource* m_TextureResource;
   ID3D10Texture2D* m_TextureInterface;
   D3DX10_IMAGE_INFO m_FileInfo;
   D3D10_TEXTURE2D_DESC m_Texture_Desc;
   bool m_bLoaded;
   bool m_Owned;

   cDirectXTexture();
   virtual bool loadFromFile(std..wstring fileName);
   virtual void free();
   void blitRectToBackBuffer(RECT Rct, int X, int Y);
};

//----------------------------------------------------------

//cSprites represents a collection of sprite objects in a
scene.
//An application may use many textures, one for each
sprite, or a single
//texture for many sprites. In either case, an
application typically
//deals with many sprites. This class allows 2D textures
to be rendered to the
//display as a sprite.

class  cSprites : public cEngineObject
{
private:
protected:
   D3DX10_SPRITE m_SpriteInfo[MAX_SPRITES];
   D3DXVECTOR2 m_Positions[MAX_SPRITES];
```

```
    D3DXVECTOR2 m_Scales[MAX_SPRITES];
    cDirectXTexture m_Textures[MAX_SPRITES];
    ID3DX10Sprite *m_SpriteInterface;

public:
    unsigned int m_NumSprites;

    cSprites();

    void setUVCoords(int ID, float Left, float Top, float
Width, float Height);
    void setColour(int ID, float R, float G, float B,
float A=1.0f);
    void setPos(int ID, float X, float Y);
    void setScale(int ID, float X, float Y);
    bool loadFromFile(int ID, std::wstring fileName);
    void free();

    void update();
};

//----------------------------------------------------------

//The DirectX mesh class represents a collection of
faces, each of which is
//an enclosed space of vertices connected by edges. This
class will use the
//vertex structure to maintain an array of vertices
constituting the mesh.

class cDirectXMesh : public cEngineObject
{
private:
protected:
public:
    ID3D10Effect* m_Effect;
    ID3D10EffectTechnique* m_Technique;
    ID3DX10Mesh* m_Mesh;
    ID3D10InputLayout* m_VertexLayout;
    ID3D10EffectMatrixVariable* m_pWorldVariable;
    ID3D10EffectMatrixVariable* m_pViewVariable;
    ID3D10EffectMatrixVariable* m_pProjectionVariable;
    D3DXMATRIX m_World;
    D3DXMATRIX m_View;
    D3DXMATRIX m_Projection;
```

```cpp
    cDirectXMesh();
    void create();
    void update();
};

//-------------------------------------------------------

//The render manager class. Responsible for managing the
graphics pipeline.

class cDirectXRenderManager : public c3DRenderManager
{
private:
protected:
        cDirectXRenderManager();
        static cDirectXRenderManager m_DirectXManager;

public:
        D3D10_DRIVER_TYPE        m_driverType;
        ID3D10Device*            m_pd3dDevice;
        IDXGISwapChain*          m_pSwapChain;
        ID3D10RenderTargetView* m_pRenderTargetView;
        D3D10_TEXTURE2D_DESC m_BackBufferInfo;
        HINSTANCE m_hInst;
        HWND m_hWnd;
        D3D10_VIEWPORT m_VP;

        cSprites m_Sprites;

        std::list<cDirectXTexture*> m_Textures;
        std::list<cDirectXMesh*> m_Mesh;

    ~cDirectXRenderManager();
     bool init(HINSTANCE hInstance, unsigned int Width,
unsigned int Height, bool fullScreen, char* WindowTitle);
        void free();
        bool update();

        static cDirectXRenderManager*
GetDirectXRenderManager();
};

#endif // DIRECTXRENDERMANAGER_H_INCLUDED

//-------------------------------------------------------
```

## Comments

- The above header file includes the complete class declarations for the 3D render manager and its three attendant classes. This header file and its source, to be created, should be seen as extensions of the work completed in earlier chapters of this book, each chapter building on the work of the one before to piece together an engine step by step.

- Notice that this header file includes the headers for the DirectX library files: d3d10.h and d3dx10.h. The former header is for the core of the DirectX library and the latter is for a set of helper functions designed to work alongside that core. Notice also that the header includes two STL headers for lists and string classes, both of which will be used throughout this chapter for handling lists of objects and Unicode strings, respectively.

- This header includes the common and popular SAFE_RELEASE macro for cleanly releasing COM interfaces. The standard method for freeing a COM interface is the Release method. This macro represents a chunk of code that will be executed whenever the macro name is encountered by the compiler elsewhere in the source. The code first checks the validity of a specified COM interface, then calls Release, and finally assigns a null pointer to the released interface. The macro might be called as any other function, as follows:

```
SAFE_RELEASE(MyComInterface);
```

- The cDirectXTexture texture class encapsulates a 2D rectangle of pixels in graphics memory, typically pixels whose colors are loaded from any valid and supported image file. Unlike a mesh, the 2D texture class has only width and height, and no depth. Thus, a texture is not truly a 3D entity. But it is used for 3D purposes, particularly as a texture that is wrapped or wallpapered onto a 3D mesh in order to color its skin. This class supports the loadFromFile method to load a texture from a file, and contains several members that will be examined in more detail later in this book. These include:

**ID3D10Resource* m_TextureResource**

Represents the raw pixel data of a texture in graphics memory.

**ID3D10Texture2D* m_TextureInterface**

Represents the COM interface of a texture through which properties can be retrieved and methods can be called.

**D3DX10_IMAGE_INFO m_FileInfo**

**D3D10_TEXTURE2D_DESC m_Texture_Desc**

DirectX structures containing information relating to the loaded texture and the file from which it was loaded such as file size, width, and height of the texture in pixels, and more.

- The cSprites class encapsulates *an array of sprites* whose size is determined by the constant MAX_SPRITES. 4096 is the maximum number of sprites supported by DirectX at any one time, and therefore the MAX_SPRITES constant has been set to this value. The cSprites object is responsible for maintaining a list of sprites and for drawing them together as a batch on each and every frame. To do this, it will use the DirectX COM interface member ID3DX10Sprite *m_SpriteInterface.

- cDirectXMesh encapsulates a single DirectX mesh object, and one instance of this class is needed per mesh in a 3D scene. The render manager will maintain a list of meshes, and it is typically the responsibility of a 3D scene manager (examined later in this book) to ensure when and where meshes are to be rendered in the scene, if they are to be rendered at all. For this chapter, however, the render manager will simply render a list of meshes in sequence without regard to their position in the scene for testing purposes. It is the duty of the scene manager and not the render manager to manage scene properties. The cDirectXMesh class features several notable members:

**ID3DX10Mesh* m_Mesh**

Refers to the DirectX COM mesh interfaces representing a mesh in graphics memory. With this interface, DirectX will act on and access the properties of a mesh in the scene. When this interface is released using the SAFE_RELEASE macro, the mesh will be destroyed.

**D3D10EffectTechnique* m_Technique**

This is a handle to the *vertex shader* used to render the mesh to the display. DirectX 10 relies heavily on vertex shaders for rendering geometry in the scene. Vertex shaders are C++-like scripts executed by the GPU (graphics processing nit) on each and every frame of the rendering loop for each and every vertex of the mesh. Using shaders a developer can apply homemade effects and stylizations to their meshes.

**ID3D10EffectMatrixVariable* m_pWorldVariable**

**ID3D10EffectMatrixVariable* m_pViewVariable**

**ID3D10EffectMatrixVariable* m_pProjectionVariable**

These three variables refer to the world, view, and projection matrices. These are used for transforming the mesh from world to view space, and from view to projection space, before it is shown on the display.

- The cDirectXRenderManager class encapsulates the render manager, the main rendering component overseeing the 3D rendering work of the engine. It is worth reiterating that this component is responsible for:

1. Creating an application window and both initializing and freeing the video hardware. It creates a window and initializes graphics hardware in the init

method. This method should be called once at application startup, and since it is where rendering work begins it constitutes the focus of the next section of the chapter. The video hardware is freed in the method free, which should be called once at application termination.

2. Loading, unloading, and processing graphics resources including textures, sprites, and meshes. The manager class will maintain a list of textures and meshes in the STL list members m_Textures and m_Mesh, and it will further maintain a pointer to a collection of sprites through the m_Sprites member. All visible meshes and sprites will be rendered to the display on each and every frame of the render loop.

3. Performing all 3D space transformations necessary for presenting scenes to the display. The work of transformation is specific to a mesh, since each and every mesh will appear at different positions and orientations in a scene. Some might appear at the origin, while others will have moved and be moving when rendered. For this reason, the work of transformation (of moving, rotating, and scaling) will be delegated to each mesh object (see the earlier description of the mesh class and its three world, view, and projection members: m_pWorldVariable, m_pViewVariable, and m_pProjectionVariable). In short, each mesh will be expected to process its own transformations.

4. Updating all graphics resources once per frame for each and every frame of the render loop. The render manager will achieve this through its update method.

## ■ 9.5   Creating a Window and Initializing the Graphics Hardware

It should be noted from the header file given above that the DirectX 3D render manager derives from the ancestor base class c3DRenderManager, just as the SDL 2D render manager derived from a general c2DRenderManager class. This ancestor class is intended only as an abstract base class and not as a class for instantiation on its own. It contains only a constructor, a virtual destructor, and three virtual methods, all of which are overridden in the descendant DirectX render manager. These are the methods: init, free, and update.

The work of the DirectX 3D render manager actually begins from the moment it is created in memory by the application, in its constructor function where it initializes all of its member variables to appropriate starting values, usually null or 0 depending on the data type. Please see the note below to view the implementation of the constructor method for this class.

NOTE. The class constructor is called once as the render manager class is created by the application. During this method the member properties of the class are initialized to starting values.

```
cDirectXRenderManager::cDirectXRenderManager() :
c3DRenderManager()
{
  m_driverType = D3D10_DRIVER_TYPE_NULL;
  m_pd3dDevice = NULL;
  m_pSwapChain = NULL;
  m_pRenderTargetView = NULL;
  m_hInst = NULL;
  m_hWnd = NULL;
  ZeroMemory(&m_BackBufferInfo, sizeof(D3D10_
TEXTURE2D_DESC));
}
```

Once the render manager class is created by an application, it should call its init method before it can expect any further rendering work to be performed. This method both creates an application window of a specified size and name to act as the canvas onto which 3D scenes will be rasterized every frame and readies the 3D graphics hardware for rendering work. Once completed, this method returns a boolean value to indicate its success. True is returned when the window is created and the 3D device is ready to use, and false is returned when an error occurrs. If false is returned, an application should either take alternative steps or exit to the desktop with an appropriate error message. To achieve its work, the init method must call on a comparatively wide selection of Windows API and DirectX functions. Both the number of functions called and the number of their expected arguments make the init method of the render manager one of the longest functions in this book. For this reason, the init method will be examined here in chunks, with each chunk of code followed by an explanation.

```
bool cDirectXRenderManager::init(HINSTANCE hInstance,
unsigned int Width, unsigned int Height, bool fullScreen,
char* WindowTitle)
{
    // Register class
    WNDCLASSEX wcex;
    ZeroMemory(&wcex, sizeof(WNDCLASSEX));
    wcex.cbSize = sizeof( WNDCLASSEX );
    wcex.style = CS_HREDRAW | CS_VREDRAW;
    wcex.lpfnWndProc = WndProc;
    wcex.cbClsExtra = 0;
    wcex.cbWndExtra = 0;
    wcex.hInstance = hInstance;
    wcex.lpszMenuName = NULL;
    wcex.lpszClassName = L"class_engine";
    if( !RegisterClassEx( &wcex ) )
        return false;
```

```
    m_hInst = hInstance;
    RECT rc = { 0, 0, Width, Height };
    AdjustWindowRect( &rc, WS_OVERLAPPEDWINDOW, FALSE );

    wchar_t *wtitle;
    mbstowcs(wtitle,WindowTitle,MAX_PATH);

     m_hWnd = CreateWindow( L"class_engine", wtitle,
      WS_OVERLAPPEDWINDOW, CW_USEDEFAULT, CW_USEDEFAULT,
   rc.right - rc.left, rc.bottom - rc.top, NULL, NULL,
   hInstance, NULL );

     if( !m_hWnd )
         return false;

     ShowWindow( m_hWnd, SW_SHOWNORMAL );
```

## Comments

- Once called, the init method sets out to create a standard application window into which the graphics device will render on each and every frame. In this sense, the window will act as a rendering canvas.

- The application window is created using a set of common Windows API functions and structures. First, a WNDCLASSEX object is created and populated with information pertaining to the type of window to be created (or *class* of window). Here, an application is expected to declare *how* windows—particular windows—of this class should appear. It details the name of the class, the font to be used for the title text, whether the window is to have a menu, and other properties. Once a style of window has been defined through the WNDCLASSEX object, this style can be registered with Windows using the RegisterClassEx function. This function *does not* create a *particular* window of this style, but only notifies the Windows OS that such a style exists and that, in the future, a window of this style is likely to be created by the registering application.

- Once a window class has been registered using the RegisterClassEx function of the Windows API, the application can then proceed to create a window object belonging to this class. The window can be created with a specified title, width, height, and position on the screen using the Windows function CreateWindow. Notice that the init method of the render manager creates a window according to the size values passed as arguments of the function. The CreateWindow function, if successful, returns an important object, called the window handle.

This object acts as the unique identifier of the window, and both DirectX and the Windows API make use of handles to identify specific window objects. The CreateWindow function does not, however, show the window on-screen after creation. The newly created window begins hidden from view, and the application must then show the window using the ShowWindow function.

NOTE. Key code segments have been highlighted in bold. Please see the information box at the end of this code segment for more information concerning DirectX objects and data types.

```cpp
HRESULT hr = S_OK;;
ZeroMemory(&rc, sizeof(RECT));
GetClientRect(m_hWnd,&rc );
UINT width = rc.right - rc.left;
UINT height = rc.bottom - rc.top;

UINT createDeviceFlags = 0;

D3D10_DRIVER_TYPE driverTypes[] =
{
    D3D10_DRIVER_TYPE_HARDWARE,
    D3D10_DRIVER_TYPE_REFERENCE,
};

UINT numDriverTypes = sizeof( driverTypes ) / sizeof
(driverTypes[0]);

DXGI_SWAP_CHAIN_DESC sd;
ZeroMemory( &sd, sizeof( sd ) );
sd.BufferCount = 1;
sd.BufferDesc.Width = width;
sd.BufferDesc.Height = height;
sd.BufferDesc.Format = DXGI_FORMAT_R8G8B8A8_UNORM;
sd.BufferDesc.RefreshRate.Numerator = 60;
sd.BufferDesc.RefreshRate.Denominator = 1;
sd.BufferUsage = DXGI_USAGE_RENDER_TARGET_OUTPUT;
sd.OutputWindow = m_hWnd;
sd.SampleDesc.Count = 1;
sd.SampleDesc.Quality = 0;
sd.Windowed = TRUE;

for( UINT driverTypeIndex = 0; driverTypeIndex <
numDriverTypes; driverTypeIndex++ )
    {
```

```
        m_driverType = driverTypes[driverTypeIndex];
        hr = D3D10CreateDeviceAndSwapChain( NULL, m_
driverType, NULL, createDeviceFlags,
                                            D3D10_SDK_
VERSION, &sd, &m_pSwapChain, &m_pd3dDevice );
        if( SUCCEEDED( hr ) )
            break;
    }

    if( FAILED( hr ) )
        return false;

    // Create a render target view
    ID3D10Texture2D* pBackBuffer;
    hr = m_pSwapChain->GetBuffer( 0, __uuidof
(ID3D10Texture2D ), ( LPVOID* )&pBackBuffer );
    if( FAILED( hr ) )
        return false;

  pBackBuffer->GetDesc(&m_BackBufferInfo);

    hr = m_pd3dDevice->CreateRenderTargetView
(pBackBuffer, NULL, &m_pRenderTargetView);
    pBackBuffer->Release();
    if( FAILED( hr ) )
        return false;

    m_pd3dDevice->OMSetRenderTargets( 1, &m_
pRenderTargetView, NULL );

    // Setup the viewport
    D3D10_VIEWPORT VP;
     VP.Width = width;
     VP.Height = height;
     VP.MinDepth = 0.0f;
     VP.MaxDepth = 1.0f;
     VP.TopLeftX = 0;
     VP.TopLeftY = 0;
     m_pd3dDevice->RSSetViewports( 1, &VP );

    m_VP = VP;

    return true;
}
```

## ■ Devices and Swap Chains

The second and final half of the init method of the render manager is responsible for initializing both the DirectX 10 library and the graphics hardware. To do this, the developer must create a Direct3D rendering device and a swap chain. These two elements of DirectX are now explained in more detail.

### Direct3D Device

The Direct3D device is a DirectX COM interface and class that encapsulates the low-level functionality of the 3D graphics hardware attached to the computer (the video card). Through the methods of this interface, developers can retrieve diagnostic information about the hardware and its capabilities such as the total number of textures it supports and the maximum width and height of textures allowed. Furthermore, the Direct3D device allows a developer to flood fill the display with specified colors and present other graphical data. In short, the Direct3D device is a crucial COM interface on which others of the SDK depend and must remain active for as long as an application intends to render to the display with DirectX.

### Swap Chain

The DirectX swap chain is a partner class to the Direct3D device. In picture form, it can be seen to *link* the graphics hardware to the canvas of the window. It is via the swap chain that graphics produced by the device are able to be shown as rasterized pixels on the canvas of the application window. By its default settings, the swap chain consists of two 2D textures in graphics memory; each texture in this case is called a *buffer* and each represents a rectangle of pixel data. One texture is *read-only*; this is called the front buffer. It represents the pixels the users sees in the application window on any one frame. The other texture is readable and writeable, and is called the *back buffer*. This buffer is not visible to the user and represents the working area onto which the graphics hardware is rendering the next frame. Once its rendering to the back buffer is completed, DirectX steps to the next frame by swapping the buffers, with the back buffer becoming the front buffer where its contents are made visible, and the old front buffer becoming the new back buffer onto which the next frame will be rendered. By flipping (or *swapping*) the buffers of the chain back and forth in this way on each and every frame, DirectX ensures smooth and continual rendering to the application window.

**Comments**

- The second and final chunk of code detailing the init method of the render manager focuses on creating and configuring a Direct3D device and swap chain in preparation for rendering graphics to the display. The previous sidebar, Devices and Swap Chains, explained in more detail what is meant by the terms "Direct3D device" and "swap chain." But in short, the Direct3D device is a COM interface that encapsulates the 3D hardware attached to the computer, and the swap chain is the means by which graphical output from the device is presented as a rasterized image to the user on the canvas of the application window.

- The first step in creating a device and swap chain for the window involves completing a DXGI_SWAP_CHAIN_DESC structure, detailing many properties of the application window and the behavior an application expects from the device when created. Here an application specifies such details as size of the window in terms of width and height in pixels, whether the application should be run full screen regardless of window size, and the window handle of the application window. DXGI_SWAP_CHAIN_DESC features many properties, and it is good practice to complete as many of them as necessary. See the DirectX Focus—Initialization Classes, Functions, and Structures sidebar later in this section for details on DirectX functions and arguments and structures.

- Once the DXGI_SWAP_CHAIN_DESC has been completed, an application can proceed to call the D3D10CreateDeviceAndSwapChain function of DirectX to create both a Direct3D device and a swap chain from the swap chain description and parameters. Calling this function is the equivalent of initializing the device. Please note that although this function should be called only once for each graphics device on the system, it is actually called here in a loop whose total number of iterations is based on the size of an enum called driverTypes, defined a few lines prior to the call. This enum specifies two driver types: HARDWARE and REFERENCE; the former refers to a hardware-accelerated device and the latter to a secondary device. The init method enters a loop when creating the device and attempts to create *only* one device, preferring the former to the latter. If the former (hardware) can be and is created, the loop is exited and the application accepts the hardware device. Otherwise, the loop will proceed to create the secondary device. In either case, the D3D10CreateDeviceAndSwapChain function (if successful) returns two COM interfaces, one for the device and one for the swap chain: ID3D10Device and IDXGISwapChain, respectively. The device interface is stored in the render manager's member m_pd3dDevice, and the swap chain interface is stored in the member m_pSwapChain.

- The D3D10CreateDeviceAndSwapChain function creates both an independent device and an independent swap chain, each object effectively having no established relationship to the other. The init method then proceeds to *configure* the swap chain by linking (or connecting) it to the device. This notifies the device of the presence of a swap chain and will configure it to allow for that chain to present the device's rendered output to the application window. The init method does this by retrieving a pointer to the back buffer of the swap chain using the GetBuffer method of the IDXGISwapChain interface and then creating a render target view object based on the back buffer and swap chain. This object is created using the CreateRenderTargetView method of the ID3D10Device interface and is stored in the member variable m_pRenderTargetView. Calling this method creates an object that contextualizes (typecasts) the back buffer texture as a valid render target view. A render target view simply modifies the back buffer to act no longer as a simple read-only texture but as a receptacle for pixel data output from the graphics device as it renders on each and every frame. Creating this object, however, still does not notify the Direct3D device that it (this particular object) should be used as the render target view. An application could have created many such objects, and could intend them to be used for different purposes and at different times. Thus, the Direct3D device requires the developer to notify it of a *specific* render target view to act as the receiver of output pixel data. In this case, the newly created render target view is suitable. This can be set as the active render target view by calling the OMSetRenderTargets method of the ID3D10Device. Setting the back buffer of the swap chain as the render target view identifies that buffer as the target (destination) onto which graphical data will be sent on each and every frame of the render loop. More information regarding these methods of DirectX and their arguments can be found in the DirectX Focus—Initialization Classes, Functions, and Structures sidebar later in this section.

- The init method of the render manager completes by creating a DirectX 10 viewport object. The viewport object is similar to a clipping (cropping) rectangle applied to the application window on each frame. The viewport structure (D3D10_VIEWPORT) defines the top, left, right, and bottom of a rectangle, which represents the region into which graphical data will be shown on each frame. Pixels that fall outside of this region will be clipped and not shown. A viewport whose size equals the size of the application window will not clip graphical data and DirectX will render to the full size of the window. The viewport can be set using the RSSetViewports method of the ID3D10Device device. The viewport settings are stored in the render manager's member variable m_VP.

### ■ DirectX Focus—Initialization Classes, Functions, and Structures

The init method of the DirectX render manager, presented earlier, calls on a selection of DirectX classes, functions, and structures to complete its work of initializing and configuring the graphics device and swap chain. The code comments for this method sketched an outline of the course execution takes and the purpose the function has, but it did not stop to detail or discuss the methods it calls and their arguments. This section details the DirectX methods and structures used by the init method of the render manager, in the order in which they are encountered.

#### Swap Chain Description Structure

This DirectX data structure is used to detail the properties of a swap chain to be created. It is intended to be passed as an argument to the function D3D10 CreateDeviceAndSwapChain.

```
typedef struct DXGI_SWAP_CHAIN_DESC {
    DXGI_MODE_DESC BufferDesc;
    DXGI_SAMPLE_DESC SampleDesc;
    DXGI_USAGE BufferUsage;
    UINT BufferCount;
    HWND OutputWindow;
    BOOL Windowed;
    DXGI_SWAP_EFFECT SwapEffect;
    UINT Flags;
} DXGI_SWAP_CHAIN_DESC;
```

#### Description

**DXGI_MODE_DESC BufferDesc**

Structure detailing the back buffer display mode. In the code sample listed throughout this section, this parameter has been left blank, which forces the function to use default values.

**DXGI_SAMPLE_DESC SampleDesc**

Structure detailing the multisampling quality of the pixel data rendered to the back buffer. This structure has two properties: Count and Quality. Count refers to the number of multisamples per pixel per frame, and Quality determines the sharpness of the output. The code sample above set the quality to 1. This value is inversely proportional to performance; the higher the quality, the lower the performance.

**DXGI_USAGE BufferUsage**

Notifies DirectX of how the developer intends to use the buffers of the swap chain. This value can be one of the following: DXGI_USAGE_ BACK_BUFFER,

DXGI_USAGE_DISCARD_ON_PRESENT, DXGI_USAGE_READ_ ONLY,

DXGI_USAGE_RENDER_TARGET_OUTPUT, DXGI_USAGE_ SHADER_INPUT, and

DXGI_USAGE_SHARED, DXGI_USAGE_UNORDERED_ACCESS. Since this application intends to use the swap chain as a receptacle of the pixel data output from the device, it uses DXGI_USAGE_RENDER_ TARGET_OUTPUT.

**UINT BufferCount**

Describes the total number of buffers in the swap chain, not including the front buffer. Since this chain contains both the back buffer and front buffer, this value should be set to 1.

**HWND OutputWindow**

Specifies the handle of the application window that is to act as the canvas on to which the swap chain will draw on each frame of the render loop.

**BOOL Windowed**

Specifies whether the application is to run in windowed or full-screen mode. If true, the application runs in a window of the size specified by the creation parameters of the window. If false, the application runs full screen regardless of the size of the window.

**DXGI_SWAP_EFFECT SwapEffect**

Determines how the back and front buffers should behave when swapped at the end of the frame. This value can be either DXGI_SWAP_EFFECT_ DISCARD or DXGI_SWAP_EFFECT_SEQUENTIAL. For this book, the default 0 is used (DXGI_SWAP_EFFECT_DISCARD).

**UINT Flags**

Can be either DXGI_SWAP_CHAIN_FLAG_NONPREROTATED, DXGI_SWAP_CHAIN_FLAG_ALLOW_MODE_SWITCH, or

DXGI_SWAP_CHAIN_FLAG_GDI_COMPATIBLE. The code of this book accepts the default settings.

**The Device and Swap Chain: D3D10CreateDeviceAndSwapChain**

Both the Direct3D device and swap chain interfaces and classes can be created together in one call to the D3D10CreateDeviceAndSwapChain function. This function creates a device based on the 3D graphics hardware attached to the computer and creates a swap chain according to the parameters passed in a DXGI_SWAP_CHAIN_DESC structure. If successful, the function returns a pointer to two valid COM interfaces, IDXGISwapChain and ID3D10Device. The former represents the swap chain and the latter the Direct3D device. The form of this function is as follows:

```
HRESULT D3D10CreateDeviceAndSwapChain(
  IDXGIAdapter *pAdapter,
  D3D10_DRIVER_TYPE DriverType,
  HMODULE Software,
  UINT Flags,
  UINT SDKVersion,
  DXGI_SWAP_CHAIN_DESC *pSwapChainDesc,
  IDXGISwapChain **ppSwapChain,
  ID3D10Device **ppDevice
);
```

**Description**

**IDXGIAdapter *pAdapter**

Pointer to a graphics adapter or null.

**D3D10_DRIVER_TYPE DriverType**

Specifies the *type* of device to be created. This can be one of the following: D3D10_DRIVER_TYPE_HARDWARE, D3D10_DRIVER_TYPE_REFERENCE, D3D10_DRIVER_TYPE_NULL, D3D10_DRIVER_TYPE_SOFTWARE, or D3D10_DRIVER_TYPE_WARP. The value D3D10_DRIVER_TYPE_HARDWARE is preferred in almost all cases since it refers to the graphics device using hardware acceleration.

**HMODULE Software**

Should be null.

**UINT Flags**

Optional parameter. Specifies a series of options for the device. Can be 0 to accept default settings, or any of the following:

D3D10_CREATE_DEVICE_SINGLETHREADED

D3D10_CREATE_DEVICE_DEBUG

D3D10_CREATE_DEVICE_SWITCH_TO_REF

D3D10_CREATE_DEVICE_PREVENT_INTERNAL_THREADING_
OPTIMIZATIONS

D3D10_CREATE_DEVICE_ALLOW_NULL_FROM_MAP

D3D10_CREATE_DEVICE_BGRA_SUPPORT

D3D10_CREATE_DEVICE_STRICT_VALIDATION

**UINT SDKVersion**

This should be D3D10_SDK_VERSION.

**DXGI_SWAP_CHAIN_DESC *pSwapChainDesc**

Pointer to a DXGI_SWAP_CHAIN_DESC structure defining the properties
of the swap chain to be created.

**IDXGISwapChain **ppSwapChain**

Pointer to a buffer to receive a valid COM interface representing the created
swap chain object.

**ID3D10Device **ppDevice**

Pointer to a buffer to receive a valid COM interface representing the created
Direct3D device object.

---

**The Swap Chain and Back Buffer**

The D3D10CreateDeviceAndSwapChain function creates two COM interfaces,
one of which is IDXGISwapChain, representing the swap chain (both the front and
back buffers). A full list of methods and properties for the COM interfaces used
here can be found in the online DirectX Documentation available from MSDN.
These declarations are not, however, provided in this chapter. However, the
GetBuffer method of the IDXGISwapChain interface is called by the init method
of the render manager, and the form of the GetBuffer method is given here:

```
HRESULT GetBuffer(
  UINT Buffer,
  REFIID riid,
  void **ppSurface
);
```

**Description**

**UINT Buffer**

Index of the buffer to which a pointer is to be retrieved. For the back buffer,
developers should typically pass 0.

**REFIID riid**

The COM interface to be used for accessing the buffer. The back buffer surface is a 2D texture. For this reason, developers should pass ID3D10Texture2D.

**void \*\*ppSurface**

Pointer to a buffer to receive the COM interface representing the specified buffer; in this case, the back buffer.

---

**2D Texture Description Structures**

Images loaded into memory from standard files and both swap chain surfaces (front and back buffer) are 2D textures, and 2D textures refer to a rectangle of pixels with width and height but not depth. However, in addition to width and height, a 2D texture can have a pixel format, miplevel properties, and other properties. This information can often be important when copying pixels between textures and when passing textures as arguments to DirectX functions. For this reason, DirectX uses the D3D10_TEXTURE2D_DESC structure to store diagnostic information regarding a texture, and the DirectX render manager maintains a D3D10_TEXTURE2D_DESC structure as a class member to describe the format, size, and other properties of the back buffer texture. This member is called m_BackBufferInfo (see the header declaration for cDirectXRenderManager). The D3D10_TEXTURE2D_DESC structure is as follows:

```
typedef struct D3D10_TEXTURE2D_DESC {
    UINT Width;
    UINT Height;
    UINT MipLevels;
    UINT ArraySize;
    DXGI_FORMAT Format;
    DXGI_SAMPLE_DESC SampleDesc;
    D3D10_USAGE Usage;
    UINT BindFlags;
    UINT CPUAccessFlags;
    UINT MiscFlags;
} D3D10_TEXTURE2D_DESC;
```

**Description**

**UINT Width**

Width of the texture in texels. If the texture is in screen space, such as a sprite, then texels correspond to pixels.

**UINT Height**

Height of the texture in texels. If the texture is in screen space, such as a sprite, then texels correspond to pixels.

**UINT MipLevels**

Number of subtextures. This book uses only 1 mipmap level for each texture.

**UINT ArraySize**

Number of textures in the array. Again, this book will use only 1.

**DXGI_FORMAT Format**

The pixel format of the texture. This is often DXGI_FORMAT_R8G8B8A8, but the value can be one of any featured in the DXGI_FORMAT enum. This enumeration is provided in Appendix C.

**DXGI_SAMPLE_DESC SampleDesc**

Specifies whether multisampling is being applied to the texture.

**D3D10_USAGE Usage**

Defines how the texture is being used. Can be one of the following values:
D3D10_USAGE_DEFAULT
D3D10_USAGE_IMMUTABLE
D3D10_USAGE_DYNAMIC
D3D10_USAGE_STAGING

**UINT BindFlags**

This further indicates how the texture is being used by DirectX; that is, whether it is being used as a render target view or as a texture on geometry in the scene. This value can be one of the following: D3D10_BIND_VERTEX_BUFFER, D3D10_BIND_INDEX_BUFFER, D3D10_BIND_CONSTANT_BUFFER, D3D10_BIND_SHADER_RESOURCE, D3D10_BIND_STREAM_OUTPUT, D3D10_BIND_RENDER_TARGET, or D3D10_BIND_DEPTH_STENCIL.

**UINT CPUAccessFlags**

Indicates whether access to the texture is read only or both read and write. Can be either or both of the following: D3D10_CPU_ACCESS_WRITE and D3D10_CPU_ACCESS_READ.

**UINT MiscFlags**

Typically, this is 0.

**Creating Render Target Views**

Typically, render target views are back buffer textures that have been modified by DirectX to receive pixel output from the graphics device on each and every frame of the render loop. A back buffer declares itself a render target view when it calls the CreateRenderTargetView method of the ID3D10Device representing the graphics device. Once called, a modified version of this texture is created, though it is not actually set as the active render target view. The render target view is set as the active render target after calling the OMSetRenderTargets method of ID3D10Device. The function declarations and descriptions for both of these functions are given here:

```
HRESULT CreateRenderTargetView
(
  ID3D10Resource *pResource,
  const D3D10_RENDER_TARGET_VIEW_DESC *pDesc,
  ID3D10RenderTargetView **ppRTView
);
```

**Description**

**ID3D10Resource *pResource**

Specifies an ID3D10Resource-derived COM interface (such as a texture) that indicates the resource to use as the render target view. In this book, the back buffer texture is used as the render target view.

**const D3D10_RENDER_TARGET_VIEW_DESC *pDesc**

Can be null. Please see the DirectX documentation for further details, if desired.

**ID3D10RenderTargetView **ppRTView**

Pointer to a buffer to receive a valid ID3D10RenderTargetView COM interface representing the target view object to receive rendered output from the graphics device.

```
void OMSetRenderTargets(
  UINT NumViews,
  ID3D10RenderTargetView *const
*ppRenderTargetViews,
  ID3D10DepthStencilView *pDepthStencilView
);
```

**UINT NumViews**

Total number of render targets to link (bind) to the graphics device. More than one render target view can be bound, but this examples binds only one—the back buffer. Therefore, this parameter should be 1.

**ID3D10RenderTargetView *const *ppRenderTargetViews**

Pointer to an array of RenderTargetView objects to be used as the render target view for the active graphics device. For this book, this array will feature only the back buffer as a render target view.

**ID3D10DepthStencilView *pDepthStencilView**

Can be null. Please consult the DirectX documentation for further details, if required.

---

**Creating Viewports**

Viewports define the rectangular region of pixels in the application window into which graphical data will be drawn by the swap chain as it receives them from the device on each and every frame. Viewports are created by the RSSetViewports method of ID3D10Device. The form of this method is given here:

```
void RSSetViewports(
  UINT NumViewports,
  const D3D10_VIEWPORT *pViewports
);
```

**Description**

**UINT NumViewports**

Total number of viewports to configure.

**const D3D10_VIEWPORT *pViewports**

Pointer to an array of D3D10_VIEWPORT structures describing the region of the viewports to apply to the application window. The D3D10_ VIEWPORT structure defines the size and extents of a viewport. This structure is as follows:

```
typedef struct D3D10_VIEWPORT {
    INT TopLeftX;
    INT TopLeftY;
    UINT Width;
    UINT Height;
    FLOAT MinDepth;
    FLOAT MaxDepth;
} D3D10_VIEWPORT;
```

## ■ 9.6   Receiving Window Messages via WndProc

The previous section examined the implementation of the init method of the DirectX render manager. This method is intended to be called once at application startup, and there it should create an application window and initialize both the graphics device and a swap chain object. Before creating an actual application window, the render manager was required to complete a WNDCLASSEX structure whose purpose was to a define a window type. One of the members of this class was named lpfnWndProc, and the render manager assigned this a pointer to an application-defined function named WndProc. By doing this, the render manager indicated to the OS that the WndProc function had been selected to be the receiver of all window message notifications sent to the created window. That is, after the application window is created, the WndProc function will be used by the OS as a callback function, called whenever an event occurs to the window that might require a response from the application. Windows has a slew of predefined window messages that are sent to the WndProc procedure to notify a window of events that occurred while that window was active. Events are generated for keyboard button presses, mouse clicks, window drags and resizes, etc. The application does not need to handle all of these events but only those of interest. Unhandled events—events ignored by the application—will invoke default behavior. Defining a WndProc function for a window is therefore a useful way of being notified about and responding to common events that occur while the application is running. The game engine created here will respond only to the WM_DESTROY message, which is sent by Windows to the WndProc function whenever the user selects to close the window and exit the application. It is therefore a notification to say that the application is about to close. When this event is received, an application should perform all freeing and cleaning up as required. The WndProc function can be implemented as follows:

> **NOTE.** Please see Appendix D for a list of the most common window messages that a Windows application can receive through WndProc. For more information on handling window messages, or for those new to this topic, the author recommends visiting the following URL for more information: http://msdn.microsoft.com/en-us/library/ms632590(VS.85).aspx.

```
LRESULT CALLBACK WndProc( HWND hWnd, UINT message, WPARAM
wParam, LPARAM lParam )
{
    PAINTSTRUCT ps;
    HDC hdc;

    switch( message )
    {
        case WM_PAINT:
            hdc = BeginPaint( hWnd, &ps );
```

```
            EndPaint( hWnd, &ps );
            break;

        case WM_DESTROY:
    //Run cleanup code here
            PostQuitMessage( 0 );
            break;

        default:
            return DefWindowProc( hWnd, message, wParam,
    lParam );
        }

    return 0;
}
```

## ■ 9.7    Managing the Render Loop (Presenting Graphics to the Display)

Downloading, installing, and configuring DirectX for a C++ IDE, and then coding a DirectX application can often seem to both newcomers and experts to involve both a prohibitive and a frustrating amount of coding for comparatively little effect. Having initialized a Direct3D device and swap chain, and having implemented a WndProc

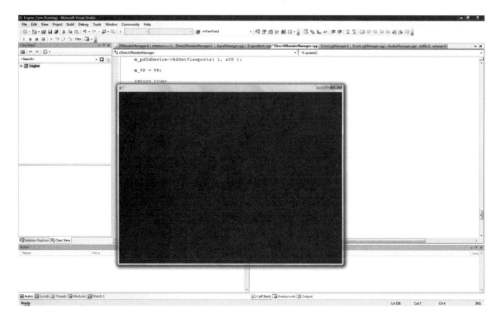

**▌FIGURE 9.15**    First run.

function, still nothing has yet been presented to the window; not even bold flood fill colors. This section implements the update method of the render manager in which the heart of the rendering work occurs and which is intended to be called once per frame. It is in the update function that the render manager will: (1) clear the back buffer of the swap chain in preparation for rendering a new frame, (2) render graphical data to the back buffer, and (3) complete the frame by flipping (or updating) the swap chain so as to present (draw) the final back buffer to the application window where it will be seen by the user. At this point, our render manager will be drawing only flood fill colors to the window since the scene is empty, and the texture, sprite, and mesh classes are still to be implemented (see Figure 9.15). However, these classes will also feature their own update methods in which they will be responsible for rendering themselves to the back buffer, and it will be the job of the render manager to call their update methods  during its own update method to ensure all data is rendered together as a frame. The update method of the render manager is as follows:

```
bool cDirectXRenderManager::update()
{
    float ClearColor[4] = { 0.0f, 0.125f, 0.3f, 1.0f }; //
red, green, blue, alpha

//Clears the back buffer. Flood fills with a specified
color.
m_pd3dDevice->ClearRenderTargetView( m_pRenderTargetView,
ClearColor );

    //Calls sprites update method
    m_Sprites.update();

    //Cycle through list of meshes
    std::list<cDirectXMesh*>::iterator list_it;

    for(list_it=m_Mesh.begin();list_it! = m_Mesh.
end();list_it++)
    {
        //Draw meshes to back buffer
        (*list_it)->update();
    }

    //End frame by flipping swap chain
    m_pSwapChain->Present( 0, 0 );

    return true;
}
```

## Comments

- The update method of the render manager should be called *once per frame on each and every frame of the render loop.*

- This method begins by calling the ClearRenderTargetView method of the ID3D10Device COM interface to flood fill the back buffer with a solid color. In effect, this is designed to clear the back buffer of any old graphical data that it may have retained from the previous frame. The details of this method are given in the DirectX Focus—Rendering Classes, Functions, and Structures sidebar at the end of this section.

- The update method then calls the update method of the sprites collection class and proceeds to call the update for each and every mesh contained in its std::list member m_Mesh. At present the reader should assume those functions are empty, since these classes are yet to be implemented. But it is important to note that it is the render manager that is responsible for invoking these methods during its render loop, between the ClearRenderTargetView method that marks the beginning of the frame and the Present method, which it calls to end the frame.

---

### ■ DirectX Focus—Rendering Classes, Functions, and Structures

In DirectX—as in SDL—rendering occurs in a loop, called the rendering loop. On each frame of the loop, programmers should call the ClearRenderTargetView method to start a frame and the Present method to end a frame, presenting it to the application window via the swap chain. Between these two calls, all objects in a scene should be rendered. The focus here is on these two methods: ClearRenderTargetView of ID3D10Device and Present of IDXGISwapChain.

```
void ClearRenderTargetView(
    ID3D10RenderTargetView *pRenderTargetView,
    const FLOAT ColorRGBA[4]
);
```

### Description

**ID3D10RenderTargetView *pRenderTargetView**

Pointer to a render target view to flood fill with a color as specified by ColorRGBA.

**const FLOAT ColorRGBA[4]**

A color with which to flood fill the render target view. This color should be in the form of RGBA (red, green, blue, alpha). Each component can be a value from 0 to 1, with 0 indicating that the component has no effect and 1 indicating that the component is fully applied. An alpha value of 0 refers to completely transparent, and an alpha value of 1 refers to fully opaque.

```
HRESULT Present(
  UINT SyncInterval,
  UINT Flags
);
```

**UINT SyncInterval**

This is typically 0 to present the scene immediately. By specifying 1, 2, 3, or 4, the presentation can be delayed until after the $n$th vertical blank.

**UINT Flags**

Should be 0. Please consult the DirectX documentation for more information, if required.

## ■ 9.8   Freeing the Render Manager

Before proceeding to the implementation details of classes outside of the render manager, such as the texture, sprite, and mesh classes, it will be useful to consider briefly the free method of the render manager. This method is called once at application termination—when the WndProc function receives a WM_DESTROY notification—and demonstrates how the COM interface members of the render manager are freed cleanly at application termination using the SAFE_RELEASE macro defined at the top of the header file. The method implementation for free is shown here:

```
void cDirectXRenderManager::free()
{
   //free all textures

   std::list<cDirectXTexture*>::iterator list_it;

   for(list_it=m_Textures.begin();list_it! = m_Textures.
end();list_it++)
         (*list_it)->free();

   for(list_it=m_Mesh.begin();list_it! = m_Mesh.
end();list_it++)
         (*list_it)->free();
```

```
    m_Sprites->free();

    //free renderer devices
    if( m_pd3dDevice ) m_pd3dDevice->ClearState();
    SAFE_RELEASE(m_pRenderTargetView);
    SAFE_RELEASE(m_pSwapChain);
    SAFE_RELEASE(m_pd3dDevice);
    }
```

There is little to state about this method that is probably not immediately clear from
the code sample. The method begins by calling the free method on all member graphics resources, including textures, sprites, and meshes. Then it proceeds to call SAFE_
RELEASE on all the key COM members of the render manager: the RenderTargetView,
the SwapChain, and the Direct3D device.

## ■  9.9    Building the DirectX Texture Resource

It will be useful here to pause and consider how far we have come in our work on the
render manager and its methods, and what remains to be created in the way of the first
resource for this manager; namely, textures. Thus far, the render manager has been
implemented to create an application window, to initialize a 3D device and swap chain
that presents graphical output to that window, and to maintain a render loop that calls the
update method of all graphics resources on each and every frame to render their content
to the back buffer. Texture resources are distinguished from many graphics resources in
that they are not 3D, since they have height and width but no depth. As such, not being
a 3D object, they cannot directly be part of a 3D scene, which is composed of 3D objects
(vertices, faces, and edges) in a unified 3D space with axes X, Y, and Z. However, textures nevertheless *do* find themselves in 3D scenes by being textured onto the skin of
3D objects through their materials. In the rendering framework designed and created in
this chapter, textures find themselves worthy of a separate class (cDirectXTexture), and
it is now appropriate to implement that class to work with the render manager. The class
cDirectXTexture will prove particularly important when creating a subsequent class,
cSprites, whose purpose is to draw textures in 2D screen space for representing 2D elements in 3D games such as health bars, notifications, and menus. To recap, the class
declaration for a 2D texture is provided here for convenience, and comments follow:

```
class cDirectXTexture : public cEngineObject
{
private:
protected:
public:
    ID3D10Texture2D* m_TextureInterface;
```

```
   D3DX10_IMAGE_INFO m_FileInfo;
   D3D10_TEXTURE2D_DESC m_Texture_Desc;
   bool m_bLoaded;
   bool m_Owned;

   cDirectXTexture();
   virtual bool loadFromFile(std::wstring fileName);
   virtual void free();
   void blitRectToBackBuffer(RECT Rct, int X, int Y);
};
```

**Comments**

- The class cDirectXTexture encapsulates a 2D texture in graphical memory. The
  member m_TextureInterface is an instance of ID3D10Texture2D, which is the
  DirectX data type for 2D textures.

- The class member D3DX10_IMAGE_INFO m_FileInfo contains diagnostic information relating to the file on disk from which the texture was loaded. This includes
  information such as the file format, the bit depth, and the mip levels. More information on this structure will be presented later in the DirectX Focus—Loading and
  Querying DirectX Treasures sidebar.

- The class member D3D10_TEXTURE2D_DESC m_Texture_Desc contains
  diagnostic information relating to the version of the 2D texture in memory. It
  contains details such as the width and height in texels, the access mode of the
  texture (read-only or read-write), and more.

- CDirectXTexture has further two properties: bool m_bLoaded and bool m_
  Owned. The former is a boolean. True indicates that the texture is currently
  loaded into memory from a file, and False indicates that the texture is currently
  not loaded. The latter member m_Owned is also a boolean. True indicates that
  the texture has been added to the render manager's list of textures (and thus will
  be removed from memory when the render manager is freed), and False indicates that the texture has not been added to the render manager's list of textures,
  and thus must be freed manually when the application closes.

  **NOTE**. The texture class begins its work in the constructor method where
  it initializes its member variables to null values. The constructor appears
  as follows:

```
cDirectXTexture::cDirectXTexture()
{
   m_TextureInterface = NULL;
```

```
  ZeroMemory(&m_FileInfo, sizeof(D3DX10_IMAGE_
INFO));
  ZeroMemory(&m_Texture_Desc, sizeof(D3D10_
TEXTURE2D_DESC));
  m_bLoaded = m_Owned = false;
}
```

## ■ 9.10  Loading Textures from Files

Though the work of the texture class technically begins in its constructor, its member values are set to default starting values that have no little or no meaning for either DirectX or the render manager. For this reason, the texture cannot be said to exist until its raw data is loaded from an image file on disk into graphics memory where it is ready to be applied. Loading will typically happen when the engine needs to read in texture data to apply to a sprite object or a mesh object in a 3D scene. The loading process is achieved through the loadFromFile method of cDirectXTexture. This function accepts a valid image file name as an argument, loads the file to a texture, and returns a boolean to indicate the success of the loading operation: true for success and false for failure. The code for this method is shown here, and comments follow:

NOTE. Key sections of code are highlighted in bold for clarity.

```
//Loads a 2D texture resource
bool cDirectXTexture::loadFromFile(std::wstring fileName)
{
    if(SUCCEEDED(D3DX10GetImageInfoFromFile(fileName.c_
str(), NULL, &m_FileInfo, NULL)))
    {
        //Retrieve pointer to render manager
        cDirectXRenderManager *RenderManager = cDirectXR
enderManager::GetDirectXRenderManager();
        ID3D10Resource* TextureRes;

        //Load texture from image file
        HRESULT hr = D3DX10CreateTextureFromFile(RenderM
anager->m_pd3dDevice,

    fileName.c_str(), NULL, NULL, &TextureRes, NULL);

        //Check loaded success
        if(FAILED(hr))
            return false;
```

```
        TextureRes->QueryInterface(__uuidof
(ID3D10Texture2D), (LPVOID*)&m_TextureInterface);
        TextureRes->Release();

        //Retrieve texture information
        m_TextureInterface->GetDesc(&m_Texture_Desc);

        m_bLoaded=true;

        if(!m_Owned)
        {
                RenderManager->m_Textures.push_back(this);
                m_Owned=true;
        }

        return true;
    }

    return false;
}
```

## Comments

- The loadFromFile method of cDirectXTexture begins by calling the
  D3DX10GetImageInfoFromFile function of DirectX to retrieve file information from the file specified by the argument fileName. Note that the
  file name of the image file is passed as an STL Unicode string. The
  D3DX10GetImageInfoFromFile function tests for the existence of the specified
  file and then returns a D3DX10_IMAGE_INFO structure containing diagnostic
  information about the file to be loaded such as the file format, the bit depth,
  and the width and height of the contained image in pixels. If the function call
  succeeds, the method continues; if it fails, the function exits by returning false.
  Information regarding both the function D3DX10GetImageInfoFromFile and the
  structure D3DX10_IMAGE_INFO can be found in the DirectX Focus—Loading
  and Querying DirectX Textures sidebar at the end of this section.

- Once file information is retrieved from the texture file on disk, the loadFromFile
  method proceeds to load texture raw data from the file. It does this by calling
  the function D3DX10CreateTextureFromFile. In short, this function accepts a
  file name to a valid image file on disk, and then loads that file on to a texture
  surface in memory. The texture in memory is encapsulated by DirectX through
  the ID3D10Resource interface. A pointer to this interface is returned by the
  D3DX10CreateTextureFromFile function.

- ID3D10Resource represents a texture in memory. Once a pointer to this interface is returned to the texture class, the loadFromFile method proceeds to *convert* (typecast) the resource object into a dedicated texture object, represented by the ID3D10Texture2D interface. It does this by calling the QueryInterface method of ID3D10Resource. This method returns a valid pointer to a ID3D10Texture2D object. This object, which now represents the texture object, is generally preferred over ID3D10Resource. This is because ID3D10Resource is a non-specific interface representing a graphics resource, and ID3D10Texture2D is a dedicated texture class, exposing methods and properties directly related to standard 2D textures.

---

### ■ DirectX Focus—Loading and Querying DirectX Textures

The loadFromFile method of class cDirectXTexture loads a texture from a file on disk to a buffer in memory. To do this, a set of DirectX interfaces, functions, and structures are called upon. First, D3DX10GetImageInfoFromFile is called to retrieve file information from the texture file into a D3DX10_IMAGE_INFO structure. Second, the D3DX10CreateTextureFromFile function is called to load a texture from a file into a buffer represented by an ID3D10Resource pointer. Then this pointer is converted to a more amenable ID3D10Texture2D object that exposes properties and methods targeted at textures specifically. Finally, the method then queries the ID3D10Texture2D interface for texture diagnostic information using the GetDesc method, and this information is returned in a D3D10_TEXTURE2D_DESC structure. These interfaces, methods, and structures are now considered further. Each is considered in the order in which it is called in the loadFromFile method.

**D3DX10GetImageInfoFromFile**
Retrieves diagnostic information from an image file on disk.

```
HRESULT D3DX10GetImageInfoFromFile(
  LPCTSTR pSrcFile,
  ID3DX10ThreadPump *pPump,
  D3DX10_IMAGE_INFO *pSrcInfo,
  HRESULT *pHResult
);
```

**Description**

**LPCTSTR pSrcFile**
Unicode string indicating the fully qualified path of the image file to be queried for information.

**ID3DX10ThreadPump \*pPump**
Can be null.

**D3DX10_IMAGE_INFO \*pSrcInfo**
Pointer to a D3DX10_IMAGE_INFO structure to receive information from the file specified by pSrcFile.

**HRESULT \*pHResult**
Can be null.

---

**D3DX10_IMAGE_INFO**
Structure for containing diagnostic information relating to an image file:

```
typedef struct D3DX10_IMAGE_INFO {
    UINT Width;
    UINT Height;
    UINT Depth;
    UINT ArraySize;
    UINT MipLevels;
    UINT MiscFlags;
    DXGI_FORMAT Format;
    D3D10_RESOURCE_DIMENSION ResourceDimension;
    D3DX10_IMAGE_FILE_FORMAT ImageFileFormat;
} D3DX10_IMAGE_INFO, *LPD3DX10_IMAGE_INFO;
```

**UINT Width**
Width of the image file in pixels.

**UINT Height**
Height of the image file in pixels.

**UINT Depth**
Depth of the image file in pixels (if the image is a 3D texture).

**UINT ArraySize**
This will be 1 for a single image.

**UINT MipLevels**
MipMap levels in the image file. For single images, such as JPEGs and PNGs, this will be 1.

**UINT MiscFlags**
This value can be one of the following:
D3D10_RESOURCE_MISC_GENERATE_MIPS
D3D10_RESOURCE_MISC_SHARED
D3D10_RESOURCE_MISC_TEXTURECUBE

D3D10_RESOURCE_MISC_SHARED_KEYEDMUTEX
D3D10_RESOURCE_MISC_GDI_COMPATIBLE

**DXGI_FORMAT Format**
This refers to the pixel format of an image, such as whether it features 8, 16, or 32 bits per channel; whether it contains an alpha channel, etc. A list of the pixel formats available in DirectX can be found in Appendix C. A common format is DXGI_FORMAT_R8G8B8A8_TYPELESS.

**D3D10_RESOURCE_DIMENSION ResourceDimension**
This value indicates the dimension of the texture: 1D, 2D, or 3D. Most textures in file formats such as BMP, JPG, and PNG will be 2D. This can be one of the following values:

D3D10_RESOURCE_DIMENSION_UNKNOWN
D3D10_RESOURCE_DIMENSION_BUFFER
D3D10_RESOURCE_DIMENSION_TEXTURE1D
D3D10_RESOURCE_DIMENSION_TEXTURE2D
D3D10_RESOURCE_DIMENSION_TEXTURE3D

**D3DX10_IMAGE_FILE_FORMAT ImageFileFormat**
Indicates the file format of the image file. This can be one of the following values:

D3DX10_IFF_BMP
D3DX10_IFF_JPG
D3DX10_IFF_PNG
D3DX10_IFF_DDS
D3DX10_IFF_TIFF
D3DX10_IFF_GIF
D3DX10_IFF_WMP

---

**D3DX10CreateTextureFromFile**
Function to load a texture from a file into an ID3D10Resource buffer.

```
HRESULT D3DX10CreateTextureFromFile(
  ID3D10Device *pDevice,
  LPCTSTR pSrcFile,
  D3DX10_IMAGE_LOAD_INFO *pLoadInfo,
  ID3DX10ThreadPump *pPump,
  ID3D10Resource **ppTexture,
  HRESULT *pHResult
);
```

**ID3D10Device *pDevice**
Pointer to a Direct3D device representing the graphics hardware.

**LPCTSTR pSrcFile**
String indicating the fully qualified path of the file to load.

**D3DX10_IMAGE_LOAD_INFO *pLoadInfo**
Can be null or a pointer to a D3DX10_IMAGE_LOAD_INFO structure indicating loading options for the texture file. Please consult the DirectX documentation for more information, if required.

**ID3DX10ThreadPump *pPump**
Can be null.

**ID3D10Resource **ppTexture**
Pointer to a buffer that will receive an ID3D10Resource COM interface, representing the newly loaded texture.

**HRESULT *pHResult**
Can be null.

---

**ID3D10Texture2D::GetDesc**
Function to retrieve diagnostic information from a texture loaded in memory.

```
ID3D10Texture2D::GetDesc(
  D3D10_TEXTURE2D_DESC *pDesc
);
```

**D3D10_TEXTURE2D_DESC *pDesc**
Pointer to a D3D10_TEXTURE2D_DESC structure. This structure, which contains diagnostic information relating to a texture loaded in memory, is often returned by calling the GetDesc method of ID3D10Texture2D. Details concerning this structure were given earlier in this chapter.

## ■ 9.11  Drawing Textures to the Display—Quick Method

The chief purpose of the loadFromFile method of the texture class is to copy the pixels of an image file on disk into a texture buffer in memory, represented by the class member m_TextureInterface. This member is a COM interface ID3D10Texture2D used by DirectX to access the pixels of a texture in memory. Through this interface, DirectX can draw textures to the screen as sprites or wallpaper them onto the surfaces of meshes via materials. The texture class as it stands supports only a method for the loading of a texture and offers no facilities for drawing it to the swap chain, from where it will be shown in the application window. The next section concentrates on building a sprites class whose main function is to draw a collection of textures to the display. But before proceeding with this class, it is worth testing the existing code for the texture class by using a quick but "dirtier" method of presenting a texture to the display. This will allow us to view the texture in the application window and thereby

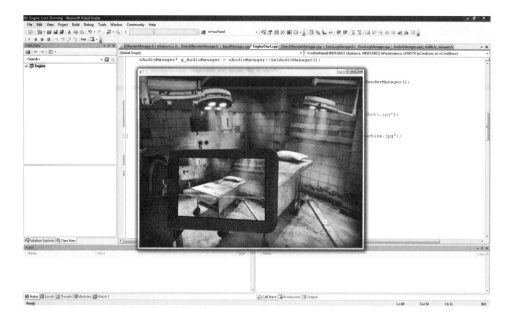

**FIGURE 9.16**    Textures drawn to the display.

confirm that it was successfully loaded by DirectX. See the application running in Figure 9.16.

It has been stated that the back buffer of the swap chain is itself a texture surface (a rectangle of pixels) onto which the graphics device outputs graphical data on each and every frame of the render loop. The device outputs data to the back buffer because the contents of this surface will become visible in the application window at the end of each frame, when the buffers are flipped. DirectX offers a convenient function that allows developers to copy a specified rectangle of pixels from one texture surface to a specified XY position on another surface, just as a graphics artist can use Photoshop to copy pixels from one image and paste them onto another. Therefore, any texture in memory can render itself to the display by copying its pixels to the back buffer texture on each frame, for as long as it wishes to remain visible. To achieve this, the blitRectToBackBuffer method has been added to the texture class. It expects three arguments: one RECT structure defining a rectangle on the source surface to copy, and both the X and Y values representing the top left position on the destination texture where pasting is to begin. This function should be called on each frame (update method) by the render manager, between the calls to ClearRenderTargetView and Present. Please note that the blitRectToBackBuffer method is not intended to be used in the final version of the engine; it is coded here only for testing and debugging purposes—to allow a developer to quickly and easily send the contents of a texture to the display. Its implementation is given here, and comments follow:

```
void cDirectXTexture::blitRectToBackBuffer(RECT Rct, int
X, int Y)
{
    cDirectXRenderManager *RenderManager = cDirectXRenderM
anager::GetDirectXRenderManager();

    ID3D10Texture2D* pBuffer;
    RenderManager->m_pSwapChain->GetBuffer(0, __uuidof
(ID3D10Texture2D ), ( LPVOID* )&pBuffer);

    //Check source rect is equal or smaller than back
buffer rect

    if(((Rct.right-Rct.left) <= RenderManager->m_
BackBufferInfo.Width) &&
        ((Rct.bottom-Rct.top) <= RenderManager->m_
BackBufferInfo.Height))
    {
        D3D10_BOX Crop;
        Crop.left = Rct.left;
        Crop.right = Rct.right;
        Crop.top = Rct.top;
        Crop.bottom = Rct.bottom;
        Crop.front = 0;
        Crop.back = 1;

RenderManager->m_pd3dDevice-
>CopySubresourceRegion(pBuffer, X, Y, 0, 0, m_
TextureInterface, 0, &Crop);
    }

    pBuffer->Release();
}
```

## Comments

- The method begins by using the GetBuffer method of IDXGISwapChain to retrieve an ID3D10Texture2D pointer to the back buffer surface of the swap chain. In effect, this call typecasts the back buffer surface as a texture object that can accept pixel transfers from other textures.

- The blitRectToBackBuffer method allows developers to specify a rectangle region on a source texture to be copied to a specified position on a destination texture. Given that each texture is a finite rectangle of pixels of a specified width and height, it is likely that different textures will be of different sizes to accommodate different images. Thus, a smaller texture could not accommodate all the pixels of a larger texture during a pixel (texel) transfer. If a developer attempts to copy a larger texture *completely* onto a smaller texture, DirectX will invoke an exception and exit on some devices. For this reason, the blitRectToBackBuffer method must compare the size of the *source* rectangle, from which pixels should be copied, with the size of the *destination* surface, where pixels will be pasted. It must deny the blit (copy and pasting) if the sizes are incompatible—that is, if the destination cannot accommodate the source.

- Once the size of the source rectangle and the size of the destination surface have been validated, the method then proceeds to perform the blit using the CopySubresourceRegion method of the graphical device (ID3D10Device), provided the destination surface is large enough to receive the pixels. Details of the CopySubresourceRegion method follow:

---

### ■ CopySubresourceRegion Details

```
void CopySubresourceRegion(
ID3D10Resource *pDstResource,
UINT DstSubresource,
UINT DstX,
UINT DstY,
UINT DstZ,
ID3D10Resource *pSrcResource,
UINT SrcSubresource,
const D3D10_BOX *pSrcBox
);
```

**ID3D10Resource *pDstResource**

Pointer to an ID3D10Resource derived interface representing the destination of the copy operation. Here, this should be a pointer to the back buffer.

**UINT DstSubresource**

Should be 0.

**UINT DstX**

The X coordinate of the point where pasting should begin on the destination.

**UINT DstY**

The Y coordinate of the point where pasting should begin on the destination.

**UINT DstZ**

Should be 0.

**ID3D10Resource *pSrcResource**

Pointer to an ID3D10Resource derived interface representing the source
texture from which data should be copied. Here, this should be a pointer to
a texture loaded from a file.

**UINT SrcSubresource**

Should be 0.

**const D3D10_BOX *pSrcBox**

A DirectX box structure representing the *3D* region of the source surface
from which data should be copied. For a 2D texture, the box represents
a rectangle. The D3D10_BOX structure looks as follows; the preceding
source code demonstrates how to convert values from a RECT to a BOX.

```
typedef struct D3D10_BOX {
    UINT left;
    UINT top;
    UINT front;
    UINT right;
    UINT bottom;
    UINT back;
} D3D10_BOX;
```

**UINT left**

The X position of the left-hand side of the box.

**UINT top**

The Y position of the top of the box.

**UINT front**

The Z position of the front of the box.

**UINT right**

The X position of the right-hand side of the box.

**UINT bottom**

The Y position of the bottom of the box.

**UINT back**

The Z position of the back of the box.

## ■ 9.12    Getting Started with the Sprites Class

The previous section demonstrated a quick method for blitting a loaded texture to the back buffer of the swap chain by using the CopySubresourceRegion method of the graphics device. However, it is not enough for a game that its engine can blit textures to the screen. An engine ought to be able to present its graphics in meaningful arrangements and offer developers control over those arrangements. Presenting textures to the screen, however, can be useful in both 2D and 3D games, for displaying health bars, status messages, and menus. But in dealing with such graphics the developer must be able to:

1. Control the *position, scale, and rotation* of the texture elements on screen. Position refers to the position of an element in 2D screen space (XY). Rotation refers to rotation about the Z axis in 2D screen space. Scaling refers to the stretching or shrinking of an element on each axis according to a scaling factor.

2. Display many elements simultaneously.

3. Do both of the above efficiently; that is, by incurring as small a performance penalty as possible.

This section aims to achieve this by creating a sprites class that allows developers to draw one or more textures to the display at the specified positions, scales, and orientations using matrix transformations. The render manager will maintain a pointer to this class and will be responsible for calling its update method on each frame to draw a batch of sprites to the display. For convenience, the sprites class to be implemented in this section is reproduced here, and comments follow:

```
#define MAX_SPRITES 4096

class cSprites : public cEngineObject
{
private:
protected:
   D3DX10_SPRITE m_SpriteInfo[MAX_SPRITES];
   D3DXVECTOR2 m_Positions[MAX_SPRITES];
   D3DXVECTOR2 m_Scales[MAX_SPRITES];
   cDirectXTexture m_Textures[MAX_SPRITES];
   ID3DX10Sprite *m_SpriteInterface;

public:
   unsigned int m_NumSprites;

   cSprites();

   void setUVCoords(int ID, float Left, float Top, float
```

```
Width, float Height);
    void setColour(int ID, float R, float G, float B,
float A=1.0f);
    void setPos(int ID, float X, float Y);
    void setScale(int ID, float X, float Y);
    bool loadFromFile(int ID, std::wstring fileName);
    void free();

    void update();
};
```

The cSprites class is designed to work alongside the render manager class and encapsulates a collection of sprite objects. That is, it is a collection of one or more textures, each of which is intended *not* to be projected to a mesh through a material but drawn *directly* to the display in screen space, at a specified position, scale, and orientation.

It might be asked at this point why the sprites class should be made to encapsulate a *collection* of sprites. Would it not have been enough to have simply modified the existing texture class with position, scale, and orientation values and have it draw itself? Drawing a collection of textures would then have simply been the result of looping through a collection of cDirectXTexture instances, drawing each individually in sequence.

It *is* true that the texture class could have been implemented in this way, and not only implemented in this way but implemented both successfully and workably. However, the third point of the three points stated above (being able to to work efficiently) requires us to find an optimum solution in terms of performance for rendering sprites to the display. Rendering them individually one after another would work, but DirectX offers an interface specifically designed for the batch rendering of collections of sprites that is fast and simple to use. For performance reasons, therefore, the cSprites class will be working with *collections* of sprites, and not individual sprites. The key properties of this class are detailed below and subsequent sections detail the class's implementation:

**D3DX10_SPRITE m_SpriteInfo[MAX_SPRITES]**
**D3DXVECTOR2 m_Positions[MAX_SPRITES]**
**D3DXVECTOR2 m_Scales[MAX_SPRITES]**
**cDirectXTexture m_Textures[MAX_SPRITES]**

These properties relate to the positions, scales, and textures of the sprites. The sprite info member contains an array of DirectX structures, featuring diagnostic information relating to a sprite. The position and scale arrays use a DirectX 2D vector structure to maintain the position and scaling information for each sprite. And finally, the m_Textures member is an array of cDirectXTexture classes, each element representing the texture to be used for a given sprite. Notice that each is an array sized to MAX_SPRITES (which is 4096). This number is the maximum number of sprites that DirectX supports to be drawn in any one batch. Thus, a single cSprites class supports the drawing of from 0 to 4096 sprites at any one time. The first sprite is at index 0, and the last sprite is at index 4095. Hence, the position of the first sprite would be m_Positions[0], and the scale of the third sprite would be m_Scales[2].

**ID3DX10Sprite \*m_SpriteInterface**

This member refers to a DirectX COM interface that is specifically designed for batch rendering sprites to the display. It features methods for rendering, positioning, and transforming sprites on each frame.

> **NOTE**. As usual, the work of the sprites class begins in the constructor where member variables are initialized to starting values. The constructor method is featured here.

```
cSprites::cSprites() : cEngineObject()
{
  for(int i=0; i<MAX_SPRITES; i++)
  {
      ZeroMemory(&m_SpriteInfo[i], sizeof(D3DX10_
SPRITE));
      m_Positions[i]=D3DXVECTOR2(0,0);;
      m_Scales[i]=D3DXVECTOR2(0,0);
      m_SpriteInfo[i].TexSize.x = 1.0f;
      m_SpriteInfo[i].TexSize.y = 1.0f;
      m_SpriteInfo[i].ColorModulate =
D3DXCOLOR(1.0f, 1.0f, 1.0f,                    1.0f);
  }

  m_SpriteInterface = NULL;
  m_NumSprites = 0;
}
```

## ■ 9.13   Implementing the Sprites Class—Load from File

The sprites class first becomes useful to an application after calling its loadFromFile method. Since the sprites class refers to a collection of sprites, loadFromFile must be called once for each sprite in the collection. The method accepts as its first argument the index of a sprite, and the second argument is the file name of the texture file to be loaded onto that sprite. The loadFromFile method appears as follows:

```
bool cSprites::loadFromFile(int ID, std::wstring
fileName)
{
   if(!m_Textures[ID].loadFromFile(fileName))
        return false;
```

```
        cDirectXRenderManager *RenderManager = cDirectXRender
Manager::GetDirectXRenderManager();

        //Creates a resource view object from a texture
        D3D10_SHADER_RESOURCE_VIEW_DESC SRVDesc;
        ZeroMemory(&SRVDesc, sizeof(SRVDesc));
        SRVDesc.Format = m_Textures[ID].m_Texture_Desc.Format;
        SRVDesc.ViewDimension = D3D10_SRV_DIMENSION_TEXTURE2D;
        SRVDesc.Texture2D.MipLevels = m_Textures[ID].m_
Texture_Desc.MipLevels;

RenderManager->m_pd3dDevice->CreateShaderResourceView(m_
Textures[ID].m_TextureInterface, &SRVDesc, &m_
SpriteInfo[ID].pTexture);

        if(!m_SpriteInterface)
            D3DX10CreateSprite(RenderManager->m_pd3dDevice,0,&m_
SpriteInterface);

        return true;
}
```

## Comments

- The function begins in familiar territory by calling on the loadFromFile method
  of the cDirectXTexture class to load a texture for the specified sprite; that is, to
  load a texture onto the texture object at array index [int ID]. It has been demonstrated in previous sections of this chapter that the cDirectXTexture class actually loads the texture from a file and into an ID3D10Texture2D object.

- The method then proceeds to create a DirectX object called a *shader resource
  view*, which is reminiscent of the name "render target view." Earlier in this chapter it was explained how creating a render target view from the back buffer texture
  was a means of *typecasting* it into a specialized render target view object. This
  object allowed the graphics device to render graphical data there on each frame.
  Similarly, creating a shader resource view is the process of typecasting a texture.
  In this case, a s*hader resource view* allows a texture to be used as a resource for
  a 3D scene. either as a sprite that can be rendered to the display or as a texture
  projected onto a 3D object. In short, a texture must be converted to a shader
  resource view object *before* it can be used in a 3D scene. The loadFromFile method of cDirectXTexture performs this conversion (or typecasting) by calling the
  CreateShaderResourceView method of ID3D10Device. This method expects to
  receive a D3D10_SHADER_RESOURCE_VIEW_DESC structure that describes
  the kind of resource object to be created; in this case, a texture resource view.

More information on this function and other objects can be found in the DirectX Focus—Shader Resource Views and Sprite Objects sidebar that follows shortly.

- Once a shader resource view is created from the ID3D10Texture2D interface of the texture class, the loadFromFile method proceeds to create a DirectX sprite object (ID3DX10Sprite) for rendering batches of sprites. It does this by a call to the function D3DX10CreateSprite. The loadFromFile method will not render data to the display; it only loads textures and prepares COM interfaces for rendering. The rendering will occur in the update method, as with all other DirectX classes created in this chapter.

---

## ■ DirectX Focus—Shader Resource Views and Sprite Objects

DirectX offers the ID3DX10Sprite sprite interface for the efficient batch rendering of textures to the display as sprite objects. This interface is created using the D3DX10CreateSprite function. However, regarding each texture rendered using the Sprite interface, DirectX expects it to have previously been converted into a shader resource view object using the function CreateShaderResourceView. This function expects a developer to provide a shader resource view description using the D3D10_SHADER_RESOURCE_VIEW_DESC structure. Thus, these three are now considered in more detail, in the order in which they are called in the loadFromFile method of cSprites: D3D10_SHADER_RESOURCE_VIEW_DESC, CreateShaderResourceView, and D3DX10CreateSprite.

**D3D10_SHADER_RESOURCE_VIEW_DESC**
This structure is passed to the function CreateShaderResourceView and describes the properties of a shader resource view to be created. The D3D10_SHADER_RESOURCE_VIEW_DESC is described in the following:

```
typedef struct D3D10_SHADER_RESOURCE_VIEW_DESC {
    DXGI_FORMAT Format;
    D3D10_SRV_DIMENSION ViewDimension;
    union {
        D3D10_BUFFER_SRV Buffer;
        D3D10_TEX1D_SRV Texture1D;
        D3D10_TEX1D_ARRAY_SRV Texture1DArray;
        D3D10_TEX2D_SRV Texture2D;
        D3D10_TEX2D_ARRAY_SRV Texture2DArray;
        D3D10_TEX2DMS_SRV Texture2DMS;
        D3D10_TEX2DMS_ARRAY_SRV Texture2DMSArray;
        D3D10_TEX3D_SRV Texture3D;
        D3D10_TEXCUBE_SRV TextureCube;
```

```
      };
  } D3D10_SHADER_RESOURCE_VIEW_DESC;
```

**DXGI_FORMAT Format**

Pixel format of the shader resource view to be created. This can be one of the values from the pixel format enumeration (DXGI_FORMAT) given in Appendix C.

**D3D10_SRV_DIMENSION ViewDimension**

For standard 2D textures, such as JPG or PNG, this should be
D3D10_SRV_DIMENSION_TEXTURE2D. Other values are:
D3D10_SRV_DIMENSION_UNKNOWN
D3D10_SRV_DIMENSION_BUFFER
D3D10_SRV_DIMENSION_TEXTURE1D
D3D10_SRV_DIMENSION_TEXTURE1DARRAY
D3D10_SRV_DIMENSION_TEXTURE2DARRAY
D3D10_SRV_DIMENSION_TEXTURE2DMS
D3D10_SRV_DIMENSION_TEXTURE2DMSARRAY
D3D10_SRV_DIMENSION_TEXTURE3D
D3D10_SRV_DIMENSION_TEXTURECUBE

**D3D10_BUFFER_SRV Buffer**

The buffer contains the following members, which are not described here. Those interested in further details concerning this buffer should consult the official DirectX documentation.
D3D10_TEX1D_SRV Texture1D
D3D10_TEX1D_ARRAY_SRV Texture1DArray
D3D10_TEX2D_SRV Texture2D
D3D10_TEX2D_ARRAY_SRV Texture2DArray
D3D10_TEX2DMS_SRV Texture2DMS
D3D10_TEX2DMS_ARRAY_SRV Texture2DMSArray
D3D10_TEX3D_SRV Texture3D
D3D10_TEXCUBE_SRV TextureCube

**CreateShaderResourceView**

This function converts (typecasts) a standard resource object (such as a texture) into a shader resource view object that can be used by the DirectX renderer in 3D scenes. The CreateShaderResourceView function is described in the following:

```
HRESULT CreateShaderResourceView(
  ID3D10Resource *pResource,
  const D3D10_SHADER_RESOURCE_VIEW_DESC *pDesc,
  ID3D10ShaderResourceView **ppSRView
);
```

**ID3D10Resource \*pResource**

Pointer to an ID3D10Resource derived interface that represents the resource object to be typecast into a shader resource view. In the case of 2D textures, this argument should refer to a ID3D10Texture2D COM interface representing a texture loaded into graphics memory.

**const D3D10_SHADER_RESOURCE_VIEW_DESC \*pDesc**

Pointer to a D3D10_SHADER_RESOURCE_VIEW_DESC structure describing the properties of the shader resource view to be created.

**ID3D10ShaderResourceView \*\*ppSRView**

Pointer to a buffer to receive a valid ID3D10ShaderResourceView interface representing the typecast version of argument pResource. Both ppSRView and pResource are separate objects and should be released individually when releasing is required.

---

**D3DX10CreateSprite**

Creates an ID3DX10Sprite object representing a sprite renderer; that is, an object that batch renders textures to the display.

```
HRESULT D3DX10CreateSprite(
   ID3D10Device *pDevice,
   UINT cDeviceBufferSize,
   LPD3DX10SPRITE *ppSprite
);
```

**ID3D10Device \*pDevice**

Pointer to an ID3D10Device object representing the graphics device.

**UINT cDeviceBufferSize**

The total number of sprites that will be used by the sprite renderer in any one pass. This value can range from 1 to 4096 (MAX_SPRITES).

**LPD3DX10SPRITE \*ppSprite**

Pointer to a buffer to receive the sprite rendering interface.

---

## ■ 9.14   Implementing the Sprites Class— Rendering and Transformations

The loadFromFile method of class cSprites is responsible for loading a specified texture from a file and for both creating and configuring the sprite rendering object, ready for the batch rendering of sprites; that is, for the rendering of textures in screen space according to a series of transformations. The term "transformation" here refers to the process of movement, rotation, and scaling. Thus, transforming a texture in screen space involves positioning it, rotating it, and scaling it according to the 2D screen coordinate system. Rendering of the sprite objects occurs inside the update method of cSprites, and this method is intended to be called by the render manager once per frame. The code for this method is as follows, with comments afterward.

**NOTE**. Key sections of code have been highlighted in bold.

```
void cSprites::update()
{
    if(m_NumSprites<=0)
        return;

    cDirectXRenderManager *RenderManager = cDirectXRenderM
anager::GetDirectXRenderManager();
    D3DXMATRIX matProjection;

    D3DXMatrixOrthoOffCenterLH(&matProjection,RenderManage
r->m_VP.TopLeftX,
                        RenderManager->m_VP.Width,
                        RenderManager->m_VP.TopLeftY,
                        RenderManager->m_VP.Height,
                        0.0f, 10);

    m_SpriteInterface->SetProjectionTransform(&matProjecti
on);

    for(int i=0; i<m_NumSprites; i++)
    {
        D3DXMATRIX Translation;
        D3DXMATRIX Scaling;

        D3DXMatrixIdentity(&Translation);
        D3DXMatrixIdentity(&Scaling);

        D3DXMatrixTranslation(&Translation, m_
Positions[i].x, m_Positions[i].y, 0);
        D3DXMatrixScaling(&Scaling, m_Scales[i].x, m_
Scales[i].y, 0 );

        m_SpriteInfo[i].matWorld = Translation* Scaling;
    }
```

```
    m_SpriteInterface->Begin(D3DX10_SPRITE_SORT_TEXTURE);
    m_SpriteInterface->DrawSpritesImmediate(m_SpriteInfo,
  m_NumSprites, 0, 0);
    m_SpriteInterface->End();
}
```

## Comments

- The update method of cSprites is designed to render a *collection* of textures to the application window, each being rendered according to a specified transformation in screen space (at a specified position, orientation, and scale in screen coordinates).

- The method begins by creating a D3DXMATRIX matrix object to represent the *projection transformation*. It was mentioned earlier that DirectX works with several forms of 3D space. Object space refers to the local 3D coordinate system that is private *for each 3D object* in a scene; its origin is typically at the center of the object. World space refers to the single unified space of a scene in which all 3D objects are situated and remain in relation to each other and to a common origin. View space refers to the position of a camera in 3D space. The purpose of view space is to transform world space so that objects of that world are brought into relationship to the camera. Projection space then projects the 3D view of a 3D world onto the flat surface of a screen. The purpose of the projection matrix then is to transform a 3D world into a 2D view. The mathematics of this process is performed by way of the projection matrix. This book assumes the reader has some familiarity with the concept of the matrix (plural: matrices). However, in short, a matrix is a grid of numbers that represents a *combination* of transformations (translations, rotations, and scales) in one structure. The matrix tells DirectX how to transform one coordinate space into another. Thus, the projection matrix instructs DirectX on how to project the contents of a 3D scene onto the flat surface of a screen. Matrices will also be used later to tell DirectX how to move and position sprites, and how to move and position meshes in a 3D scene. It is not necessary for the reader to have a complete understanding of the mathematics of matrices in order to perform many common transformations, since DirectX provides a series of helper functions that can be used to build matrices, as we shall see shortly. Readers looking for more information on matrices and transforming 3D space with matrices might want to consult the mathematics book recommended earlier in this chapter or to consider the following book: *Introduction to Game Programming with C++* by Alan Thorn (ISBN: 1598220322).

- The update method then calls the DirectX matrix helper function D3DXMatrixOrthoOffCenterLH to build a projection matrix. This function accepts several arguments: the left and top of the viewport, and the width and height of the viewport. It also requires near and far clipping distances, which refer to the horizon lines beyond which 3D objects cannot be seen.

• Once the projection matrix is created in the D3DMATRIX variable matProjection, the update method proceeds to call the SetProjectionTransform method of ID3DX10Sprite. This function binds the newly created projection matrix to the sprite object as the *active projection matrix*. This means that all sprites rendered with *this instance* of ID3DX10Sprite will be transformed by that projection matrix when rendered, *until* that matrix is overwritten by another in a subsequent call to SetProjectionTransform. This method *does not* render data to the screen, but only prepares the projection transformation of the sprite object for rendering.

• Once the projection matrix has been set, the update method of cSprites prepares the sprite objects to be rendered by ID3DX10Sprite. It does this by cycling through its collection of textures, and for each of them it prepares a world transformation matrix. This matrix is responsible for positioning, rotating, and scaling the texture in world space—all according to a common origin and in relation to each other. Positioning a sprite in *world* space corresponds to positioning it on the screen, since (for sprites) there is a 1:1 correspondence between world space and screen space. If an object is to appear at 100 pixels by 100 pixels from an origin in the top left corner of the screen, then (100,100) is the texture's position in world space. For each and every texture of the collection, the update method positions and scales the textures. It starts by creating a unique matrix object for each form of transformation: positioning and scaling. Then it sets each matrix to the identity matrix (that is, to a starting matrix; a blank canvas). It does this using the DirectX matrix function D3DXMatrixIdentity. Then it proceeds to build a matrix for each transformation, storing the result in its respective matrix structure. It builds a translation (positioning) matrix using the D3DXMatrixTranslation function, and a scaling matrix using the D3DXMatrixScaling function. To build the translation matrix, the D3DXMatrixTranslation function is passed the X, Y, and Z positioning values representing the position of the texture in world space. The scaling matrix is built according to the X and Y scaling values. Both the position and scaling data is maintained in the class member properties m_Positions and m_Scales.

• The final step of transforming the textures of the cSprites class involves *combining* each world transformation matrix into one complete transformation. This occurs by multiplying the matrices (the position and scaling matrices) and storing the resultant matrix. That matrix represents the combination of its factors. The resultant matrix is assigned to a member variable (matWorld) of the DirectX structure D3DX10_SPRITE. This structure is used by DirectX to represent a unique sprite, and an application should maintain as many instances of this structure as there are sprites, one for each sprite. The matWorld member of this structure represents the world matrix transformation, and will be used later by the DirectX sprite renderer (ID3DX10Sprite) to correctly position and scale the texture on screen each frame.

• The preceding paragraph explained that for each texture in the collection, there should be position and scaling values and a descriptive D3DX10_SPRITE structure that is to contain the world transformation matrix for its respective texture. This matrix will be used by ID3DX10Sprite when rendering sprites to position and scale them correctly. Once the world transformation matrix has been created for each member, it is the duty of ID3DX10Sprite to render all sprites in the collection as a batch—a batch render. It achieves this by way of three methods: Begin, DrawSpritesImmediate, and End. Once the End method is called, sprite rendering is completed and the rendered data will appear when the graphics device calls the Present method of the swap chain, during the update method of the render manager.

---

### ■ DirectX Focus—Matrix Transformations

Matrices are one of the core mathematical structures used by DirectX to both express and apply affine transformations to objects in 2D and 3D space. Such transformations are said to be *affine* because they involve only the combination of rotation, scaling, and translation. Such transformations do not adjust or amend the structure of the thing transformed. A banana that is moved, scaled, or rotated still remains an intact banana *after* the transformation. Thus, it is affine. But a banana that is squished beneath the force of a falling weight does not emerge intact. Therefore, being squished is not an *affine* transformation, though it is a transformation. Mathematically, a matrix is a grid of numbers, and DirectX provides a slew of functions for building, editing, and combining them. Rather than give the function declaration for each matrix math function, this section will list the matrix building functions available, and the reader can examine them in further detail by consulting the DirectX documentation. The matrix functions are:

```
D3DXMatrixAffineTransformation
D3DXMatrixAffineTransformation2D
D3DXMatrixDecompose
D3DXMatrixDeterminant
D3DXMatrixIdentity
D3DXMatrixInverse
D3DXMatrixIsIdentity
D3DXMatrixLookAtLH
D3DXMatrixLookAtRH
```

```
D3DXMatrixMultiply
D3DXMatrixMultiplyTranspose
D3DXMatrixOrthoLH
D3DXMatrixOrthoOffCenterLH
D3DXMatrixOrthoOffCenterRH
D3DXMatrixOrthoRH
D3DXMatrixPerspectiveFovLH
D3DXMatrixPerspectiveFovRH
D3DXMatrixPerspectiveLH
D3DXMatrixPerspectiveOffCenterLH
D3DXMatrixPerspectiveOffCenterRH
D3DXMatrixPerspectiveRH
D3DXMatrixReflect
D3DXMatrixRotationAxis
D3DXMatrixRotationQuaternion
D3DXMatrixRotationX
D3DXMatrixRotationY
D3DXMatrixRotationYawPitchRoll
D3DXMatrixRotationZ
D3DXMatrixScaling
D3DXMatrixShadow
D3DXMatrixTransformation
D3DXMatrixTransformation2D
D3DXMatrixTranslation
D3DXMatrixTranspose
```

**The Sprite Description Structure (D3DX10_SPRITE)**

One of the structures used by the cSprites class to describe a unique sprite in the textures collection is D3DX10_SPRITE. There should be as many instances of this structure as there are sprites to be rendered, one per sprite. Each structure describes the properties of a sprite. This structure is used by the DrawSpritesImmediate method of the ID3DX10Sprite interface; that is, DrawSpritesImmediate expects to receive an array of such structures, one for each unique sprite. The details of this structure follow:

```
typedef struct D3DX10_SPRITE {
    D3DXMATRIX matWorld;
    D3DXVECTOR2 TexCoord;
    D3DXVECTOR2 TexSize;
    D3DXCOLOR ColorModulate;
    ID3D10ShaderResourceView *pTexture;
    UINT TextureIndex;
} D3DX10_SPRITE;
```

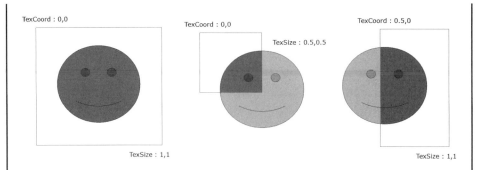

**FIGURE 9.17**   Texture coordinates.

### D3DXMATRIX matWorld
The world transformation matrix to be applied to the sprite.

### D3DXVECTOR2 TexCoord
### D3DXVECTOR2 TexSize
TexCoord refers to the upper left texture coordinate of the sprite, while TexSize refers to the width and height of the sprite in texture coordinates. If the entirety of the texture should be rendered as the sprite, then TexCoord should be (0,0) and TexSize (1,1). However, the texture coordinates can be changed so as to render only a cropped rectangular selection of the texture. Consider Figure 9.17, which illustrates the use of texture coordinates.

### D3DXCOLOR ColorModulate
Specifies a color that is to be used to tint the sprite.

### ID3D10ShaderResourceView *pTexture
Pointer to a shader resource view texture to be applied as the texture of the sprite.

### UINT TextureIndex
Can be 0.

### Using the ID3DX10Sprite Interface
The update method of cSprites calls upon the ID3DX10Sprite interface to batch render a collection of sprites to the back buffer of the swap chain, each sprite according to a specific world and projection transformation. To do this, it calls upon a total of four methods belonging to the ID3DX10Sprite interface: Begin, End, SetProjectionTransform, and DrawSpritesImmediate. These methods are now considered in more detail.

## SetProjectionTransform

This method sets the projection matrix to apply to all subsequently rendered sprites.

```
HRESULT SetProjectionTransform(
  D3DXMATRIX *pProjectionTransform
);
```

## D3DXMATRIX *pProjectionTransform

Pointer to a matrix structure representing the projection transformation matrix.

---

## Begin

The Begin method should be called during the render loop. It prepares ID3DX10-Sprite for drawing a collection of sprites.

```
HRESULT ID3DX10Sprite::Begin(
  UINT flags
);
```

## UINT flags

This flag determines the order in which sprites are rendered to the window. This order affects their depth; that is, affects which sprite will appear on top and which below, assuming that the extents of some sprites will overlap. It can be one of the following values:

D3DX10_SPRITE_SORT_DEPTH_BACK_TO_FRONT
D3DX10_SPRITE_SORT_DEPTH_FRONT_TO_BACK

Draws sprites in the order of their depth (z values).

D3DX10_SPRITE_SORT_TEXTURE

Draws sprites according to their texture so that all sprites in the collection sharing the same texture will be rendered together.

---

## DrawSpritesImmediate

This method renders a specified collection of sprites to the back buffer of the Direct3D swap chain.

```
HRESULT DrawSpritesImmediate(
  D3DX10_SPRITE *pSprites,
  UINT cSprites,
  UINT cbSprite,
  UINT flags
);
```

**D3DX10_SPRITE *pSprites**
Pointer to an array of D3DX10_SPRITE structures representing the collection of sprites to render.
**UINT cSprites**
Indicates the total number of sprites in the array (pSprites).
**UINT cbSprite**
Should be 0.
**UINT flags**
Should be null.

## ■ 9.15   Completing the Sprites Class

The core of the cSprites class consists of the loadFromFile and update methods. Together, these two methods allow a developer to load a collection of textures from files and then to render them to the display. Though the update method configures a world transformation matrix for each texture in the array, allowing each texture to be moved and scaled, it does not yet offer accessor methods that allow developers to set the position and scale properties. As a result, the world transformation matrix will always be built from the default starting position and scale values set inside the class constructor. In addition to the accessor methods for setting sprite positions and scales, the class requires a destructor function inside which the array of textures and the sprite object must be released. The implementations of these functions are straightforward, and are as shown here. These complete the sprites class, and the sidebar Using the cSprite Class demonstrates how a developer might use them to load a sprite object. The sample code for this class as well as the others can also be found in the book's companion code. The next section considers the implementation of the 3D mesh class.

```
//------------------------------------------------------

//Destroys a sprite object
void cSprites::free()
{
   //Release sprite interface
   SAFE_RELEASE(m_SpriteInterface);

   //Release texture array
   for(int i=0; i<MAX_SPRITES; i++)
```

```
            SAFE_RELEASE(m_SpriteInfo[i].pTexture);
}

//-----------------------------------------------------

void cSprites::setUVCoords(int ID, float Left, float Top,
float Width, float Height)
{
   //Set UV coords for specified sprite
   m_SpriteInfo[ID].TexCoord.x = Left;
   m_SpriteInfo[ID].TexCoord.y = Top;
   m_SpriteInfo[ID].TexSize.x = Width;
   m_SpriteInfo[ID].TexSize.y = Height;
}

//-----------------------------------------------------

void cSprites::setColour(int ID, float R, float G, float
B, float A)
{
   //Set colour for specified sprite
   m_SpriteInfo[ID].ColorModulate = D3DXCOLOR(R,G,B,A);
}

//-----------------------------------------------------

void cSprites::setPos(int ID, float X, float Y)
{
   //Set position for specified sprite
   m_Positions[ID].x=X;
   m_Positions[ID].y=Y;
}

//-----------------------------------------------------

void cSprites::setScale(int ID, float X, float Y)
{
   //Set scale for specified sprite
   m_Scales[ID].x=X;
   m_Scales[ID].y=Y;
}

//-----------------------------------------------------
```

### ■ Using the cSprite Class

The cSprites class is intended to work alongside the render manager class, the latter being responsible for calling the update method of the former on each frame. Indeed, the render manager class features a member declared in the header file as "cSprites m_Sprites;". Thus, applications can add a collection of sprites to their scenes by calling the methods of this instance belonging to the render manager. Consider the following example that uses the m_Sprites member and its methods to load a sprite from a 2D PNG texture file. Furthermore, the update method of the render manager will ensure this sprite collection is drawn to the back buffer on each frame.

```
m_DirectXRenderManager->m_Sprites.m_NumSprites=1;
m_DirectXRenderManager->m_Sprites.loadFromFile
(0, L"MyImg.png");
```

> **NOTE.** Notice how our hard work in coding a DirectX render manager and rendering framework has led to a render manager class that is simple to use, requiring only two lines of code to successfully render an image to the display.

## ■ 9.16    Getting Started with Meshes

A mesh is a 3D model formed from vertices, edges, and faces. By using only these three constituents, 3D artists can produce almost limitless complexity and arrangements to approximate real-world objects such as houses, cars, people, monsters, weapons, and more. For this reason, meshes form the greater part of 3D worlds within games; almost every item existing there is a mesh. Meshes are typically produced using a 3D software package such as 3ds Max or Maya, and, when completed, are then *imported* into a 3D game engine. Once imported, the mesh becomes the responsibility of the programmer, who must ensure that their engine renders the mesh appropriately and does not buckle beneath the weight of the mesh's total number of polygons. DirectX supports mesh objects through its ID3DX10Mesh interface, representing a complete mesh object. The term "complete" here means a mesh containing vertices, edges, faces, textures, and texture coordinates. This DirectX mesh interface and its properties, methods, and attendant objects will be encapsulated in the custom-made engine class cDirectXMesh. This class will work alongside the render manager to render a mesh, with one instance of cDirectXMesh per mesh in the scene. It follows therefore that there must be as many cDirectXMesh classes as there are meshes in the scene. The render manager will maintain a list of these mesh objects through its member m_Meshes, and it will ensure that the update method of each mesh is called each and every frame to render the mesh to the back buffer. The class declaration for the mesh class is reproduced here, and then several notable properties of the class are discussed:

```
struct vertex
{
    D3DXVECTOR3 Pos;
    D3DXVECTOR4 Color;
};

class cDirectXMesh : public cEngineObject
{
private:
protected:
public:
    ID3D10Effect* m_Effect;
    ID3D10EffectTechnique* m_Technique;
    ID3DX10Mesh* m_Mesh;
    ID3D10InputLayout* m_VertexLayout;
    ID3D10EffectMatrixVariable* m_pWorldVariable;
    ID3D10EffectMatrixVariable* m_pViewVariable;
    ID3D10EffectMatrixVariable* m_pProjectionVariable;
    D3DXMATRIX m_World;
    D3DXMATRIX m_View;
    D3DXMATRIX m_Projection;

    cDirectXMesh();
    void create();
    void update();
};
```

**ID3D10Effect* m_Effect**
**ID3D10EffectTechnique* m_Technique**
These two members refer to the vertex shader to be applied to the mesh class when rendered. As mentioned, a vertex shader is a program, coded in HLSL (High Level Shader Language), that is run on the graphics hardware for each and every vertex of the mesh on each and every frame. Using the shader, developers can have fast and efficient access to the mesh at the vertex level. This allows effects and specific kinds of mesh deformations to be applied. Coding shaders in HLSL is not within the scope of this book, though this book will use a basic and standard shader for the purposes of demonstrating the rendering of a mesh object. The HLSL code for this shader will be provided in full in a later section of this chapter. For more information on HLSL and vertex shaders, readers are encouraged to consult the following book:

*Introduction to 3D Game Programming with DirectX 9.0c: A Shader Approach* by
Frank D. Luna (ISBN: 1598220160).

**ID3DX10Mesh\* m_Mesh**
**ID3D10InputLayout\* m_VertexLayout**
These two related members represent the mesh loaded into memory. The first COM
interface refers to the mesh object as a collection of vertices, edges, and faces. The second object is descriptive of the first in the sense that it describes how the vertex information of the mesh is structured in memory. The simplest vertex contains only XYZ
position information, but additional information can be added to a vertex: color information, texture coordinate information, and more. The vertex layout object is therefore
used to tell DirectX in which order it is to expect the information for each vertex.

> **NOTE.** The work of the mesh class begins in the constructor, even though
> this method simply initializes the member variables to starting null values.
> For completeness, this method is provided here:

```
cDirectXMesh::cDirectXMesh()
{
  m_Effect = NULL;
  m_Technique = NULL;
  m_Mesh = NULL;
  m_VertexLayout = NULL;

  m_pWorldVariable = NULL;
  m_pViewVariable = NULL;
  m_pProjectionVariable = NULL;
  D3DXMatrixIdentity(&m_World);
  D3DXMatrixIdentity(&m_View);
  D3DXMatrixIdentity(&m_Projection);
}
```

## ■  9.17   Creating and Loading Meshes

The great majority of mesh files used for games approximate real-world objects. Each
mesh can use thousands, perhaps hundreds of thousands, of vertices in order to resemble
real-world detail and smoothness. Due to this level of detail therefore, a mesh is typically created using a 3D modeling package with an approachable mouse-driven GUI, and
not created manually in a text file where a programmer or artist must list each and every
one of the vertices. However, the exact format of a mesh file—the file to which an artist
exports their mesh from 3D software for importing into an engine—varies from game
to game, from engine to engine, and from development studio to development studio.

Some engines use their own proprietary mesh format, while others use a set of long established standards or emerging standards, some of which include the X file format, 3DS format, and COLLADA Format (DAE). Due to the variation among formats and the impact this has on coding work for loading meshes, this chapter will avoid all standards and instead explain how to create meshes from scratch on a vertex basis, so that the reader will be equipped to apply that knowledge to either developing their own custom mesh format or parsing a file belonging to an existing standard. Chapter 10, which focuses on OGRE, will examine how to load mesh objects into 3D scenes using a real-world, freely available, and popular graphics engine for 3D games.

Since the cDirectXMesh class does not load an existing mesh from a file but creates a mesh from scratch (in this case, creates a cube), it features not a loadFromFile method but a create method. This method creates the necessary vertex, edge, and face data for the mesh, defines a basic vertex shader, and creates an ID3DX10Mesh COM interface representing that mesh as a complete entity in a scene. The code for this method follows:

```
void cDirectXMesh::create()
{
//Get render manager
cDirectXRenderManager *RenderManager = cDirectXRender
Manager::GetDirectXRenderManager();

//Load vertex shader from file
D3DX10CreateEffectFromFile( L"MyShader.fx", NULL, NULL,
"fx_4_0", D3D10_SHADER_ENABLE_STRICTNESS, 0,
                                        RenderManager-
>m_pd3dDevice, NULL, NULL, &m_Effect, NULL, NULL );

    m_Technique = m_Effect->GetTechniqueByName( "Render"
);

    D3D10_INPUT_ELEMENT_DESC layout[] =
    {
        { "POSITION", 0, DXGI_FORMAT_R32G32B32_FLOAT,
0, 0, D3D10_INPUT_PER_VERTEX_DATA, 0 },
        { "COLOR", 0, DXGI_FORMAT_R32G32B32A32_FLOAT,
0, 12, D3D10_INPUT_PER_VERTEX_DATA, 0 },
    };

    UINT numElements = sizeof( layout ) / sizeof(
layout[0] );

    D3D10_PASS_DESC PassDesc;
    m_Technique->GetPassByIndex( 0 )->GetDesc( &PassDesc
```

```
);

    RenderManager->m_pd3dDevice->CreateInputLayout(
layout, numElements, PassDesc.pIAInputSignature,
                                       PassDesc.
IAInputSignatureSize, &m_VertexLayout );

    RenderManager->m_pd3dDevice->IASetInputLayout( m_
VertexLayout );

//Create vertices

vertex v[] =
{
{ D3DXVECTOR3( -1.0f, 1.0f, -1.0f ), D3DXVECTOR4( 0.0f,
0.0f, 1.0f, 1.0f ) },
{ D3DXVECTOR3( 1.0f, 1.0f, -1.0f ), D3DXVECTOR4( 0.0f,
1.0f, 0.0f, 1.0f ) },
{ D3DXVECTOR3( 1.0f, 1.0f, 1.0f ), D3DXVECTOR4( 0.0f,
1.0f, 1.0f, 1.0f ) },
{ D3DXVECTOR3( -1.0f, 1.0f, 1.0f ), D3DXVECTOR4( 1.0f,
0.0f, 0.0f, 1.0f ) },{ D3DXVECTOR3( -1.0f, -1.0f, -1.0f
), D3DXVECTOR4( 1.0f, 0.0f, 1.0f, 1.0f ) },
{ D3DXVECTOR3( 1.0f, -1.0f, -1.0f ), D3DXVECTOR4( 1.0f,
1.0f, 0.0f, 1.0f ) },
{ D3DXVECTOR3( 1.0f, -1.0f, 1.0f ), D3DXVECTOR4( 1.0f,
1.0f, 1.0f, 1.0f ) },
{ D3DXVECTOR3( -1.0f, -1.0f, 1.0f ), D3DXVECTOR4( 0.0f,
0.0f, 0.0f, 1.0f ) },
            };

//Create indices

    UINT numVertices = sizeof(v)/sizeof(v[0]);

            DWORD i[] =
            {
                3,1,0,
                2,1,3,

                0,5,4,
                1,5,0,

                3,4,7,
                0,4,3,
```

```
                      1,6,5,
                      2,6,1,

                      2,7,6,
                      3,7,2,

                      6,4,5,
                      7,4,6,
            };

    UINT numIndices = sizeof(i)/sizeof(i[0]);

    if(SUCCEEDED(D3DX10CreateMesh(RenderManager->m_
pd3dDevice, layout, numElements, "POSITION", numVertices,
                             numIndices/3, D3DX10_
MESH_32_BIT, &m_Mesh)))
      {
            m_Mesh->SetVertexData(0, v);
            m_Mesh->SetIndexData(i, numIndices);
            m_Mesh->CommitToDevice();
      }
}
```

## Comments

- The create method of cDirectXMesh begins by loading a specified effect file into an ID3D10Effect buffer using the DirectX function D3DX10CreateEffectFromFile. This function reads and parses the script (HLSL) of an effect file and loads a compiled version into memory as an effect buffer, stored in the class member m_Effect. The effect file can contain a collection of vertex shaders. In short, the effect file can consist of one or more *techniques* that are to be applied to the mesh *on each frame of the render loop.* Each technique can contain one or more *passes,* and each pass can contain one or more *shaders.* Thus, a technique refers to a *collection of passes.* A pass represents a method (style) for rendering 3D geometry (such as a mesh). A pass can contain *one or more* vertex shaders, and these shaders will be run for that pass.

A vertex shader is responsible for rendering the vertices of the mesh on each frame. For each frame of the render loop, a technique must be selected, and then a pass. Once a pass is selected, the associated vertex shaders will be executed once per vertex of the mesh. Each vertex is passed to the shader function as an argument, and the shader is responsible for processing the argument, applying any transformations required, and then outputting a resultant vertex. It is this resultant vertex that is passed onto DirectX as the final vertex to be rendered. The shaders in the effect file loaded in this example do nothing except output the same input vertex intact, and thus the mesh renders in its default state; that is, with no change applied. Please note that the effect file is not executed at the time of loading. It is run once every frame for each object to which it is applied. The effect file that will be used for this sample is listed here:

```
    matrix World;
    matrix View;
    matrix Projection;


struct VS_OUTPUT
{
    float4 Pos : SV_POSITION;
    float4 Color : COLOR0;
};

// Vertex shader
//----------------------------------------------------

VS_OUTPUT VS( float4 Pos : POSITION, float4 Color : COLOR
)
{
    VS_OUTPUT output = (VS_OUTPUT)0;
    output.Pos = mul( Pos, World );
    output.Pos = mul( output.Pos, View );
    output.Pos = mul( output.Pos, Projection );
    output.Color = Color;
    return output;
}

// Pixel shader
//----------------------------------------------------

float4 PS( VS_OUTPUT input ) : SV_Target
{
    return input.Color;
}


technique10 Render
{
    pass P0
    {
```

```
            SetVertexShader( CompileShader( vs_4_0, VS() ) );
            SetGeometryShader( NULL );
            SetPixelShader( CompileShader( ps_4_0, PS() ) );
        }
    }
```

- Once an effect file is loaded into the buffer m_Effect, it proceeds to extract from that buffer a render technique of a specified name. This is achieved by a call to GetTechniqueByName, and the technique extracted in this case is called render. It is noted that the shader file defined earlier declares this technique. The technique has one pass (p0), and this pass features a vertex shader and a pixel shader.

- For this example, each and every vertex of the mesh features both positional data (XYZ) and color data (RGBA), though vertices *can* contain even more data than this, including application-specific data. Given the flexibility of the format in which a vertex can be represented to DirectX, it is necessary that an application declares to DirectX the structure of the vertex format being used for any item of 3D geometry. An application must declare to DirectX the order in which the elements of a vertex data structure will be encountered when parsed in memory. This is to ensure that DirectX can know in advance the size in bytes of each vertex in the vertex array (vertex buffer), and can know which segment of that data includes positional information. An application notifies the API of a vertex format by creating an input layout object. It creates this object by first declaring the input layout description, which is a description of the vertex format. The following code has been extracted from the create function. It defines both a "position" value and a "color" value, giving a data type for each, and it defines the position *before* the color. Notice that this structure declaration corresponds to the vertex data structure (struct vertex), declared at the top of the render manager header file:

```
    D3D10_INPUT_ELEMENT_DESC layout[] =
    {
        { "POSITION", 0, DXGI_FORMAT_R32G32B32_FLOAT,
0, 0, D3D10_INPUT_PER_VERTEX_DATA, 0 },

        { "COLOR", 0, DXGI_FORMAT_R32G32B32A32_FLOAT,
0, 12, D3D10_INPUT_PER_VERTEX_DATA, 0 },
    };
```

- Once the vertex format has been described using the standard DirectX D3D10_INPUT_ELEMENT_DESC structure, the method continues by first creating a layout object using the CreateInputLayout method of the Direct3D render device and then by registering this created object with the rendering pipeline using the method IASetInputLayout. The former method populates a member buffer (m_

VertexLayout) with a pointer to a valid input layout object. The latter method registers this object as the active layout, to be used by DirectX when parsing the vertex data of all 3D objects.

- It has been stated that the purpose of the layout object is to register a vertex format definition with the rendering pipeline so that DirectX can iterate through all the vertices of a mesh. Having created the layout object, a developer should proceed to create the vertex data itself. Conventionally, the vertex data of a mesh is loaded from a proprietary file that was created using a 3D modeling program. But given that no single mesh standard is so firmly entrenched in the contemporary games industry as are the standards for 2D images (such as JPG and PNG), this book does not make assumptions about the format of mesh files that might be used by the reader. Instead, it examines how to manually create the mesh vertex data in code, piecing together a mesh and allowing the reader to code a parser for the format of their choice.

- At first, the creation of a mesh might seem to start by creating an array of vertex objects, with each element of the array representing a single vertex in the mesh. In this way, a single array holds each and every vertex of the mesh. Stated like this, however, the solution would not be optimum because it would involve duplication of data, as this array would be storing duplicate vertices wherever any two faces meet. Any single vertex represents one of the end points of an edge, and thus is a corner point for any two adjoining faces. For this reason, for every two adjoining faces of the mesh there will be a shared vertex at the point where their edges touch. Thus, the vertex array of the mesh should contain not *all* vertices but all *unique* vertices. Consider Figure 9.18.

In addition to such an array (*a1*), it will be necessary to declare a second array (*a2*) defining which of the vertices from *a1* form the corner points of the same face. DirectX must be told, for example, that any face *f* is formed by three

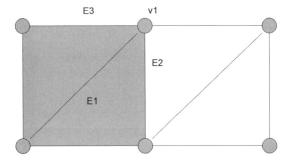

Edges E1, E2, E3 Share a vertex v1

**FIGURE 9.18**    Shared vertices.

vertices *v1*, *v2*, and *v3*. It must be told this for each and every face in the mesh. This is achieved using an index buffer (array) where every three elements of the array define the three vertices for a unique face. Each single element of the index buffer represents the index (array offset) of a vertex in the vertex array.

> NOTE. Chapter 10 considers the loading of meshes from existing files using the open source 3D rendering engine OGRE.

- The final stage of building the mesh begins with a call to the DirectX function D3DX10CreateMesh. This function accepts as arguments the vertex format layout structure for the vertices of the mesh, the total number of vertices in the mesh, the total number of indices, and a pointer to a buffer that is to receive an ID3DX10Mesh mesh interface representing the newly created mesh. The returned mesh class features no vertices or indices; this function simply creates a blank mesh, ready to populate with vertices in the corresponding vertex format. The function then proceeds to call three mesh creation methods, each applied to the newly created mesh. The first is SetVertexData. This method is used to fill the mesh with the vertices defined earlier. The next is SetIndexData, used to fill the mesh with index information relating to the vertices. The last is CommitToDevice, which effectively saves (or registers) the changes made to the mesh class. After the CommitToDevice method is called, the new mesh is ready to render.

---

### ■ DirectX Focus—Mesh Creation

The create method of class cDirectXMesh is responsible for manually building a mesh structure in a 3D scene. It does this by: (1) creating and configuring a vertex shader for mesh rendering, (2) defining a vertex format to be used for storing mesh data, (3) registering that format with DirectX, (4) creating a vertex and index buffer representing the geometry of the mesh, and (5) creating a mesh object based on that data. This process is achieved by calling a series of DirectX functions, the most important of which are now detailed here for convenience and clarity.

**Vertex Shaders**
As will be demonstrated shortly, mesh rendering depends for its success on a vertex shader, even when the shader does nothing but output the vertices unchanged. Vertex shaders are loaded using the D3DX10CreateEffectFromFile function of DirectX 10.

```
HRESULT D3DX10CreateEffectFromFile(
   LPCTSTR pFileName,
   CONST D3D10_SHADER_MACRO *pDefines,
```

```
        ID3D10Include *pInclude,
        LPCSTR pProfile,
        UINT HLSLFlags,
        UINT FXFlags,
        ID3D10Device *pDevice,
        ID3D10EffectPool *pEffectPool,
        ID3DX10ThreadPump *pPump,
        ID3D10Effect **ppEffect,
        ID3D10Blob **ppErrors,
        HRESULT *pHResult
    );
```

**LPCTSTR pFileName**

The fully qualified path of the file containing the vertex shader and effect information to be parsed and loaded.

**CONST D3D10_SHADER_MACRO *pDefines**

Can be null.

**ID3D10Include *pInclude**

Can be null.

**LPCSTR pProfile**

A string defining the profile (or shader version) to be used when parsing the loaded shader. For standard DirectX 10 projects, this value should be "fx_4_0."

**UINT HLSLFlags**

Typically, this will be D3D10_SHADER_ENABLE_STRICTNESS.

**UINT FXFlags**

This can be 0. Please see the official documentation for more information regarding this value, if required.

**ID3D10Device *pDevice**

Pointer to an ID3D10Device graphics device.

**ID3D10EffectPool *pEffectPool**

**ID3DX10ThreadPump *pPump**

These can be null.

**ID3D10Effect **ppEffect**

Pointer to a buffer that will receive a valid ID3D10Effect interface when and if the function returns successfully.

**ID3D10Blob **ppErrors**

**HRESULT *pHResult**

These can be null.

**Input Layouts**

The input layout object is created to define a vertex structure prior to its use. By creating this object, an application can create and load 3D geometry whose vertex information is in this format. The input layout object is created by calling the CreateInputLayout method.

```
HRESULT CreateInputLayout(
  const D3D10_INPUT_ELEMENT_DESC
*pInputElementDescs,
  UINT NumElements,
  const void *pShaderBytecodeWithInputSignature,
  SIZE_T BytecodeLength,
  ID3D10InputLayout **ppInputLayout
);
```

**const D3D10_INPUT_ELEMENT_DESC *pInputElementDescs**

An array whose elements in total describe the format of the vertex data to be used when rendering. Each element in the array corresponds to a unique field of the format. The first might be "Position," representing a 3D position vector, and the second might be color or texture coordinate data.

**UINT NumElements**

The total number of elements in the array specified by pInputElementDescs.

**const void *pShaderBytecodeWithInputSignature**
**SIZE_T BytecodeLength**

The input signature identifying a vertex shader and its bytecode length. These values can be obtained by calling the GetDesc method of the ID3D10Effect-Technique interface representing a technique in the shader effect file.

**ID3D10InputLayout **ppInputLayout**

Pointer to a buffer to receive a pointer to a valid ID3D10InputLayout interface if the function call is successful. This interface represents the vertex format.

**Mesh Objects**

A mesh is a collection of vertices, edges, and faces. It can be either created from scratch or loaded from a file on disk. To create a mesh from scratch, D3DX10CreateMesh is used. This function creates an empty mesh ready to be populated with vertex and index data using the SetVertexData and SetIndexData methods, respectively.

```
HRESULT D3DX10CreateMesh(
  ID3D10Device *pDevice,
```

```
      CONST D3D10_INPUT_ELEMENT_DESC *pDeclaration,
      UINT DeclCount,
      LPCSTR pPositionSemantic,
      UINT VertexCount,
      UINT FaceCount,
      UINT Options,
      ID3DX10Mesh **ppMesh
    );
```

**ID3D10Device *pDevice**

Pointer to an ID3D10Device device.

**CONST D3D10_INPUT_ELEMENT_DESC *pDeclaration**

Vertex format description to be applied to the vertices of the mesh.

**UINT DeclCount**

Total number of elements in the declaration array specified by pDeclaration.

**LPCSTR pPositionSemantic**

String defining the name of the element containing positional information—the core data of a vertex. This value depends on the name given by the developer to the positional data. For this chapter, the name "POSITION" is used.

**UINT VertexCount**

The total number of vertices of the mesh.

**UINT FaceCount**

The total number of faces of the mesh.

**UINT Options**

Typically, this will be D3DX10_MESH_32_BIT.

**ID3DX10Mesh **ppMesh**

Pointer to a buffer to receive a valid mesh object if the function call is successful.

```
    HRESULT SetVertexData(
      UINT iBuffer,
      CONST void *pData
    );
```

**UINT iBuffer**

Total number of vertices in the buffer specified by pData.

**CONST void *pData**

Pointer to an array of vertices to be used for the mesh.

```
    HRESULT SetIndexData(
      CONST void *pData,
```

```
    UINT cIndices
  );
```

**CONST void *pData**
Pointer to an array of indices.
**UINT cIndices**
Total number of indices in the array specified by pData.

## ■ 9.18   Rendering Meshes

The previous section explained how a developer can create a mesh manually by defining the vertex, edge, and face data using a combination of vertex and index buffers, and the ID3DX10Mesh interface. ID3DX10Mesh represents a complete mesh in a 3D scene and, once created, that mesh can be rendered to the display on each frame of the render loop. The cDirectXMesh class supports the rendering of a mesh in its update method, which is intended to be called once by the render manager on each and every frame. The code for this method is given here, and comments follow:

```
void cDirectXMesh::update()
{
   //Gets render manager object
   cDirectXRenderManager *RenderManager = cDirectXRender
Manager::GetDirectXRenderManager();

   m_pWorldVariable = m_Effect->GetVariableByName
( "World" )->AsMatrix();
   m_pViewVariable = m_Effect->GetVariableByName( "View"
)->AsMatrix();
   m_pProjectionVariable = m_Effect->GetVariableByName(
"Projection" )->AsMatrix();

   // Initialize the view matrix
   D3DXVECTOR3 Eye( 0.0f, 1.0f, -5.0f );
   D3DXVECTOR3 At( 0.0f, 1.0f, 0.0f );
   D3DXVECTOR3 Up( 0.0f, 1.0f, 0.0f );
   D3DXMatrixLookAtLH( &m_View, &Eye, &At, &Up );

   // Initialize the projection matrix
   D3DXMatrixPerspectiveFovLH( &m_Projection, ( float )
D3DX_PI * 0.5f,
   RenderManager->m_VP.Width / ( FLOAT )RenderManager->m_
```

```
VP.Height, 0.1f, 100.0f );

    m_pWorldVariable->SetMatrix(m_World);
    m_pViewVariable->SetMatrix(m_View);
    m_pProjectionVariable->SetMatrix(m_Projection);

    D3D10_TECHNIQUE_DESC techDesc;
     m_Technique->GetDesc(&techDesc);
     for( UINT p = 0; p < techDesc.Passes; ++p )
     {
         m_Technique->GetPassByIndex( p )->Apply( 0 );
          m_Mesh->DrawSubset(0);
     }
}
```

## Comments

- The update method begins by retrieving pointers to the world, view, and projection matrices to be applied to the mesh in order to transform world space into view space and view space into projection space where the mesh will be rendered to the display, provided it is within sight of the camera. The matrix variables are declared and used by the vertex shader in the effect file. Once pointers to these

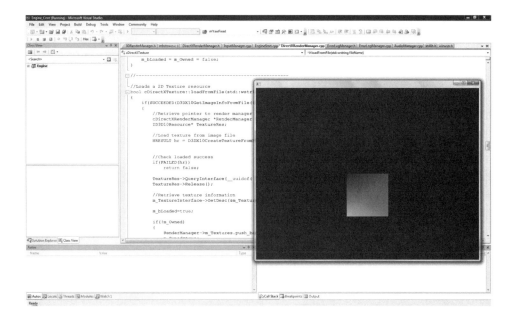

**FIGURE 9.19**    Rendering a mesh.

matrices are obtained the method proceeds to edit them as appropriate, building a suitable view and project matrix, and also a world transformation matrix that can be used to move, rotate, and scale the mesh in world space. The matrices are applied to the mesh through repeated calls to the setMatrix method, once per matrix kind: view, world, and projection.

- The final stage of rendering involves iterating through all *passes* for the render technique of the vertex shader associated with the mesh. For each pass, the pass will be applied to (run on) the mesh, and the mesh DrawSubset method is finally called to render the mesh to the back buffer of the swap chain; that is, to render the mesh to the window at the end of the frame (when Present is called by the render manager). See Figure 9.19 in which an application is rendering a cube mesh to the application window.

## ■ 9.19 Using the Render Manager

The render manager and its attendant class framework created in this chapter now support the following features: the loading and unloading of textures, their rendering to the display as 2D screen elements, and the loading and rendering of meshes in a unified 3D world space. Much has been said of DirectX 10 in its capacity for rendering graphics, and much also has been said of the implementation details of the four classes that constitute the 3D rendering framework for our incipient engine. These classes are: cDirectXTexture, cSprites, cDirectXMesh, and cDirectXRenderManager. However, in discussing the implementation details of these classes, little has been said of their usage, of how a developer is supposed to call on the methods of these classes to render data to the screen. It was shown earlier how a developer might use the framework to render sprites, but it has not yet been demonstrated how to use the framework to render meshes. The following code shows how to do this in the initialization function of an application:

```
//Get render manager
cDirectXRenderManager* m_DirectXRenderManager = cDirectX
RenderManager::GetDirectXRenderManager();

//Initialize render manager
m_DirectXRenderManager->init(hInstance, 800,600,false,"My
Window");

//Create mesh class
cDirectXMesh Mesh;
```

```
//Build or load vertex data
Mesh.create();

//Add mesh to render manager mesh list
m_DirectXRenderManager->m_Mesh.push_back(&Mesh);
```

> **NOTE.** Notice how far the engine classes go toward abbreviating the pro-
> cess of mesh creation and rendering. In a few straightforward lines of code,
> a mesh is created and ready to render. This mesh is rendered by calling the
> update method of the render manager on each frame of the render loop. The
> render manager is internally responsible for calling the update method of all
> its renderable member objects such as meshes, textures, and sprites.

## ■ 9.20   Chapter Summary

This chapter focused on creating a DirectX 10 3D render manager component for an
engine. This rendering framework consisted of a total of four classes, representing
textures, sprites, meshes, and the manager overseeing their operation. The manager
component itself delegates much of the loading and rendering work to other classes and
is chiefly responsible for both initializing and uninitializing the graphics hardware
that is to sustain the rendering of graphics to the application window. It is important to
note, however, that the 3D render manager as it stands presently is very limited in its
scope and is by no means feature-filled. Rendering meshes to the display is certainly a
start toward building content-rich 3D worlds, but it is not enough in itself to render those
worlds efficiently. The current 3D render manager does not, for example, include any
methods for optimizing mesh geometry managing the objects in 3D scenes, or optimizing the rendering process by excluding meshes that are not immediately visible to the
camera. It neither offers support for advanced texturing techniques, such as normal or
bump mapping to enhance the realism of 3D scenes, nor does it currently support particle
systems for creating effects like rain and snow. The next chapter takes us forward in this
direction toward 3D scene management, and it does so not by extending the work of the
DirectX render manager—valuable though that is—but by opening up the hood on an
existing graphics rendering engine, called OGRE (Object-Oriented Graphics Rendering
Engine). This open source and generally free-to-use engine is now firmly established in
the contemporary games industry, having powered many commercial game projects. By
examining how OGRE addresses the issue of 3D scene management, readers will have
the opportunity to both learn how to use OGRE for their own projects and take inspira-
tion from its current design so as to more effectively meet the challenge of implementing similar features in their own engines using the DirectX render manager.

# 10 Scene Management and OGRE 3D

## Overview

After completing this chapter, you should:

- Appreciate the importance of scene management for 3D games
- Understand the concept of octrees, scene graphs, animation keying, and frustrum culling
- Be able to set up and use OGRE 3D for rendering 3D graphics
- Load mesh objects from files exported from 3D applications
- Have gained a grasp of materials and lighting in 3D games as well of 3D scene management

The previous chapter was dedicated to building a 3D render manager framework using the DirectX 10 SDK. The 3D render manager was intended to be a 3D counterpart to the 2D SDL render manager coded earlier in this book. As such, it shared with the SDL render manager the purpose of initializing the graphics hardware, sustaining a render loop, and drawing 3D graphics to the application window on each and every frame. The term "3D graphics" is here meant to indicate mesh data in a unified world space consisting of vertices, edges, and faces, of which the latter can be "skinned" with materials and textures. In order to draw such graphics to the window, it was necessary for the developer to implement an additional set of classes associated with the render manager, including the texture, the sprite, and the mesh classes. The texture class encapsulated a 2D image loaded into memory from a file, the sprite class was intended to draw such textures to the display in 2D screen space to represent 2D elements such as health bars and messages, and the mesh class was built to encapsulate a mesh object in 3D space. However, in creating all of these items—important though they were and still are—the DirectX render manager still suffered some severe limitations. Specifically, the following three key problems were identified in the 3D render manager:

- It cannot load mesh data from files.

  Though the 3D render manager framework supports a mesh class for representing mesh data in a scene, this class does not support the loading of mesh data from a file on disk. At present, a developer must manually build a mesh in code by defining an array of vertices, specifying a position value for each and every vertex. Though this method works insofar as it can be used to build basic 3D primitives such as cubes, spheres, and cylinders, it is not generally suitable for building complex objects with perhaps many thousands of polygons such as monsters, buildings, and vehicles. To build these items, an artist would be unlikely to just blindly type in positional values for all vertices of the mesh but rather would use a GUI-driven 3D modeling package such as 3ds Max, Maya, or Blender. With this software, an artist can interactively build a mesh with its modeling tools, receiving immediate visual feedback on their actions. Building a mesh in such software, however, incurs the problem of data migration, for both artists and programmers need a means of exporting mesh data *from* modeling software *to* the game engine, where it can be featured inside the scenes of a 3D game. This migration usually occurs by way of a *mesh file*. The artist builds a mesh and then exports that data into a mesh file of a specified format, and the engine then imports that data by parsing the file. This, however, depends on the 3D modeling software and the engine sharing a common understanding as to the file format to be used for storing the mesh data. At the time of writing, there is no standard file format in the games industry for storing meshes. Rather, engines tend to use their own proprietary formats and provide exporter plug-ins for a selection of 3D software packages. Rather than spend time looking into the creation of a custom-made mesh file format, this chapter will consider OGRE and the features it offers for loading meshes from files, complete with texture and material data. It will also examine an exporter plug-in for three common 3D modeling packages so that artists can export their meshes to this format.

- It offers no support for 3D scene management.

  An earlier chapter explained the importance of scene management in the world of 2D scenes, and what was said regarding its importance for 2D scenes applies no less to 3D scenes. The render manager as it stands supports the loading and transformation of meshes in 3D space, but this alone is not enough for building 3D scenes efficiently. The loading of a single mesh and its positioning at the origin in 3D space does not pose a scene management problem. Being a lone mesh and being at the origin means the camera can view the entirety of the scene at a glance without the need to move elsewhere, and the mesh exists in no relation to any other mesh in the scene. However, most 3D games feature substantially more content than that in their scenes. For example, consider a first-person shooter game, in which the camera of the scene represents the player's view into the 3D world. A typical "level" (or scene) in a sci-fi first-person shooter might allow the player to roam an abandoned space station environment, complete with smoke-filled corridors, swinging platforms, and strange bubbling lava pits in the engine room. In such an environment, the player will need to move around in order to explore areas not immediately in view and to find roaming enemies who will themselves be moving around. Thus, because a game designer when building a level is not limited to only what the player can see from their view at any one point, it follows that in theory game environments can stretch on almost without limit. However, the memory of any one computer and its capacity to hold scene information is by no means limitless. Thus, the potentially limitless scenes on the one hand and the most certainly limited memory of a computer on the other pose a scene management problem—how to create massive 3D environments (or to create the illusion of massive 3D environments) by limited means. This represents one of the many scene management problems. Another is the management of the relationships that exist between 3D objects in a shared space. It is true that each 3D object has its own position, scale, and orientation. These are set in DirectX, as we have seen, by the world transformation matrix. However, none of these values for any one object can be said to be entirely independent of those of other objects in the scene. An environment with swinging platforms onto which the player and enemies may leap and walk makes this problem clearer. The platforms may swing back and forth at their own momentum while the player moves around on the ground below; neither has an effect on the other. But as the player steps away from stable ground and onto a moving platform, his or her position is no longer independent of that of the platform. By stepping onto a platform, the position of the player is brought into relation with the position of the platform. The player is indeed free to move around in the local space of the surface of the platform, but as the platform swings from left to right and right to left, the position of the player is locked with it. The result is that the player moves in world space along with the platform, swinging back and forth. The player is not unrealistically hovering in the air unaffected by the movement of the platform, but swings with the platform as it moves, and this occurs for as long as the player remains on the platform. Thus, the second problem of scene management is the representation of relationships between objects in a scene. This chapter will examine how OGRE resolves both problems in 3D.

- It does not support 3D lighting.

The DirectX render manager displayed its meshes and scenes using only the default ambient light, which is a light that pervades the scene, casting light uniformly in all directions and whose intensity does not diminish with distance, unlike real-world lighting. The result is that meshes put into the scene under default lighting will be illuminated from all sides regardless of their position in 3D space, since ambient light shines everywhere at equal intensity. Though such an ambient lighting method can be useful for both programmers and artists as a diagnostic tool—for previewing both their meshes as a whole and their arrangement in the scene without either darkening or shadows—it does not make for realistic-looking scenes when presented to the user in this way. In real-world scenarios—both in interior and exterior scenes—light has both a position and a size. In exterior daytime scenes, the key (brightest) light is usually the sun; the sun is also the key light for interior day scenes. For interior night scenes, however, the key light is usually an artificial light such as a lamp or a torch. Regardless of the light source, however, the light can be said to have position in space and a size (in terms of the size of the area that is casting the light) as well as intensity and color. The intensity of a light refers to its brightness, and this diminishes with distance. In real-world lights, intensity diminishes at an inverse square ratio, but computer lights often diminish linearly for performance reasons. This chapter will examine how lights work in 3D using OGRE.

## ■ 10.1    Moving Forward with OGRE 3D

The previous section identified three fundamental problems with the DirectX render manager that relate to 3D scene management: (1) loading meshes from files, (2) maintaining relationships between objects in a scene, and (3) 3D lighting. These problems are not inherent to the DirectX SDK but to the manager component of the engine. For example, DirectX does offer support for 3D lighting and also offers a few methods for optimizing 3D scenes such as back-face culling. A game engine, though, is generally supposed to provide its own scene management features, either homemade features or features provided through an additional third-party library such as OpenSceneGraph. Without these scene management features, the render manager can still render meshes and present 3D scenes, but its ability to do so both efficiently and with realism is greatly limited. In order to inspire the reader to resolve these issues in the DirectX render manager, this book considers a fully featured and widely used graphics rendering engine called OGRE. This engine already features support for rendering meshes from files, creating scene hierarchies and relationships, and 3D lighting, as well as for texturing, vertex shaders, particle systems, scene optimizations, and other effects. By examining these features of OGRE, this chapter will demonstrate how issues such as lighting, scene management, and mesh loading are handled in 3D engines as well as give the reader a basic grounding in the use of OGRE itself. Furthermore, OGRE is open source, meaning the reader can examine, learn from, and extend upon its source code, and this book will demonstrate how to download and compile OGRE from source. Before proceeding further into coding details, it will be necessary to pause and consider OGRE as a whole: what it is, for whom it is intended, and why it is used, and also what it is not. Having considered this, it will also become necessary to flesh out a rough design as to exactly what this chapter seeks to achieve with OGRE, on a feature-by-feature basis. Overall, this chapter will more likely read as a guide to OGRE than as a guide to encapsulating it into a separate scene manager component for an engine. But it is by presenting the material in this way that the widest ground and the greatest detail can be covered concerning OGRE. Once a firm grounding in the OGRE library has been given, with a clear and dedicated focus on its feature set, the reader will be that much more equipped to apply their newly gained knowledge either to their own engine or to extending an existing engine, depending on their needs.

## 10.2   Introducing OGRE 3D

OGRE 3D has been used to power many commercial games, including Zero Gear (see Figure 10.1), Jack Keane, Torchlight™, and Zombie Driver (see Figure 10.2). The official OGRE 3D website defines OGRE as follows:

What Is OGRE? OGRE (Object-Oriented Graphics Rendering Engine) is a scene-oriented, flexible 3D engine written in C++ designed to make it easier and more intuitive for developers to produce applications utilising hardware-accelerated 3D graphics. The class library abstracts all the details of using

**FIGURE 10.1**   Made with OGRE: Image from Zero Gear. Courtesy of David Marsh, NimbleBit.

**FIGURE 10.2**    Made with OGRE: Image from Zombie Driver™. Courtesy of EXOR Studios™.

the underlying system libraries like Direct3D and OpenGL and provides an interface based on world objects and other intuitive classes.

Source: http://www.ogre3d.org/about

OGRE is an acronym for Object-Oriented Graphics Rendering Engine, and its purpose is to provide an open source and platform-independent class library for rendering real-time 3D graphics to the display using hardware acceleration. That is, OGRE is in effect a high-level collection of classes that together wrap (encapsulate) both the DirectX and OpenGL libraries, and also extends the feature set offered by these libraries in providing its own scene management features. In short then, OGRE can be used to build real-time 3D scenes, complete with textured meshes loaded from files, 3D lighting and particle systems, and scene management. For our purposes, it will be important to note one of the keywords in the OGRE name, specifically "Graphics." OGRE is *not* a game engine—and our Chapter 1 definition of an engine will not find it to be so either. This is because OGRE is concerned almost exclusively with the rendering of graphics to the display. It does not include features for reading input from input devices, for calculating physical reactions and collisions, or for playing audio on sound hardware. The focus of OGRE is graphics rendering. This means that developers seeking to compile a complete engine using third-party libraries should supplement OGRE (as the renderer) with other libraries for input, audio, physics, etc.

NOTE. Appendix A features a list of available libraries for piecing together a complete engine.

In addition to being open source and to rendering graphics, by encapsulating both DirectX *and* OpenGL into a platform-independent class library, OGRE also lends itself to being cross-platform; indeed, OGRE has been compiled and run on a variety of platforms using a variety of IDES and compilers. Platforms include Windows, Linux, and Mac. Compilers include GNU Compiler and Microsoft Visual C++ Compiler. IDEs include Visual Studio, Code::Blocks, Qt™, Eclipse, and Xcode®. There are also efforts being made to port OGRE to the iPhone platform. At the time of writing, OGRE 3D is released under the MIT license, which grants developers the right to use OGRE for both their free and commercial projects without charge. The MIT license is provided in Appendix F and also here for convenience.

In short, as a render engine, OGRE includes many features for rendering 3D graphics; the following are the most notable for our purposes:

• OGRE features an extensible framework of classes, including those for mathematics, mesh, texture, and animation functionality. From these, developers can derive their own classes, customizing OGRE to suit the needs of their projects.

---

■ **MIT License**

Copyright © <year> <copyright holders>

Permission is hereby granted, free of charge, to any person obtaining a copy of this software and associated documentation files (the "Software"), to deal in the Software without restriction, including without limitation the rights to use, copy, modify, merge, publish, distribute, sublicense, and/or sell copies of the Software, and to permit persons to whom the Software is furnished to do so, subject to the following conditions:
The above copyright notice and this permission notice shall be included in all copies or substantial portions of the Software.

THE SOFTWARE IS PROVIDED "AS IS", WITHOUT WARRANTY OF ANY KIND, EXPRESS OR IMPLIED, INCLUDING BUT NOT LIMITED TO THE WARRANTIES OF MERCHANTABILITY, FITNESS FOR A PARTICULAR PURPOSE AND NONINFRINGEMENT. IN NO EVENT SHALL THE AUTHORS OR COPYRIGHT HOLDERS BE LIABLE FOR ANY CLAIM, DAMAGES OR OTHER LIABILITY, WHETHER IN AN ACTION OF CONTRACT, TORT OR OTHERWISE, ARISING FROM, OUT OF OR IN CONNECTION WITH THE SOFTWARE OR THE USE OR OTHER DEALINGS IN THE SOFTWARE.

- OGRE can load textures from files in the following file formats: BMP, DDS, EXR, GIF, HDR, ICO, IFF, JBIG, JNG, JPEG/JIF, KOALA, MNG, PBM/PGM/PPM, PCX, PFM, PICT, PNG, PSD, SGI, TGA, TIF, and XBM. This also includes 1D textures, volumetric textures, cubemaps, and compressed textures. Texture data can also be *updated* in real time (animated), either by manual pixel editing or by streaming video feeds (live or from movie files) onto the texture surface (as a video texture). Blitting video to textures often involves the use of a third-party library for decoding video files in the first place; these libraries include the now obsolete DirectShow® and Theora (http://www.theora.org/). Later in this book we will examine a complete commercial game engine that supports video textures out of the box.

- OGRE offers a converter application to transform standard XML data into a binary format that it can parse. This converter can be used to convert mesh XML data into binary mesh data, which can then be imported into OGRE and rendered. OGRE thereby offers the ability to load mesh and material data from a binary file that has been converted from XML. The OGRE website also offers a selection of third-party tools and plug-ins for exporting mesh data from modeling software to an XML file. In this way, the XML converter acts as a bridge between exported mesh XML data and binary mesh data suitable for importing. Furthermore, OGRE supports both *progressive meshes* and *skeletal meshes* (*skinned meshes*). See Figures 10.3 and 10.4. The former refers to meshes whose level of detail (face count) depends on its distance from the camera in a 3D scene; the level of detail (LOD) of a progressive mesh is inversely proportional to its distance from the camera. The latter refers to a mesh that is linked to an underlying hierarchy of bones representing an integrated structure of connections, joints, and hinges to which the mesh conforms (such as a standard model of a human skeleton). As the bones of the structure are rotated about their sockets, so the associated mesh bends and adapts to match the skeleton.

- OGRE features real-time 3D lights, each of which can be positioned in 3D space, can be targeted in specific directions, and can cast shadows. Together these settings allow developers to simulate a variety of light sources, including natural lights, like the sun and moon, and artificial lights, like torches, ceiling lights, and desk lamps.

- OGRE offers a scene hierarchy interface that allows developers to express and parse the relationships between objects in the scene via a *node tree*. Using a tree structure, each and every object in the scene can be attached to a *node*, and a node can be described as being a parent, child, or sibling of another node. In this relationship, child nodes inherit the transformations of their parents, as we shall see.

  **NOTE.** For a more complete list of OGRE features, please visit the OGRE features homepage at: http://www.ogre3d.org/about/features.

## Progressive and Skinned Meshes

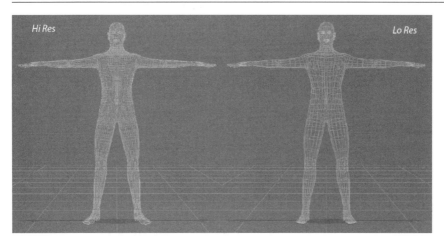

**FIGURE 10.3**   Progressive meshes—meshes whose detail changes based on the distance of the camera from the mesh.

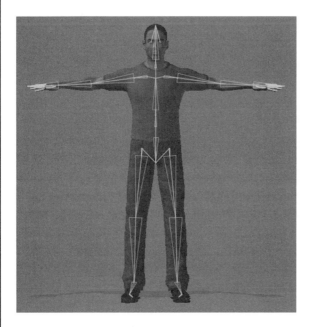

**FIGURE 10.4**   Skinned mesh. Skinned meshes feature two components, mesh data and an underlying skeleton. By adjusting the skeleton, the pose of the mesh will conform.

## ■ 10.3    Planning to Work with OGRE 3D

Three core features have been found to be missing in the DirectX render manager created using DirectX 10 in the previous chapter. Specifically, these are the ability to load textured, complex meshes from files exported from 3D software; the ability to understand, express, and manage the relationships between objects in a common 3D world space; and the ability to position light sources and to control their properties regarding their intensity, position, color, direction, and attenuation (the latter referring to how the intensity of a light diminishes with distance). Rather than extend the work of the previous chapter by implementing these features in the DirectX render manager, this chapter instead switches its focus to OGRE 3D and examines how it handles these issues along with a selection of others commonly found in contemporary game engines. Specifically, the following points detail the ground covered on OGRE in this chapter:

- This chapter will highlight how to download, install, and configure the OGRE SDK for the Windows platform. It will explore in detail how OGRE creates application windows, initializes graphics hardware, reads text configuration files, writes to log files, and both creates and sustains a render loop for presenting graphics to the display on each frame.

- It will explore the FrameListener and WindowListener classes, explaining how they can be used to receive important notifications from OGRE when key events occur such as when a frame begins and ends, and when the user resizes or closes an application window.

- This chapter will also consider the OGRE resource framework for loading and unloading game resources such as textures and meshes, comparing the OGRE resource framework to our resource manager class created in an earlier chapter.

- In addition, it will explore a series of third-party plug-in tools that allow developers to export textured and animated meshes from their 3D modeling software (such as 3ds Max, Maya, and Blender) into XML files, and from there to OGRE binary files. Once in binary form, the mesh data can be loaded, parsed, and rendered by OGRE.

- This chapter will investigate the OGRE material structure, how it relates to meshes in the scene, and how materials can be edited and created through the use of script files external to the application executable.

- It will consider texture mapping issues that determine how a texture is mapped onto 3D geometry and will also examine 3D lighting, discussing how OGRE lights are created, configured, and even animated using the animation key framework.

- Additionally, scene hierarchies and object relationships will be considered. Here, the chapter will illustrate how the OGRE scene node tree—that is, the scene node hierarchy—can be used to transform objects in 3D space (akin to the DirectX world matrix), while also maintaining their relationships to other objects.

- Finally, this chapter will examine how to download, amend, and compile the OGRE source code, and how the example applications bundled with the OGRE SDK should be approached and used as learning material for making further progress in working with OGRE.

## ■ 10.4  Downloading, Installing, and Configuring the OGRE SDK

Developing applications with OGRE begins by downloading and installing the latest OGRE SDK, available from the official OGRE homepage. OGRE features an active online community whose members discuss the engine and offer support and advice to each other. Furthermore, the OGRE software versions are actively maintained by a small team of developers and contributors. This means that OGRE is updated frequently. For this reason, the latest version of OGRE at the time of writing this book (Shoggoth 1.6.5) will almost certainly *not* be the latest version at the time this book is published. This, however, should not prove problematic because much of the structure of OGRE's class framework, its function names, and the arrangement of its data structures are honored from version to version. Specific functions might be improved, some classes extended, and some bugs fixed, but the overall interface into the OGRE library has remained more or less similar across all versions throughout the past several years, meaning that the guidance and instruction given here will not lose its relevance. This section now offers step-by-step guidance in downloading and installing the OGRE SDK:

Step 1.  Navigate a web browser to the OGRE homepage at http://www.ogre3d. org/ and click the **Download** button in the left-hand margin of the page (see Figure 10.5). This presents a page featuring a series of download options for the OGRE SDK; these are: Download a prebuilt SDK, Download a source package, and Retrieve the source from Mercurial. This chapter will return later to this download menu in order to download the latest OGRE source. However, for now readers should select **Download a prebuilt SDK** to download the latest SDK for building OGRE applications.

Step 2.  From here, readers should select an OGRE SDK suitable for their IDE. At the time of writing, supported IDEs include Code::Blocks, Visual C++ 2003, 2005, and 2008, and Xcode for Mac. Once downloaded, run the prebuilt OGRE installer to install the OGRE libraries, documentation, and example applications to the local computer (see Figure 10.6).

**FIGURE 10.5**    OGRE homepage.

**FIGURE 10.6**    Downloading OGRE.

Step 3.  The OGRE installer will install a series of files and subfolders to the specified installation folder. The names of these files and subfolders follow, along with a description of each:

bin
docs
include
lib
media
samples

**bin**

Bin is an abbreviation of "binary," and refers to the default destination folder where OGRE executables will be built by the compiler. Inside the bin folder are two further subfolders: debug and release. The former contains all OGRE executables built in debug mode, while the latter contains those built in release mode. This folder starts empty except for the essential run-time files required by all OGRE applications, and will shortly be populated by executables as the bundled example applications are compiled. The next section will explain how to do that.

**docs**

The docs folder contains the official OGRE reference documentation as a standard Windows HTML help file, a user manual in HTML format, and licensing information in a series of Windows text files. Once the reader has completed the work in this chapter, the author recommends they continue reading the OGRE manual and also keep the reference guide available. The reference documentation lists all classes belonging to the OGRE SDK and their associated functions, members, properties, and events. The reference is an ideal place to retrieve information regarding OGRE structures and functions, especially when the name of a function is known and the programmer simply requires details of the arguments expected.

**include**

The include folder features all of the C++ header files belonging to the OGRE SDK. This folder should be added to the include path of header files in the C++ IDE, either in Code::Blocks or Visual Studio; Chapter 2 details how to do this. The header file ogre.h is the main header file, which all OGRE applications should reference in their projects.

**lib**

The lib folder contains all of the C++ precompiled lib files required to compile and link OGRE applications into executables. As with the include folder, the lib path should be added to the list of library paths in the C++ IDE, either Code::Blocks or Visual Studio; Chapter 2 details how to do this. All release OGRE applications should link to OGREMain.lib, and all debug applications to OGREMain_d.lib.

**media**

The media folder contains a collection of material scripts, vertex shaders, mesh files, image files, and effect files that are used by the example applications and are useful to OGRE newcomers for instructive purposes.

**samples**

The samples folder contains the C++ project and source files for all the example applications that bundle with the SDK. For the Visual Studio IDE, the complete collection of sample projects can be opened and compiled together in the IDE by opening the Samples.sln file. Once the project samples are compiled in either debug or release mode, the resultant executables will reside in the respective release and debug subfolders of the bin folder.

## ■ 10.5    Building the OGRE Sample Applications—A Guided Tour

As mentioned, the OGRE SDK ships with a selection of sample applications in source code form, each demonstrating a specific feature of OGRE. This example framework represents a suitable place to begin work with OGRE for several reasons: (1) the sample applications provide an interesting showcase for OGRE and its feature set, demonstrating particle systems, binary space trees, volumetric textures, skeletal animation, and more, (2) an examination of the example source code can be instructive in learning how to use many advanced OGRE features, and (3) a successful compilation of the OGRE sample applications in both debug and release mode confirms that the OGRE SDK is configured correctly on the system. Building the sample application framework involves little more than opening up the samples project in the C++ IDE and clicking the Build or Compile option, once for both debug and release mode. Compilation might take several minutes; during this process the compiler might flag several warnings in the debug output window, but it should display no error messages. The following sections demonstrate some notable example applications.

### 10.5.1    OGRE Lighting

The lighting sample application is intended to demonstrate OGRE lights, but it actually demonstrates far more (see Figure 10.7). It features mesh loading—the loading of an ogre head mesh—animated grass, a skybox (to create the surrounding night sky), and animated lights that change color as they move around the scene. This sample

Current  FPS:  60.9636
Average  FPS:  58.0984
Worst  FPS:  45.4545  117  ms
Best  FPS:  60.9636  1  ms
Triangle  Count:  1132
Batch  Count:  35

**❙ FIGURE 10.7**   Lighting demo.

depends on the files inside the media folder, including texture files for the grass, head, and sky as well as the material information contained in a script file (.material). Material scripts are discussed later in this chapter in more detail.

## ■ Skybox Details

A *skybox* refers to a textured cube with inverted normals that centers itself on the camera. A *normal* determines the direction in which a polygon of a mesh is facing. In the world of 3D, polygons are one-sided, and a polygon whose normal points toward the camera is visible, while a polygon whose normal faces away is not visible. A cube with *inverted normals* that is centered on the camera is a cube that *surrounds* the camera, showing all of its sides. By texturing a seamless six-sided texture onto the interior of the cube, one texture per side—such as a sky or environment—the artist can create the illusion that the camera is surrounded by an environment.

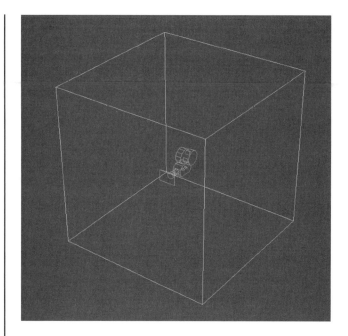

**I FIGURE 10.8**    Sky boxes create the illusion of surrounding environments.

### 10.5.2    OGRE Shadows

The OGRE shadow sample shows a scene featuring a warrior statue standing at a marina, surrounded by pillar objects (see Figure 10.9). Both the statue and pillars are casting real-time shadows on the ground based upon a light in the scene that is positioned behind the camera at roughly 45 degrees above the objects. In addition to demonstrating both lighting and shadows, the shadow sample also exhibits mesh loading for the scene objects, a skybox object for the sky and horizon line, and GUI elements containing edit boxes and check boxes that allow users to configure the light's shadow casting parameters.

### 10.5.3    OGRE BSP

The BSP sample throws the player into a first-person scenario in which they can explore the corridors and recesses of a classic and large FPS environment using the keyboard arrow keys (see Figure 10.10). BSP is an acronym for an algorithm known as *binary space partition*, and the purpose of the sample is to demonstrate how a BSP algorithm can be used to expedite the rendering process to render large environments efficiently. In addition to featuring a working example of a BSP algorithm, the BSP sample features mesh and texture loading, real-time lighting, first-person camera movement, and script parsing.

**▎ FIGURE 10.9**   Shadows demo.

**▎ FIGURE 10.10**   Binary space partition demo.

## 10.5.4    OGRE Render to Texture

Previous samples have demonstrated OGRE's ability to read in resources—such as textures and meshes—from scripts and files in the media folder and then to render them to the window as a scene. The Render to Texture sample goes beyond this functionality to write (render) to a texture for the purposes of creating reflections in the water (see Figure 10.11). The scene in this sample features an ogre head mesh and some twisted torus-shaped primitives hovering above a flat plane object representing a surface of water. The sample renders this scene at least twice on each frame: once for the view as seen from the scene camera and another view as seen from the angle of reflection above the water. The second rendering is *textured* (projected) onto the plane of water beneath the mesh and torus objects, and is updated every frame in order to create the appearance of reflection.

> **NOTE.** Notice how each OGRE sample application first displays the standard OGRE configuration dialog menu at startup. This dialog allows a user to specify the settings that are to apply to the application for this instance. Using the list box and drop-down controls, a user can specify the graphics hardware to be used (if more than one option is present on the computer), along with the resolution, bit depth, and VSync settings at which the sample

**FIGURE 10.11**    Render to Texture demo.

will be run. By default, this dialog will appear for all OGRE applications, giving the user the opportunity to run their application according to their own preferences. However, a developer has the ability to override this dialog by passing in their own settings at application startup. A later section of this chapter will examine how this can be done.

## ■  10.6    Configuring an OGRE Project from Scratch

As mentioned, the OGRE SDK bundles with a series of sample applications that together demonstrate a variety of features of the engine, from mesh loading and lighting to texture rendering and scene optimizations. Compiling and running the sample applications from source is useful for at least two reasons: (1) for confirming that the OGRE SDK is installed correctly on the computer, and (2) for educational purposes, since the source of each project demonstrates common usage of the engine. However, after viewing the sample applications, a developer is likely to want to both create and compile their own OGRE applications from scratch. Doing this involves several steps, the first of which is to configure the C++ IDE options for compiling OGRE projects. Initially, this involves adding both the header and lib paths to the header and lib directories list in the IDE options menu. (Instructions on how to do this can be found in Chapter 2.) The purpose of adding the paths is to notify the C++ compiler of all the source locations in which header file and lib file information may be found when and if it is required. Though OGRE applications cannot compile without the developer performing this step, this is not all that must be done to compile OGRE applications. In addition, developers should consider the following issues when compiling and running OGRE applications:

- All OGRE applications—in both debug and release modes—require the presence of a set of run-time libraries (DLLs) to run successfully, regardless of the computer on which they are executed. Some of the libraries vary, depending on the OGRE features being used, but some are required by all OGRE applications. These files should be located in the same folder as that of the application executable. The *essential* files include the following:

For release mode:

    OgreMain.dll

    RenderSystem_Direct3D9.dll

    RenderSystem_GL.dll

For debug mode:

    OgreMain_d.dll

    RenderSystem_Direct3D9_d.dll

    RenderSystem_GL_d.dll

**NOTE**. These run-time libraries, and others, can be found in the OGRE installation directory in their respective release and debug subfolders of the bin folder.

Though the above files are required by even the simplest of OGRE applications, usually more are required. The OgreMain.dll represents the engine core of the OGRE run-time, including such engine subsystems as the resource manager, the scene manager, the log manager, and the error manager. The RenderSystem DLL files represent the render manager components, one render manager for DirectX and another for OpenGL. Most OGRE applications, however—including the sample applications—require more run-time libraries than these since their feature set extends beyond the basic OGRE core. Other DLL run-time libraries that *might* need to be included (depending on the application) are as follows:

For release mode:

CEGUIBase.dll

CEGUIExpatParser.dll

CEGUIFalagardWRBase.dll

cg.dll

OgreGUIRenderer.dll

OIS.dll

Plugin_BSPSceneManager.dll

Plugin_CgProgramManager.dll

Plugin_OctreeSceneManager.dll

Plugin_OctreeZone.dll

Plugin_ParticleFX.dll

Plugin_PCZSceneManager.dll

For debug mode:

CEGUIBase_d.dll

CEGUIExpatParser_d.dll

CEGUIFalagardWRBase_d.dll

Cg_d.dll

OgreGUIRenderer_d.dll

OIS_d.dll

Plugin_BSPSceneManager_d.dll

Plugin_CgProgramManager_d.dll

Plugin_OctreeSceneManager_d.dll

Plugin_OctreeZone_d.dll

Plugin_ParticleFX_d.dll

Plugin_PCZSceneManager_d.dll

- In addition to the run-time DLL libraries, most OGRE applications—again, including the samples—require a selection of text configuration files; some are used to specify a selection of engine settings, such as resolution, whether it is to run in full-screen mode, etc.; and others specify the path names of folders where resources are to be found such as textures, meshes, and scripts. OGRE cannot and does not see the whole of the file system. It must therefore be told explicitly via a config file each and every one of the folder paths where data is to be read or written. Paths *not* listed in that file (resources.cfg) will be ignored by OGRE. The resources.cfg file will be considered later in this chapter. For now it is enough to appreciate that many—perhaps most—OGRE applications require the presence of a selection of text-based configuration files in order to run successfully. If an application does not need resources at all (unlikely), and can run at any size and resolution specified by the user (also unlikely), then no such files are required. The following configuration files might be used by some OGRE applications, both debug and release:

    Plugins.cfg

    quake3settings.cfg

    resources.cfg

    media.cfg

    **NOTE**. The first sample OGRE application created in this chapter requires only the core engine files: OgreMain.dll, RenderSystem_Direct3D9.dll, and RenderSystem_GL.dll.

- The presence of the necessary run-time libraries and configuration files ensures OGRE applications execute successfully once compiled. But compilation of OGRE applications requires the developer to perform some steps in addition to simply setting the include and lib directories. These steps vary depending on the C++ IDE used to compile OGRE and are now considered in further detail. They are presented as a step–by-step tutorial for creating a blank OGRE application, ready to start coding.

### 10.6.1   Configuring OGRE for Code::Blocks

Step 1.  Compiling OGRE in Code::Blocks requires the MinGW GCC compiler, which ships by default with Code::Blocks. Thus, Code::Blocks should already be using this compiler, unless it has been changed manually by the user.

The active Code::Blocks compiler can be changed by selecting the menu item **Settings | Compiler and Debugger Settings**. See Figure 10.12.

Step 2. Once the active Code::Blocks compiler is set to MinGW GCC, the developer should proceed to create a new, blank project, then set a selection of compiler options for that project. This can be achieved by clicking the menu item **Project | Build Options**.

From this dialog, click the **Other Options** tab to specify compiler switches. See Figure 10.13. In the edit box, enter the following:

mthreads

fmessage-length=0

fexceptions

fident

Step 3. Next, from the **Build Options** menu, click the **Linker Settings** tab (see Figure 10.14). In the **Other Linker Options** edit box, enter the following linker switches:

**| FIGURE 10.12**    Accessing compiler settings.

**FIGURE 10.13** OGRE compiler switches.

**FIGURE 10.14** OGRE linker options.

**I FIGURE 10.15**    Setting #defines for OGRE.

-Wl,—enable-auto-image-base

-Wl,—add-stdcall-alias

Step 4. From the **Build Options** menu, click the **Compiler Settings** tab. From there, click the **#defines** subtab (see Figure 10.15). In the edit box, enter the following defines:

WIN32

NDEBUG

_WINDOWS

Step 5. Click **OK**. Code::Blocks is now configured to build an OGRE application.

## 10.6.2    Configuring OGRE for Visual Studio.NET 2005 or Above

**NOTE**. Visual Studio.NET 2005 users should note that in order to compile OGRE applications, the Visual Studio 2005 Service Pack is required. This can be downloaded for free from the official Microsoft website at:

**I FIGURE 10.16**    Creating a new project for OGRE.

http://www.microsoft.com/downloads/details.aspx?FamilyId=BB4A75
AB-E2D4-4C96-B39D-37BAF6B5B1DC&displaylang=en.

Step 1.  Start Visual Studio and create a new, empty Windows project. To do this:

Click **File | New Project**. Select **Win32 Project** from the project Templates
list, specifying the Name, Location, and Solution Name details. Once completed, click **OK**. See Figure 10.16.

The project configuration menu appears, allowing users to fine-tune the
starting parameters of their project. Make sure the **Windows Application**
radio button is selected and also that the **Empty Project** check box is checked.
Click the **Finish** button to create the project skeleton. See Figure 10.17.

Step 2.  Create a new and empty source file, and add it to the project by right-clicking
the project title in the project explorer tree view pane. Select **Add | New
Item**, and use the Add New Item dialog to add a new source file. Once
added, the Visual Studio project should look something like the following
Figure 10.18.

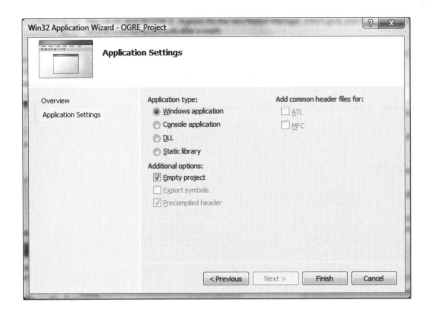

**FIGURE 10.17**    Creating a project skeleton for OGRE.

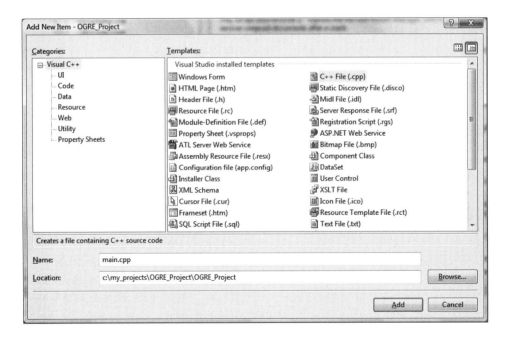

**FIGURE 10.18**    Adding new project items.

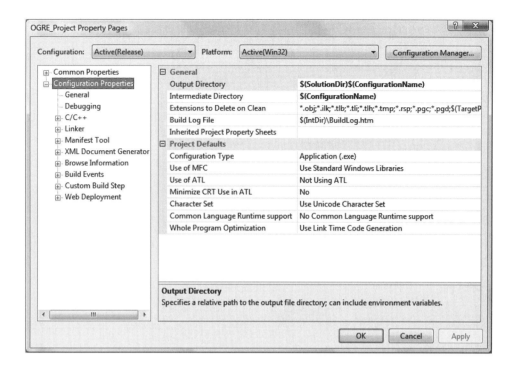

**FIGURE 10.19**   Accessing project options.

Step 3.  Save the project, and right-click the project title in the project explorer tree view pane. A context menu appears. From here, select **Properties** to view the OGRE_Project Property Pages dialog. See Figure 10.19.

Step 4.  From this options screen, select **C/C++ | Code Generation** from the left-hand tree view. Ensure the Runtime Library option is set to Multi-threaded DLL (/MD), as shown in Figure 10.20.

Step 5.  Select **Linker | General**, and ensure the Output File setting points to the path that contains the OGRE essential run-time files mentioned earlier in this section. This path represents the location to which the compiled executable will be copied and run once compiled. See Figure 10.21.

Step 6.  Select **Linker | Input**, and ensure Additional Dependencies lists the OGRE lib files for linking, as shown in Figure 10.22.

Step 7.  Click **OK**. The project is now configured for compiling OGRE applications.

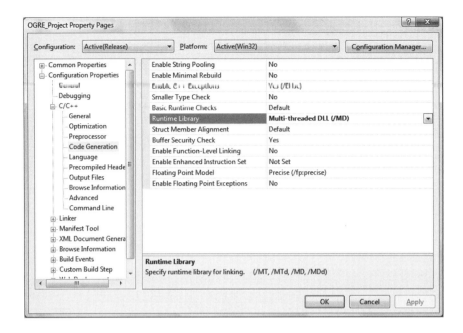

**FIGURE 10.20**    Setting compiler options.

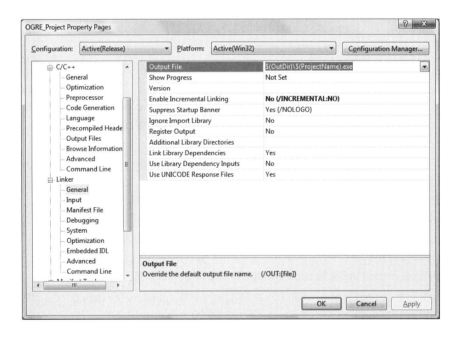

**FIGURE 10.21**    Building to the output path.

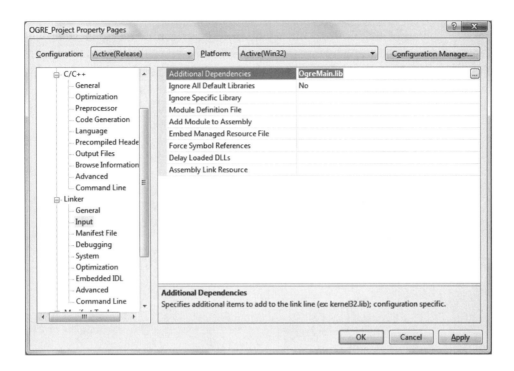

**FIGURE 10.22**   Linking to the OGRE libraries.

## ■ 10.7   Building an OGRE Application—Getting Started

It has been stated that compiling OGRE source projects in a C++ IDE requires the compiler to work according to specific settings, and the execution of compiled OGRE applications typically requires the presence of a set of run-time libraries and text-based configuration files. Once a compiler is appropriately configured and the necessary run-time libraries are in place, a developer can start coding an OGRE project in C++. This section and several that follow consider in detail how to code a basic OGRE application that will: (1) show a configuration dialog at application startup, (2) initialize graphics hardware according to the settings provided in that dialog, and (3) sustain a render loop that shows nothing but a black screen. True, this application is not in itself glamorous in comparison to the sample applications that ship with the SDK, but it will serve as the foundation on which further and more complex OGRE applications will be based.

> **NOTE.** The project files for this chapter can be found in the book's companion code at http//www.jblearning.com/catalog/9780763784515/.

The coding of this project will begin where execution of the application will begin: with a standard Windows main function. Coding this will allow us to compile and run the application on demand. Over the course of the subsequent sections, this function will be refined, amended, and improved until the project conclusion, at which point there will be an application that achieves steps 1, 2, and 3 above. Thus, the project begins with a WinMain function in a source file (main.cpp) as follows:

```cpp
//Compiled with OGRE 1.6.5 Visual C++ 2005
#include <Windows.h>
#include "OgreApplication.h"
//----------------------------------------------
INT WINAPI WinMain( HINSTANCE hInst, HINSTANCE, LPSTR
strCmdLine, INT )
{
    try
    {
        cOgreApplication T;
        T.init();
    }
    catch( Exception& e )
    {
        MessageBoxA( NULL, e.getFullDescription().c_str(),
"An exception has occurred!", MB_OK | MB_ICONERROR | MB_
TASKMODAL);
    }
    return 0;
}
//----------------------------------------------

//Application entry point
INT WINAPI WinMain( HINSTANCE hInst, HINSTANCE, LPSTR
strCmdLine, INT )
{
    try
    {
        //Code will be added here
    }
    catch( Exception& e )
    {
//Catch OGRE exception

        MessageBoxA( NULL, e.getFullDescription().c_str(),
"An exception has occurred!", MB_OK | MB_ICONERROR | MB_
TASKMODAL);
    }
```

```
    return 0;
}

//----------------------------------------------
```

NOTE. Compile and run this application. It should compile without error or warning, but will execute and finish so quickly as to be hardly visible. This is because execution falls through the main function, since no application loop exists to keep the application alive. If the application does not compile, revisit the configuration steps in the previous two sections before proceeding, to ensure that each step was performed correctly. If the application still fails to compile, visit and search the OGRE community forums for helpful advice. The OGRE forums can be found at: http://www.ogre3d.org/forums/.

**Comments**

- Notice that this file includes the ogre SDK header file using the #include preprocessor directive, and also declares that the OGRE namespace is to be applied to the code throughout this file. This prevents the coder from having to prefix all OGRE commands with "OGRE::" (e.g., OGRE::Vector2).

- The main function contains little code but that code does rely on the OGRE SDK, specifically on the error management framework. OGRE throws exceptions of type Exception when errors occur. This application will catch these exceptions and display a message box showing error information. Consider the OGRE Exception class listed in the following sidebar.

---

■ **Ogre Focus—Exception Class**

The OGRE Exception class raises one of the first parallels between OGRE and the engine foundations coded in this book. In Chapter 3, an error framework was coded in which a custom-exception class was thrown by an error manager as exceptions were raised. The OGRE framework adopts a similar strategy, passing its custom-made class as exceptions are raised. By using the methods and properties of this class, developers can determine the nature of the error raised by OGRE. The following are the public methods of this class:

```
    class Exception
    {
    //Constructors
```

```
Exception (int number, const String &description,
const String &source) ;
Exception (int number, const String &description,
const String &source, const char *type, const char
*file, long line) ;
Exception (const Exception &rhs);

//Other methods
virtual const String &  getFullDescription (void)
const ;
virtual int  getNumber (void);
virtual const String &  getSource () const;
virtual const String &  getFile () const ;
virtual long  getLine () const ;
virtual const String &  getDescription (void) const;
};
```

**Description**

An instance of the Exception class or a derivative is passed as an argument to *catch* each exception that is thrown by OGRE. This class describes the last error that occurred. It features three constructors used for building the class to represent an error. Developers can thus use this class to define their own custom exceptions and errors in addition to those raised by OGRE. Other methods are detailed below:

**virtual const String & getFullDescription (void) const;**

Returns a string describing the exception, including the line number and source file name from which the error was raised and a human-readable description of the error.

**virtual int  getNumber (void)**

Returns a unique integer identifying the error raised.

**virtual const String & getSource () const**

Returns the name of the function in which the exception was raised.

**virtual const String & getFile () const**

Returns the name of the source file in which the exception was raised.

**virtual long  getLine () const**

Returns the line number in the source file from which the exception was raised.

**virtual const String & getDescription (void) const**

Returns a string containing *only* the description of an error, without the source file name or line number.

### 10.7.1   Showing a Configuration Dialog and Selecting a Render System

OGRE is a rendering engine that features two render managers natively (or render systems, in OGRE terminology), one system per graphics library: DirectX and OpenGL. Given that the OGRE class framework is both open and extensible, it is possible for developers to extend that set by creating their own customized render system, but many OGRE applications and this book will use only the default render systems provided with OGRE. The purpose of the OGRE render system is almost identical to the purpose of the 2D and 3D render managers created in earlier chapters: to create an application window, to initialize graphics hardware, to load graphics resources, and to sustain a render loop that renders graphics to the application window on each frame. To create an OGRE render system, an application must provide OGRE with a range of parameters describing both the system to be created and the conditions under which it is to work once created; these include the size of the window to be created, the graphics card to use (if more than one is connected to the computer), whether the application is to run in full-screen mode, and a selection of additional parameters, some of which are specific to the DirectX or OpenGL render systems. These parameters can be provided manually by the developer in code or can be read from a config file, or an application can show the default OGRE configuration dialog that offers a GUI interface for inputting these creation parameters. Consider the amended WinMain function that follows. It initializes the OGRE library, initializes the graphics hardware according to the settings provided by the standard configuration dialog or to the settings provided manually (depending on a boolean value), and then finally creates an application window associated with the initialized graphics device.

```
//Global variables

Root *g_Root = NULL;
RenderWindow* g_Window=NULL;
bool showDialog=true;

//Application entry point
INT WINAPI WinMain( HINSTANCE hInst, HINSTANCE, LPSTR
strCmdLine, INT )
{
    try
    {
        //Initialize OGRE lib

        //Create OGRE Root object
        g_Root = OGRE_NEW Root("","");

        //Loads the RenderSystem DLLs
        g_Root->loadPlugin("RenderSystem_Direct3D9");
```

```
            g_Root->loadPlugin("RenderSystem_GL");

            if(showDialog)
{
   //Show dialog and create window
               if(g_Root->showConfigDialog())
            g_Window = g_Root->initialise(true, "Window");
}
else
{
   //Create graphics and window manually

   //Retrieve pointer to a default render system.
   //Can be either DirectX or OpenGL.
   //Depends on developer preference.
   //DirectX is selected here.

   RenderSystem *rs = g_Root->
getRenderSystemByName("Direct3D9 Rendering Subsystem");

   //If DirectX available
   if(rs)
   {
        g_Root->setRenderSystem(rs);
   }
   else
   {
        //Choose OpenGL
        rs = g_Root->getRenderSystemByName("OpenGL
Rendering Subsystem");

   //VERY IMPORTANT. Sets selected render system as
active.
        if(rs)
            g_Root->setRenderSystem(rs);
   }

   rs->setConfigOption("Full Screen", "No");
   rs->setConfigOption("Video Mode", "800 x 600 @ 32-bit
colour");

   g_Window = g_Root->initialise(true, «Window»);
}

   }
```

```
catch( Exception& e )
{
//Catch OGRE exception

    MessageBoxA( NULL, e.getFullDescription().c_str(),
"An exception has occurred!", MB_OK | MB_ICONERROR | MB_
TASKMODAL);
    }

    return 0;
}
```

## Comments

- The reader will likely notice the changes made to the top of the source file, which features three global variables. The first is g_Root, which represents the OGRE Root object—the heart of an OGRE application that should be deleted only after usage of OGRE has stopped. The next is g_Window. This member belongs to the class RenderWindow and represents both the initialized graphics device and the application window into which graphical data is rendered on each and every frame. The last member is a boolean that can be set to either true or false to indicate whether the application should show an OGRE config dialog at startup or should create the device and window manually without prompting the user.

- The WinMain function begins by creating an OGRE Root object, and this is the first step all OGRE applications should perform. The Root object is the core of OGRE, and using its methods, developers can terminate an application; start, stop, and pause the rendering process; poll system hardware for supported graphics devices; create application windows; load and unload plug-in DLLs; and much more. The complete details for this class can be found in the OGRE reference documentation. The constructor for the Root object requires several arguments pertaining to external text-based configuration files, and these will be considered in further detail later in this chapter. It is, however, possible to instruct OGRE to ignore these files by simply passing empty strings as arguments to this function. Notice also that this line uses the OGRE macro OGRE_NEW, which equates to the standard new operator in C++. The reasons for overloading this operator are beyond the scope of this book, but it is enough here to state that calling OGRE_NEW will act identically to the new keyword. A valid instance of the Root object is returned in the global member g_Root.

- Once an OGRE Root object has been created, the function proceeds to load the render system DLL components with a call to the loadPlugin method of the Root object. This method does not initialize the graphics hardware, nor does it create an application window; it only loads the render system components from external DLLs and prepares them for use in later calls.

- The method then checks the showDialog boolean value to determine whether it should present the user with a configuration dialog and then create the graphics device and window object based on the settings provided there, or create the device from settings passed in code. By default, this boolean is set to true to show the configuration dialog.

- The OGRE configuration dialog (shown in Figure 10.23) is shown with a call to the method showConfigDialog of the Root object. This method accepts no arguments and returns a boolean value: true indicating that the user confirmed the dialog settings by clicking OK or false indicating that they pressed the Cancel button. If the user clicked OK, the settings chosen are recorded by OGRE and will be used internally later when creating the render device and application window.

- Once showConfigDialog has been called and returned with a true value, the method can proceed to create both the device and window in one call to the initialise method of the Root object. This function accepts two arguments: the first to indicate whether an application window should be automatically created and the second specifying the name to be shown in the window title bar if the first

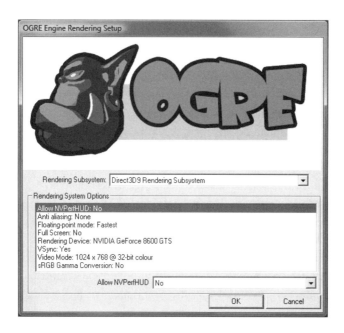

**▌FIGURE 10.23**  OGRE config dialog.

parameter is true. After calling this function, OGRE will internally have created both a graphics device and a window; in other words, it will have created two distinct objects: the render system and the application window. If successful, the initialise method returns a pointer to a window object (RenderWindow) representing the newly created application window. If the function fails, null is returned.

- The previous two comments explained how both a window and a render manager component can be created in one call after the OGRE configuration dialog has been shown and used. This occurs when the global boolean variable showDialog is set to true. It might be the case, however, (and often is) that a developer will want to show either their own custom dialog instead of the default one or no dialog at all, specifying the graphics settings manually in code to OGRE. In short, if no dialog is shown, the developer must manually provide OGRE with all the information necessary to create a render manager and window object. To do this, the WinMain function starts by querying the Root object to see which devices (render systems) are supported by the hardware attached to the computer. In this case, the function calls the getRenderSystemByName method of the Root object to test whether a DirectX device is supported. This method could have equally started by checking for the presence of an OpenGL device or for another custom device. For this test to succeed, however, a developer must have previously loaded the render system as a plugin with a previous call to the loadPlugin method. The call getRenderSystemByName (if successful) retrieves a pointer to the specified render manager (class RenderSystem), or else null. This method does not initialize the graphics hardware nor does it create a window; it simply returns a pointer to an appropriate but as yet uninitialized render manager that represents the specified renderer, either DirectX or OpenGL.

- If the call to getRenderSystemByName fails, the method proceeds to fall back on the OpenGL render system as a secondary option. It does this by calling getRenderSystemByName again, this time passing the string "OpenGL Rendering Subsystem" as an argument. Again, it should be emphasized here that it is not my intention to suggest that OpenGL is somehow inferior to or less than DirectX by referring to it as a "secondary option." For the purposes of this example, which must choose between two render systems, one must invariably come before the other, and since DirectX has been the focus of some of our work throughout this book I decided to prioritize DirectX (see Figure 10.24). If both attempts to retrieve a render manager fail, then the application must exit since it cannot render data via either system. But in most cases, this process will succeed and lead to the application retrieving a pointer to one render manager or the other, either DirectX or OpenGL.

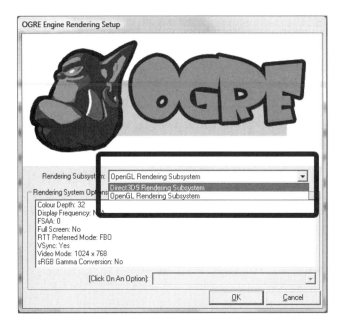

| FIGURE 10.24    OGRE options.

- Once a pointer to a render system is retrieved, the application is then able to compensate for the absence of the config dialog by calling the setConfigOption method of the render system for each unique setting that is to be applied to that render system. Calling the setConfigOption method for each setting is tantamount to setting the configuration values using the dialog box (see Figure 10.25). This function accepts two string arguments representing field and value pairs, respectively.

    The first string specifies the option to set, and the second refers to the value that is to be applied to the selected setting. The string values supplied here should resemble those featured in the OGRE configuration dialog box. To set the resolution, for example, an application should pass the following two values: ("Video Mode," "800 × 600 @ 32-bit colour"). To set whether the application is to run in full-screen mode, it should pass the following two strings: ("Full Screen," "No"). Notice how the string arguments correspond to the option names in the config dialog, as shown in Figure 10.25.

    > NOTE. Compiling this application should produce neither errors nor warnings, but at execution time the application will create a window that disappears almost instantly as the application exits. Again, this is because execution falls through the WinMain function since no loop exists to sustain the life of the application.

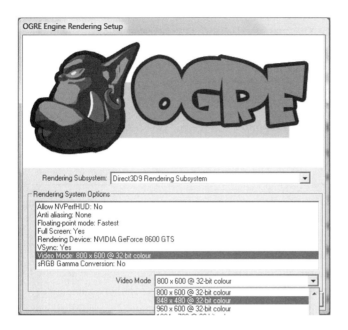

Rendering Subsystem: Direct3D9 Rendering Subsystem

Rendering System Options

Allow NVPerfHUD: No
Anti aliasing: None
Floating-point mode: Fastest
Full Screen: Yes
Rendering Device: NVIDIA GeForce 8600 GTS
VSync: Yes
Video Mode: 800 x 600 @ 32-bit colour
sRGB Gamma Conversion: No

Video Mode  800 x 600 @ 32-bit colour

800 x 600 @ 32-bit colour
848 x 480 @ 32-bit colour
960 x 600 @ 32-bit colour

**I FIGURE 10.25**   Setting OGRE config values.

## ■ OGRE Focus—Retrieving Render Systems, Setting Configuration Options, and Initializing

Manually creating a render system in OGRE generally involves a three-stage process: (1) retrieve a pointer to an uninitialized render system of a specified name, (2) set the configuration options for that system, and (3) initialize that render system and create the associated application window. Each of these three steps corresponds to the following function calls, respectively, and they are now considered in more detail: getRenderSystemByName, setConfigOption, and initialise.

### Retrieving Render Systems
Every unique render system in OGRE is identified by its name and, in the case of the DirectX and OpenGL renderers, their names appear in the Rendering Subsystem drop-down box in the standard configuration dialog. Retrieving a pointer to a specific render system is achieved by calling the getRenderSystemByName method of the OGRE Root object. When specifying render systems using this function, developers must take care that the string argument of the function (the name of the renderer) appears exactly as it is written in the dialog box, as shown in Figure 10.25.

```
RenderSystem* Root::getRenderSystemByName(const
String &  name)
```

**Arguments**

**const String &  name**

String representing the name of the renderer for which a pointer is to be retrieved. The function returns a pointer to the specified renderer, if found; else null is returned. Notice that the name parameter is of type String, which is an OGRE-defined type and a typecast of std::string.

---

### Setting Config Options

The RenderSystem class represents a unique render system object that can be used by OGRE for rendering graphics to the application window. Each object supports a setConfigOption method that allows developers to configure the device before its creation in the initialise method of the Root object. The setConfigOption method needs to be called only if the user will not be specifying options in either a standard or custom dialog that appears at application startup; it is used for manually configuring a render system. This function accepts two string arguments in the form of [field, value], and the strings should appear as they are written in the OGRE config dialog.

```
void Ogre::RenderSystem::setConfigOption  (const
String &  name, const String &  value)
```

**Arguments**

**const String &  name**

String representing the name of the setting (property or field) to set.

**const String &  value**

String representing the value that should be assigned to the property specified by the name parameter.

---

### Initializing Graphics Hardware and Window Creation

Once a pointer to a render system has been retrieved and its settings configured, an application can proceed to initialize the device and create an associated render window. This is achieved by a call to the initialize method of the Root object. Calling this method initializes the graphics hardware and creates a window into which graphics will be rendered. It does not, however, start or sustain a render loop. That is to be created in a later section of this chapter. Details for the initialize method follow:

```
RenderWindow* Ogre::Root::initialise  (bool
autoCreateWindow,
```

```
  const String &  windowTitle = "OGRE Render
Window",
  const String & customCapabilitiesConfig =
StringUtil::BLANK
  )
```

**Arguments**

**bool autoCreateWindow**

Boolean indicating whether to automatically create an application window associated with the render device. If true, OGRE automatically creates a window. If false, no window is created. Windows can be created manually by calling the createRenderWindow method of the Root object. This book, however, considers only cases where windows are created automatically.

**const String & windowTitle**

If autoCreateWindow is true, then this value specifies the title to appear in the window title bar.

**const String & customCapabilitiesConfig**

This is an optional value and can be null.

## 10.7.2   Creating a Scene Manager, Camera, and Viewport

Once a render device and application window are created using OGRE, a developer can proceed to create a scene manager, a camera, and a viewport. Note that the latter two objects correspond almost exactly to their DirectX counterparts with identical names. A camera object in a 3D game is akin to a camera in a movie studio—it represents the window and perspective from which objects, events, and actions in a game world are observed. The perspective into that world can be changed by adjusting the camera, and a camera can be adjusted in a number of ways, as we shall see. The OGRE viewport corresponds to a clipping (or cropping) region into which the contents of the camera view will be rendered in the window on each frame. By default, the size of the viewport matches the size of the window, meaning the window is entirely filled with graphical data, but the viewport can be cropped so as to limit the area into which data is rendered. The OGRE scene manager is not an object with a DirectX counterpart, and it is an especially important object in the OGRE framework. The scene manager component of the OGRE SDK represents the scene graph (or hierarchy of a scene)—a single unified world space. It is through the methods of the SceneManager class that meshes and textures are added to a scene, transformed, oriented, animated, and removed. An object, such as a mesh, cannot be rendered to the display in OGRE without first being *added* to the scene; that is, it must become a member of the scene coordinate system. In effect, the scene represents everything that can be rendered. A later section examines the scene manager in further detail; this section focuses only on the creation of the SceneManager class, alongside the Camera and Viewport objects. Consider the following code that does this; assume this code is a continuation of the WinMain function presented in the previous section:

```
//Added following members to source file top
//SceneManager *g_SceneManager=NULL;
//Camera *g_Camera=NULL;
//Viewport *g_Viewport=NULL;

//Create scene manager
g_SceneManager = g_Root->createSceneManager(ST_GENERIC,
"Default SceneManager");

//Create scene camera
g_Camera = m_SceneManager->createCamera("Camera");
g_Camera->setPosition(Vector3(0,0,500));
g_Camera->lookAt(Vector3(0,0,-300));
g_Camera->setNearClipDistance(5);

//Create viewport object
// Create one viewport, entire window
g_Viewport = g_Window->addViewport(m_Camera);
g_Viewport->setBackgroundColour(ColourValue(0,0,0));

// Alter the camera aspect ratio to match the viewport
 g_Camera->setAspectRatio( Real(g_Viewport->
getActualWidth()) / Real(g_Viewport->
getActualHeight()));
```

## Comments

- This function depends on the addition of three global members: g_SceneManager, representing an OGRE SceneManager object, g_Camera an OGRE Camera object, and g_Viewport an OGRE Viewport object. These variables are initialized to null but will later receive pointers to valid objects.

- The first object to be assigned a value is g_SceneManager, representing a hierarchical graph of nodes (objects) in 3D space. The WinMain function calls the createSceneManager method of the Root object to create an instance of the SceneManager class, and the created object begins empty; that is, begins as an empty scene. It is important to create the scene manager *before* both the camera and the viewport, and it is important to create the camera *before* the viewport. This is because of class dependence: The camera depends on the scene manager and the viewport on the camera. The camera represents *a view into* an *existing* scene, and the viewport represents a region into which an *existing* camera will render its contents on each frame. The createSceneManager method returns a pointer to a SceneManager class, if successful; otherwise, it returns null. The method accepts two main arguments; the first argument describes the type of scene manager to create, and the second specifies a name to be assigned to the scene manager (an application can create more than one scene manager). Scene managers can be of various types, ranging from a generic manager to an octree manager, with each scene manager suited to specific kinds of game scenes such as large outdoor environments or claustrophobic indoor environments. More is discussed later on the issue of scene type, but for now this sample will create an instance of a generic scene manager that is suitable for most scenes.

- Once a scene manager has been created using createSceneManager, the WinMain method continues by creating a camera object and a viewport object. The Camera object is created with a call to the createCamera method of the SceneManager, which returns a pointer to a newly created camera if successful; otherwise, it returns null. The returned camera represents a single camera (view) in the scene. It has both a *position* and *orientation* in 3D space; that is, a look at position and near clip distance. Position refers to the camera's absolute XYZ position from the origin in a 3D coordinate system, and orientation refers to the angle by which it has been rotated on each local axis (local X, local Y, and local Z). The look at position refers to the 3D point in the scene on which the camera is focused, and the near clip distance gives the camera some depth by specifying a maximum distance from its center that forms a region inside which objects will not be rendered. In other words, if a 3D object in the scene is close enough to the camera as to fall between the camera center and the near clip distance, the camera will clip (ignore) that object. The position, look at, and near clip distance options of the camera can be set using the setPosition, lookAt, and setNearClipDistance methods of the Camera class.

- The Camera object is created using the createCamera method of the SceneManager, and based on that camera a developer must also create a viewport. The Viewport object represents the rectangular region in the application window inside which the contents of the camera view will be projected on each frame of the render loop. The Viewport object is created from a call to the addViewport method of the Window object. That method requires as an argument in its constructor a pointer to the camera to be associated with the viewport. Once created, an application can proceed to flood fill the viewport with a specified starting color using the setBackgroundColour method of the Viewport object, and can also set the aspect ratio of the camera, passing the width and height of the viewport as arguments. The viewport size in terms of width and height in pixels is set to match the size of the application window.

---

### ■ OGRE Focus—Scene Managers, Cameras, and Viewports

The above addition to the WinMain function of an OGRE application created in sequence: a scene manager, a camera for the scene, and a viewport based on the camera. To do this, it needed to call on a selection of OGRE classes and methods, including root::createSceneManager, SceneManager::createCamera, and RenderTarget::addViewport. These methods are now considered in further detail.

---

#### The createSceneManager Method
In OGRE the SceneManager class is an essential object for building scenes that contain objects. It represents a hierarchical scene graph of invisible nodes, and is considered hierarchical because each node can be the parent, child, or sibling of another. The nodes themselves do not render but are intended to act as *dummy objects*; that is, as objects that affect others that are visible. Scene geometry, such as meshes, can be attached to nodes and the nodes can then be transformed. As a node is transformed, all attached objects will conform to its transformation. Scene managers are discussed in detail later in this chapter. A single instance of a scene manager can be created using the createSceneManager method of the Root object.

```
SceneManager* Root::createSceneManager (const
String &  typeName,
  const String &  instanceName = StringUtil::BLANK)
```

#### Arguments
##### const String &  typeName
String object representing the type of scene manager to be created. OGRE ships with a selection of types, and developers can also derive from the SceneManager class and implement their own. This chapter will consider only the ST_GENERIC scene manager type for general scenes. Other types native to OGRE include:

ST_EXTERIOR_CLOSE

ST_EXTERIOR_FAR

ST_EXTERIOR_REAL_FAR

ST_INTERIOR

> **NOTE**. OGRE will throw an exception if the type argument is not recognized.

**const String &  instanceName**
String object representing the unique name of the scene manager to create. This value can be left blank, in which case OGRE will assign a unique name automatically.

---

## The createCamera Method

The camera is a view into a scene and therefore depends on a scene manager for its existence. For this reason, SceneManager objects must be created before cameras. Camera objects have a position and orientation in a scene as well as a look at position and a near clip distance. In OGRE, cameras are encapsulated into the Camera class. A camera is created using the createCamera method of the SceneManager class. The prototype for this function appears as follows:

```
Camera* SceneManager::createCamera  ( const String &
name   )
```

**Arguments**

**const String &  name**
String object representing the unique name to be assigned to the new camera.

---

## The addViewport Method

OGRE encapsulates viewports—rectangular crop regions in the render window—into the Viewport object. Viewports are created from cameras, and therefore the Camera object must be created before the viewport. The viewport is both created and added to a render window by calling the addViewport function of the render window. All arguments of this function are optional, except the first.

```
virtual Viewport* Ogre::RenderTarget::addViewport (
Camera *  cam,
int   ZOrder = 0,
float  left = 0.0f,
float  top = 0.0f,
float  width = 1.0f,
float  height = 1.0f
)
```

**Arguments**

**Camera * cam**

Pointer to the Camera object whose view contents will be rendered to the viewport rectangle in the render window.

**int ZOrder**

This is an optional argument. For applications that use only one viewport, this value will be 0. However, applications can create more than one viewport to provide picture-in-picture effects or minimap effects; in these cases, it is necessary to ensure each viewport is drawn in the appropriate order. Higher orders are rendered *on top* of lower orders.

**float left**

**float top**

**float width**

**float height**

These are optional values and refer to the dimensions of the viewport. Left at their defaults, the viewport left and top values are 0,0 (top left of the window) and the width and height values are (1,1), which refer to the width and height of the window. In OGRE, screen coordinates are relative in that a width of 1 always refers to the width of the window, 0.5 refers to half the width, 2 is twice as much, etc. Using these relative values, the size of the viewport can be adjusted if required.

## 10.7.3   Catching Scene Events with Frame Listeners

The responsibility of an OGRE application is to build the scene graph by creating nodes and attaching objects to those nodes such as meshes, lights, cameras, sprites, etc., and the responsibility of OGRE itself is to parse and render that scene. OGRE does this through a render loop, much like the render loop created for the DirectX and SDL render managers. The next section will explain how the OGRE render loop can be started using the SDK function startRendering. This function is a self-contained loop, and when this method is called, OGRE enters a while loop whose every iteration represents a unique frame. On each frame, the OGRE scene manager and render system are together internally responsible for performing whatever work is required to render a 3D scene to the application window. At present, however, if the startRendering method is initiated without adding further code to the application, a developer would find their application trapped inside an infinite loop from which there is no escape. This is because the startRendering method never exits, being a while loop, and the application has not yet configured a means by which notifications can be received *from* OGRE and also by which messages can be sent *to* OGRE during the render loop. An application is likely to want to receive a notification from OGRE at the beginning of each frame in order to update game data, animate objects, and amend the scene graph as required. Additionally, an application will also want to instruct OGRE to pause, stop, and shut down whenever the need arises. OGRE allows such a channel of communication with the application through its FrameListener class. The FrameListener class is an abstract base class that developers should *not* instantiate directly but should use as a *base class* from which to derive a descendent class, overriding the ancestor's methods with custom functionality. A developer, then, *registers* instances of the derived listener class with the OGRE Root object, and OGRE calls all those registered listeners at both frame start and frame end for each and every frame. Consider the following example code as an extension of the WinMain function; comments follow:

```
class MyListener: public FrameListener
{
private:
protected:
public:
    RenderWindow* m_Window;

    bool frameRenderingQueued(const FrameEvent& evt)
    {
        //Exit if user clicks on window close button
        //Returning false instructs OGRE to exit
        return !m_Window->isClosed();
    }
};

//-------------------------------- WINMAIN function

g_Listener = new MyListener();
g_Listener->m_Window = m_Window;

g_Root->addFrameListener(g_Listener);
```

## Comments

- The above sample begins by creating a class derived from FrameListener, called MyListener. FrameListener exposes the following three virtual methods, which a descendent may override with custom behavior: frameStarted, frameEnded, and frameRenderingQueued. The first method is called as a new frame begins, the second is called after the back buffer is flipped and the scene finally presented to the display, and the third method is called after the scene has rendered but before the back buffer is drawn to the application window. Each of these methods is expected to return a boolean value; returning true will instruct OGRE to continue rendering as normal, and returning false will instruct OGRE to terminate the render loop and thus exit from the startRendering function, which is called at application startup to begin rendering, as the next section will demonstrate.

- The MyListener class is descended from the OGRE base class FrameListener, and it overrides only one method: frameRenderingQueued. This method will be called once per frame by OGRE after the listener is *registered*. The implementation of this method is short and checks only to see whether the user has clicked the standard window close button to exit the application. It checks this with a call to the isClosed method of the RenderWindow. If is Closed returns true, the function exits by returning false; and if isClosed returns false, the function exits by returning true. As mentioned, the return value is checked by OGRE to determine whether it should exit the render loop.

- Finally, the WinMain function is responsible for creating a new instance of the derived class MyListener and proceeds to register it with OGRE using the method addFrameListener of the Root object.

  NOTE. FrameListeners can be unregistered using the removeFrameListener method of the Root object.

---

### ■ OGRE Focus-Frame Listeners

Frame listeners are abstract base classes designed to be overridden with application-specific behavior. OGRE will recognize these classes as callback classes and will invoke three of its methods on each frame to notify an application of three key events: when a frame begins, when a frame ends, and when a frame is ready to be presented to the window. Each of these three functions should return a boolean, and OGRE uses this value to determine whether it should continue rendering or terminate the render loop. The following code lists the class declaration for the FrameListener class:

```
namespace Ogre
{

struct FrameEvent
{
Real timeSinceLastEvent;
Real timeSinceLastFrame;
};

class _OgreExport FrameListener
{
public:
virtual bool frameStarted(const FrameEvent& evt) {
return true; }
virtual bool frameRenderingQueued(const FrameEvent&
evt) { return true; }
virtual bool frameEnded(const FrameEvent& evt) {
return true; }
virtual ~FrameListener() {}
};
}
```

**NOTE**. Each of the three callback functions of FrameListener accepts an argument of type FrameEvent whose declaration is also given here. This structure features two properties that are updated automatically by OGRE, and applications can use them to keep track of time. Perhaps the most important member of the structure is timeSinceLastFrame, which indicates using a floating-point value how many seconds have elapsed since the previous frame.

## 10.7.4   Starting the Render Loop

The render loop represents the "heart" of a game application; it is the loop that keeps a game running until the user exits. Each iteration of the loop constitutes a frame, and on each frame an OGRE application will seek to render graphical data to the application window. Once an application has registered at least one FrameListener with the OGRE Root object, it can safely proceed to start the render loop using the startRendering method. Calling this function will begin the loop and keep an OGRE application alive and updating. The following code features the complete OGRE application created so far, including the call to startRendering. Compiling and running this application will result in a window that remains on-screen until the user exits

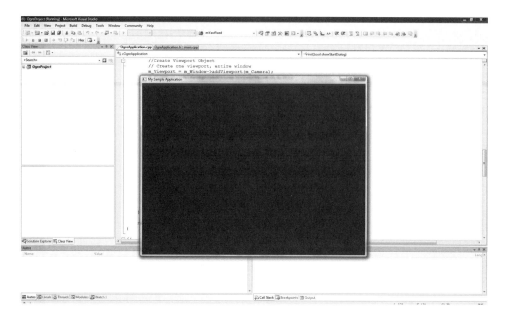

**I FIGURE 10.26**   First OGRE application.

(see Figure 10.26). It will, however, show only a black and empty window, since the OGRE scene is currently empty.

```
//FrameListener class
class MyListener: public FrameListener
{
private:
protected:
public:
    RenderWindow* m_Window;

    bool frameRenderingQueued(const FrameEvent& evt)
    {
        //Exit if user clicks on window close button
        //Returning false instructs OGRE to exit
        return !m_Window->isClosed();
    }
};

Root *g_Root = NULL;
RenderWindow* g_Window=NULL;
MyListener *g_Listener = NULL;
```

```
SceneManager *g_SceneManager=NULL;
Camera *g_Camera=NULL;
Viewport *g_Viewport=NULL;
bool showDialog=true;

//Application entry point
INT WINAPI WinMain( HINSTANCE hInst, HINSTANCE, LPSTR
strCmdLine, INT )
{
    try
    {
        //Initialize OGRE lib

        //Create OGRE Root object
        g_Root = OGRE_NEW Root("","");

        //Loads the RenderSystem DLLs
        g_Root->loadPlugin("RenderSystem_Direct3D9");
        g_Root->loadPlugin("RenderSystem_GL");

        if(showDialog)
{
   //Show dialog and create window
            if(g_Root->showConfigDialog())
          g_Window = g_Root->initialise(true, "Window");
}
else
{
   //Create graphics and window manually

   //Retrieve pointer to a default render system.
   //Can be either DirectX or OpenGL.
   //Depends on developer preference.
   //DirectX is selected here.

   RenderSystem *rs = g_Root-
>getRenderSystemByName("Direct3D9 Rendering Subsystem");

   //If DirectX available
   if(rs)
   {
        g_Root->setRenderSystem(rs);
   }
   else
   {
```

```
        //Choose OpenGL
        rs = g_Root->getRenderSystemByName("OpenGL
Rendering Subsystem");

    //VERY IMPORTANT. Sets selected render system as active.
        if(rs)
            g_Root->setRenderSystem(rs);
    }

    rs->setConfigOption("Full Screen", "No");
    rs->setConfigOption("Video Mode", "800 x 600 @ 32-bit
colour");

    g_Window = g_Root->initialise(true, «Window»);
}

//Create scene manager
g_SceneManager = g_Root->createSceneManager(ST_GENERIC,
"Default SceneManager");

//Create scene camera
g_Camera = m_SceneManager->createCamera(«Camera»);
g_Camera->setPosition(Vector3(0,0,500));
g_Camera->lookAt(Vector3(0,0,-300));
g_Camera->setNearClipDistance(5);

//Create viewport object
// Create one viewport, entire window
g_Viewport = g_Window->addViewport(m_Camera);
g_Viewport->setBackgroundColour(ColourValue(0,0,0));

// Alter the camera aspect ratio to match the viewport
 g_Camera->setAspectRatio( Real(g_Viewport->
getActualWidth()) / Real(g_Viewport->getActualHeight()));

g_Listener = new MyListener();
g_Listener->m_Window = m_Window;

    g_Root->addFrameListener(g_Listener);

    g_Root->startRendering();
    }
    catch( Exception& e )
    {
    //Catch OGRE exception
```

```
        MessageBoxA( NULL, e.getFullDescription().c_str(),
"An exception has occurred!", MB_OK | MB_ICONERROR | MB_
TASKMODAL);
    }

    return 0;
}
```

■ **10.8   OGRE and Resources**

The OGRE application developed throughout the previous section was not extravagant, for it rendered no meshes, lights, or textures. It simply created an application window, initialized a graphics device, and both created and sustained a render loop. When compiled and run, however, the application shows nothing but a blank window representing an empty 3D scene. As uninspiring as this application might appear to some, it nevertheless represents a firm foundation—a framework—on which to build subsequent OGRE applications featuring more elaborate scenes. A scene in OGRE comprises a collection of meshes, lights, and other objects in a unified 3D space, and these objects are usually loaded by an application at run time from external resource files; that is, from files on disk and not from those already loaded into memory. As mentioned in an earlier chapter, such files are termed "resource" files because they represent the raw materials (or assets)—such as textures, audio, meshes, and scripts—from which an engine assembles a game. Please refer to Chapter 4 for more information on the concept of resources and resource managers. OGRE too has its own resource management system that is responsible for finding, loading, and unloading resources from external files, and it is necessary to consider this system before resources can be loaded for display in 3D scenes using OGRE. The OGRE resource system consists of resource paths, resource groups, and resources.

### Resource Paths

A resource path is a string representing a local file system that contains one or more resource files. The file system can be a standard folder or even a compressed archive such as a ZIP file. At application startup, OGRE can be configured to read a list of resource paths from a text file on disk (resources.cfg), each path specifying a unique file system. This list—once loaded—will represent the extent of OGRE's knowledge of the computer's file system. When OGRE is requested to load a resource by file name (such as MyImage.png), it will scan only through the list of resource paths to find that file. OGRE will not search on paths not listed in the resource path list. Furthermore, since OGRE scans all resource paths for files of specified names, it follows that all files on those paths must have a unique name. Conventionally, Windows requires all files in a single folder to have a unique name but does allow files of the same name to exist in different folders. OGRE, however, requires all files across the resource path list to have unique names. The following code lists the contents of a sample resources.cfg file, representing a list of resource paths—both folder paths and ZIP files—that an OGRE application will load into a list at startup. OGRE will not at this stage automatically load any resource data found on those paths but loads only the string representations of those paths. Notice that path names are specified relatively to the folder in which the application executable is contained, and that zip paths are prefixed with "Zip=" and folder paths with "FileSystem=".

```
# Resource locations to be added to the 'bootstrap' path
# This also contains the minimum you need to use the OGRE
example framework
[Bootstrap]
Zip=../../media/packs/OgreCore.zip

# Resource locations to be added to the default path
[General]
FileSystem=../../media
FileSystem=../../media/fonts
FileSystem=../../media/materials/programs
FileSystem=../../media/materials/scripts
FileSystem=../../media/materials/textures
FileSystem=../../media/models
FileSystem=../../media/overlays
FileSystem=../../media/particle
FileSystem=../../media/gui
FileSystem=../../media/DeferredShadingMedia
FileSystem=../../media/PCZAppMedia
Zip=../../media/packs/cubemap.zip
Zip=../../media/packs/cubemapsJS.zip
Zip=../../media/packs/dragon.zip
Zip=../../media/packs/fresneldemo.zip
Zip=../../media/packs/ogretestmap.zip
Zip=../../media/packs/skybox.zip
```

**Resource Groups**

The resources configuration file listed above contains two resource groups—Bootstrap and General—with each group containing the resource paths listed beneath its title. OGRE allows developers to divide its list of resource paths into groups, each group containing one or more paths, according to their needs; often that division is based on the relationship that member resources have to one another. For example, a developer might have divided their game resources into several folders based on their type: audio resources in one folder (audio), graphics resources in another (graphics), and text resources in another (text). To reflect this division of resources across separate folders in the OGRE resource system, a developer might create one similarly named resource group for audio resources that represents all audio resource paths and another group for graphics that represents all graphics resource paths. An alternative approach to grouping resources might be to group them according to their use during the game. This might lead a developer to create one group for all level 1 resources, another for level 2 resources, and so on. As we shall see, all the resources of a group can be loaded and unloaded as a group, not just individually. This therefore makes resource groups a convenient system for loading and unloading large batches of resources in one call. It is important to recognize that there are no hard-and-fast rules about the right or wrong way to use resource groups in OGRE. The resource group feature of the OGRE resource framework is simply there to offer a convenient mechanism for grouping resources.

**Resource**

The resource is the basic unit of currency within the OGRE resource system. A resource represents a unique and identifiable game asset that the engine may be required to load, unload, and use on request during game play. For OGRE, resources typically come in the form of textures, materials, meshes, particle systems, and shaders. The resource as an entity typically contains two faces with regard to the data it represents: *metadata* and *raw data*. The metadata refers to information *about* the resource raw data, and the raw data represents the main body of the resource itself. For bitmap images, the metadata will describe the file name of the image file, the width and height of the image in pixels, the pixel format and color depth of the image, and whether the image contains an alpha channel, etc. The raw data refers to the actual pixel data of the image and typically constitutes the most sizable portion of data. For this reason, when loading resource information and resource paths, OGRE will by default load *only* metadata and *no* raw data.

> **NOTE.** OGRE automates much of the resource loading process. It will automatically load all appropriate resource data whenever it detects that a given resource is required for a scene, provided that resource can be found on one of the available resource paths. It is therefore important that an application configures and loads the resource paths correctly. This subject is the focus of the next section.

## 10.8.1   Loading Resource Paths

Games can be said to be resource-intensive applications in two senses: First, they often make heavy demands on the hardware resources of the computer on which they run; and second, and more relevantly, a game relies heavily on the digital resources (assets) necessary to represent a world of imagination to the player. In this latter sense, a resource represents a game asset (such as a texture, mesh, or script), and for an OGRE application to use such resources in its scenes, it must first configure a list of resource paths. This list tells OGRE of all possible locations where resources for the application will be found when required. The resource list in this sense represents the extent of OGRE's knowledge of the local file system because OGRE will not search elsewhere for resources if none with a matching name are found on any of the resource paths. Once the resource path list is loaded, OGRE can then proceed to search those paths for resources as and when required. The resource path list is typically loaded at application startup, and can be either created manually in code or loaded from a text-based configuration file on disk. The following code uses the OGRE library to load a resource path list from a configuration file, and comments follow:

```
// Load resource paths from config file
//Config File object OGRE class

ConfigFile cf;
cf.load("resources.cfg");

// Go through all sections & settings in the file
ConfigFile::SectionIterator seci =
cf.getSectionIterator();

String secName, typeName, archName;
while (seci.hasMoreElements())
{
    secName = seci.peekNextKey();
    ConfigFile::SettingsMultiMap *settings = seci.
getNext();
    ConfigFile::SettingsMultiMap::iterator i;
    for (i = settings->begin(); i != settings-
>end(); ++i)
    {
        typeName = i->first;
        archName = i->second;

    //Add resource path
        ResourceGroupManager::getSingleton().
addResourceLocation(
        archName, typeName, secName);
    }
}
```

```
//Initialize all groups once all resource paths are added
ResourceGroupManager::getSingleton().
initialiseAllResourceGroups();
```

## Comments

- The code sample starts by creating an OGRE ConfigFile class. This class is part of the OGRE framework and is not application specific. It encapsulates a text-based configuration file and supports methods for iterating through sections of that file and for reading field names and field values. A unique section of the file is marked by the [] symbols, and between them appears the name of the section in the form [SectionName]. Lines beginning with the hash symbol (#) are understood to be comments and—like blank lines—are ignored by the ConfigFile class. Field-title and Field-value pairs are in the form of FieldTitle=FieldValue (e.g., FileSystem=../../media). The ConfigFile class will be used to load and read the settings of a text-based configuration file for loading a list of resource paths.

- The code then calls the load method of the ConfigFile class to load a config file of a specified name. This function simply readies the class for the parsing of the specified file.

- Once loaded, the code retrieves a pointer to a section iterator, which allows developers to iterate though all sections of the file one by one, starting from the first and ending with the last. For each section found in the file, the code should cycle through all elements of the section. An element refers to a field name and field value pair, and many such elements may belong to a section. An application loads the resource path list of OGRE by creating a resource group for each section of the file and by loading all elements of that section as resource paths of that group.

- For each section found in the file, the above code creates a local variable, ConfigFile::SettingsMultiMap. This represents a map of the section—a collection of member elements. It then retrieves a pointer to a SettingsMultiMap iterator representing the first element of the section, and using that iterator the code cycles through each and every element. For each element, it records the first and second parameters (the field name and the field value, respectively). Having obtained those values it calls ResourceGroupManager::getSingleton(). addResourceLocation. That is, it calls the addResourceLocation method of a singleton object that OGRE exposes, called ResourceGroupManager. This object is initialized automatically by OGRE when the Root object is created. Since OGRE maintains only one resource system per application, this object is exposed as a singleton object, and a pointer to the one valid instance can be accessed in any function by calling the ResourceGroupManager::getSingleton() method. The addResourceLocation method of this singleton object registers a new resource path with the OGRE resource system. The arguments and details of this function are considered in the OGRE Focus—Resource Paths sidebar as follows.

- The sample code above calls addResourceLocation for each element of every section in the config file to add a valid resource path to the OGRE resource system. Once all paths are added, it calls the initialiseAllResourceGroups method of the ResourceGroupManager singleton object. This method completes the resource path loading process and readies the resource system for use with those paths. It does not load any raw resource data.

### ■ OGRE Focus—Resource Paths

A resource path specifies to OGRE a local file system in which resource data may be found during application execution. A resource path can be a standard folder containing files and further subfolders, which are not automatically added to the resource path, or it can contain compressed ZIP files that in turn contain resource files. It is also possible to extend the OGRE source so as to support custom formats and compression types, though this book is concerned only with the types native to OGRE. The key method for adding resource paths into the OGRE resource system is the addResourceLocation method of the singleton object ResourceGroupManager. Its details follow.

```
void addResourceLocation  (
  const String &  name,
  const String &  locType,
  const String &  resGroup = DEFAULT_RESOURCE_GROUP_
NAME,
  bool  recursive = false
  )
```

**Arguments**

**const String & name**
An OGRE string specifying the name of the resource location to be added to the resource group specified by the argument resGroup. This will be either the absolute or the relative path to a folder (such as c:\my_resources) or a ZIP file (such as myzip.zip). This value corresponds to the field value parameter read from the element of a section in the config file.

**const String & locType**
An OGRE string indicating the resource type that is specified by the name
argument. This value corresponds to the field title parameter read from the
element of a section in the config file. This could be "Zip" or "FileSystem."

**const String &  resGroup = DEFAULT_RESOURCE_GROUP_NAME**
An OGRE string specifying the name of the resource group to which the
resource path specified by the name parameter should be added. This can be
left null, in which case the resource is added to a default resource group. If
specified, the resource will be added to that group if it exists. If a group of
the specified name does not exist, then one will be created. This value corresponds to the section name of the config file.

**bool  recursive**
Boolean to determine whether subdirectories of the path specified by the
name parameter should be indexed and registered as valid resource paths.
This argument has a default value of false.

## ■  10.9   Meshes, Materials, and Material Scripts

The previous section demonstrated how text-based configuration files are used to
specify a collection of resource paths using a series of sections and elements. These
paths define the limit of OGRE's vision of the local file system, and OGRE will search
these paths for a file of a specified name whenever it is necessary to load, access, and
use that resource data for the purposes of rendering a scene. One scenario in which
OGRE will need to resort to the resource system is in the loading and rendering of
meshes. In the case of textured meshes, it will need to access the resource system
twice—once to find and load the mesh file (featuring vertices, edges, and polygons)
and a second time to access and load the texture data to be skinned onto the mesh. This
section considers the use of meshes, materials, and textures, and their definition in
material scripts. Before diving into the details of material scripts, however, this section
demonstrates how to load and show a premade and pretextured mesh provided with
the OGRE SDK. Though this loading sample will take much for granted in the way
of assuming that a mesh will already have been created, textured, and exported to an
OGRE format, and had a material script defined, it nevertheless is a helpful introduction to demonstrating how mesh files can be loaded, rendered, and added to the scene
graph. Details of mesh exporting and material scripts are given later in this section,
and the scene graph is considered in more detail in the next section. The following

code loads a mesh file and adds it to the scene. Once added, OGRE will render the mesh on each frame. Comments follow the code.

> **NOTE**. For this sample to work, the mesh loading code should be called after OGRE initialization and before the render loop is started using the startRendering method.

> **NOTE**. OGRE uses the term "entity" to refer to a mesh.

```
m_SceneManager->setAmbientLight(ColourValue(1, 1, 1));

Entity *ent1 = m_SceneManager->createEntity( "head",
"ogrehead.mesh" );

SceneNode *node1 = m_SceneManager->getRootSceneNode()-
>createChildSceneNode( "HeadNode" );

node1->attachObject(ent1);

node1->translate(Vector3(0,0,250));
```

## Comments

- The code begins with a call to the method setAmbientLight, passing 1 for each of its three RGB color values, where 0 is blackness and 1 is full intensity. A value of 1 for all components results in the color white. The setAmbientLight method of the scene manager sets the ambient light in the scene. Ambient light is an all-pervading light shining with equal intensity in all directions of the scene, and it does not cast shadows. It does not therefore make for realistic lighting in scenes since real-life light has both position and direction and loses intensity with distance at an inverse square ratio. However, it is useful for illuminating all areas of a scene in order to examine meshes and their textures under neutral conditions. By default, the ambient light is set to 0, and thus the scene begins in complete darkness. For this reason, meshes added to a scene in darkness will not render since there exists no light to illuminate them. Thus, it is necessary here to set the ambient lighting. It would not be necessary, however, if an application added its own custom lights, in which case a developer is likely to want ambient light set to 0 to ensure it does not conflict with their own setup.

- Once a light is added to the scene, an application loads a mesh from a resource file using the createEntity method of the SceneManager class. Note that OGRE uses the term "entity" to refer to a mesh. This method requires two arguments: a unique name for the entity in the scene and the file name of the mesh file from which the entity is to be loaded. This function will search all resource paths for a file with a matching name. If no file is found, an exception is thrown. If the function is successful, a valid entity object is returned. It is important to note that the createEntity method does not *add* the entity to the scene; it simply creates an entity in memory and encapsulates it through the methods of the entity class.

• OGRE provides access to a scene through the properties and methods of the scene manager, and this manager in short represents a scene graph. The scene graph is a hierarchical structure of scene nodes by which OGRE understands and describes the arrangement of objects in a scene. A scene node refers to a nonvisible anchor object that exists in a hierarchy of other nodes—each node has a parent, and can have siblings and children. The node itself is not visible and is an anchor to which one or more visible objects may be attached. The node has position, orientation, and scaling properties, and all objects attached to the node are affected by those properties for as long as they remain attached. To move a mesh in a scene, a developer should attach the mesh to a scene node and then move that node. To add a mesh to a scene therefore, a developer must first *create a scene node* and then *attach the mesh to that node*. Creating a scene node is achieved as follows: First, the getRootSceneNode method of the SceneManager is called to retrieve a SceneNode pointer to the *root* node of the scene; that is, to the topmost node to which all other nodes in the scene are descended either directly or indirectly. Once retrieved, the createChildSceneNode method of the SceneNode is called. This creates a direct child node to be associated with the mesh whose parent is the root node. The method createChildSceneNode returns a pointer to a newly created scene node, and the mesh is attached by calling its attachObject method, passing a pointer to the entity as an argument. The mesh is now added to the scene and can be rendered by OGRE on the next frame, provided it is visible to the scene camera. Notice how the position of the mesh in the scene can be adjusted by calling the translate method of the mesh scene node.

> **NOTE.** Compiling and running this sample will show an application window featuring a textured mesh object in a scene with ambient lighting. The entity is a 3D mesh of the OGRE logo. Please note that OGRE automatically loaded the appropriate mesh and associated texture resources; this is because the mesh and material script files contain the names of material and texture data assigned to this mesh. Thus, it was not necessary for the application to load the resources as a separate step prior to loading the mesh. See Figure 10.27.

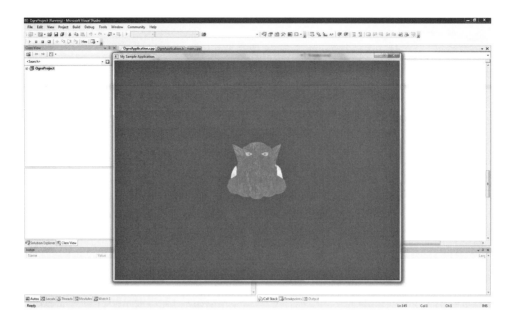

**❙ FIGURE 10.27**   OGRE head sample.

## 10.9.1   Materials and Material Scripts

The previous section demonstrated how a premade mesh with material and texture information can be loaded from a file on disk as an entity in a 3D OGRE scene. As mentioned, the process of mesh loading relies on OGRE being made aware of a set of resource paths on which it will find resource data such as mesh files and texture information. To load a mesh and present it in a scene, the sample code called upon the createEntity method of the SceneManager and on the SceneNodes class, respectively, and although the mesh rendered correctly with a material when compiled and run as an application, the previous section did not examine exactly how the details of the material framework operate, nor how material information in a script file was referenced automatically by OGRE to texture the mesh. This section pauses to consider how OGRE material scripts work and explains how they can be adjusted to affect the skin of the ogre head mesh loaded in the previous section.

The OGRE SDK ships with an impressive range of sample applications that rely on a shared media folder containing resources for those applications. This folder contains scripts, meshes, textures, shaders, and more. For the purposes of illustration and to help the reader disentangle themselves from the mass of samples and sample resources, the book's companion code features a much reduced mesh loading example project that ships with only those resources necessary for successful execution of the

■   **OGRE Focus—Entity Loading**

OGRE draws a subtle but not unimportant distinction between a mesh and an entity. The term "mesh" refers only to a collection of vertices, edges, and faces compose a model. The term "entity" refers to a mesh *complete* with texture and material data, and shader data where appropriate. An entity is loaded into memory from a mesh file on disk using the createEntity method of the SceneManager class, and is subsequently added to a scene using scene nodes. Notice from the code sample above that a mesh is loaded into the scene from a binary and proprietary file format (.mesh). The format .oof is also supported. It should be reiterated that createEntity only *creates* an entity object from a file and does not automatically add that object to a scene. The form of the createEntity method follows:

```
Entity* Ogre::SceneManager::createEntity
(
const String &  entityName,
const String &  meshName
)
```

**Arguments**

**const String &  entityName**

OGRE string to specify the unique name of the entity to be created. An exception is thrown if the entity name is already in use.

**const String &  meshName**

OGRE string specifying the full file name of the mesh file from which the entity is to be loaded. This mesh file should be located on any of the resource paths.

compiled application. It contains an ogre head mesh file and a material script defining the default materials to be used for that mesh when loaded and rendered in a scene. Reducing the sample data and code to the minimum in this way will help illustrate exactly what is necessary when working with an OGRE application that loads meshes and uses materials.

An OGRE application that loads a mesh from a file also loads material data, if material data is defined, and it often reads this material data from a .material script file. Again, it should be remembered that a material is an algorithm or "recipe" instructing the OGRE renderer on how to render the skin of a mesh when illuminated by scene lighting. A material can indicate the color of a mesh surface, its shininess, its reflective properties, its roughness, and perhaps most importantly the *texture map* to be applied to the skin; that is, the image that will define the mesh's appearance. In the sample application created in the previous section, an OGRE application was coded to load a mesh file with material information defining the green skin of an ogre head. The mesh file itself contains only limited material data: It contains information about the *name* of the material to be applied to the mesh (since OGRE identifies a material by its unique name) and the texture coordinates of the texture map. The texture coordinates define how a flat 2D texture image is to be wallpapered and tiled and stretched onto the surface of the mesh. The material name (as a string argument) is then used by the OGRE library to (1) find a matching material in a separate material script file (2) then to read its properties regarding color and shininess, and also to load the actual 2D image file to be used as the texture map. A material script file is a standard text-based file that can define one or more materials using an OGRE scripting language. As with other resources like images and meshes, the script files should be located on an OGRE resource path, and as the resource paths are initialized, OGRE will automatically index all material information found on those paths for reference. The material script file for the materials of the sample ogre head mesh (ogrehead.material) contains four materials: one material for the skin (Ogre/Skin), one for the tusks (Ogre/Tusks), one for the earring (Ogre/Earring), and one for the eyes (Ogre/Eyes). The material script for these materials is given below and then comments follow:

```
material Ogre/Earring
{
   technique
   {
      pass
      {
         ambient 0.5 0.5 0
         diffuse 1 1 0

         texture_unit
         {
            texture spheremap.png
            colour_op_ex add src_texture src_current
            colour_op_multipass_fallback one one
            env_map spherical
         }
      }
   }
}
```

```
material Ogre/Skin
{
   technique
   {
      pass
      {
         ambient 0.7 0.7 0.7
         cull_hardware none

         texture_unit
         {
            texture GreenSkin.jpg
            tex_address_mode mirror
         }
      }
   }
}
material Ogre/Tusks
{
   technique
   {
      pass
      {
         ambient 0.5 0.5 0.4
         diffuse 1 1 0.8

         texture_unit
         {
            texture dirt01.jpg
            colour_op_ex add src_texture src_current
            colour_op_multipass_fallback one one
         }
      }
   }
}
material Ogre/Eyes
{
   technique
   {
      pass
      {

         texture_unit
         {
```

```
                texture WeirdEye.png
            }
        }
    }
}
```

## Comments

- The above material script file contains four uniquely named materials, one for each section of the mesh. The mesh file references those materials by name and contains the texture coordinates to be used when mapping the texture map onto the mesh skin. The material script file contains further information about the material such as its color and the file name of the texture map file to be used. It is worth noting that since the texture coordinate information is stored separately from the file name of the texture file, an application can map different images onto the mesh by changing texture maps; although the images can change, the mapping coordinates will remain constant.

- Each new material begins with the keyword "material," followed by the material name. Each material consists of techniques, passes, and texture_units. Each material can feature one or more techniques; each technique can feature one or more passes; and each pass can feature one or more texture_units.

### Techniques

A technique refers to a style or method for rendering an object, and the simplest material contains only the minimum one technique needed for rendering. However, since hardware varies from computer to computer, and since the conditions under which an application executes varies even on the same computer, a developer must be sure that all systems can render the material under the one technique if they choose to define no more than one. Often, for simple materials that map a standard 2D texture to a mesh and do little else, an application is in no danger that its technique will not be supported. It helps to think of techniques as contingency plans. OGRE will seek to use the first technique it encounters to render the selected material; if that technique is not supported, it will fall back onto another, and will repeat until either a supported technique is found or no more techniques remain. If there is no technique of a material supported by the hardware at run time, then the material will render blank.

### Passes

Passes belong to techniques, and one pass represents one *render* per frame of the object to which the material is applied. A material can have from 1 to 16 passes, and a material with 16 passes requires OGRE to render it 16 times on each frame.

Passes are used to create specific texture effects such as bump mapping, normal mapping, and other reflection or specular effects. Each effect is produced through a unique pass. It follows that the number of passes per technique is directly proportionally to the performance penalty incurred for rendering. The materials considered in this book feature only one pass. During the pass stage, a material can define properties such as specular, diffuse, and emissive to define the color of the material and how it responds to light.

---

### ■ Material Pass Properties

The following properties can be defined in the material pass. Please consult the OGRE documentation for further details on each property.

ambient
diffuse
specular
emissive
scene_blend
separate_scene_blend
depth_check
depth_write
depth_func
depth_bias
iteration_depth_bias
alpha_rejection
alpha_to_coverage
light_scissor
light_clip_planes
illumination_stage
transparent_sorting
normalise_normals
cull_hardware
cull_software
lighting
shading
polygon_mode
polygon_mode_overrideable
fog_override

colour_write
max_lights
start_light
iteration
point_size
point_sprites
point_size_attenuation
point_size_min
point_size_max

### Texture Units

Texture units belong to passes and are used to describe which 2D texture file is to be mapped onto whatever mesh or meshes are assigned to a material. The texture unit section can also be used to amend texture mapping, to adjust texture tiling, and to apply other texturing effects. It is in the texture unit stage that a material script actually defines which 2D texture image is to be used for this pass. This value is supplied using the texture command. The following texture command assigns a file as the texture for this material: texture dirt01.jpg. The file dirt01.jpg should exist on the resource location paths.

> **NOTE**. The material of a mesh can be changed to a specified material on-the-fly using the method setMaterialName of the Entity class, as follows:

```
ent1->setMaterialName("MyMaterial");
```

### ■ Texture Unit Properties

The texture unit stage of the material script supports the properties listed below. Please consult the official OGRE documentation for more information on each property.

texture_alias
texture
anim_texture
cubic_texture
tex_coord_set

```
tex_address_mode
tex_border_colour
filtering
max_anisotropy
mipmap_bias
colour_op
colour_op_ex
colour_op_multipass_fallback
alpha_op_ex
env_map
scroll
scroll_anim
rotate
rotate_anim
scale
wave_xform
transform
binding_type
content_type
```

The material of a mesh can be cleared and set to a blank white material using the setMaterialName function as follows:

```
ent1->setMaterialName("BaseWhiteNoLighting");
```

BaseWhiteNoLighting is a standard name recognized by OGRE for blank white materials.

## 10.9.2   Scene Nodes and the Scene Graph

For created entities to be rendered to the application window on each frame, they must be added to the OGRE scene, which is a common 3D space of XYZ axes, inside which objects can be oriented, translated, scaled, and edited. The origin of that space is at (0,0,0), and to a camera located at the origin, positive Z will appear to stretch onward into the distance, while negative Z will reach backward behind the camera. The X axis is aligned horizontally and Y vertically, each axis perpendicular to the other. In this 3D space, objects are situated in relation to each other, and it is the job of game designers and level designers to populate and arrange this space with interesting assets to make a complete and functional game. It is the job of the engine developer to make this space manageable and accessible to these designers.

Earlier chapters of this book and earlier sections of this chapter mentioned some of the problems encountered by developers when seeking to manage game scenes and specifically 3D scenes. Foremost among these problems is the issue of managing relations and dependencies between objects in a scene and the implications these relations have for the motion and position of objects in 3D space. This problem can be reiterated here succinctly by referring to the example of Aladdin and his magic carpet. Aladdin can walk around on the surface of his carpet and thereby change his position in 3D space. But as the carpet takes flight and moves through the air, it carries Aladdin along with it. Aladdin can still walk about the surface of the carpet as it moves through the air, but the trajectory of the carpet affects the world position of Aladdin because Aladdin is dependent on the carpet. Aladdin's movement on the surface of the carpet does not affect the position of the carpet, but the movement of the carpet affects the position of Aladdin. This is by no means the only kind of example that demonstrates a relationship between two objects in 3D space, for there are innumerable more, but it highlights the need to manage such relationships. If Aladdin and the carpet were separate meshes added to the scene independently of one another, there would exist no linking mechanism to tie the position of one to the other. In this case, as the carpet moved, the application would be responsible for moving Aladdin manually. Though this system could work, it would not be optimal, especially where many such relations existed. OGRE resolves this problem and related problems using the hierarchical scene graph, an example of which is shown in Figure 10.28.

The scene graph allows both OGRE and engine developers to express, manage, and represent objects in a 3D scene. The graph's top-level functionality is encapsulated into the SceneManager class, and developers can create and manipulate *scene nodes* using this class. Scene nodes are the building blocks of a scene, and the scene graph represents a hierarchical collection of scene nodes. A scene node is an invisible anchor point (or dummy object) that has one parent and can have one or more children and sibling nodes, and the topmost node in the hierarchy is called the root node. It is to scene nodes generally that visible objects, such as meshes and sprites, attach themselves in order to exist in a 3D scene. To be attached to a scene node is to be in the scene, and to be detached from a scene node is to be removed from the scene. Each scene node has a position, orientation, and scale in 3D space, which applies to all objects attached to that node; as one node is transformed, so all attached objects transform to match the node. Furthermore, transformations applied to one node are inherited downward through the graph, cascading relatively onto dependent nodes (see Figure 10.28). This means that transformations applied to the root node affect all nodes in the scene since all other nodes trace their ancestry to this node. To resolve the

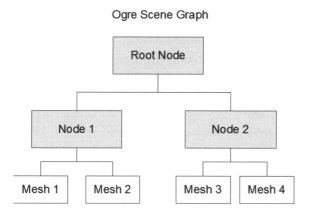

**| FIGURE 10.28**   OGRE scene graph.

Aladdin and carpet problem using scene nodes, a developer would create two scene nodes, one for the carpet and one for Aladdin. The Aladdin node would be a child of the carpet node. This would ensure that carpet transformations cascaded downward to Aladdin but also that Aladdin transformations did not affect the carpet, because transformations to child nodes do not cascade upward to parents. The scene node concept need not be restricted to meshes and graphics; it could be extended to include 3D sounds attached to objects, so that the volume level of sounds adjusted according to their position in 3D space, growing louder as they approached the player character and fainter as they moved farther away. Furthermore, encoding a scene into a scene node hierarchy (or tree) offers additional benefits to an engine developer. Since the tree can be traversed programmatically—that is, since each node can be visited through recursive looping—a developer can "serialize" the contents of a scene. This means developers can easily export and import scenes to and from external files respectively, such as XML. Being able to save and load scenes in this way opens up the scene and engine to new development possibilities, specifically the possibility of creating world editors and GUI game development tools that developers can use to interactively build scenes, exporting them to formats that interface with the scene graph.

Putting the thoughts of these possibilities and potentials aside for a moment, it is now necessary to consider how the scene graph can be built manually in code using OGRE. The earlier mesh-loading sample code demonstrated this functionality at work in order to add a mesh to a scene via a scene node, and now this section considers this functionality and the SceneNode class in more detail. It does this by exploring a set of methods, classes, and functions for manually building scene graphs.

### 10.9.3    The SceneNode Class

OGRE encapsulates a scene node of the graph in the SceneNode class. Through this class a single node can be translated, rotated, scaled, renamed, severed from its current parent and attached to another, and attached to objects in the scene. In addition, as the node is transformed, OGRE will automatically cascade the transformation downward to all child nodes. The root node represents the top node of the scene graph—the ultimate ancestor node—whose transformation cascades downward to all other nodes. A pointer to this node can be retrieved by a call to the getRootSceneNode method of the SceneManager class. This method accepts no arguments. Some key methods of this class are listed in the following class declaration and then the usage of some are demonstrated in more detail throughout the following sections of this chapter. For a complete reference to the SceneNode class, please consult the official OGRE documentation that ships with the SDK.

```
class SceneNode
{
public:
unsigned short  numAttachedObjects (void) const;
void  attachObject (MovableObject *obj);
MovableObject *  getAttachedObject (unsigned short index);
MovableObject *  detachObject (unsigned short index);
virtual bool  isInSceneGraph (void) const;
AxisAlignedBox &  _getWorldAABB (void);
void  yaw (const Radian &angle, TransformSpace
relativeTo=TS_LOCAL);
void  roll (const Radian &angle, TransformSpace
relativeTo=TS_LOCAL);
void  pitch (const Radian &angle, TransformSpace
relativeTo=TS_LOCAL);
void  setPosition (Real x, Real y, Real z);
void  setScale (Real x, Real y, Real z);
void  translate (Real x, Real y, Real z, TransformSpace
relativeTo=TS_PARENT);
Node *  createChild (const String &name, const
Vector3 &translate=Vector3::ZERO, const Quaternion
&rotate=Quaternion::IDENTITY);
void  addChild (Node *child);
Node *  removeChild (unsigned short index);
};
```

### 10.9.4    Creating and Adding Scene Nodes

The getRootSceneNode method of the SceneManager class returns a pointer to the topmost scene node of the scene graph. This scene node is especially important in that transformations to this node cascade downward, affecting all other nodes in the scene. If, for example, a developer were creating a beat-'em-up game, similar to Street Fighter® IV, they might implement a camera shake or world shake effect in their scenes. This effect occurs when a heavy punch is delivered from one character to another or when a character is thrown to the floor. On these occasions, the camera (or world) shakes to emphasize the damage that occurred and to add dramatic effect to the action. Such an effect could be recreated using the scene graph by transforming the root node to shake back and forth, thereby shaking all objects in the scene. Most transformations, however, will not and do not occur at the root node level, because many objects of the scene are intended to move independently of each other. To do this, a node should be created for each object or group of objects that are designed to move and transform as one unit. For example, the components of a car (wheel, seats, doors) would likely be attached to a single node to ensure all parts move together as a compete and integrated car. Creating a new child node involves calling the createChildSceneNode method of the SceneNode class; this method should be called on the node that is to be the parent of the newly created node. In a scene that contains only the root node, the first child to be created will be a child of the root node. The form of the createChildSceneNode is listed here and an example follows:

```
SceneNode* Ogre::SceneNode::createChildSceneNode
(
const String &  name,
const Vector3 &  translate = Vector3::ZERO,
const Quaternion &  rotate = Quaternion::IDENTITY
 )
```

**Arguments**

**const String &  name**

OGRE string specifying the unique name of the child node to be created.

**const Vector3 &  translate = Vector3::ZERO**

Optional parameter specifying the starting position of the node in world space.

**const Quaternion &  rotate = Quaternion::IDENTITY**

Optional parameter specifying the starting orientation of the node in world space. The orientation is defined as a quaternion, which is a mathematical structure used to define rotations. Unlike standard angles as measured in degrees or radians, a quaternion describes a specified *rotation* about a specified *axis*. Quaternions pertain to 3D mathematics and are outside the scope of this book. More information can be found on quaternions and their usage in OGRE at the following URL:

http://www.ogre3d.org/wiki/index.php/Quaternion_and_Rotation_Primer.

**Example: Creating a Child Scene Node**

```
//Get root node
SceneNode *RootNode = m_SceneManager->getRootSceneNode();

//Create child node of the root node
SceneNode *MyNode = RootNode->createChildSceneNode(
"MyNode" );
```

## 10.9.5   Attaching and Detaching Objects

It was mentioned earlier that scene nodes are invisible in the sense that they do not render to the display. They exist in the scene and have an effect on visible objects, but they do not themselves render. For this reason, if nothing visible is attached to those nodes it is possible for a scene to render blank even when it is full of nodes. The purpose of the node is to act as a *dummy object* (or an anchor point) to which visible objects are attached. Scene nodes can be transformed (translated, scaled, and rotated), and all attached objects inherit that transformation. For a visible object to be affected by a node therefore, it must first be *attached* to that node. Nodes can be attached to one or more objects, but any one object should be attached to no more than one node. The process of attachment binds an object to a node, and the process of detachment unbinds the object and node. Attachments and detachments between objects and nodes are made through a call to the attachObject and detachObject methods of the class SceneNode. These methods should be called on the node to or from which a specified object should be attached or be detached, respectively. It is important to note also that for objects the process of attachment represents their addition to the scene, and detachment their removal. It is through scene nodes that objects exist in scenes, and therefore unattached objects are not considered to be in the scene even though they may exist in memory. The form of these functions are shown here and then an example of their use follows:

```
void Ogre::SceneNode::attachObject  (MovableObject*  obj)
```

**Arguments**

**MovableObject * obj**

Pointer to an object that should be attached to the specified node. This object can be of any OGRE class derived from MovableObject, which includes entities (meshes), cameras, lights, and particle systems as well as custom objects derived from MovableObject. The attached object will inherit node transformations.

```
MovableObject* Ogre::SceneNode::detachObject (const
String &  name )
```

**Arguments**

**const String &  name**

OGRE string specifying the name of the object to detach from the node. If an object of the specified name is not attached to the node, an exception is returned. This function returns a pointer to the object detached from the node. Detaching an object from a node *does not* delete the object from memory. A detached object can still be accessed, edited, and reattached to either the same node or a different node.

**Example: Attaching and Detaching an Object**

```
//Get root node
SceneNode *RootNode = m_SceneManager->getRootSceneNode();

//Create child node of the root node
SceneNode *MyNode = RootNode->createChildSceneNode
("MyNode" );

//Attach object
MyNode->attachObject(MyEntity);

//Retrieve the number of objects attached to this node
unsigned short numAttachedObjects = MyNode->
numAttachedObjects();

//Detaches the object named "MyNode"
MyNode->detachObject("MyNode");
```

NOTE. The numAttachedObjects method can be called to retrieve the total number of objects attached to the node at the time of the call. The getAttachedObject method can also be called to retrieve a pointer to a specified attached object without detaching that object from the node.

## 10.9.6   Editing the Scene Node Hierarchy

Scene nodes exist in a tree-like hierarchy that begins with the topmost root node, each node below having *one* parent and either none, one, or more child nodes. The parent of a node is the node directly above it in the tree, and child nodes are those directly below. Furthermore, transformations that are applied to one node cascade downward to all nodes below it in the hierarchy; that is, to all its descendant nodes: children, grandchildren, and so on. Using this structure, a multitude of relationships can be expressed about objects existing in a unified 3D world space. In an earlier section, it was shown how new child scene nodes can be *created* using the createChildSceneNode method of the SceneNode class. This method is useful for creating a *new* scene node as the child node of a *preexisting* scene node. However, there will be occasions when OGRE developers require more than simply the ability to create new child nodes. For this reason, it is therefore important to become familiar with other graph building methods, such as those that allow a developer to delete and remove scene nodes from the graph, remove nodes from their current parent, and add existing nodes to another node as a child. Using a combination of all of these methods, a developer can completely rebuild the scene graph according to their needs. A child node in the graph can be removed with a call to the removeChild method, a node can be removed and deleted with a call to removeAndDestroyChild, and an existing node can be connected to another as its child with a call to the addChild method. These methods are now considered in further detail and an example of their use follows.

> **NOTE.** Removing nodes and deleting nodes refer to two distinct processes in OGRE. Removing a node means to disconnect it and its children from the node hierarchy of the scene but does not delete the node in memory. After removal, the node remains in memory and can be reconnected to other nodes elsewhere in the graph. The deletion of a node, however, deletes it from memory. Developers should be careful to ensure that a node is removed from the graph before deletion.

---

### ■ Node Editing Functions

```
Node* Ogre::Node::removeChild(const String &  name)
```
**Arguments**

**const String &  name**
OGRE string specifying the name of the child node to remove; that is, to detach from this parent. The node is not deleted, only removed from the hierarchy, potentially to be reattached as a child of a node elsewhere. It is important to also note that a specified node is detached from its parent, along with all its child nodes.

---

```
void Ogre::SceneNode::removeAndDestroyChild ( const
String &  name   )
```
**Arguments**

**const String &  name**
OGRE string specifying the name of the child node to both *remove* from the hierarchy and *delete* from memory. This function also removes and deletes any and all child nodes of the specified node.

```
void Ogre::SceneNode::addChild (Node *child)
```

**Arguments**

**Node *child**

Pointer to a node that is to be added as a child node. The specified node should not already be the child of an existing node.

**Example: Rebuilding the Scene Graph**

```
//Create a node
SceneNode *node1 = m_SceneManager->getRootSceneNode()-
>createChildSceneNode( "TestNode" );

//Remove node from parent
m_SceneManager->getRootSceneNode()->
removeChild("TestNode");

//Creates a second node
SceneNode *node2 = m_SceneManager->getRootSceneNode()->
createChildSceneNode( "TestNode2" );

//Adds TestNode as child of TestNode2

TestNode2->addChild(node1);

//Removes and deletes TestNode2 and children
m_SceneManager->getRootSceneNode()->removeAndDestroyChild
("TestNode2");

//Return number of child nodes. Should be 0.
unsigned short numChildren = m_SceneManager->
getRootSceneNode()->numChildren();
```

## 10.9.7   Transforming Scene Nodes

Scene objects are attached to scene nodes and inherit their transformations. Furthermore, transformations cascade downward through the hierarchy to descendant nodes. Transformations can represent one or a combination of translation, rotation, and scaling. The first pertains to movement within 3D space; a change of position from the current position to another represents a *translation*. The second is *rotation* and refers to the amount of turn applied to an object; rotation can be represented in OGRE using angles in degrees or in radians, or using a quaternion structure. *Scaling* refers to a change in size and comes in two forms: uniform scaling and nonuniform scaling; the first preserves the proportions of the object after the scale, and the latter does not. Uniform scaling refers to the stretching or shrinking of an object on all axes (XYZ) equally, while nonuniform refers to the scaling of an object by different factors on all axes. For translating a node, OGRE offers several methods, of which two are the most notable: setPosition and translate. The first method sets the absolute XYZ position of a node in world space as measured from its origin. The second moves the node in X, Y, and Z as a *relative offset from* its current position; if the node's current position is (0,0,0), then both setPosition and translate have the same effect. However, if a node were already positioned at (5,5,5), then each of the two functions would act differently. Translating this node by (5,5,5) would move it to the absolute world position of (10,10,10). Using a setPosition of (5,5,5) would appear to have no effect as the node is already located at (5,5,5). As with translation, OGRE offers several methods for rotation: roll, pitch, yaw, and setOrientation. The first three methods constrain rotation about a single axis and work relatively to the node's current orientation, while the latter method allows free rotation on all axes and works in absolute terms. The roll method rotates a node a specified number of radians about the local Z axis, the pitch method rotates a node by a specified number of radians about the local X axis, and yaw method by a specified number of radians about the local Y axis.

In each case, pitch, roll, and yaw rotate an object by default about a *local axis* and not a world axis. Local Y, for example, always points upward relative to the object. If the object is rotated, the local Y axis rotates accordingly. The world space Y axis, however, remains pointing upward regardless of the rotation of nodes. The pitch, roll, and yaw functions can be customized to rotate a node about the world space X, Y, and Z axes. Consider Figure 10.29, which illustrates the distinction between world and local axes.

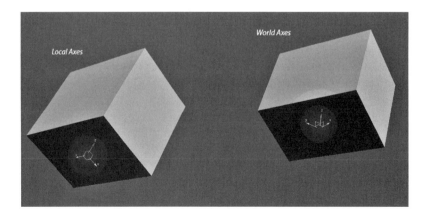

**❘ FIGURE 10.29**    3D axes.

The setOrientation method rotates a node in world space according to a specified quaternion, which can represent combined rotations about any combination of axes. Finally, OGRE offers the Scale method to scale a node on each axis according to a specified scaling factor; in uniform scaling, the scaling factor is equal for all axes, and in nonuniform scaling, the scaling factor is different across the axes. These methods are now considered in further detail, and then an example of their usage follows:

```
void Ogre::Node::setPosition
(
Real   x,
Real   y,
Real   z
)
```

**Arguments**

**Real  x**

An OGRE real value (float) indicating the absolute X position in world space for the translation.

**Real  y**

An OGRE real value (float) indicating the absolute Y position in world space for the translation.

**Real  z**

An OGRE real value (float) indicating the absolute Z position in world space for the translation.

```
virtual void Ogre::Node::translate
(
Real   x,
Real   y,
Real   z,
TransformSpace   relativeTo = TS_PARENT
 )
```

**Arguments**

**Real  x**

An OGRE real value (float) indicating the X position relative to the TransformSpace argument by which the node should be translated.

**Real  y**

An OGRE real value (float) indicating the Y position relative to the TransformSpace argument by which the node should be translated.

**Real z**

An OGRE real value (float) indicating the Z position relative to the TransformSpace argument by which the node should be translated.

**TransformSpace relativeTo = TS_PARENT**

By default this value is set to TS_PARENT, indicating that translations to the specified node are made relative to the position of the parent node. This value can also be TS_WORLD or TS_LOCAL, indicating world and local space respectively.

**Example: Translating a Node**

```
//Create a node
SceneNode *node1 = m_SceneManager->getRootSceneNode()->
createChildSceneNode( "TestNode" );

node1->translate(15,0,0, TS_WORLD); //Sets world position
node1->translate(15,0,0, TS_LOCAL);  //Moves object from
last position
```

---

**NOTE.** Angles can be converted in OGRE from degrees to radians as follows:

```
float AngleInDegrees = 90;
Radian(Degree(AngleInDegrees));

void Ogre::Node::roll
(
const Radian &  angle,
TransformSpace  relativeTo = TS_LOCAL
 )
```

**Arguments**

**const Radian & angle**

Angle in radians by which to rotate around the local Z axis, or the axis specified by the TransformSpace argument.

**TransformSpace relativeTo = TS_LOCAL**

Z axis by which rotation should occur. This can be TS_WORLD, TS_LOCAL, or TS_PARENT.

```
void Ogre::Node::pitch
(
const Radian &  angle,
TransformSpace  relativeTo = TS_LOCAL
```

)

## Arguments

### const Radian &  angle

Angle in radians by which to rotate around the local X axis, or the axis specified by the TransformSpace argument.

### TransformSpace  relativeTo = TS_LOCAL

X axis by which rotation should occur. This can be TS_WORLD, TS_LOCAL, or TS_PARENT.

```
void Ogre::Node::yaw
(
const Radian &  angle,
TransformSpace  relativeTo = TS_LOCAL
)
```

## Arguments

### const Radian &  angle

Angle in radians by which to rotate around the local Y axis, or the axis specified by the TransformSpace argument.

### TransformSpace  relativeTo = TS_LOCAL

Y axis by which rotation should occur. This can be TS_WORLD, TS_LOCAL, or TS_PARENT.

```
void Ogre::Node::setOrientation
(
const Quaternion &  q
)
```

## Arguments

### const Quaternion &  q

The quaternion representing the rotation for the specified node. The quaternion class features four components: x, y, z, and w. Consult the rotation tutorial mentioned earlier if more information on quaternions is required.

### Example: Rotating a Node

```
//Create a node
SceneNode *node1 = m_SceneManager->getRootSceneNode()->
createChildSceneNode( "TestNode" );
```

```
node1->yaw(Radian(Degree(75)));

//performs same rotation using quaternions on world Y
axis.
node1->setOrientation(Quaternion::FromAngleAxis(Radian
(Degree(75)),
Vector3(0,1,0)));
```

---

```
void Ogre::Node::setScale
(
Real  x,
Real  y,
Real  z
)
```

**Arguments**

**Real x**

OGRE real (float) indicating the scaling factor to be applied to the X axis. 0 shrinks the object to its minimum extents, 1 is to default extents, 2 to twice its extents, and so on. Negative values invert the scale of the object.

**Real y**

OGRE real (float) indicating the scaling factor to be applied to the Y axis. 0 shrinks the object to its minimum extents, 1 is to default extents, 2 to twice its extents, and so on. Negative values invert the scale of the object.

**Real z**

OGRE real (float) indicating the scaling factor to be applied to the Z axis. 0 shrinks the object to its minimum extents, 1 is to default extents, 2 to twice its extents, and so on. Negative values invert the scale of the object.

**Example: Scaling a Node**

```
//Create a node
SceneNode *node1 = m_SceneManager->getRootSceneNode()->
createChildSceneNode( "TestNode" );

node1->scale(0.5, 1, 2.0);
```

## 10.9.8    Bound Volumes, Culling, and Optimization

Scene nodes are nonvisible anchor objects to which visible objects, such as meshes and particle systems, are attached. They have position, orientation, and scale in 3D space, and these transformations apply to attached objects. Furthermore, they also have a *bounding*

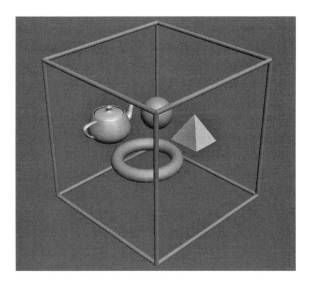

**‖ FIGURE 10.30**   Bounding box.

*box volume.* The bounding box of a node is a nonvisible box defined by its corner points that is always sized exactly so as to contain (or enclose) all objects attached to the node (see Figure 10.30). The box is sized and resized as objects are added and removed. It proves useful in performing various scene queries and calculations. For example, if a developer wanted to test to see whether any of the meshes of one node intersected (collided) with any of the meshes of another, there would be several checks they could perform in order to reach a conclusion, but not all of them would be optimal and lead toward smooth performance. The developer could cycle through all the vertices and edges of each mesh belonging to one node and test them against all the vertices and edges of the meshes of the other to see whether edges overlapped. This method might be the most accurate of them all, but the cost of that accuracy is a performance penalty likely to hinder the smoothness of the application. For this reason, most games approximate mesh sizes using bounding volumes and simply compare the bounding volumes in order to test for collisions. This makes sense because a bounding box that is equal in width, height, and depth can be defined by only two corner points, each at one extent of the box. Thus, by comparing the two bounding boxes for intersection—one box for each of the two compared meshes—an application can quickly reach decisions about the collision status of two objects in a scene.

Though bounding boxes are frequently used for collision detection between scene objects, there is also another use to which they can be put, this time regarding the optimization of scene rendering. Most 3D engines in the contemporary games market are called upon to render large, expansive environments that the player can explore, often at their leisure. However, given that the hardware resources and processing power at the disposal of an engine is finite and that by comparison a game environment is potentially infinite, there arises a potential performance problem that must be managed if an engine is not to buckle beneath the total weight of textures and meshes needed for a large game world. Consider a large environment for a MMORPG (massively multiplayer online role-playing game) whose meshes and materials total over 50 GBs of data; that is quite large by contemporary standards. It would not at present be possible for most engines to load this environment in its entirety and render it to the screen as a complete unit without serious performance penalties that would leave the game unplayable on all but the fastest of machines. To render such a world, it would be necessary for the engine to break down (disassemble) the environment into equally sized segments or chunks, each segment streamed into memory as and when required, with some segments loaded and some not, some eligible for rendering, some not. As some segments enter memory, some are deleted, and so on. The basis on which an engine decides whether any section of the environment must be loaded and rendered is determined by the position of the player in the scene. Imagining the entire level topographically as a map, the game engine would mark the position of the player and trace out a radius around their position. Segments of the environment that fall within that radius are considered immediately necessary since the player can see those areas directly or in the distance from their current position, or because those areas are adjacent to the region in which they are currently standing and can therefore be accessed quickly should the player travel there. Areas of the environment outside of this radius can be safely unloaded for the time being.

One quick but promising way to start implementing this method in OGRE would be to make use of node bounding boxes. Using this technique, a developer would divide the complete environment into several mesh files, attaching each to a separate scene node. The engine then records the position of the player on each frame, marking out a surrounding bounding circle or box for their field of view. Then the engine proceeds to determine which regions of the environment should be visible by comparing the bounding box of the player to the bounding boxes of each node. Nodes that intersect the camera and viewing region should be visible, and nodes outside of that region can be hidden or unloaded. This technique is similar to the technique of *octrees* and *quadtrees*, which work by subdividing the level into boxes (or regions) of either eight or four, respectively, testing to see whether the camera and its viewing area intersects the bounding volume of those regions. Intersected regions are visible to the camera and should be rendered, and regions outside the viewing area can be ignored by the renderer. "Ignored" as used here means that the renderer does not need to process the mesh and texture data for those areas on the current frame. In this way, an engine can optimize the scenes and render only nearby data. Consider the following code that retrieves a bounding box for a scene node:

```
//Get root node
SceneNode *RootNode = m_SceneManager->getRootSceneNode();

//Create child node of the root node
SceneNode *MyNode = RootNode->createChildSceneNode
("MyNode" );

//Attach object
MyNode->attachObject(MyEntity);

//Get bounding box for node
AxisAlignedBox AABB = MyNode->_getWorldAABB();
```

The AxisAlignedBox class encapsulates a bounding box for the scene node, but once the box is retrieved how should an application go about using it to test for collisions and intersections? The following class declaration lists some of the most notable methods of the bounding box class, and each method is examined in some detail:

```
class AxisAlignedBox
{
public:
void  setExtents (const Vector3 &min, const Vector3
&max);
void  merge (const AxisAlignedBox &rhs);
bool  intersects (const AxisAlignedBox &b2);
bool  intersects (const Sphere &s);
bool  intersects (const Vector3 &v);
bool  contains (const AxisAlignedBox &other);
};
```

**void  setExtents (const Vector3 &min, const Vector3 &max)**

The setExtents method sets the size of the bounding box from two vector parameters, each representing the new corner extents of the bounding box. This method also has a counterpart getExtents method for retrieving the corner points of a bounding box.

**void merge (const AxisAlignedBox &rhs)**

The merge method resizes a given bounding box by merging it with a second one. The result is that the resized bounding box is large enough to contain both volumes—the original volume plus the merged volume.

**bool  intersects (const AxisAlignedBox &b2)**

The first variation of the intersects method compares one bounding box to another and returns true if the boxes are found to intersect one another. An intersection occurs when one bounding box is either partially contained or fully contained by another.

**bool  intersects (const Sphere &s)**

The second variation of the intersects method compares one bounding box to a sphere volume and returns true if the two volumes are found to intersect one another. An intersection occurs when the sphere is either partially contained or fully contained by the bounding box.

**bool intersects (const Vector3 &v)**

The third variation of the intersects method compares one bounding box to a point in 3D space and returns true if the point intersects the box. An intersection occurs when the point is contained by the bounding box.

**bool  contains (const AxisAlignedBox &other)**

The contains method returns true *only* if one bounding box is entirely contained within the other. Intersections between boxes—such as partial overlapping—will return false.

---

## ■  10.10    Exporting and Importing Meshes

Meshes are typically created by game artists using 3D modeling software, of which the most common in the contemporary games industry include:

- 3ds Max:
  http://usa.autodesk.com/adsk/servlet/pc/index?siteID=123112&id=13567410
- Maya:
  http://usa.autodesk.com/adsk/servlet/pc/index?id=13577897&siteID=123112
- Cinema 4D:
  http://www.maxon.net/products/cinema-4d.html
- Softimage:
  http://usa.autodesk.com/adsk/servlet/pc/index?siteID=123112&id=13571168
- Blender:
  http://www.blender.org/

Using the modeling tools offered by any one of these applications, artists can interactively build, texture, and light meshes using a GUI. However, each application saves mesh data in its own application-specific formats, and these formats are not natively compatible with OGRE. This means that unless an artist or programmer develops their own exporter plug-in or downloads a third-party plug-in to bridge the gap between 3D software and engine, the artist cannot transfer their mesh data from their modeling software and into OGRE. Thankfully, to bridge this gap, the OGRE community offers a set of plug-ins for different 3D software packages that add features to export meshes to formats that OGRE can recognize. For more information on the mesh exporting facilities for all supported 3D modeling packages, please visit the following OGRE URL: http://www.ogre3d.org/wiki/index.php/OGRE_Exporters. See Figure 10.31.

**NOTE.** At the time of writing, OGRE features mesh export facilities for the following 3D modeling tools (given in alphabetical order):

- 3ds Max
- Blender
- Cinema 4D
- Google™ Sketchup™
- LightWave®
- Maya
- MilkShape 3D
- RenderMonkey™
- Softimage XSI
- trueSpace

**FIGURE 10.31**   OGRE Exporters wiki page.

- VRML
- Wings 3D

## 10.10.1    Exporting Meshes with 3ds Max

This section offers a step-by-step insight into how to download, install, and configure the OGRE mesh exporter for use with Autodesk 3ds Max. This guide assumes the reader has an installed and working copy of 3ds Max 2010 or higher on their system.

> **NOTE**. The OGREMax exporter is available in both free and commercial versions. The free version is subject to the following limitations:
>
> - It is intended for noncommercial use only.
> - Only one texture coordinate set can be exported per mesh.
> - Only one texture unit can be exported per material.
> - No technical support is provided.
>
> For more details on version info, please visit: http://www.ogremax.com.

Step 1.  Navigate a web browser to the URL http://www.ogremax.com/. From there, click the **Exporters** link at the top left and select the installer appropriate for your version of 3ds Max. Click **Download**. See Figure 10.32.

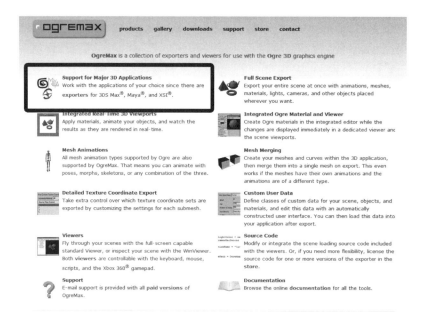

**FIGURE 10.32**    Downloading exporter.

Step 2.   Once downloaded, close any open and running versions of 3ds Max. Then extract the contents of the zip package and run the installer to install the exporter to the local computer. The installer should automatically configure the plug-in for 3ds Max. See Figure 10.33.

Step 3.   Once installed, the plug-in is ready to use in 3ds Max. Start 3ds Max and load or create a mesh. To export the mesh to an OGRE mesh, select the mesh in the 3ds Max editor and then use the main menu to select **File | Export Selected**. See Figure 10.34.

Step 4.   The **Select File to Export** dialog appears. Use this dialog to name the exported mesh file, and use the Save as Type drop-down box to select **OgreMax Mesh** as the export format. After exporting the mesh, the export plug-in will have created both a mesh file and an associated material file that are compliant with OGRE. See Figure 10.35.

Step 5.   Finally, create an OGRE application and load the teapot mesh as any other mesh. Consider the mesh loading sample given earlier for the ogre head. See Figure 10.36.

**I FIGURE 10.33**   Installing exporter.

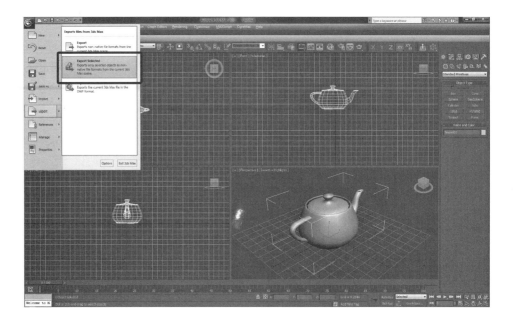

**FIGURE 10.34** Using the exporter in 3ds Max.

**FIGURE 10.35** Saving the mesh file.

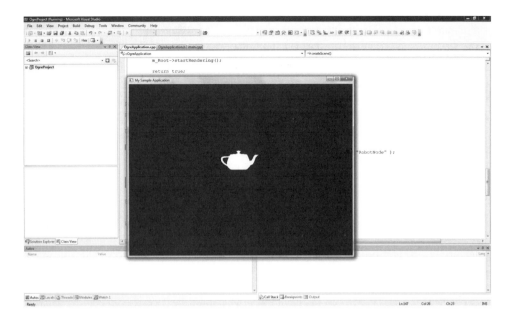

**| FIGURE 10.36**   Loading a teapot.

## ■ 10.11   Lights

The samples created in OGRE thus far have used the default scene ambient light, and the intensity of this light can be set using the setAmbientLight method of the SceneManager class. This method expects three arguments for the color channel components of red, green, and blue to define the color intensity of the light. When all three components are set to 1, the light is white; when all components are set to 0, the light is black. Ambient light is useful for illuminating a scene so as to view all of its content from any angle in a neutral condition. It is, however, problematic for creating realistic scenes because ambient light does not act like real-world lighting in that it casts light in all directions and at an equal intensity that does not dissipate with distance. The result of this lighting method is that scene geometry can look flat and staged because the light is not responding to the geometry of the scene. That is, the light is cast everywhere, equally. To enhance the realism of a scene, a developer often looks to light as a sculpting tool that adds depth and weight. Using lights and shadows and by adjusting the direction in which a light is cast, a scene designer can impart a dramatic feel to a scene and add detail where otherwise there would have been none. Since the ambient light can serve none of these purposes—has no specific position, direction, or shadow casting abilities—it is often disqualified as a lighting system for final scenes presented to the gamer.

Thankfully, OGRE users are not constrained to using only the default ambient light, for there are other lighting types available. These include point lights, spot lights, and directional lights; each is considered in more detail shortly. Ambient light differs from these latter three types in several ways: First, a scene contains only one ambient light that applies scenewide, whereas a scene can contain one or more of the instances of the other types. Second, the ambient light is not part of the scene in the sense that it has no specific position or direction in 3D space, unlike the other types. These new lighting types are now considered in turn.

## 10.11.1    Spot Lights

The spot light is the next least computationally expensive light after the ambient light. It works akin to a standard spot light in a theater, shining light of a specified color and intensity in a specified direction (see Figure 10.37). The spot light has the following properties:

### Position

Refers to the XYZ point in 3D space at which the light *source* is positioned; that is, the point from which light is emitted. Computer spot lights differ from real-world spot lights by casting light from a single *point* in 3D space, whereas real-world spot lights cast light from a bulb that has tangible dimensions in terms of width,

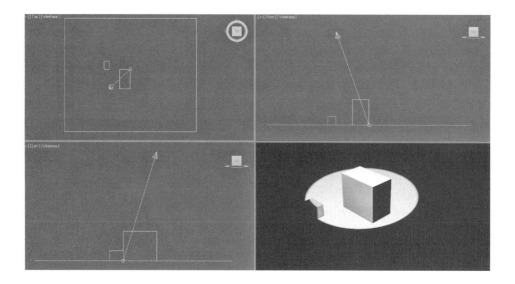

**▌ FIGURE 10.37**    Spot light.

height, and depth. This difference in the structure of the light source has surprisingly important implications for the realism of a light, and offers the lighting artist a particular challenge when attempting to use spot lights to achieve realistic lighting. Nevertheless, spot lights—when positioned and set appropriately—can provide an efficient mechanism for achieving spectacular effects.

**Direction**

In addition to position, a spot light also has direction expressed using a normalized direction vector. This XYZ vector indicates the direction in which the light source is pointing. In combination with the intensity, attenuation, and range properties, direction indicates which items in a scene will and will not be illuminated by this light.

**Color and Intensity**

The spot light has both color and intensity. The former refers to the color of the light in terms of its red, green, and blue components, and the latter refers to the brightness (or strength) at which the light shines at the light source position. Black light will appear to cast no light (and thus have an intensity of 0), while white light gives the appearance of full intensity. Colors other than white can be used (such as red or blue), which helps create the appearance that a colored filter has been placed over the light source.

**Range**

The range property of a spot light works with its direction property to determine the total potential volume of a scene over which the light can have influence. The range of a light begins at the position of the light source and traces its volume in the direction in which the light is facing, and ends at a specified distance away from the source. Objects within this range *can* fall under the illumination of the light, and objects outside the range will *not* be affected by the light.

**Attenuation**

The attenuation of a spot light determines how the intensity of the light (full intensity being 1) diminishes with distance across its range. The intensity of most real-world light attenuates at an inverse square ratio, while computer lights often attenuate linearly, meaning they diminish in proportion to the distance from the light source. The intensity at the light source is often 1, and this linearly attenuates to 0 at the far end of the light range.

## 10.11.2   Point Lights

The point light is the second most computationally expensive light in OGRE, after the directional light (considered next). The point light is in some sense a specialized

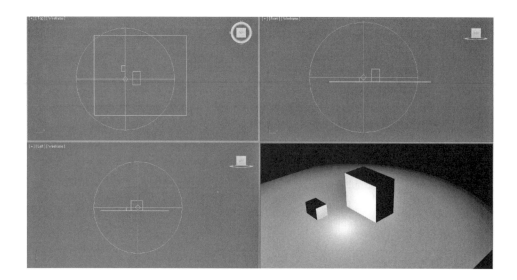

**FIGURE 10.38**   Point light.

version of the ambient light in that it starts from a single point in 3D space and casts its light outward in all directions. The difference between the point light and ambient light, however, is that a point light has position, range, and attenuation properties (see Figure 10.38). The position in this case refers to the point at which light casting begins, and the attenuation sets the distance at which the light intensity will reduce to 0 in all directions from the source. Refer to the previous light source for more information on the position, range, and attenuation properties. The point light source can be useful for simulating light bulbs, camp fires, and explosions.

## 10.11.3   Directional Light

The directional light is the most computationally expensive light source in OGRE. It casts light as an array of parallel rays traveling in the same direction rather than from a single point in 3D space. The directional light is useful for simulating distant and natural light sources such as the sun or the sun reflected from the moon at night. This light source has color, intensity, direction, and attenuation but no position. See Figure 10.39.

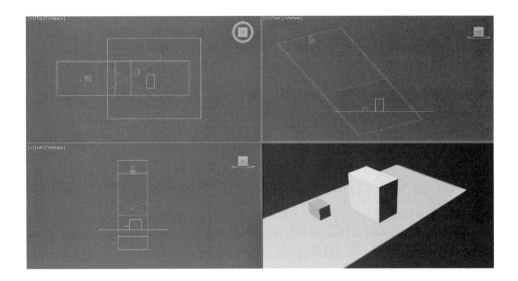

**❙ FIGURE 10.39**   Directional light.

## 10.11.4   Direct and Global Illumination

The standard OGRE lights consist of the ambient light, point lights, spot lights, and directional lights. Using one or more of these types of lights, a game developer can produce interesting and generally realistic scenes, but it is important to be aware of the limitations of real-time 3D lighting in comparison to real-world lighting; the most notable of these pertains to global illumination (GI). Lights in OGRE work according to a direct illumination system, meaning that OGRE does not by default simulate light bounces, diffuse interreflections, reflections, or refractions. The result of this is that an OGRE light illuminates only that which falls within its range, and objects outside of this range or objects whose faces are pointed away from the light source will not be illuminated, and hence will appear completely black. This model is called *direct illumination* because only polygons that are directly accessible to the light source appear illuminated. This has severe implications for creating realism in real-time 3D because real-world lights do not act like this. Consider a standard bedroom in a family home; such rooms have a window through which sunlight pelts, illuminating some areas directly, such as walls and parts of the floor. However, this room also contains areas that are not directly in view of that light but still do not appear completely black. Look under the bed and notice that though this region is typically darker than other regions, it is to some extent illuminated. Here, these regions are illuminated by indirect light—sunlight that has bounced from the walls and floors has reflected from shiny surfaces, or has refracted through glass. Such bounced light also

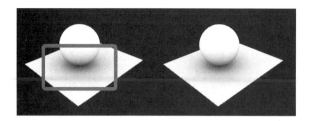

**I FIGURE 10.40**    Ambient occlusion.

inherits some of the color of the object from which it bounced. Thus, a white floor beside a red brick wall on a sunny day will take on a reddish tint from the light that has bounced from the wall. This model is known as *global llumination*, and though it can be simulated effectively using rendering software such as 3ds Max or Maya, it has not (for performance reasons) extended far into the realm of real-time 3D, where other techniques, such as *texture baking* and *ambient occlusion*, are typically used to simulate these effects. *Texture baking* with regard to lighting refers to the process of precalculating lighting and shadowing effects in a modeling package such as 3ds Max, and then saving out those details into the model texture map. In this way, many lighting effects are prerendered (already made) in the texture map itself.

The term "ambient occlusion," however, refers to "contact shadows," as shown in Figure 10.40. Such shadows appear around the edges of objects when they make contact with another object, and adding this effect to 3D models can help emphasize depth in a 3D scene. Ambient occlusion details are typically texture baked into the model texture along with lighting details (see Figure 10.40). The next section considers how lights can be used in OGRE.

## 10.11.5   Creating and Using Lights in OGRE

The standard lights in OGRE are point lights, directional lights, and spot lights, all working according to a direct illumination model. Point lights cast light in all directions from an infinitesimal point in 3D space. Spot lights similarly cast light from an infinitesimal point in 3D space but in a specified direction and across a specified range according to attenuation parameters. Finally, the directional light casts parallel rays of light in a single direction for a specified range. Each of these can be created using the createLight method of the SceneManager. Calling this method will both return a pointer to a newly created light and add the light to the scene independent of a scene node, although lights can be added to scene nodes in order to control their position in relation to scene objects. Consider the following code samples for creating a light of each type: point, spot, and directional.

**Example: Creating a Point Light and Adding it to a Scene**

```
//Disable ambient light
m_SceneManager->setAmbientLight(ColourValue(0, 0, 0));

//Create a red point light
Light* light = m_SceneManager->createLight("Light1");

//Set light type
light->setType(Light::LT_POINT);

//Set position
light->setPosition(Vector3(0, 150, 700));

//Set specular color (color reflected by nonshiny
sections of objects)
light->setDiffuseColour(1.0, 0.0, 0.0);

//Set diffuse color (color reflected by shiny sections of
objects)
light->setSpecularColour(1.0, 0.0, 0.0);
```

**Example: Creating a Spot Light and Adding it to a Scene**

```
//Disable ambient light
m_SceneManager->setAmbientLight(ColourValue(0, 0, 0));

//Create a blue spot light
Light* light = m_SceneManager->createLight("SpotLight");

//Set light type
light->setType(Light::LT_SPOTLIGHT);

//Set position
light->setPosition(Vector3(0, 150, 700));

//Set diffuse color (color reflected by nonshiny sections
of objects)
light->setDiffuseColour(0.0, 0.0, 1.0);

//Set specular color (color reflected by shiny sections
of objects)
light->setSpecularColour(1.0, 0.0, 0.0);


//Set light direction at 45 degree angle downward.
```

```
light->setDirection(-1, -1, 0);

//Set size of spotlight range. Inner range and outer
range.
light->setSpotlightRange(Degree(30), Degree(70), 1.0);
```

**Example: Creating a Directional Light and Adding it to a Scene**

```
//Disable ambient light
m_SceneManager->setAmbientLight(ColourValue(0, 0, 0));

//Create a green directional light
Light* light = m_SceneManager->createLight("Direction_
Light");

//Set light type
light->setType(Light::LT_DIRECTIONAL);

//Set position
light->setPosition(Vector3(0, 150, 700));

//Set diffuse color (color reflected by nonshiny sections
```

### ■ OGRE Focus—Light Creation

The createLight method of the SceneManager is responsible for creating all of the OGRE standard lights. This method differs from other creation methods, like createEntity, in that it both *creates* a light and then *adds* the created light to a scene. The position of the light in the scene is by default independent of any one scene node, and can be set using the setPosition method of the Light class. However, a light can also be *attached* to a scene node, much like meshes, and be as much subjected to their transformations. Attaching lights to scene nodes is useful in situations where lights are expected to move with geometry; for example, car headlights are intended to move along with a car mesh as it drives along a road. In this case, it would be both useful and desirable to attach the lights to a car scene node. However, in cases where a light should be positioned and oriented in absolute world coordinates and will not move regardless of the position of scene objects, there appears no compelling reason to attach it to the scene node hierarchy. In addition to the positioning features of lights, a light also supports other methods and properties whose usage depends on the light type. The light type is set using the setType method; it accepts any valid OGRE light type provided in the Light::LightTypes enum structure. Once the light is created and its type set, its properties should be configured. For point lights, this includes setting its color and position; for directional lights their direction and color; and for spot lights their position, direction, color, range, and attenuation. Some of the light creation methods are now considered in further detail; these methods are createLight, setSpotlightRange, and setDirection.

> **NOTE.** The LightTypes enum indicates the light types supported by OGRE. These values are passed to the setType method of the Light class when setting the light type. The enum include constants for point lights, spot lights, and directional lights. It appears as follows:

```
enum LightTypes
{
LT_POINT = 0,
LT_DIRECTIONAL = 1,
LT_SPOTLIGHT = 2
};
```

```
Light* Ogre::SceneManager::createLight
(
const String &  name
)
```

**Arguments**

**const String &  name**
OGRE string indicate the unique name of the light to be created.

This function returns a pointer to a valid Light class object encapsulating an OGRE light in the scene. It is important to note that calling this function both creates a light and adds the created light to the scene.

---

```
void Ogre::Light::setSpotlightRange
(
const Radian &  innerAngle,
const Radian &  outerAngle,
Real  falloff = 1.0
)
```

**Arguments**

**const Radian &  innerAngle**

**const Radian &  outerAngle**

A spot lights casts light from a point in a specified direction across a specified range and loses intensity over that range according to an attenuation parameter. Within that range, the light casts rays of two intensities: an inner intensity and an outer intensity. The inner intensity refers to the angular volume within the range of the light that falls directly beneath the light source and is therefore the brightest. The outer intensity refers to the borders of the light range where the intensity of the light dissipates toward 0 on each side since it is farther away from the source. The two InnerAngle and OuterAngle parameters specify the size of each region. The nearer these two values are to one another, the sharper the edges of the circle of light cast by the spot light, creating a sharp contrast between the line cone and the darkness outside. Bringing these values further apart will result in a light cone with smoother edges since there is a greater distance between the center and edge for the light falloff. Each value is a radian specifying the angular region from the source that represents the inner cone and the outer cone. The outer cone should be equal to or larger than the inner cone.

**Real Falloff**

The falloff value indicates how the light is to fade in the outer cone. A value of 0 indicates no falloff and a value of 1 (default) specifies a linear falloff where the light intensity ranges from 1 at the center of the cone to 0 at the edge. Values higher than 1 reduce the distance at which the light falloff occurs.

```
void Ogre::Light::setDirection
(
const Vector3 &  vec
)
```

**Arguments**

**const Vector3 &  vec**

A normalized 3D vector indicating the direction in which the light is shining. For example, a value of (0,1,0) indicates a direction of up (directly along the Y axis), a value of (1,0,0) indicates a direction of right (directly along the X axis), and a value of (0,0,1) indicates a direction of forward (directly along the positive Z axis). Negative values are used to express the reverse direction.

```
of objects)
light->setDiffuseColour(0.0, 1.0, 0.0);

//Set specular color (color reflected by shiny sections
of objects)
light->setSpecularColour(1.0, 0.0, 0.0);

//Set light direction along Z axis
light->setDirection(0, 0, -1);
```

NOTE. The OGRE Light class supports a range of methods and properties for editing lights in an OGRE scene. The most notable methods were listed here, but the Light class supports additional methods that are beyond the scope of this book. One of these is setPowerScale, which can be used to heighten or reduce the intensity of a light. Consult the official OGRE documentation for more information on the Light class.

■  **10.12  Animation—Focusing on the Camera Track Sample**

This chapter so far has examined a variety of OGRE features that are of interest not only to developers planning to use the OGRE library for their own applications but also to those looking to learn from OGRE in the hope of extending it or improving their own engine. This chapter has examined how to configure an OGRE application and how to use that library to create a window, configure a device, load resources, create scene graphs, add meshes and lights to that scene, and apply materials from material scripts. At present, however, the scenes created using these techniques are not animated; that is, they contain no motion over time. It is, however, possible to add animation easily to our scenes by transforming objects over time (frame by frame) using concepts such as speed, velocity, and direction vectors. With these ingredients, a developer could engineer their own custom animation framework, always being mindful of the relationships between objects in the scene. It is especially true when the issue of animation becomes pressing that a developer can appreciate the benefits of the scene graph, as the motion of objects in the scene do not occur independently. A car, for example, does not move independently of its passengers; they are expected to move with the car as it drives along the road. Yet in a 3D scene, the car and its passengers might be separate objects with unique position values. It has been mentioned how the scene graph fixes this problem by creating parent–child connections between nodes in the scene and by cascading those transformations downward through the hierarchy. In this way, objects such as cars can easily be transformed through animations, and an application can be certain that such transformations will automatically trickle downward to all attached child nodes, such as passenger objects. The term "automatically" is used here to mean that OGRE will handle the cascading of transformations through the scene graph. However, in addition to standard scene graph features offered by OGRE, it also features its own key frame-based animation system for playing prekeyed animations. Using this system, applications can build a series of animations and then apply them to objects in the scene. This section considers the OGRE animation system in more detail by focusing on the Camera Track sample application provided with the OGRE SDK. The source code and project files for this application can be found in the samples folder of the OGRE installation.

The OGRE animation system is key frame-based. This means that a developer builds an animation by defining several "key" states in that animation (such as a start frame, middle frame, and end frame), and OGRE then plays back the animation, interpolating (blending) between those key frames. For example, the animation of a human character walking along the street might be expected to play for 30 seconds, during which time many frames will pass. Depending on the hardware and frame rate of an application (and VSync), the number of frames passed over 30 seconds could be more than 5000. To play such an animation, a developer would not usually define each and every frame of the animation, frame by frame, but instead would specify only the key points of that animation and have OGRE "fill in" the intervening frames. Thus, the first key frame might be (and usually is) the first frame of the animation (at time 0), which is used to specify the starting state—in this case, the human character perhaps standing in a neutral position at one end of the road. The next *key* frame might be at time 10 seconds and will have seen the character make a few steps and reach a third of the way along the street. The next key frame might be at 20, and then the last at 30, defining the end state of the animation at which the player has returned to a neutral posture and reached the end of the street. As the animation plays back, OGRE will pass through each and every frame throughout the duration of the animation from 0 seconds to 30 seconds, but the developer defined only the key frames that were to occur, those being: 0 seconds, 10 seconds, 20 seconds, and 30 seconds. In this way a key frame animation was created.

The Camera Track sample in the OGRE SDK (see Figure 10.41) provides a working demonstration of the key frame animation framework in OGRE. It does this by creating a scene featuring a ground plane, an ogre head positioned on that plane, and a camera. The camera remains focused on the ogre head mesh. The key frame animation works by smoothly moving the camera between a series of points in 3D space at each key frame, interpolating the camera position between key frames. Thus, as the animation plays, the camera remains in motion but is always focused on the ogre head mesh at the center of the scene, offering the viewer a guided tour of the mesh from all angles. To see how this was achieved, open the sample Camera Track project and start by compiling and running the sample to see the effect. The main bones of this

**FIGURE 10.41**   Camera Track sample.

application can be found in the createScene method of the file cameratrack.cpp. The whole of this method is shown here both to highlight the use of the animation system and to pull together much of the material that has been discussed throughout this chapter, comments then follow:

```
void createScene(void)
{
    // Set ambient light
    mSceneMgr->setAmbientLight(ColourValue(0.2, 0.2,
0.2));

    // Create a skydome
    mSceneMgr->setSkyDome(true, "Examples/CloudySky",
5, 8);

    // Create a light
    Light* l = mSceneMgr->createLight("MainLight");
    l->setPosition(20,80,50);

    Entity *ent;
```

```
        // Define a floor plane mesh
        Plane p;
        p.normal = Vector3::UNIT_Y;
        p.d = 200;
        MeshManager::getSingleton().createPlane(
            "FloorPlane", ResourceGroupManager::DEFAULT_
RESOURCE_GROUP_NAME,
            p, 200000, 200000, 20, 20, true, 1, 50, 50,
Vector3::UNIT_Z);

        // Create an entity (the floor)
        ent = mSceneMgr->createEntity("floor",
"FloorPlane");
        ent->setMaterialName("Examples/RustySteel");
        // Attach to child of root node; better for
culling (otherwise bounds are the combination of the two)
        mSceneMgr->getRootSceneNode()->
createChildSceneNode()->attachObject(ent);

        // Add a head, give it its own node
        SceneNode* headNode = mSceneMgr->
getRootSceneNode()->createChildSceneNode();
        ent = mSceneMgr->createEntity("head", "ogrehead.
mesh");
        headNode->attachObject(ent);

        // Make sure the camera track is on this node
        mCamera->setAutoTracking(true, headNode);

        // Create the camera node & attach camera
        SceneNode* camNode = mSceneMgr->
getRootSceneNode()->createChildSceneNode();
        camNode->attachObject(mCamera);

    //Create animation

        // set up spline animation of node
        Animation* anim = mSceneMgr->
createAnimation("CameraTrack", 10);
        // Spline it for nice curves
        anim->setInterpolationMode(Animation::IM_SPLINE);
        // Create a track to animate the camera's node
        NodeAnimationTrack* track = anim->
createNodeTrack(0, camNode);
        // Set up key frames
```

```
        TransformKeyFrame* key = track->
createNodeKeyFrame(0); // start position
        key = track->createNodeKeyFrame(2.5);
        key->setTranslate(Vector3(500,500,-1000));
        key = track->createNodeKeyFrame(5);
        key->setTranslate(Vector3(-1500,1000,-600));
        key = track->createNodeKeyFrame(7.5);
        key->setTranslate(Vector3(0,-100,0));
        key = track->createNodeKeyFrame(10);
        key->setTranslate(Vector3(0,0,0));
        // Create a new animation state to track this
        mAnimState = mSceneMgr->createAnimationState("Cam
eraTrack");
        mAnimState->setEnabled(true);

        mSceneMgr->setFog(FOG_EXP, ColourValue::White,
0.0002);

    }
```

## Comments

- The createScene method of the sample application Camera Track is called once at application startup to position and configure the elements of the scene. It does this by setting the ambient light and then by creating a point light at the center of the scene.

- After creating two light objects at the scene center, the method proceeds to create a floor plane object using the createPlane method of an OGRE class called the MeshManager. This manager component often works internally with other OGRE managers to manage mesh data in the scene. It also offers a series of methods for creating "out of the box" 3D primitives. These are createManual, createPlane, createCurvedIllusionPlane, createCurvedPlane, and createBezierPatch. Consult the OGRE documentation for more information on these methods, if required.

- The next scene object to be created and added to the scene is the ogre head mesh. This is loaded as an entity object from a mesh file via the createEntity method of the SceneManager, and the loaded mesh also references a set of sample material scripts for the skin, eyes, earring, and teeth parts. The material definitions for this mesh were given in an earlier section of this chapter. Once created, the head is added to the scene by being attached to a node that is a child of the root scene node.

- The createScene method also calls the setAutoTracking method of Camera. This method accepts two arguments, the first a boolean indicating whether camera tracking should be enabled or disabled, and the second a pointer to a scene node that is to be *tracked*. When a camera is set to track a node, it will always look at that node, and when either the node or camera moves, the look at direction of the camera will change to ensure it continues looking at the node. After this, the createScene method attaches a camera to an independent scene node. Thus, *the camera position will be affected by the node position*. This will play an important role in the animation that will be created for this sample, because the animation will apply to the scene node and not to the camera.

- Thus far the Camera Track sample has configured lighting for the application and created two mesh objects—a ground plane and ogre head—both of which have been added to the scene by way of being attached to two independent nodes that are children of the root node. Furthermore, the application has also created a camera that is to track the ogre head node, and the camera itself has also been attached to an independent scene node. Having established this setup of scene objects, the application proceeds to create a key frame animation that will apply to the camera node.

- Creating the key frame animation involves several stages. The first step is a call to the createAnimation method of the SceneManager. This method creates an Animation object of the specified unique name. If successful, it returns a pointer to an Animation object representing an empty animation; that is, an animation featuring no key frames. Once an application retrieves a pointer to this object, it can proceed to build an animation. It does this by creating an *animation track*. The animation track is used to specify which object in the scene is to be animated; in this case, the camera node. This is because the sample application intends to move the camera about the scene for a guided tour of the ogre head mesh. It creates an animation track with a call to the createNodeTrack method of the Animation object. This function returns a NodeTrack object to which key frame information can be added for the camera node. Each unique key frame of the animation is represented by an instance of the TransformKeyFrame object, and this sample code creates as many TransformKeyFrame objects as there are key frames in the animation. It calls the createNodeKeyFrame method to create a unique key frame at the specified time in seconds; the time value is passed as an argument of the function. For each key frame created, the sample code sets a translation state, defining the position of the camera node in 3D space *at that key frame*. Thus, it creates a starting key frame at 0 seconds, the next at 2.5, the next at 5, the next at 7.5, and the final key frame at time 10. For each of these key frames, it sets a unique translation value. Once all key frames are created, the main body of the animation is completed.

- To finalize the newly created animation, the sample code calls the createAnimationState method to create an animation state object. The Animation object created earlier and the key frame definitions that followed helped build an animation *template*. Based on this template, an application can create *animation states*, each state representing a *running* instance of that template. An application can create as many animation states as required based on a single animation template. The animation state in essence represents the media controls of a template—the play, stop, and pause controls. Animation playback is initiated with a call to the setEnabled method of the animation state.

• However, the createScene method given above is not enough to sustain the life of the animation over time. If a developer were now to compile and run the sample application based only on the createScene method, they would likely find that the animation did not run at all even though it was told to run by calling the setEnabled method of the animation state. Despite this, the camera node would still remain static and lifeless. This is because OGRE applications must perform an additional step on each frame in order to *notify* the Animation object of a new frame. In this case, by notifying the Animation object on each frame of the render loop, it can keep track of the elapsed time and calculate the appropriate translation state that is to be used for transforming the camera node for the current frame. The sample application updates the status of the animation on each frame through the frameRenderingQueued method of the OGRE FrameListener class.

NOTE. Please revisit the frame listener description given earlier in the chapter if a refresher is needed. In short, the FrameListener class is an abstract base class that developers are intended to override with custom behavior. Developers register listener classes with OGRE in order to receive notifications from the OGRE renderer once per frame of frame start and frame end events. Consider the frame listener class in the following code that updates the timing of an animation of each frame.

```
    class CameraTrackListener: public ExampleFrameListener
{
protected:
public:
    CameraTrackListener(RenderWindow* win, Camera* cam)
        : ExampleFrameListener(win, cam)
    {
    }

    bool frameRenderingQueued(const FrameEvent& evt)
    {
    if( ExampleFrameListener::frameRenderingQueued(evt) ==
false )
```

```
                return false;

    //Update animation
            mAnimState->addTime(evt.timeSinceLastFrame);

            return true;
        }
    };
```

---

### ■ OGRE Focus—Animation

The purpose of animation in OGRE is to create motion among the objects of 3D scenes. Animation in OGRE is made simple for two main reasons: First, the hierarchical scene graph of nodes and their ability to cascade transformations means that objects not only can be added to scenes but also can be brought into relation with other objects, and these relations can hold even when the objects are animated. Second, OGRE offers a key frame-based animation system. Using this system, applications can create an animation template representing a collection of key frames; that is, transformation states at key points in the animation. Based on this template, applications create animation state instances to play back that animation on scene objects. To use the animation feature set, a total of four OGRE classes are used: Animation, AnimationState, NodeAnimationTrack, and TransformKeyFrame. These classes offer a range of methods for creating and editing animations, of which the most notable are detailed here.

```
Animation* Ogre::SceneManager::createAnimation
(
const String &  name,
Real  length
)
```

This function returns a valid pointer to an empty animation object.

**Arguments**

**const String & name**

OGRE string representing the unique name of the animation to be created. If the name is not unique, an exception is thrown.

**Real length**

Total length of the animation in seconds.

```
void Ogre::Animation::setInterpolationMode
(
InterpolationMode   im
)
```

Instructs OGRE on the method of interpolation to be used when tweening (blending) between frames. Since a developer specifies only key frames in the animation, OGRE is expected to fill in intervening frames between those keys. The interpolation method specifies the method of interpolation to be used.

**Arguments**

**InterpolationMode im**

Specifies the interpolation mode to be used when blending between key frames of an animation. This can be IM_LINEAR or IM_SPLINE. The former interpolates linearly between the previous key frame and the next, and the latter adds a "curvature" to the interpolation to produce a smoother but computationally more expensive result. It is recommended that readers experiment with these two values to observe the effect each setting has on their animation.

```
TransformKeyFrame* Ogre::NodeAnimationTrack::createNodeKeyFrame

(
Real   timePos
)
```

This function creates a transform key frame for the animation.

**Arguments**

**Real timePos**

Specifies the time in seconds at which the key frame is to occur.

> **NOTE.** The transform key frame represents a single key frame in a key frame-based OGRE animation. Each key frame encapsulates an instruction about how a node should be transformed at that frame. Transformations consist of translation, rotation, and scaling. The Camera Track sample uses only translation, and it sets the translation value via the setTranslate method of the TransformKeyFrame class. However, this class also supports additional methods for transformation: setRotation and setScale. The former method accepts a quaternion by which to rotate the node and setScale accepts a 3D vector to use for scaling.

## ■ 10.13    Compiling OGRE from Source

This chapter concludes with the subject of compiling OGRE from its source code. OGRE is an open source engine, which means its source code can be examined, edited, and recompiled for those who wish to do so. Given that OGRE is feature filled already, it might be the case that a developer has no intention of extending the OGRE code, but even so the code offers a fountain of information and insight to those looking to learn more about game engine development using C++—from structuring an engine into manager components to writing quick and efficient algorithms for splines and quaternions. For this reason, readers intending to code their own engine from scratch should view the OGRE source code at the earliest opportunity. This section offers a step-by-step guide on downloading, configuring, and compiling OGRE from source:

Step 1.  Navigate a web browser to the OGRE homepage and click **Download** in the left-hand margin. This provides the user with options to download a prebuilt SDK or to download the OGRE source. Select **Download a source package** to move to the source download page, which offers an array of source packages to download, each targeted toward a specific IDE.

Step 2.  Visual Studio users will need to download two packages and Code::Blocks users one package. For Visual Studio, it will be necessary to download the

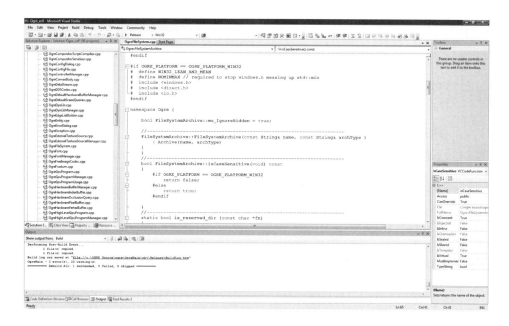

**FIGURE 10.42**    Compiling OGRE from source.

| Name |
| --- |
| OGRE 1.6.5 Source for Linux / OSX |
| OGRE 1.6.5 Source For Windows |
| Mac OSX Universal Precompiled Dependencies |
| Visual C++.Net 2003 (7.1) Precompiled Dependencies |
| Visual C++.Net 2005 (8.0) SP1 Precompiled Dependencies |
| Visual C++.Net 2008 (9.0) Precompiled Dependencies |
| Code::Blocks + MingW Precompiled Dependencies |

**❘ FIGURE 10.43**   Visual Studio source package.

| Name |
| --- |
| OGRE 1.6.5 Source for Linux / OSX |
| OGRE 1.6.5 Source For Windows |
| Mac OSX Universal Precompiled Dependencies |
| Visual C++.Net 2003 (7.1) Precompiled Dependencies |
| Visual C++.Net 2005 (8.0) SP1 Precompiled Dependencies |
| Visual C++.Net 2008 (9.0) Precompiled Dependencies |
| Code::Blocks + MingW Precompiled Dependencies |

**❘ FIGURE 10.44**   Code::Blocks source package.

Windows Source Package and also the Visual Studio precompiled dependencies (one package is available for each version of Visual Studio). See Figure 10.43. Code::Blocks users should download the Code::Blocks MinGW package that comes bundled with the precompiled dependencies. See Figure 10.44.

Step 3.   Once downloaded to the computer, both Code::Blocks and Visual Studio users should extract the source code package to a folder of their choice. Visual Studio users should take the extra step of also extracting the dependencies package into the same source code folder. Once extracted, the OGRE source project should be configured and ready to compile in the C++ IDE. To do this, simply open up the OGRE 3D project in either Visual Studio or Code::Blocks and click the **Compile** button. The OGRE project can be compiled in either debug or release mode. Successful compilation in debug mode produces an OgreMain_d.dll file; in release mode, it is OgreMain.dll. As stated, this file constitutes the core of the engine and should be present in the application folder alongside the executable when it is run.

## ■ 10.14   Chapter Summary

This chapter considered OGRE in some detail. It started by detailing the steps involved in downloading, installing, and configuring a precompiled OGRE SDK from the OGRE homepage, and then proceeded to detail how to set up an application window and initialize the graphics device for rendering. Having done this, it moved on to examining the resource system. Specifically, it explained how OGRE relies on a collection of resource paths when searching for resource data, and these paths represent the entirety of OGRE'S knowledge of the resource system. Files outside of those paths will not be found. Then the chapter proceeded to demonstrate mesh loading from files using the createEntity method and mesh exporting, and also discussed how meshes are tightly integrated into the material system that relies on scripts defined in files (.material files). Meshes are added to the scene by becoming part of the scene graph, and the scene graph was found to be a collection of scene nodes; that is, a hierarchical tree of nodes with the topmost node being the root node, and each node below having a parent node and possibly child nodes. The scene node system plays an important role in ensuring that animations play successfully, with each mesh moving appropriately in relation to the other. Finally, the chapter closed by considering how OGRE can be compiled from source; doing this is a useful exercise both for the developer that intends to use OGRE and for the developer that intends to learn from OGRE. The next chapter considers the issue of physics with Bullet Physics.

# 11 Rigid Body Physics with Bullet Physics

## Overview

After completing this chapter, you should:

- Appreciate the purpose of game physics
- Understand how to download, install, and compile the Bullet SDK
- Understand how to code and compile a basic physics application
- Know some tips and tricks on how to integrate physics into an engine

The previous chapter of this book considered the OGRE 3D graphics library in the context of scene management and demonstrated the importance for an engine of a node-based and hierarchical scene graph to express and honor the relationships between objects in a scene. The scene graph was found to be useful for cascading transformations downward through the hierarchy so that each node of the graph was transformed relative to its parent. In essence, this chapter extends on our work from the previous chapter regarding scene management. It does so in the sense that *game physics* relates to the laws that govern the relationships and motion of objects in the scene. Whereas the previous chapter considered the act of transformation itself—of moving, rotating, and scaling objects—this chapter focuses on specific and patterned transformations, those that are the result of physics. This chapter should, however, be considered only as an introduction or as a "getting started" primer to using a physics library in an engine. The purpose of this chapter is to show how a physics framework can be built and integrated into a game engine, and not to explain the intricacies or the mathematics behind physical interactions between solid objects (rigid bodies). However, for those interested in more information regarding the mathematics involved, or for those looking for more detailed information on using physics libraries, there are references to two books related to these subjects at the end of the chapter. This chapter focuses on explaining the place of a physics system in an engine, and also on downloading, compiling, and getting started with a free and open source physics library called Bullet Physics.

## ■ 11.1   Physics and Game Engines

The engine framework created thus far allows developers to create a node-based scene graph representing a 3D scene in which objects exist in a unified world space measured in terms of XYZ. The role of a physics system within that framework is to perform real-time detection of collisions between objects, and to "resolve" the motion and transformations of those objects on each frame of the render loop. These two terms—collision detection and world transforms—are considered in further detail.

### 11.1.1   Collision Detection

The term "collision detection" refers to the process of detecting *when* the volumes of any two scene objects intersect each other. Usually this means detecting when the bounding volumes (bounding box or sphere) of any two objects intersect or come into contact. The moment of intersection is called a *collision*, and engines respond to collisions in different ways, depending in part on the types of objects that collide and on the speed at which they were traveling when the collision occurred. For collisions between a game character and a wall, the engine will likely prevent the movement of the character any further in that direction to ensure the character does not pass through that wall. For collisions between a game character and a hazardous lava pit, the engine will typically respond by reducing the health of the player either until such a collision no longer remains or until the players health has depleted. These are examples of collisions, and such collisions demand *responses* from the engine when *detected*. Of these two—detection and response—the physics manager is responsible primarily for detecting the collision and notifying the engine. It might be the case however, that such a collision between two objects entails a physical reaction such as when a bouncing ball collides with a wall and is deflected away from the wall at an angle. In these cases, the physics manager is also responsible for managing the trajectory of objects in motion; this is related to the world transform aspect of the physics framework.

### 11.1.2   World Transforms

Objects in the scene that collide often react to one another, and the reaction that occurs often differs depending on the object's mass, its speed and trajectory, its inertia, the properties of its surface, and any other forces that might be being applied to it at the time such as gravity and wind. The result is that the position and rotation of objects in the scene exist in a continual state of flux according to the laws of physics. These govern how any one object reacts to contact with others and to any applicable forces. The existence of collisions and forces means that many objects could always be on the move, and it is the duty of the physics manager to manage (or resolve) these motions and transformations on each frame to ensure the engine renders a live (real-time) and believable view of the scene and its contents.

## ■ 11.2   Engines and Physics Managers

It was mentioned in the first chapter that in terms of design, an engine can be sub-divided into a series of components (subsystems or managers), each component dedicated to a unique function: one for 2D rendering, one for 3D rendering, one for audio and music, and others for scene management, error handling, and input reading. Physics is no exception to this rule in the sense that an engine will typically feature a physics manager. Its chief function is to both detect collisions and resolve world transforms of objects. This role, however, as a manager of collisions and transformations of scene objects, means that it must work much more closely with the scene manager and its node hierarchy than any other manager works with another. In order to know about the content of scenes and to transform the objects according to physical reactions, the physics manager must interface with the SceneManager class. In this sense therefore, the physics manager *depends* on the scene manager because the scene objects (their positions in 3D space) are the raw materials on which the physics engine makes it calculations. Thus, before a developer proceeds to implement a physics manager using a physics library, it is helpful to consider exactly which features of the library will be encapsulated into the Physics Manager class and which will extend into other classes, such as the scene manager and scene nodes, that are intended to work with the physics manager. A potential solution to distributing physics work across engine components is outlined in the following two points. These points should be interpreted as recommendations rather than as clearly established facts beyond dispute. As with all components of an engine, the design and implementation details can and do vary depending on the engine being developed, the needs of the developer, and the tools being used.

- The game engine should feature a singleton physics manager component that is ultimately responsible for detecting collisions, resolving scene object transforms, and "stepping" (or updating) the physics world on each frame. This class should also offer an enable/disable switch for enabling and disabling physics, respectively.

- Each 3D object in a scene that is to be part of the physics simulation should feature associated collision information. The collision information contains *position*, *scale*, and *orientation* data as well as *collision shape* data, the latter defining a bounding box or an approximation of the 3D object to be used by the physics manager when detecting collisions. Note that the actual mesh data of an object—its vertices, faces, and edges—are not used in collision detection for performance reasons, even though doing so would be the most accurate method of collision detection. It would be ideal to detect a collision by comparing all the vertices of one object with all of those from another, but performing such comparisons for all scene objects on each frame would be performance prohibitive. Therefore, simpler mesh approximations are used to represent the volume of the mesh, bounding boxes and bounding spheres being notable examples.

## ■ 11.3   Getting Started with Physics

When preparing to implement a physics framework into their engine, the first decision a developer must make is whether to code the physics system from scratch on the basis of their knowledge of physics or to use an established and ready-made physics framework developed by a third party. Of these two, the latter option is the most common in the contemporary games industry, with the majority of developers choosing any one of an established selection of physics libraries. At the time of writing, the most prominent physics libraries for video games include (in no particular order):

- **nVidia®PhysX®** (http://www.nvidia.com/object/physx_new.html)

  PhysX is a cross-platform and proprietary physics SDK owned and developed by nVidia Corporation. It is available free of charge to registered users for PC Windows, PC Linux, Mac, and Sony PlayStation® 3, and other licenses are available for Nintendo Wii and Xbox 360. It has been used on a wide selection of video games including Gears of War®, Unreal Tournament 3, and Tom Clancy's Splinter Cell Double Agent™.

- **Havok Physics™** (http://www.havok.com/)

  Havok Physics is a cross-platform physics SDK developed by Havok Software that, like some other physics libraries, includes features for rag doll physics, soft body dynamics, and other animation features. It is available for the following platforms: PC Windows, PC Linux, Mac, GameCube™, Wii, PlayStation 2, PlayStation 3, PSP®, Xbox®, and Xbox 360. It has been used on a wide selection of video games and simulations including Halo® 3, Half-Life 2, and StarCraft II.

- **Bullet** (http://bulletphysics.org/)

  Bullet is an open source and cross-platform physics SDK developed by Erwin Coumans and other developers, and is the main focus of this chapter. The Bullet Physics library is released under the zlib license and is free to use for commercial game development. (More information can be found at the Bullet Physics website, and the zlib license is reproduced in Appendix G.) It supports the following platforms: PC Windows, PC Linux, Mac, Wii, Xbox 360, PlayStation 3, and iPhone. It has been used on a wide selection of video games and simulations including Grand Theft Auto IV, Madagascar Kartz, and Regnum Online.

- **ODE** (http://www.ode.org/)

  ODE is an acronym for Open Dynamics Engine™, a C++ physics SDK developed by Russell Smith. It is open source and claims to be platform independent in the sense that the code can be compiled and used on any platform supporting the C++ language. It features support for both rigid body dynamics and collision detection. It has been used on a wide selection of video games and simulations including BloodRayne™ 2, Call of Juarez®, and S.T.A.L.K.E.R.

- **Box2D (2D Physics)** (http://www.box2d.org/)

  Box2D differs from the physics SDKs mentioned above in that it is dedicated not to 3D physics but to 2D physics; that is, to physics in 2D space. For this reason, Box 2D is frequently used to power the physics frameworks of 2D games such as side-scrolling platformers and isometric RPGs. Box2D is free to use and released under the MIT license, and is open source and cross-platform, having been used for games on PC Windows, Nintendo DS, Nintendo Wii, and the iPhone. It has been used on a wide selection of video games and simulations including Crayon Physics Deluxe, Fantastic Contraption™, and IncrediBots.

### 11.3.1   Bullet Physics

The previous section listed a selection of physics SDKs that are both popular and established in the contemporary games industry. Of these libraries, this book has chosen to introduce Bullet in more detail, demonstrating how to download the SDK, compile the source code, run the samples, and create a basic application, while offering both advice and clarification along the way. The selection of Bullet as opposed to others in no way should be taken as criticism of the others, for all of the above libraries are used for game development, and the selection of a physics SDK depends in part on preference and in part on the needs of a project. Bullet was chosen as the focus for this chapter for several reasons: First, it was chosen in favor of Box2D since the author assumes most readers intend to create *3D* games and *3D* engines. Second, it was chosen in favor of Havok Physics and PhysX because it is both open source and free for commercial use on all platforms. Being open source in this case allows readers to explore the source code and to learn from its implementation. Use of the Bullet SDK is now considered in further detail.

### ■ 11.4   Getting Started with Bullet Physics

The main focus of this chapter is the open source and cross-platform Bullet Physics SDK. To develop with this library, the developer must first download both the SDK and source code from the Bullet Physics website and then configure and compile that source code into a form that can be used with standard Visual Studio C++ projects.

The following step-by-step guide demonstrates how to download Bullet Physics and also explores the contents of the downloaded source package. The next section goes on to explain how to automatically compile and configure the source code into a Visual Studio-compliant project using the freely available Windows utility CMake.

Step 1.   Navigate a web browser to the Bullet Physics website at http://bulletphysics. org/wordpress/ (see Figure 11.1). From there, click the **Bullet Download** link at the top left and download the latest ZIP source package from the list

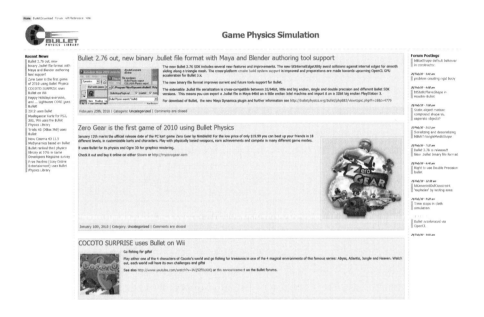

**❙ FIGURE 11.1**   Bullet website.

**❙ FIGURE 11.2**   Selecting a Bullet package.

(see Figure 11.2). This package typically appears as the topmost item in the list. The latest version of Bullet at the time of writing is version 2.7.6.

Step 2.  Once downloaded, extract the contents of the package to a unique folder on the local file system (e.g., C:\BulletSDK). The package should contain the following folders; a description of each follows in Table 11.1.

Demos

Extras

Glut

lib

msvc

src

| **Demos** | The Demos subfolder contains all C++ header, source, and object files for the sample applications bundled with the Bullet Physics SDK. The sample applications are intended to be both a showcase of the Bullet library features and a learning tool. Each sample is a showcase because when compiled and run, it demonstrates a unique set of bullet features; it is a learning tool because its source code demonstrates how to code and work with those features. The SDK does not ship with compiled versions of the sample applications; rather, developers should compile the samples themselves. A later section of this chapter will explore how to compile and run the sample applications. |
|---|---|
| **Extras** | The Extras folder contains a variety of code and tools for use with Bullet. It contains an alternative set of source files for compiling the sample applications on Mac as well as a set of plug-in exporters for 3D modeling software such as Maya and Blender. These exporters allow artists to associate sections of their mesh objects with Bullet-compliant physics information such as collision detection information and mass and inertia data. This data can then be imported into Bullet, where it works with the meshes of a scene. |
| **Glut** | The Glut folder features a Bullet dependency, the OpenGL Utility Toolkit library. Developers will not typically need to access or edit the contents of this folder. It is referenced by both the Bullet library and the sample applications at compile time. |
| **lib** | This folder often contains no files. It will not figure in our work with the Bullet SDK. |
| **msvc** | MSVC is an acronym for Microsoft Visual C++. Depending on the version and specific release of the Bullet SDK, this folder might contain premade Visual C++ project files for both the Bullet source code and the Bullet sample applications. If present, the user can reference these project files in their own applications in order to use the Bullet library. This book does not make the assumption that these files have been prepared already. Instead, it discusses—in the next section—how the user can create these Visual C++-compliant projects themselves using CMake. |
| **src** | The src folder contains all the C++ source and header files for the core components of the Bullet SDK. These components are the Collision, Dynamics, Multithreaded, Soft Body, and Math modules. Applications intending to use the Bullet SDK will need to reference these modules in their C++ projects. |

**▌ TABLE 11.1**  Bullet SDK Folders

## 11.4.1   Configuring the Bullet Core and Samples with CMake

The Bullet Physics library is open source in the sense that its complete source code both ships with the library and can be edited, examined, and compiled by the user of the library. Two sets of source code ship with Bullet: the source code for the sample applications using the Bullet Core and the Bullet Core itself, which consists of several unique modules. Each Bullet application must reference the Bullet Core, just as an OGRE application must reference OGREmain. Unlike OGRE, however, the Bullet SDK does not ship with a set of precompiled run-time libraries to which an application links at run time, but only with a set of source and header files and projects to which an application links statically at compile time. However, the source code for both the Bullet Core and the sample applications are provided in an IDE-independent form; that is, the source and header files are provided without additional proprietary and application-specific IDE project files that tell a compiler how to piece together the source files into a project. Specifically, the SDK does not always ship with Microsoft Visual C++ project files that allow the source code to be instantly loaded into and compiled by that IDE. If those project files are provided, they are found in the msvc folder, but some versions ship with this folder empty. In such cases, the developer is intended to prepare and compile the source files themselves into a form that Visual C++ will recognize. To do this—to compile together the source and headers of a project into a Visual C++ project—a developer can use the free and open source CMake utility. This utility reads "make" files (common to open source projects) that tell a compiler how to build an open source project and converts this into a form Visual C++ can use. The following step-by-step instructions illustrate how to download and use the CMake utility to prepare the Bullet SDK for compilation and use in Microsoft Visual C++:

Step 1.   Navigate a web browser to the CMake homepage at http://www.cmake.org/ (see Figure 11.3). From there, select **Download** to go to a downloads page, download the Windows installer package (as shown in Figure 11.4), and install CMake to the computer.

Step 2.   Once installed, create a folder inside the Bullet SDK directory named **Build**. This folder will contain Visual C++ project files generated by CMake from the Bullet SDK source code and make file.

Step 3.   Start CMake (see Figure 11.5). Enter into the topmost edit box (labeled "Where is the source code") the fully qualified path of the Bullet SDK where the make file is to be found. In this case, the make file is in the Bullet SDK root folder. In the second edit box, specify the path where the generated project files should be output. This location should correspond to the Build folder created in Step 2. Once these settings are specified, click the **Configure** button.

Step 4.   The configure dialog allows users to specify the IDE for which the project should be generated (see Figure 11.6). This dialog supports a range of IDEs,

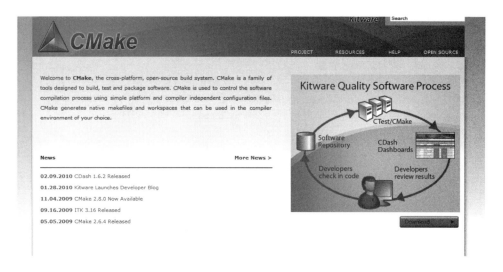

**FIGURE 11.3** CMake homepage.

Binary distributions:

| Platform | Files |
| --- | --- |
| Windows (Win32 Installer) | cmake-2.8.0-win32-x86.exe |
| Windows ZIP | cmake-2.8.0-win32-x86.zip |
| Mac OSX Universal (.dmg installer for Tiger or later) | cmake-2.8.0-Darwin-universal.dmg |
| | cmake-2.8.0-Darwin-universal.tar.gz |
| | cmake-2.8.0-Darwin-universal.tar.Z |
| Linux i386 | cmake-2.8.0-Linux-i386.sh |
| | cmake-2.8.0-Linux-i386.tar.gz |
| | cmake-2.8.0-Linux-i386.tar.Z |
| SunOS Sparc | cmake-2.8.0-SunOS-sparc.sh |
| | cmake-2.8.0-SunOS-sparc.tar.gz |
| | cmake-2.8.0-SunOS-sparc.tar.Z |
| IRIX64 64 | cmake-2.8.0-IRIX64-64.sh |
| | cmake-2.8.0-IRIX64-64.tar.gz |
| | cmake-2.8.0-IRIX64-64.tar.Z |
| IRIX64 n32 | cmake-2.8.0-IRIX64-n32.sh |
| | cmake-2.8.0-IRIX64-n32.tar.gz |
| | cmake-2.8.0-IRIX64-n32.tar.Z |
| HPUX 9000/785 | cmake-2.8.0-HP-UX-9000_785.sh |
| | cmake-2.8.0-HP-UX-9000_785.tar.gz |
| | cmake-2.8.0-HP-UX-9000_785.tar.Z |
| AIX powerpc | cmake-2.8.0-AIX-powerpc.sh |
| | cmake-2.8.0-AIX-powerpc.tar.Z |
| | cmake-2.8.0-AIX-powerpc.tar.gz |

**FIGURE 11.4** Downloading CMake.

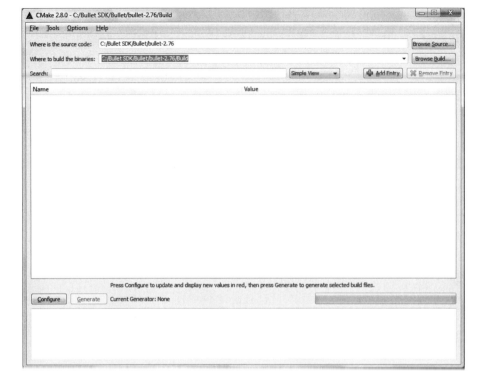

**FIGURE 11.5**    Configuring CMake.

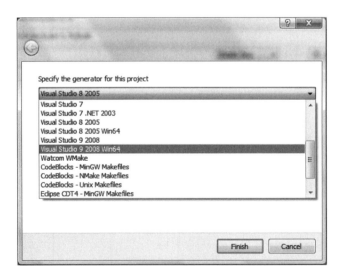

**FIGURE 11.6**    Configuring a compiler with CMake.

including Visual Studio and Code::Blocks, and users should select the item suitable for their IDE of choice. This book assumes either Visual Studio or Code::Blocks. Once selected, click the **Finish** button.

Step 5.   The main menu now displays a list of options and check boxes detailing the settings for the project to be generated. Typically, these defaults can be accepted. From here, click the **Generate** button. CMake will then generate the appropriate projects for the selected IDE in the specified Build folder (see Figure 11.7).

Step 6.   The Build folder should appear similar to Figure 11.8 for a Visual Studio C++ IDE. It features a complete Visual Studio solution for the Bullet Core and demo applications (BULLET PHYSICS.SLN) and separate C++ projects for each application and module of the core. The core projects are in the src subfolder of the Build directory.

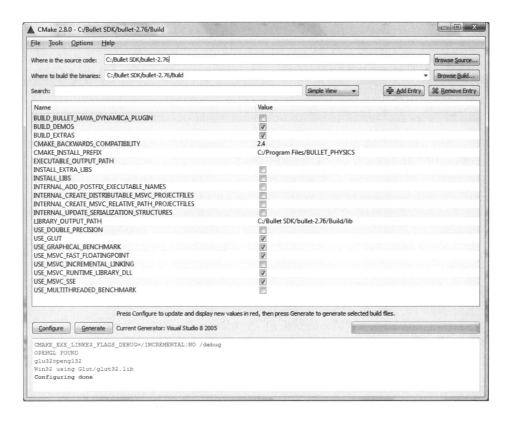

**| FIGURE 11.7**   Finalizing settings with CMake.

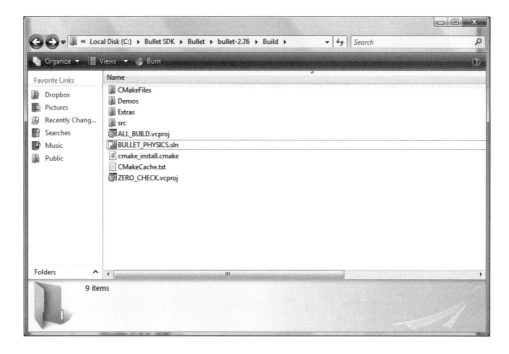

**I FIGURE 11.8**    Creating a project with CMake.

## 11.4.2    Compiling the Sample Applications

The CMake utility features mentioned in the previous section can generate proprietary and application-specific project files based on a make file, common to many
open source projects. Here, the CMake utility was used to generate a series of either
Code::Blocks or Visual C++ projects based on the Bullet SDK and Bullet sample
applications. Using the generated projects, a developer can proceed to compile both
the Bullet SDK Core and the sample applications. In order to provide the reader with
an introduction to the Bullet library and its features, this section considers how to
build and run the sample applications.

To compile the samples, open the generated project file named BULLET
PHYSICS. This project represents a collection of all bullet projects, both the core
modules and the sample projects. Compiling this project compiles the entirety of all
source and headers provided with the Bullet SDK. Users should be able to open this
project file in their IDE of choice and compile out of the box without having to tweak
settings further. Compilation time will vary from system to system, and once completed all sample applications will be built for testing (see Figure 11.9).

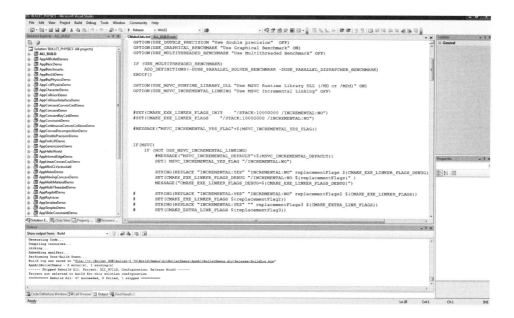

**FIGURE 11.9** Building the demo applications.

**NOTE.** The compiled demo executables are output by default to either the release or debug subfolder of the sample application project folder, depending on whether the project was built in release or debug mode, e.g., the Basic Demo executable will be output to BulletSDK\Build\Demos\ BasicDemo\Release. The demo applications *depend* on the run-time GLUT and GLEW DLLs (cross-platform libraries for displaying graphics), and these DLLs must be present in the application folder when the application is executed. These DLLs ship with the Bullet SDK and can be found in the root folder.

## 11.4.3 Exploring the Sample Applications

Bullet ships with approximately 45 demo applications (see Figure 11.10), each demonstrating either a unique feature or a unique combination of features, and most of them depend on the run-time GLEW and GLUT libraries. In addition, most of the samples feature a common set of keyboard shortcuts that allow a user to toggle console visibility and to manually step the physics world frame by frame in order to preview the results of the simulation more clearly. Several sample applications are now considered in more detail.

**FIGURE 11.10**    Demos folder.

---

### ■ Common Keyboard Shortcuts for the Demo Applications

h—Toggles the visibility of the help text on the screen

Space bar—Resets the simulation

Alt+mouse move—Rotates view

q—Quits

Arrow keys—Move camera

i—Toggles the simulation; pressing "i" once pauses and pressing again resumes

s—Manually steps to the next frame of the simulation; used in combination with i

**| FIGURE 11.11**  Basic Demo.

## 11.4.4  Basic Demo

The Basic Demo shows collision detection, gravity effects, and rigid body dynamics in action (see Figure 11.11). It features a scenario in which a stack of boxes is arranged in juxtaposition so as to form a cube resting atop a plane textured with a checkered texture. The user can rotate the camera view using either the keyboard or mouse and can also fire box objects as though they were bullets from a gun. When a fired box strikes the cube object at the center of the view, the constituent pieces of the cube that were hit—the box components—are blasted out of position. The amount of disturbance is determined by the speed and size of the fired box and by the angle at which the impact occurs. When impact occurs, the disturbance cascades to the surrounding boxes, and thus there is potential for the cube to come tumbling down to the ground like a house of cards.

## 11.4.5  Rag Doll Demo

The Rag Doll Demo demonstrates the Bullet rag doll physics system (see Figure 11.12). Rag doll physics is often used in games for simulating character death sequences or scenarios in which an unconscious character must fall limply to the ground.

**FIGURE 11.12**    Rag Doll Demo.

Conceptually, rag doll physics works by defining an underlying bone structure of a character and assigning each bone of the skeleton a series of constraints that define how it may move and rotate in relation to both joints and other bones. By specifying the bone and joint constraints of the skeleton so as to imitate real human skeletons, a physics engine ensures the game character acts realistically as it falls to the ground under the effects of gravity. The rag doll sample demonstrates two figures that fall to the ground; notice how the skeleton and joint constraints are observed as the character falls.

## 11.4.6    Soft Body Demo

The Soft Body Demo illustrates the soft body dynamics features of the Bullet SDK (see Figure 11.13). Soft bodies simulate bodies whose forms are malleable and changeable to pressure and forces; these include objects such as soft cushions, foam, rubber, elastic, and jelly. A soft body stands in contrast to a rigid body, which can be moved and rotated but does not morph or bend or contract in response to pressure. Rigid bodies are to that extent resistant to forces; these include objects such as cars, steel blocks, tables, chairs, televisions, and other hard and solid objects. The Soft Body Demo of the Bullet SDK features a soft foam-like cube that starts by falling to

**FIGURE 11.13**   Soft Body Demo.

the ground under the effects of gravity, and afterward can be blasted with cubes fired from a gun at the control of the user. Here, the user can observe how the soft body reacts to pressure—bending, squishing, distorting, contracting, etc.

## 11.4.7   Configuring an Application for Use with Bullet

The previous sections examined a selection of three Bullet sample applications, and the reader is encouraged to examine them all at least once before proceeding to build their first bullet application. Building a Bullet application involves linking to a series of three fundamental Bullet project files, compiled in earlier sections of this chapter. The following step-by-step instructions detail how to do this in Visual C++:

Step 1.  Create a new Visual Studio project (Win 32 Console Application) or load an existing project such as an OGRE sample.

Step 2.  Three Bullet Core projects must be added to the Visual Studio solution as dependencies of the main application project. To do this, in the project tree view, highlight the topmost item representing the Visual Studio Solution. Right-click with the mouse to view a context menu and select **Add Existing**. Use the browser to find the three Bullet Core projects in the **Build | Src folder**

**❘ FIGURE 11.14**    Project dependencies.

(see Figure 11.14). Add the following projects: BulletCollision, LinearMath, and BulletDynamics. Projects intending to use soft body dynamics should also add BulletSoftBody.

Step 3.   The newly added Bullet Core projects should now become *dependencies* for the main application project, meaning the main project relies on the Bullet Core. To do this, select the main application project in the project tree view. Right-click with the mouse to view a context menu and select **Project Dependencies**. In the dialog that appears, check all Bullet Core projects and click **OK**.

Step 4.   To complete the configuration process, the source code of an application should be linked to the Bullet SDK by including its main header file as follows: #include <btBulletDynamicsCommon.h>. The project is now configured to build Bullet applications.

## ■   11.5   Building a Bullet Application

Bullet-powered applications are, as we have seen, capable of collision detection, rigid body dynamics, rag doll physics, and soft body simulation. Together, these components represent a recipe for enhancing the believability of games, ensuring objects in the scene behave similarly to real-world objects when set in motion and when affected by other objects and similar forces. The previous section examined the steps necessary in configuring an application for use with the Bullet Physics library, and this section introduces the functions, classes, and methods of a basic Bullet application, and also highlights some key techniques of which Bullet developers should be aware. It does this by considering the hello world sample application featured in the Bullet documentation and which is recommended as the starting project for all newcomers to the Bullet library looking to get a first taste of its use. This chapter, however, will extend upon the sample provided there by taking a slower and more detailed glimpse at the processes involved, rather than offering only source code. The full source code of the hello world sample application for Bullet is presented shortly. The rest of this chapter is dedicated to unraveling this sample and to explaining the purpose and importance of its classes, functions, and properties.

NOTE. Memory Allocation. Unlike OGRE, the Bullet Physics library works strictly on the principle that the creator of objects should also be their destroyer. For this reason, any and all objects instantiated with the new keyword must also be deleted when no longer required. Developers should not rely on Bullet to release objects that they created.

NOTE. The following sample application should constitute the complete body of the main function, or WinMain function.

```
//Create main heart of physics collision detection engine
- broadphase object
//This object is used to detect collisions between any
pair of bounding regions
btBroadphaseInterface* broadphase = new
btDbvtBroadphase();

//Create object for handling memory allocation of
collision information
btDefaultCollisionConfiguration* collisionConfiguration =
new btDefaultCollisionConfiguration();

//Object featuring required algorithms for detection
collisions between both
//convex and concave regions
btCollisionDispatcher* dispatcher = new btCollisionDispat
cher(collisionConfiguration);

//The Sequential Impulse Constraint Solver serves to
ensure that scene
//objects are affected appropriately by forces and
motions in the scene
btSequentialImpulseConstraintSolver* solver = new
```

```
btSequentialImpulseConstraintSolver;

//dynamicsWorld is a high-level object representing the
"world" of
//the physics simulation
btDiscreteDynamicsWorld* dynamicsWorld - new
btDiscreteDynamicsWorld
(dispatcher,broadphase,solver,collisionConfiguration);


//Set world gravity
dynamicsWorld->setGravity(btVector3(0,-10,0));

//Create new bounding region for ground plane
btCollisionShape* groundShape = new btStaticPlaneShape
(btVector3(0,1,0),1);

//Create new bounding region for a sphere object
btCollisionShape* fallShape = new btSphereShape(1);

//A MotionState object that associates a collision shape
and a position
//with a rigid body object
btDefaultMotionState* groundMotionState = new btDefault
MotionState(btTransform(btQuaternion(0,0,0,1),btVector3
(0,-1,0)));

btRigidBody::btRigidBodyConstructionInfo groundRigidBodyCI
(0,groundMotionState,groundShape,btVector3(0,0,0));

//Add plane to scene as ground floor
btRigidBody* groundRigidBody = new
btRigidBody(groundRigidBodyCI);
    dynamicsWorld->addRigidBody(groundRigidBody);

btDefaultMotionState* fallMotionState =
    new btDefaultMotionState(btTransform(btQuaternion
(0,0,0,1),btVector3(0,50,0)));

//Set mass and inertia of sphere

btScalar mass = 1;
btVector3 fallInertia(0,0,0);
fallShape->calculateLocalInertia(mass,fallInertia);
```

```
btRigidBody::btRigidBodyConstructionInfo fallRigidBodyCI
(mass,fallMotionState,fallShape,fallInertia);

//Add sphere to scene
btRigidBody* fallRigidBody = new
btRigidBody(fallRigidBodyCI);
    dynamicsWorld->addRigidBody(fallRigidBody);

//Represents render loop
for (int i=0 ; i<300 ; i++)
{
    //Should be called in main game loop
     dynamicsWorld->stepSimulation(1/60.f,10);

   //Retrieve world Y position of sphere in 3D space
        btTransform trans;
        fallRigidBody->getMotionState()-
>getWorldTransform(trans);

        std::cout << "sphere height: " << trans.
getOrigin().getY() << std::endl;
}

    //Creators of objects must also destroy
    dynamicsWorld->removeRigidBody(fallRigidBody);
    dynamicsWorld->removeRigidBody(groundRigidBody);

    delete fallRigidBody->getMotionState();
    delete fallRigidBody;
    delete groundRigidBody->getMotionState();
    delete groundRigidBody;
    delete fallShape;
    delete groundShape;
    delete dynamicsWorld;
    delete solver;
    delete collisionConfiguration;
    delete dispatcher;
    delete broadphase;
```

## 11.5.1   The btBroadPhaseInterface, btDefaultCollisionConfiguration, and btCollisionDispatcher Objects

The sample Bullet application begins by creating a btBroadPhaseInterface object. The purpose of this object is to be the main engine for detecting collisions between pairs of bounding boxes for objects in a scene. Thus, for a scene with lots of objects, each object approximated by a bounding box, btBroadPhaseInterface has the main duty of detecting when any two bounding regions intersect. The Bullet SDK also offers additional implementations of the broadphase class that are specialized in their functionality, detecting collisions between specific types of objects and according to specific algorithms. It should also be noted that btBroadPhaseInterface, along with all other objects used in the sample, are created using the new keyword and must be deleted at application termination with a corresponding call to delete.

Once the broadphase class has been created, the sample proceeds to create two further objects: btDefaultCollisionConfiguration and btCollisionDispatcher. The former object is a helper object used internally by the Bullet SDK for managing the allocation of memory for collision objects and for collision detection algorithms. The latter is a helper object used internally by the Bullet SDK, which acts as a repository of collision detection algorithms for detecting collisions between both convex- and concave-shaped bounding regions. Given two bounding regions that are to be tested, the collision dispatcher finds the appropriate algorithm for testing.

## 11.5.2   Creating the Constraint Solver and the Dynamics World

The first three objects created are responsible primarily for collision detection and are used internally by the Bullet SDK for achieving this successfully. The first is for overseeing collision detection, the second for handling memory management, and the third for finding appropriate collision detection algorithms given a pair of bounding regions to be tested. Once this framework is initialized, the next class to be created in the sample is btSequentialImpulseConstraintSolver. This class relates less to collision detection than it does to rigid body dynamics and is a helper object used by the Bullet SDK for ensuring all bodies in a scene are affected accurately by the scene's pervading motions, collisions, and forces. If the ground plane is removed from beneath a sphere object in the scene, the sphere would then proceed to fall under the effects of gravity, and its fall would accelerate with distance, continuing until it reached another ground surface or indefinitely if no further ground plane existed to make contact. The btSequentialImpulseConstraintSolver is in part responsible for ensuring that objects behave appropriately in this way, acting and responding according to physical laws. Once the solver is created, the sample proceeds to create one of the most important objects for a Bullet developer: the dynamicsWorld class (btDiscreteDynamicsWorld). This object encapsulates the world simulation and is thereby similar to the OGRE scene graph in that its purpose is to add objects to and remove objects from the simulation. Creating this object requires pointers to the other helpers created in earlier steps, and the class offers methods for setting the strength of the world gravity, for adding motion constraints, for adding and removing objects, and for adding and clearing forces. In short, it is through the methods of the dynamicsWorld class that a developer accesses the world of the simulation. Important methods for the btDiscrete-DynamicsWorld class are listed in the following code:

```
class  btDiscreteDynamicsWorld
{
   public:
   //Called each frame to update physics world

   virtual int stepSimulation (btScalar timeStep, int
maxSubSteps=1,       btScalar fixedTimeStep=btScalar(1.)/
btScalar(60.));

   //Contraints restrict the motion of objects along
specific axes or in
   //specific directions. The add and remove constraint
methods
   //can be used to add and remove constraints within
world space

   virtual void addConstraint (btTypedConstraint
*constraint, bool    disableCollisionsBetweenLinkedBodies
=false);

   virtual void removeConstraint (btTypedConstraint
*constraint);

   //Actions refer to initiators of motion and forces
   //such as game characters and vehicles
   //These can be added to a scene using the add
   //and remove action methods

   virtual void addAction (btActionInterface *);
   virtual void removeAction (btActionInterface *);

   //The set and get gravity functions set and get the
strength
   //of the gravity that affects the dynamics world.
   //The set gravity function accepts a director vector
whose
   //position indicates the direction of the gravity and
whose
   //magnitude the strength

   virtual void setGravity (const btVector3 &gravity);
```

```
virtual btVector3        getGravity ();

//The add and remove rigid body methods are
responsible for
//adding and removing rigid bodies in a scene.
//A rigid body refers to a solid object resistant to
changes
//in its morphology; that is, a solid body that cannot
be deformed.

virtual void addRigidBody (btRigidBody *body);
virtual void removeRigidBody (btRigidBody *body);

//Clears forces in scene
virtual void clearForces ();

//Should be called once per time-step (frame)
//to update effects of gravity in a scene
virtual void applyGravity ();
;}
```

NOTE. A complete reference for all classes featured in the Bullet SDK can be found online at the following URL: http://bulletphysics.com/Bullet/BulletFull/.

## 11.5.3    Configuring the World and Adding Objects

The Constraint Solver class is responsible for solving and resolving physical reactions between rigid bodies within a specified 3D world space, and the dynamicsWorld object is responsible for representing that world to the developer. It is through the interface of the dynamicsWorld object that a developer can set some of the most important properties of that world. They can set the strength of gravity and both add rigid body objects to and remove them from the world space; that is, to and from the simulation. The preceding sample code proceeds to configure the simulation: first, by setting the strength of gravity using the setGravity method, and second, by creating two rigid body objects between which collisions will be detected—one object representing a ground plane and the other a sphere. It creates and configures two objects for the simulation via a series of discrete steps. The code to do this is reproduced here, and comments follow:

```
dynamicsWorld->setGravity(btVector3(0,-10,0));
btCollisionShape* groundShape = new btStaticPlaneShape
```

```
(btVector3(0,1,0),1);

btCollisionShape* fallShape = new btSphereShape(1);


btDefaultMotionState* groundMotionState = new btDefaultMo
tionState(btTransform(btQuaternion(0,0,0,1),btVector3
(0,-1,0)));

btDefaultMotionState* fallMotionState =
    new btDefaultMotionState(btTransform(btQuaternion
(0,0,0,1),btVector3(0,50,0)));

btRigidBody::btRigidBodyConstructionInfo groundRigidBodyCI
(0,groundMotionState,groundShape,btVector3(0,0,0));

btRigidBody* groundRigidBody = new
btRigidBody(groundRigidBodyCI);
    dynamicsWorld->addRigidBody(groundRigidBody);

btScalar mass = 1;
btVector3 fallInertia(0,0,0);
fallShape->calculateLocalInertia(mass,fallInertia);
btRigidBody::btRigidBodyConstructionInfo fallRigidBodyCI
(mass,fallMotionState,fallShape,fallInertia);
btRigidBody* fallRigidBody = new
btRigidBody(fallRigidBodyCI);
dynamicsWorld->addRigidBody(fallRigidBody);
```

## Comments

- The sample creates two collision shape objects, one for each object it intends
  to create for the scene. The Bullet Physics library draws a distinction between
  a rigid body and a collision shape; the former refers to the actual object in the
  scene with its own position, scale, and orientation, and the latter refers to the
  bounding volume associated with that object. This volume will be used by
  Bullet when testing for collisions. A separation is made between a collision
  shape and a rigid body since all rigid bodies in the scene will have a unique
  position, scale, and orientation, but many of those bodies will share the same
  collision shape, being sufficiently similar in form and size. For this reason,
  any single simulation will typically feature fewer collision shapes than there
  are rigid bodies. Consider, for example, a side-scrolling platformer game
  that features a main character, several enemy clones, and some platforms

onto which characters can jump. Each unique entity in the scene constitutes a unique body or collection of bodies, for each has its own position, orientation, and scale—one for the player, one for each enemy, and one for each platform. However, all enemy clones—being clones—will share the same collision shape. The sample produced here creates only two rigid bodies, and it starts by creating their shapes. A collision shape is encapsulated in the btCollision-Shape class, and instances of this class are returned by the btStaticPlaneShape and btSphereShape functions. The former produces a plane collision shape and the latter a sphere. More information on collision shape creation can be found in the Bullet Focus—Creating Rigid Bodies sidebar at the end of this section.

- Once a collision shape is created for each unique object to be created in the scene, the sample code proceeds to create a MotionState object for each rigid body, one for the plane and one for the sphere. MotionState encapsulates the world transformation matrix for each unique and moveable rigid body in the scene. Bullet will internally update and apply transforms to this matrix where appropriate on each step of the simulation (on each frame). However, this object features two methods for developers who want to set and get the world transform manually: getWorldTransform and setWorldTransform. The former is used to retrieve the current transformation matrix for the selected object, and the latter to set its matrix. In Bullet, matrices are encapsulated in the btTransform object.

- The collision shape and MotionState objects are important components (or properties) of a rigid body, the former defining its bounding volume and the latter its transformation in 3D space. But these objects together do not constitute a complete rigid body in a scene. Creating both collision shape and MotionState objects does not *add* a rigid body to the simulation; rather, it creates only those two objects in memory, in preparation for creating a rigid body. A rigid body is created in memory: first, by instantiating a btRigidBody::btRigidBodyConstructionInfo structure, and then by passing this structure as a parameter to the constructor of a class btRigidBody during the new statement. The structure btRigidBodyConstructionInfo defines the properties of a rigid body to be created; it specifies a pointer to a btCollisionShape to be used as its shape, a pointer to a MotionState object to be used for its world transformation, and also a 3D vector expressing the body's starting position in 3D space. These values are passed to the btRigidBody class as its creation parameters, and the result is a newly created rigid body based on those settings. Finally, the created rigid body is *added* to the simulation by calling the addRigidBody method of class btDiscreteDynamicsWorld. This class was created in an earlier step.

### ■ Bullet Focus—Creating Rigid Bodies

Rigid bodies exist at a specified position and orientation in 3D space and refer to *nondeformable* solid objects. The term "nondeformable" is used to mean that such objects are resistant to pressure and forces and are the antithesis of soft bodies. As mentioned, rigid bodies include objects like cars, tables, chairs, cups, boxes, and more. Soft bodies include objects like cushions, jelly, foam, rubber, skin, elastic, and more. In Bullet, a rigid body object is created in four distinct stages: (1) a collision shape is instantiated, defining the bounding volume of the body for collision detection purposes, (2) a MotionState object is created to represent the world transformation matrix that is to be applied to the rigid body in 3D space, (3) a btRigidBodyConstructionInfo is instantiated to specify the creation parameters for a rigid body, and (4) the rigid body is created according to the creation parameters. These four stages require the developer to call on a selection of functions and classes, including btStaticPlaneShape, btSphereShape, btDefaultMotionState, btRigidBody, and the addRigidBody method of class groundRigidBody.

**Collision Shapes**

The sample code uses two collision shape creation functions to create bounding volumes for collision detection, one for a plane and one for a sphere. These functions are btStaticPlaneShape and btSphereShape. Bullet offers these and other methods for creating a wide selection of collision shapes. The following list details some of the collision shape creation functions available:

    btBoxShape

    btCapsuleShape

    btConeShape

    btCylinderShape

    btSphereShape

    btStaticPlaneShape

    btTetrahedronShapeEx

    btTriangleMeshShape

**Rigid Body Objects**

A unique rigid body in a simulation is encapsulated in the class btRigidBody. This class represents the primary interface through which developers access and edit rigid bodies in a simulation. An abbreviated declaration of this class follows, and it highlights some of the class's most important methods, providing comments where appropriate:

```
class btRigidBodyConstructionInfo
{
    public:
        //Sets extra gravity to apply to this object
        void    setGravity (const btVector3 &acceleration)

        //Sets trajectory damping
        void    setDamping (btScalar lin_damping, btScalar ang_damping)

        //Returns a pointer to an associated collision shape object
        //This object is the same as that specified in the creation
        //parameters given to the class constructor.
        btCollisionShape * getCollisionShape () const

        //Sets the body's center of mass
        void    setCenterOfMassTransform (const btTransform &xform);

        //Applies forces to an object. The force is specified
        //as a 3D vector. Direction indicates the direction of the
force
        //and magnitude indicates the strength.
        void    applyCentralForce (const btVector3 &force)
        void    applyForce (const btVector3 &force, const btVector3
&rel_pos)

//Applies a spin about an axis
void    applyTorque (const btVector3 &torque)

//Erases all forces being applied to the object
        void    clearForces ()

        //Retrieves current orientation of body as a quaternion
        btQuaternion   getOrientation () const

        //Retrieves the current linear velocity of a body as a 3D
vector
        const btVector3 & getLinearVelocity () const

        //Retrieves the current angular velocity of a body as a 3D
vector
        const btVector3 & getAngularVelocity () const

        //Sets the current linear velocity of a body as a 3D vector
        void    setLinearVelocity (const btVector3 &lin_vel)

        //Sets the current angular velocity of a body as a 3D vector
        void    setAngularVelocity (const btVector3 &ang_vel)

        //Translates a body to a specified position in space.
```

```
          //Position is specified as a 3D vector
          void    translate (const btVector3 &v)

   //Retrieves the bounding box for the body
   void    getAabb (btVector3 &aabbMin, btVector3 &aabbMax)

   //Retrieves the world transformation matrix object for the body
          const btMotionState *  getMotionState () const

          //Sets a MotionState object as the current world transformation
          //for this body
          void    setMotionState (btMotionState *motionState)

          //Returns true if the body exists within the 3D space of a
          //dynamics object. False if otherwise.
          bool    isInWorld () const
```

### 11.5.4  Stepping the Simulation

The point of a physics simulation is to enhance the realism of scenes by ensuring that collisions between objects are detected and handled appropriately as and when they occur; and that the motion, responses, and trajectories of objects are resolved according to established physical laws, such as those of gravity and inertia. The concepts of motion, response, and trajectory, however, depend on concepts such as speed, acceleration, and distance, all of which are often defined in terms of their relation to time. Objects move at a specified speed, and speed refers to the distance that is traveled within a specified time. In short, motion occurs over time, and thus a physics simulation must work across the frames of the render loop. To convey a sense of motion in game scenes therefore, it is not enough to present only one frame in isolation. The simulation must be updated on each and every frame in order to show the latest snapshot (or *state*) of the world. The sample code given in an earlier section updates the simulation in a rather contrived for-loop designed explicitly to demonstrate how the world is stepped using Bullet Physics. For most game applications, this for-loop should correspond to the standard game loop. This section of code is reproduced here, and comments follow.

```
for (int i=0 ; i<300 ; i++)
{
        dynamicsWorld->stepSimulation(1/60.f,10);

        btTransform trans;
```

```
        fallRigidBody->getMotionState()
->getWorldTransform(trans);

std::cout << "sphere height: " << trans.getOrigin().
getY() << std::endl;
}
```

**Comments**

- The code begins by initializing a for loop for 300 iterations, each iteration intended to correspond to a frame (or group of frames) of the game render loop. For each iteration, it 'steps' the simulation, updating the dynamics-World object with the latest transformation and collision information. The next step simply demonstrates how to retrieve a world transformation matrix from the sphere in order to read its position on the world Y axes as it changes over time, falling under the effects of gravity until it collides with a ground plane.

  **NOTE.** Notice how the sample code ends with a series of delete statements, one for each object created. This is in line with the Bullet policy of making the creator of objects also be their destroyer.

## ■ 11.6   Chapter Summary

This chapter provided a brief taste of how a game developer approaches the task of integrating a physics framework into a game engine using a third-party physics library, namely Bullet Physics. It started by highlighting the distinctive components of a physics library in terms of collision detection and world transformation, in addition to soft body and rigid body dynamics. Rather than focus on implementing a physics manager from scratch using these concepts, it discussed them while considering the basics of the Bullet Physics library such as how to download and install the SDK, how to configure and compile the source code, and how to compile and run the sample applications, and also offered a commentary of the standard hello world application. Having taken this first step toward game physics development, the reader is equipped to explore the SDK source code and sample applications to use the techniques presented in this book to encapsulate the library into a manager component. The next chapter turns to the issue of game scripting which is especially important for creating artificial intelligence, and also to the importance of time-saving engine tools such as fully featured GUI level editors. It does this by considering an established and popular game engine called DX Studio.

# ■ References

Millington, Ian. *Game Physics Engine Development*. San Francisco: Morgan Kaufmann Publishers, 2007.

Bourg, David. *Physics for Game Developers*. Sebastopol, CA: O'Reilly & Associates, Inc., 2002.

# 12 | Focus on DX Studio: Engine Tools, Editors, and Scripting

## Overview

After completing this chapter, you should:

- Appreciate the benefits of increasing the accessibility of an engine through engine tools and scripting languages
- Be able to recognize the benefits of scripting for customizing game behavior and for creating aspects such as artificial intelligence
- Understand how to harness the power of the SpiderMonkey JavaScript engine for use in a game engine
- Be familiar with the basics of the game engine DX Studio

The final chapter of this book considers the variety of tools, extensions, and scripting mechanisms used by developers to interface with their engines and to improve their engine's versatility and customizability. Each chapter of this book thus far has focused on a unique building block of engine development including audio playback, graphics rendering, error and input handling, scene and resource management, and physics simulation. Each of these components can be encapsulated into a unique manager subsystem (or class), and once brought together into a cohesive whole, this collection of managers constitutes the foundation of a game engine, the infrastructure necessary for building a video game. From this foundation a developer can proceed to elaborate on the engine by introducing additional classes and manager components that boast of features tailored to particular game genres: minimap components for RTS (real-time strategy) games, line of sight and visibility features for RPG (Role Playing Games) games, or inventory objects and path finding classes for adventure games. By elaborating on the engine in this way—that is, by branching from this foundation—a developer travels along the road of specialization, of creating an engine dedicated to a particular genre of game. This process often proves very useful to developers intending either to market their engine to other developers or to create a series of games in the same genre, or both. The extra comprehensiveness added to an engine by such features, however, tends to increase the complexity of its use for the game developer, and thus there arises the problem of engine accessibility. The term "engine accessibility" is used here not to refer to accessibility features (such as onscreen keyboards, text-to-voice, and subtitles), important though these are. Instead, it is used to refer to the accessibility of an engine's feature set to the developer intending to make a game. Thus, the accessibility of an engine describes its "usability" (or ease of use) to a game developer, and the ease of use of an engine is an important factor in ensuring that a game is developed both efficiently and on a timely basis. It might be that an engine sports a plethora of advanced features and yet offers no clear documentation or examples of their use and offers no presentable interface, editor, or tools by which some of the tedium of game development can be relieved. In this case, the developer already has a strong reason to avoid using that engine for their game—not because the engine lacks features but because it lacks accessibility, particularly to those game developers who are not also the developer of the engine. Before proceeding to discuss some of these helpful tools as an answer to a developmental problem, it is first necessary to say more about the problem: the tedium of game development.

## ■ 12.1   The Problems of Game Development

It was stated in Chapter 1 that a computer game is *powered* by its engine and also that the engine does not constitute the whole of a game. The work of the game developer begins rather than ends with a completed engine, because the engine is the infrastructure that supports the game. Once the engine is built, the development of a game can begin on that foundation. In addition to its engine, a game also consists of resources (or assets), those being graphical (such as meshes and textures), audio (such as music and sound), and informational (such as XML configuration files and level/scene data). The art and science of game development requires the game designer to manage and assemble those assets into a meaningful whole, in the same way an author of fiction must assemble their imagination, skill, and writing into a whole that conveys a story. The game designer must arrange graphical and audio elements into a scene and also define the behavior of that scene. This might involve arranging the layout for a castle or dungeon scene in an RPG, arranging *where* elements are positioned in 3D space including the positions of walls and doors as well as those of enemies and power-ups. The designer might also define *how* the entities within that scene are to behave in response to the actions of the player such as whether an enemy should flee or hold ground when attacked. The designer should also specify *when* specific events should be triggered during game play such as when a giant and powerful enemy should come crashing through the wall to attack the gamer. Thus, the design aspects of *where*, *how*, and *when* are the three core axes around which game design occurs and asset use is managed. For this reason, it is important for an engine to be *accessible* to these three aspects—accessible to the extent that it allows developers the opportunity to define the where, how, and when of a game easily and intuitively.

The accessibility of an engine is improved when it does all of this without requiring the developer to have a working knowledge of the internals of the engine.

The engine developed thus far in this book already offers a slew of features in terms of graphical rendering and scene management, and thus the reader might be tempted to think that it is already accessible to these three aspects. In some senses this is true, because a game developer can use the engine's scene graph and its node-based structure to define much of the where and how of a game, and can also use some timing and animation features to define the when. But despite this, a strong case can be made to suggest the engine is not nearly accessible enough. This case can be based on the following drawbacks, all of which apply to our game engine as it stands.

> **NOTE**. This chapter uses the two terms "engine developer" and "game developer" to mean two distinct entities, though they might in practice refer to one and the same person. *Engine developer* refers to the creator of a game engine, and *game developer* refers to someone who uses an engine to make games.

- The game developer must hard code the behavior (the how and when) of a game directly in compiled C++ using the scene graph methods provided by the scene manager component. The developer must call upon the scene graph methods to load a mesh at a specified position in 3D space and to configure the nodes of the graph to bring that mesh into a relationship with others in the scene. There are three main problems with this method: First, the game developer must recompile the game code for each edit made to game behavior or to the scene, e.g., each time the speed of a unit or creature is amended. Second, the developer cannot interactively and *visually* preview their edits to the scene prior to compiling and running the game. The developer cannot, for example, interactively position and arrange the meshes, lights, and textures of a scene at design time with immediate visual feedback. Instead, the developer must hard code the arrangement of a scene and then compile the engine to preview its appearance. Third, the game developer must have a working knowledge of C++ and of compilers to interface with the scene manager component and compile the application, respectively.

- In the case of OGRE, the game developer must tediously edit text-based material scripts and configuration files whenever the appearance of objects must be changed, and once edited there is no editor or preview window to show visual feedback. To preview the changes made to these files, the developer need not recompile the application but still must restart it for the new settings to take effect.

The above drawbacks to the engine are: (1) the absence of immediate visual feedback when changes are made to scenes, (2) the inability to make scene-level changes with an editor and without recompilation, and (3) reliance on text-based configuration files whose effects cannot be visualized without running the game. Together, these three drawbacks do not conclusively prohibit the developer from making a game using an engine, since such an engine could be used to make a game, even with those drawbacks. But they do severely impact the developer's productivity, on their ability to make games efficiently and on a timely basis. They do this by increasing both the time and work required to make even the simplest of changes to a game's scenes. One way to resolve this problem is to create a set of intuitive engine tools to internally handle all of the tedium the developer would rather avoid where possible. Such tools represent an interface between the developer and the engine, and they allow game developers to build games through scripting windows and drag-and-drop user interfaces. The next section examines engine tools in more detail.

## ■ 12.2    Increasing Productivity through Engine Tools

The previous section highlighted the obstacles to productivity that can arise for a game designer when using an engine that does not offer a set of supplementary engine tools for building games. These tools often include script editors, scene designers, and material preview windows, as we shall see. Engines that lack these tools are by no means useless or unusable, since games can be and are made with them. But such engines increase the time and work required of the developer when building a game, and both this time and work could be reduced. For this reason, engine developers can make their engines easier to use and more marketable for selling when they create a set of tools to use with them. The following tools are some of the most common that accompany game engines:

- **Map or Scene Editor**

  Perhaps the most popular and prevalent tool for an engine is the map editor. This tool allows developers to interactively view, preview, and edit the scenes of their game using a graphical user interface. Using the map editor, developers can intuitively add meshes, textures, and other objects to the scene in real time, building a map of their game and receiving immediate visual feedback on the scene as it will appear when run in the game. When the scene is saved in the editor, the editor caches the scene to a file that can be loaded and parsed by the engine at application startup, whereupon the engine will recreate the scene as defined in the file. Thus, each edit made in the editor potentially saves the developer both the time and work that would otherwise have been invested in recompiling and rerunning the game executable after the scene change had been made. See Figure 12.1.

- **Scripting Frameworks**

  Most engines support an interpreted scripting language, such as JavaScript or Lua, that developers can use on-the-fly to customize the behavior of both the engine and their game without having to recompile the game executable (see Figure 12.2). This is because the engine both reads and parses the scripted

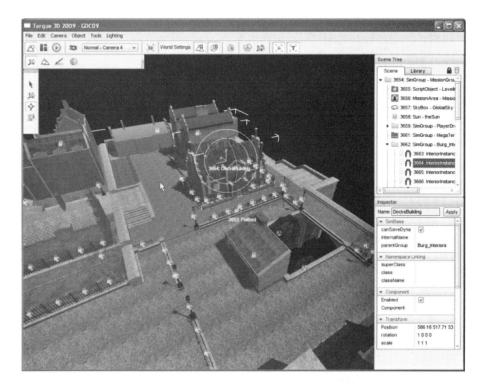

**FIGURE 12.1**   Map editor.

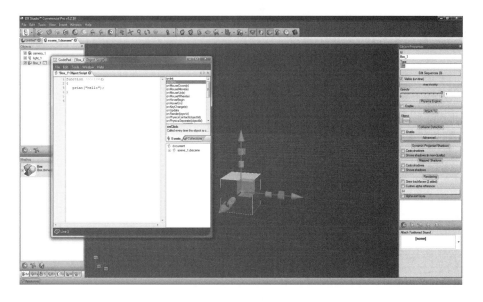

**FIGURE 12.2**   Script editor.  Courtesy of Chris Sterling, Worldweaver, Ltd.

code as and when it is executed. This offers developers the benefits of programmatic control over game elements without the burden of the lengthy compile times involved with compiled languages, though it often incurs performance penalties.

- **Material Preview Windows**

  A material refers to the skin applied to the surface of a mesh. A material defines how the surface reacts to light as well as to the texture maps that are wallpapered

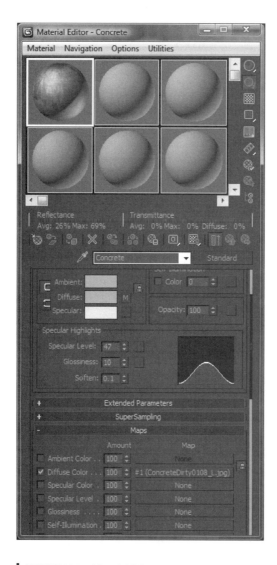

**I FIGURE 12.3**    Material Editor.

EXERCISE 12.1

**Q.** List at least one benefit of game engine tools for both the engine developer and the game developer. Justify your answer with reference to the concepts of time and work, and to either map editors, scripting frameworks, or material editors.

**A.** Your answer might include the following:

For the game developer:

- **Increases Productivity**—Map editors, scripting frameworks, and material previews reduce time, money, and cost required to develop games.

For the engine developer:

- **Increases Marketability**—Given that engine tools increase development productivity, engines that ship with such tools therefore increase their market value.

onto the surface. Building a material for an object involves trial and error, skill, talent, and judgment. Some engines ship with a material editor tool that allows developers to interactively build and preview their materials before applying their final versions to meshes in the scene. See Figure 12.3.

## ■ 12.3 Introducing Game Tools through DX Studio

Engine tools are provided by engine developers to reduce the tedium of specific game development tasks and to make the game development experience both more fun and productive. By using drag-and-drop GUIs, scripting windows, material editors, and other tools to build games, developers save time and money because they are able to receive real-time previews and visualizations of the changes they make. This chapter elaborates further on game tools, both on their uses and their benefits, by considering a game engine called DX Studio. DX Studio is a cross-platform 2D and 3D game engine that ships with a complete integrated editor, featuring map designing features, mesh import facilities, a scripting system, and a material browser, among other features. By comparing the workflow of game development in DX Studio with the workflow of our engine developed thus far, readers should be able to appreciate the benefits of game engine tools and have developed ideas about the tools suitable for their own engine. In considering the features of DX Studio, this chapter discusses topics such as:

- Integrated scripting with JavaScript
- Creating maps and scenes using a map editor

- Importing game assets, such as meshes and textures, into the engine via the editor

- Compiling a single game project to specific output formats: EXE, web browser plug-in, Windows Vista® gadget, etc.

- Outputting game data to open standards such as XML using the editor

> **NOTE.** DX Studio is available under different licenses depending on how the developer intends to use the games created with the engine. DX Studio is available in Freeware, Standard, and Professional editions. Visit the DX Studio website for more information (http://www.dxstudio. com/).

## ■  12.4    Getting Started with DX Studio

Third-party game engines typically fall into one of two categories: those that are intended to be integrated into an application as an SDK, such as the OGRE library, and those that work on a standalone basis; that is, those in which the editor tools and the engine are tightly integrated into a single IDE and do not require the developer to compile it with their application like an SDK. DX Studio is of the latter kind in that it offers all the tools necessary to build a game in one complete integrated package; the developer does not need to have Visual Studio and does not need to manually compile their application. Instead, DX Studio provides its own editor that developers use to build applications with the DX Studio engine, just as Flash developers use Adobe Flash to build their own custom presentations for the Flash player. There are both advantages and disadvantages to so tight an integration between both editor and engine. The advantage is simplicity, since the developer need not have prior knowledge of an existing IDE, has all the tools required to build applications with the engine, need not compile open source projects nor link to specific libraries, and does not need to learn the intricacies of an SDK function set. However, the chief disadvantage in comparison to an open source SDK-delivered engine is a lack of customizability and flexibility, since the developer must work within the parameters of the editor provided with the engine. They cannot simply edit the engine source code to suit their needs, nor, for example, can they replace its audio playback framework with an audio library of their choice, or its rendering framework with a rendering engine of their own making. Thus, the out of the box engine that is fully equipped and ready to build games through its own editor has both pros and cons, and both the reader and game developers generally will need to consider these points carefully when deciding on which engine to use for their particular project.

DX Studio markets itself as a complete and integrated 3D toolkit for making video games and 3D simulations. Applications created with the DX Studio engine can be built as a standalone executable for Windows PC or as an embedded plug-in in a web browser. There are also efforts being made by the DX Studio team and community to widen the platform support of the engine to both Mac and Linux systems, but at the time of writing these implementations are in development. This section details instructions on where to find DX Studio, how to download and install it, and where to find helpful reference documentation on its use. The next sections then proceed to detail the basics of a DX Studio project and how to use the editor tools to build standalone DX Studio applications.

## 12.4.1    Installing DX Studio

The DX Studio engine is divided into two components, each of which can be downloaded separately—the player component and the editor component. The player component represents the run-time framework necessary to run a DX Studio application either as an executable or as an embedded presentation inside a web browser such as Internet Explorer®, Firefox®, or Opera. Users of DX Studio-powered games must have the DX Studio Player installed on their system if their games are to run correctly. The DX Studio Player can be downloaded and installed from the DX Studio website, and developers can also distribute the DX Studio Player seamlessly in an installer alongside their games. The DX Studio Editor component stands in contrast to the player in that it is intended not for gamers but for the developers of DX Studio-powered games. It represents the complete DX Studio package featuring both the player and the editor tools, the first being necessary to run DX Studio games and the latter being necessary to build them. To download the DX Studio Editor, navigate a web browser to the URL http://www.dxstudio.com/. Once there, click the Download button to view the download page and download the DX Studio Editor. It downloads in the form of an installer. Once downloaded, the installer can be run to install DX Studio to the computer.

## 12.4.2    DX Studio Documentation and Support

Engine developers intending to market their engines for use by other developers often overlook the importance of clear, accessible, concise, and regularly updated documentation of their engines; that is, documentation aimed not at *engine developers* but at *users of the engine*. Engine documentation is useful to users of all levels and especially to new users, both for reference purposes and for guidance and instruction. For this reason, documentation helps to make an engine more accessible to its users. The DX Studio engine comes with three main forms of documentation and support: an online reference guide, online community constructed wiki, and the community forum.

- **Reference Guide**

   The DX Studio reference guide complements the wiki in that it offers a comprehensive list of all DX Studio objects, methods, and function calls that can be accessed via the JavaScript scripting language. As we shall see, the DX Studio engine supports JavaScript as a scripting language. The reference guide can be found at http://www.dxstudio.com/guide.aspx. See Figure 12.4.

- **Wiki**

   The wiki component of the DX Studio documentation is constructed and maintained by the DX Studio community. It differs from the reference in that it is presented less as a reference and more as learning materials and tutorials. The wiki features getting started lessons and other useful tips and tricks. The wiki can be found at http://www.dxstudio.com/guide.aspx. See Figure 12.5.

- **Forums**

   DX Studio features a lively, helpful, and sizable community in which users come together and share ideas, thoughts, and advice on the engine. Here, help is both offered and received. The DX Studio forums can be found at http://www.dxstudio.com/community.aspx. See Figure 12.6.

**FIGURE 12.4**   DX Studio reference guide. Courtesy of Chris Sterling, Worldweaver, Ltd.

**FIGURE 12.5**    DX Studio wiki. Courtesy of Chris Sterling, Worldweaver, Ltd.

**DX Studio** 3.2

home » forums

Forums

Report Abuse

FAQ

# Forums

Welcome to the new DX Studio Discussion Forums! Please feel free to comment, ask and respond to questions here, and hopefully this will build into a useful resource for DX Studio users. Make sure to read and understand the forum rules before posting.

Please choose a forum from the list below, or for all sections combined, try the All Forums section or the Watched Topics

| 7746 registered forum users, 236 online now | Topics |
|---|---|
| **General Discussion**<br>The default forum for all DX Studio related chat that doesn't fall into one of the specific categories below. | 1478 |
| **New Users**<br>If you're a new user or just have some basic questions, this is the place to be. | 430 |
| **Feature Requests**<br>Have an idea that would make DX Studio even better? Post it here. | 833 |
| **Scripting**<br>Need help with writing DX Studio script? This is where you need to be. | 1603 |
| **Announcements**<br>All minor release information is posted here. | 115 |
| **User Projects and Ideas**<br>See what others are doing with DX Studio (screen shots, examples, etc), share your ideas and get feedback. | 434 |
| **Import/Export and Modeling**<br>Questions about the best tools and tricks to use for getting files into or out of DX Studio, or modelling and other asset generation discussions. | 263 |
| **Competitions**<br>If you're entering a DX Studio sponsored competition, or would like to set up your own, use this forum. | 43 |
| **SDK/COM**<br>For advanced users. The new C++ Player SDK and ActiveX interfaces should be discussed here. | 13 |
| **Bugs**<br>Post any suspect bugs you've found in a public DX Studio release here. | 37 |
| **Advertising and Jobs**<br>If you're selling model packs or services, or looking to recruit coders or artists, then this is the forum to use. | 68 |

**FIGURE 12.6**    DX Studio forums.

## ■ 12.5   The Anatomy of a DX Studio Document

DX Studio is a *project-based* engine in the same way that both Visual Studio and Code::Blocks are project-based applications. That is, the software works by allowing users to build a project from a collection of related but unique files and assets, from XML documents and configuration files to textures and audio files. The DX Studio Editor allows users to assemble, view, and edit the files of the project seamlessly, and saving the project ensures that a new and separate file is created that records the settings of the project. In DX Studio, however, the term "document" is used in place of the term "project," and thus a DX Studio project is called a DX Studio document. The DX Studio Editor can be used to work on one document at any one time and is responsible for creating, editing, saving, and compiling documents, and the DX Studio Player is responsible for running them. In the context of game development, one DX Studio document would typically equate to a single game.

> **NOTE.** The reader is now encouraged to launch the DX Studio Editor and to work with it alongside this book, following through the tutorials and exercises presented here. On launching DX Studio, the user is given the opportunity to either create a *new* DX Studio document or load an *existing* document. For the purposes of this chapter, the reader should create a new document. See Figure 12.7.

**❘ FIGURE 12.7**   DX Studio welcome page. Courtesy of Chris Sterling, Worldweaver, Ltd.

## 12.5.1   DX Studio Documents

A DX Studio document is created using the DX Studio Editor and represents a collection of assets and files that together constitute a game application, which can be run either as a standalone Windows executable or as an embedded presentation in a web browser. A DX Studio document is composed of the following elements: layers, scenes, objects, and resources. These are described in more detail as follows:

- **Layers**

  Layers in DX Studio fulfill a similar function to the layer objects found in some photo-editing applications such as Photoshop or GIMP. A DX Studio document contains one or more layers in a stack, and each layer matches the size of the document in terms of width and height and represents a transparent film or Perspex® sheet onto which pixel data can be rendered or blitted. Regions containing pixel data are nontransparent regions, and regions with no pixel data are transparent, thus showing the contents of the layer beneath it in the stack. On each frame of the render loop, the layer stack is presented to the application window as seen from the top, with the topmost layer appearing in front of those farther down the stack and the bottommost layer appearing at the back. Each layer has a Z-order that corresponds to its position in the stack, and the order of a layer can be changed by adjusting its Z-order value. Each layer in a DX Studio application is associated with no more than one scene at any one time, and it is the scene that determines what is rendered in its associated layer.

- **Scenes**

  A scene can be either 2D or 3D, representing a 2D or 3D scene, respectively. A scene in DX Studio corresponds to our existing understanding of a scene, as established in previous chapters. A 3D scene represents a 3D coordinate space that can feature lights, cameras, meshes, shapes, and other effects. A 2D scene represents a 2D space and features flat 2D bitmaps drawn one atop the other in screen space. A DX Studio document object can contain one or more scenes, and for a scene to be visible—that is, for the contents of the scene to be rendered to the application window—it must be attached to a layer in the stack; only one scene can be attached to one layer at any one time, though a document can have as many layers as necessary. Thus, it is the layer stack that is rendered on each frame by the DX Studio Player, and each layer in the render stack is associated with one scene. Each scene encapsulates either a 2D or 3D space, and inside that space there can exist none, one, or more scene objects.

- **Objects**

  An object (or scene object) can be a camera, light, mesh, primitive object, particle system, or other special object in either a 2D or 3D scene. An object thus encapsulates a "thing" (any unique thing) that can exist within the coordinate space of a scene. Therefore, each object has a position, orientation, and scale and is subject to transformations in the form of translation, rotation, and scaling.

- **Resources**

    Resources refer to the assets of a game (such as textures, meshes, and sounds) that must be loaded and cached by the DX Studio Player in order to present scenes successfully. Resources can exist at two separate levels, which refer to the "lifetime" or "scope" of a resource; these levels are document level or scene level. Document-level resources are those global resources that exist throughout the lifetime of a DX Studio application and are shared throughout all scenes. Such resources might include cursor images, main character sprites, and gun and footstep sounds. Scene-level resources are those whose scope is scene limited and whose lifetime equates to the lifetime of the scene. Scene resources are loaded as the scene is created and are unloaded as the scene is removed. A resource can also be either embedded or linked. An embedded resource is one that is compiled into the document at compile time and thus the document contains the resource. Linked resources, however, remain external to the document at run time, and the DX Studio Player must access the external file as and when it must be loaded. More will be said of the properties of resources later in this chapter.

## ■ 12.6    Creating a Hello World Application Using the DX Studio Editor

It has been stated that DX Studio documents consist of layers, scenes, objects, and resources. The layer stack represents the queue of items to be rendered on each frame in turn, with the topmost layer of the stack being rendered in front of all layers beneath and each layer beneath rendered in sequence from top to bottom. Each layer depends on an associated scene object, and the scene object determines what is rendered inside the associated layer. The scene encapsulates either a 2D or 3D scene and contains a set of scene objects existing in a 2D or 3D coordinate space, respectively. This section offers a tutorial on how to create a simple DX Studio application that features one layer and one scene that contains a textured cube that will print the message "hello world" to the window when clicked with the mouse. This is a useful starting application because it demonstrates: (1) how to navigate the DX Studio Editor GUI and how to use its tools to build a simple scene; (2) how to load a texture asset as a scene resource; (3) how to use the material browser to texture a cube object in the scene; (4) how to position and orient a camera in 3D space to view the cube at an appropriate angle and distance; (5) how to use the JavaScript coding editor to script a behavior that will run when the user clicks the mouse button; and (6) how to compile and run the completed application as a standalone executable.

## 12.6.1   Creating a New 3D Scene

DX Studio documents begin empty insofar as they feature neither layers nor scenes. Figures 12.8 and 12.9 illustrate the sidebars that appear in the editor on the starting page of the document.

**I FIGURE 12.8**   Layers and Tasks panes. Courtesy of Chris Sterling, Worldweaver, Ltd.

**FIGURE 12.9**    Layer Properties and Scenes panes. Courtesy of Chris Sterling, Worldweaver, Ltd.

1. The Layers pane lists all active layers in the current document, and the Z-order of layers corresponds to the order in which they are listed in this list, from top to bottom.

2. The Tasks pane provides the first set of creation options when beginning a new document. From this menu, users can choose to create a new and empty document

or to add a new scene to the document. A layer is automatically created and associated with the newly created scene.

3. The Layer Properties pane appears on the right-hand side of the editor window. The topmost pane (3 in Figure 12.9) lists the editable properties of the currently selected layer, including the layer's name and absolute top left position of the layer in screen coordinates. The Scene drop-down list allows the users to specify the scene to be associated with the selected layer.

4. The Scenes pane lists all scenes in the document, and the buttons at the bottom provide controls for adding, editing, removing, and uploading scenes, respectively; the latter option allows users to upload scenes to an online community library where it can be downloaded and viewed by other members.

To begin the Hello World sample, proceed with the following steps:

Step 1.   Create a new 3D scene in the document by clicking the **Scene button** in the Tasks panel shown in Figure 12.8. Doing so will open the **New Scene** dialog (shown in Figure 12.10) from which the user can choose to create a 3D or 2D scene or to create a scene based on a scene template in the online community scene library.

Step 2.   For this sample, users should select **Create a new 3D scene** to create both a new 3D scene and its associated layer. Users can confirm the creation has

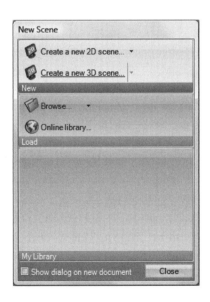

**I FIGURE 12.10**   Creating a new scene. Courtesy of Chris Sterling, Worldweaver, Ltd.

occurred successfully by ensuring that a new layer is listed in the layer list and that a new scene is listed in the scene list.

Step 3.    Once created, view (edit) the scene contents in the editor either by double-clicking the scene item in the list or by selecting the scene item in the list and then clicking the edit button at the bottom of the panel. Doing this displays the Scene Editor in the editor. From here, users can interactively create and edit scenes for their game and preview them to see how they will appear when executed.

## 12.6.2    Editing a 3D Scene

The Scene Editor tab allows developers to add, remove, position, edit, and script objects in a scene, and it is perhaps the place where developers will spend most of their time, since much of game development consists of scene editing and scripting. A newly created scene begins empty by default with the exception of two objects: a camera and a light; the former provides the view that will be used when the document is run, and the latter provides the key light for the scene and does not by default cast shadows. The Scene Editor view features three main panels: a left panel (Scene Objects), center panel (World View), and right panel (Selected Object Properties). Descriptions of the left and center panels are provided.

### Scene Objects Panel

1.    The Objects pane of the Scene Objects panel lists all objects in the scene (see 1 in Figure 12.11). In this example, it lists three: a light, a camera, and a box. However, a newly created scene will list only a camera and a light. Each object in the scene is expected to have a unique name, and selecting the object in the list will both select the same object in the world view and display a list of object-specific properties in the Object Properties panel on the right-hand side of the application window. The check mark assigned to each object in the list determines whether that object is enabled in the scene. Disabled objects are both nonvisible and do not cast shadows when illuminated by light. The Add and Remove buttons at the bottom of the Objects pane add objects to and remove objects from the scene, respectively. The next section discusses how to add an object.

2.    The Scene Objects panel also features a lower, tabbed pane (see 2 in Figure 12.11). The tabs appear at the bottom of the pane and can be used to cycle through a selection of lists. The tabs are in order from left to right: Meshes, Particles, Sounds, Environments, Fonts, Modules, and Controls. These tabs and their lists together represent a list of scene resource templates. A resource template is distinguished from a standard resource in that it can be instanced. For example, a mesh is a

**FIGURE 12.11**   Scene Objects panel. Courtesy of Chris Sterling, Worldweaver, Ltd.

resource template because, once loaded, an application can populate a scene with many instances of that mesh. An instance is not a clone, since a clone can be edited and adjusted without affecting all other clones of the same kind. Each instance, however, does affect all other instances in the sense that if the vertices of a mesh instance were adjusted, those adjustments would apply to all other instances, too. Thus, the bottom pane of the Scene Objects panel represents resource templates in the abstract, and the Objects pane above (1 in Figure 12.11) represents the specific instances of those templates in the scene. Later, when a mesh is added to the scene, it will be added first to the templates, and then based on that template an instance will be created in the scene.

> **NOTE.** Like OGRE 3D, DX Studio supports three light types: point, directional, and spot. (Review Chapter 10 for more information on these light types.)

### World View Panel

The World View panel (see Figure 12.12) in the editor is a designer view of a 3D scene insofar as it is used by developers to view, edit, and position objects in that 3D world space using the keyboard and mouse. When the document is run as an application, the scene is rendered from the view of the scene camera, and that view might differ from the view the game developer saw when designing the scene in the editor. This is because the position of the camera and the position of the editor view can and often do differ.

**▌FIGURE 12.12**   World View panel. Courtesy of Chris Sterling, Worldweaver, Ltd.

Most of the time this is not a problem since the game developer will want to view the scene from a selection of perspectives other than those allowed by the game camera. However, the developer can synchronize the editor and camera views using the Camera Settings toolbar button. Clicking this button will match the camera to the viewport settings, ensuring that the scene as it appears in the editor viewport will appear exactly the same to the user when the document is run as an application.

## 12.6.3   Adding an Object to the Scene

To summarize: The Hello World sample application developed in this tutorial will feature one layer containing a 3D scene with a textured cube at the world origin of (0,0,0). This cube will print the words "hello world" to the application window when clicked upon with the mouse. The previous steps together focused on creating a new DX Studio document and on creating a new 3D scene in that document, the scene being generated with two scene objects: a light and a camera. Having created this scene, a developer can then proceed to add the box mesh object. DX Studio supports two kinds of meshes: parametric primitives and meshes loaded from files exported in the Collada framework; that is, files exported from 3D software such as 3ds Max and Maya. The parametric primitives are simple 3D objects (boxes, spheres, cylinders, and planes) that DX Studio can generate automatically on the basis of some width and height parameters (hence, the term "parametric"). This tutorial will create a parametric box using the Mesh Generator tool. To access the Mesh Generator tool, click the Mesh Generator icon on the DX Studio toolbar, as shown in Figure 12.13. From the drop-down list that appears, select the Cube option to display a cube generator window.

The Mesh Generator tool (see Figure 12.14) is dedicated to creating parametric meshes, and the cube variant to generating cubes. It allows the user to specify the width, height, and depth of the cube in world units, and the created cube is automatically positioned at the world origin of (0,0,0). Once the mesh is generated, the scene features *two* new entities, a mesh *template* and a mesh object *instance* based on that template; only the latter exists within the coordinate space of the scene. The instance has *position*, *orientation*, and *scale*. The position of the cube can be adjusted interactively using the XYZ gizmo that appears in the world view window. Dragging the mouse along any axis will translate the cube in that direction.

**FIGURE 12.13**   Mesh Generator icon. Courtesy of Chris Sterling, Worldweaver, Ltd.

| Name | Box |
| Width | 1 |
| Height | 1 |
| Depth | 1 |

**I FIGURE 12.14**   Mesh Generator tool. Courtesy of Chris Sterling, Worldweaver, Ltd.

## ■ Object Properties

Notice then when an object (such as the box, light, or camera) is selected in the scene, a context-sensitive panel called Object Properties is shown on the right side of the editor window. The contents of this panel change depending on the current selection in the world view, always showing properties appropriate to the selection. Consider Figure 12.15. For mesh objects, editable properties include Visible, Opacity, Casts Shadows, Draw Backfaces, and Position Sound. These properties are described in more detail as follows.

### Visible

Boolean value determining the object's visibility in the scene. False refers to invisible and true to visible.

### Opacity

Scalar value from 0 to 1 describing the opaqueness of an object. 0 refers to an object that is completely transparent, and 1 to an object that is completely opaque; fractional values between these set the object to be partially transparent to that extent. Thus, 0.5 refers to an object that is half transparent and half opaque.

### Casts Shadows

Boolean value indicating whether the selected object is to cast shadows when affected by a light in the scene.

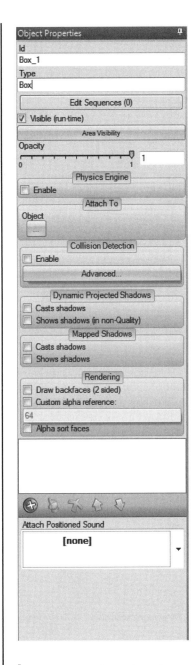

**I FIGURE 12.15**   Object Properties panel. Courtesy of Chris Sterling, Worldweaver, Ltd.

**Draw Backfaces**

Boolean value indicating whether the object is *two-sided*, and *not* whether the backfaces of an object (the faces whose normals point away from the camera) are culled.

**Position Sound**

Allows media files (such as MP3s and OGG files) to be attached to the selected object in 3D space to utilize 3D sound. Attaching a sound to an object means that a sound shares its position, scale, and orientation in 3D space. Objects with sounds attached sound louder when closer to the camera, and their volume grows fainter as the distance between camera and object are increased.

NOTE. All properties that can be changed in the editor can also be animated and changed via JavaScript at run time.

## 12.6.4    Adding a Texture Resource to the Scene

The previous section involved the creation of a parametric cube primitive at the origin of a 3D scene. The surface of the created cube, however, is colored using a standard material applied to the object by default. This material can be changed and customized to suit the needs of the game. It will be remembered that a material is a procedure that defines how the surface of a mesh will appear and specifically how it will react to light. It defines the shininess of an object (specular component), the roughness or bumpiness of an object (bump component), and the general appearance of the skin of an object when illuminated by a light (diffuse component). The diffuse component is typically the component to which people refer when they talk of the "look" or "skin" of an object. This Hello World sample application will load a texture map (a bitmap

**FIGURE 12.16**   Resources. Courtesy of Chris Sterling, Worldweaver, Ltd.

object) into the diffuse component of the material to wallpaper the loaded image over the surface of the cube mesh. To begin the texturing process, a valid image that is to act as the texture must first be loaded into the engine as a resource of the scene. The following steps describe how to add a texture resource to the scene:

Step 1.   Access the scene Resources sheet (or Resources panel. See Figure 12.16.) by clicking on the **Resources** button in the bottom left corner of the editor window. This panel displays all resources used for the current scene; each scene by default references the header.xml file as a resource (discussed later). In short, this file represents an XML definition of the contents of a scene. If the cube has been added to the scene, it will also reference a .dxmesh file; both the XML file and .dxmesh file are "embedded resources." That is, these resources will be compiled into the application executable rather than referenced externally by the application at run time.

Step 2.   To add a new texture resource as an embedded resource, click the green + button on the bottom panel. To add the texture as a linked (external) resource, right-click the mouse over the Resources sheet, and from the context menu that appears choose **Add Linked Resource**. Remember that embedded resources will be compiled into the executable, while external resources will remain external to the application and will be loaded at run time as and when required. Either route (embedded or linked resource) will lead the user to a file selection dialog from which they should choose any valid image file to be used as a texture. DX Studio supports the following image formats: PNG, BMP, JPG, TGA, DDS, TIF, GIF, and DXSprite.

---

### ■ DX Studio—Resource Types

The Resources sheet (see Figure 12.16) is the place where resources can be added, edited, and moved to and from a DX Studio scene. A resource added at the *document level* is a global resource insofar as it remains "alive" and accessible throughout the lifetime of an application, and a resource added at the *scene level* is local insofar as its lifetime and reach are restricted to the scene. DX Studio supports the following resource types:

- **Textures**

  A texture refers to any standard 2D image file that can be either mapped onto 3D geometry, such as a mesh, or drawn "as is" in 2D screen space in a 2D scene. To maximize compatibility with older video hardware, textures are often sized (in terms of width and height) in "power of 2" dimensions, e.g., 16×16, 32×32, 64×64, 128×128, 256×256, 512×512, 1024×1024, and 2048×2048.

- **Meshes**

  3D scenes in DX Studio support the importing of 3D mesh assets in a variety of established 3D formats, including 3DS and (Collada) DAE. Many 3D modeling programs can export to these formats, including 3ds Max, Maya, Blender, Softimage, and LightWave 3D.

- **Environment Maps**

  Environment maps are cubic textures often used to create backgrounds for 3D environments. An environment map is said to be a cubic texture because it consists of six unique images intended to be arranged together to form the inside faces of a cube, each image representing one face of that cube. The textured cube is then configured so as to always surround the game camera wherever it moves, ensuring the camera is always at its center. Seen from its center, the cube creates the illusion of one seamless space extending in all directions. In DX Studio, cubic environment textures are simply ZIP files containing six images and an XML file defining which image is to be associated with which cube face.

- **Audio**

  DX Studio supports the loading and playback of audio resources from files in the following formats: WAV, MP3, and OGG Vorbis. An audio file can be loaded entirely into memory and played as a *sample*, or loaded and played in chunks as a *stream*.

- **Movies**

  DX Studio also supports the loading of movie files as resources. These resources can then be used as animated textures for scene geometry; that is, movie files (including those with audio tracks) can be mapped onto 3D objects and then played as an animated texture. Supported movie formats are those compatible with the Microsoft DirectShow framework, and movie files encoded with the patent free and open source OGG Theora Codec.

- **Particle Systems**

  Particle systems are used in game development for special effects purposes to create the effect of particles in motion. Typically, particle systems are used to simulate rain, fog, dust, sandstorms, fairy dust, lightning bolts, and motion trails.

## 12.6.5   Applying a Material to the Cube Using the Material Editor

The previous section explained how to use the Resources sheet to load a standard image file into the scene as a scene-level texture resource. Doing this, however, *did not* automatically texture map the texture onto the cube mesh, since a scene could have contained many such meshes and DX Studio was not instructed as to how the texture should be used once loaded. To texture map the loaded texture onto the cube, a material must first be created and then the texture applied to the material's diffuse channel. Materials are created in the Material Editor, and this window can be accessed through the right-click context menu for the selected object in the scene. The following instructions detail how to texture an object:

Step 1.   Select the mesh to be textured (in this case, the cube). The cube can be selected either by clicking with the mouse cursor hovering over it in the world view of the scene or by selecting the object by name from the scene objects list in the leftmost panel.

Step 2.   With the cube selected, right-click the mouse to show a properties context menu for the selected object. From this menu, select **Edit Materials**. This displays the Material Editor through which materials are built and applied to objects. More information on the Material Editor can be found in the Material Editor sidebar that follows these steps.

Step 3.   In the Material Editor, ensure **Default** is selected in the Materials list box. For this material, set both the Diffuse and Ambient colors to white: RGB (1,1,1). Then click the **Default Maps** tab.

Step 4.   The maps tab lists all textures assigned to the map channels of the selected material. The map channels for a material are: Texture Map, Opacity Map, Bump Map/Normal Map, Specular Map, and Emissive Map. The topmost item (Texture Map) defines the color (or appearance) of the surface of an object; other maps define both how that surface responds to light and the roughness of the surface. To texture map the cube using the loaded texture resource, that resource must be assigned to the texture map channel of the selected material. At present, the Texture Map box reads "none" to indicate that no texture resource is currently applied to this channel, and clicking on the drop-down arrow for this list will show nothing. To find the loaded texture resource, the user must first specify the scope in which the resource resides. Scene level resources reside in scene scope, and thus the user must select the option **Scene** in the drop-down box in the Texture Map area (next to the Add Resource button). Once the scope filter is set, the texture resource can be selected in the Texture Map drop-down box. Select this item and click the **Apply** button to apply the texture map to the cube. The cube surface should update in the editor world view.

## ■ Material Editor

A material defines through textures and other properties how the surface of an object both responds to light and appears to the camera where illuminated. The Material Editor features a selection of pages to build, edit, and apply materials to selected objects in 3D scenes. The Material Editor allows developers to define textures and mapping coordinates, to set the shininess and bumpiness of an object, and to determine the opacity of an object. The tabs of the Material Editor are Basic, Default Maps, Multitexture, Light, Surface Detail, and Effects; this book only considers the Basic and Default Maps tabs. Figures 12.17 and 12.18 illustrate these two tabs.

1. The Material Editor can be used to create, edit, and delete one or more materials from the selected object. The top left box represents a preview

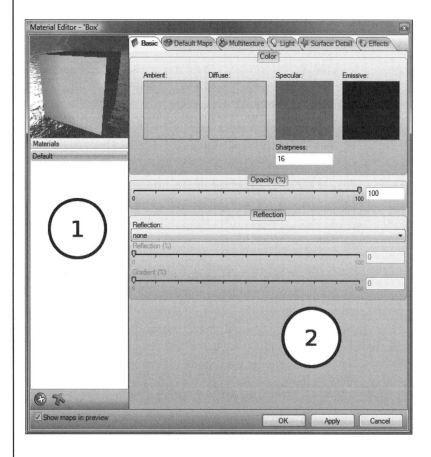

**FIGURE 12.17**    Material Editor Basic tab. Courtesy of Chris Sterling, Worldweaver, Ltd.

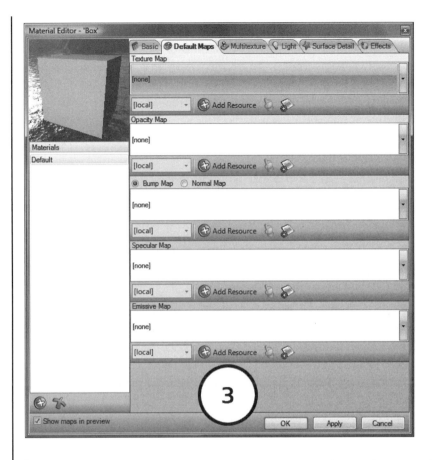

**FIGURE 12.18** Material Editor Default Maps tab. Courtesy of Chris Sterling, Worldweaver, Ltd.

of the selected material, and the Materials list below constitutes the list of materials applied to the selected object. Materials can be added using the green **Add** button and removed using the orange **Delete** button. By default, only the topmost material in the list (the default material) is applied to all the faces of an object. However, objects can be edited in script (as we shall see) so that different materials can be applied to different faces if required.

2. The Color, Opacity, and Reflection panels of the Material Editor are the main factors (along with maps) that influence how the material appears when applied to the surface of an object. The Ambient color determines the color of the object when in areas of shadow, and the Diffuse color is used to tint or shade an object a specific color and is *combined* with (not overridden by) any maps in the map channels such as texture maps and specular maps. The Specular color determines the color of shiny highlights on the

material, and the Emissive color adds self-illumination to an object; that is, artificially adds a glow to the object regardless of the lighting in the scene. The Opacity value determines the opacity of the material and is different from the Opacity setting examined earlier in the Object Properties panel. The Opacity setting specified in the Object Properties panel determines the visibility of an object regardless of its material properties, while the Material Editor Opacity setting sets the opacity of an object only for as long as that material is applied to it.

3. The Default Maps tab is used for assigning texture map resources to the map channels of a material, and a material has several map channels. However, none of them are obligatory insofar as the Diffuse, Ambient, Specular, and Emissive colors will be substituted in bold wherever there is an associated map missing. The available map channels for a material are as follows:

**Texture Map**

The *texture map* is typically understood to be the main color or look of an object, because it specifies the texture that is to be directly wallpapered over the surface of a mesh according to the mesh mapping coordinates. For example, a photo of bricks might be assigned to the Texture Map channel so as to be wallpapered onto a mesh intended to be a brick wall. For this reason, the Texture Map channel is generally the most significant map of a material.

**Opacity Map**

The Opacity Map channel relies on a grayscale image that is mapped to the mesh to determine the extent to which areas of the mesh are transparent. Unlike the Opacity setting, which applies a uniform transparency across the entire mesh, the opacity map uses the pixels of a map and its shades between white (fully visible) and black (fully transparent) to determine which regions of the mesh should be transparent, visible, or semitransparent. Applying a completely black texture to the Opacity Map channel of a material will turn the whole of an object invisible (Opacity = 0), and applying a completely white image will conversely turn the whole of an object visible (Opacity = 1). However, the opacity map is generally not useful when it features pixels of a uniform color, since the Opacity setting is more suitable for setting uniform opacity. Instead, the opacity map is often used for effects.

**Bump Map**

The Bump Map channel expects to receive a grayscale image whose pixels define the *bumpiness* (or roughness) of the material. Regions of the image that are white appear to be raised or protruding, and regions that are black appear to be depressed or recessed.

**Specular Map**

Like both the Opacity Map and Bump Map channels, the Specular Map channel relies on a grayscale image. The pixels of this image determine the shininess and dullness of the material when illuminated by a light source in the scene. White pixels define the shiniest regions, and black regions will not shine at all regardless of the intensity of the light.

**Emissive Map**

The emissive map refers to a texture whose color values define which regions of the material are to appear illuminated regardless of the lighting conditions in the scene, even when no light is shining upon the object. This channel is therefore especially useful for texturing meshes intended to represent light sources, since light sources remain bright and almost unshaded for as long as the light is on; these sources include light bulbs, the sun, car headlights, and candles.

## 12.6.6   Scripting the Cube for Hello World

The Hello World sample created thus far features a 3D scene with a textured cube sitting at the world origin position, but it does not and will not at present print the words "hello world" to the application window when the cube is clicked upon using the mouse. To do this, the developer must script this behavior; that is, must code that functionality using the integrated JavaScript language. The following steps explain how to code this behavior:

Step 1.   Select the cube object in the world view, and right-click mouse to view the object properties context menu. From this menu, select **Edit Script**. The JavaScript scripting window appears.

Step 2.   The JavaScript window features three main panels: the code editor, the events view, and the document tree. More information on the scripting window is provided in the following side box. Double-click the **OnMouseUp** event to create a new OnMouseUp function in the code editor. In the body of this function in the code editor, enter the following code:

```
print("hello world");
```

**NOTE.** This code will print the words "hello world" to the application window when the application is run and the box is clicked upon using the mouse. See Figure 12.19.

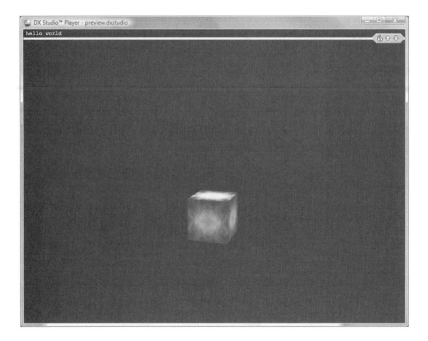

**I FIGURE 12.19**    Sample application. Courtesy of Chris Sterling, Worldweaver, Ltd.

## ■ The JavaScript Scripting Window

The JavaScript scripting window is used for creating and editing JavaScript scripts that customize the behavior of DX Studio scenes at run time, for both 2D and 3D scenes. JavaScript is integrated into the engine and editor and thus all engine coding occurs through the scripting window; developers do not need to use additional coding tools such as Visual Studio or Code::Blocks. The scripting window is shown in Figure 12.20 and more details follow:

1. The Code Editor is where scripters and programmers will spend most of their time, implementing and editing functions and classes in the JavaScript language. Developers can both create their own custom functions and implement a set of DX Studio recognized events, such as mouse clicks and keyboard presses, to handle these events as they occur at run time.

2. The Events window lists all available events for the selected object, whether that object is a scene, a scene object, or another object. Events refer to a set of recognized functions that developers can implement with custom, application-specific behavior. DX Studio then calls these functions as appropriate events

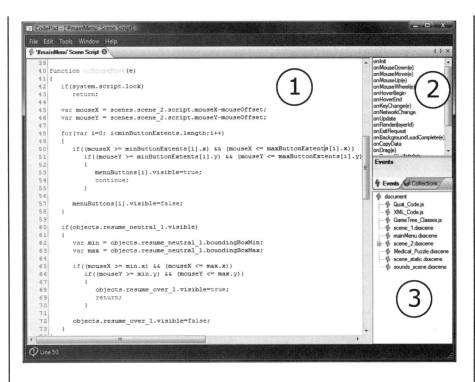

**FIGURE 12.20**   JavaScript scripting window. Courtesy of Chris Sterling, Worldweaver, Ltd.

occur at run time. Thus, it calls mouse down events when users, press the mouse button, and keyboard change events when users press or release keys on the keyboard. By implementing these functions with custom behavior, developers handle application events according to the needs of their application. To handle any available event, double-click an event from the event list and DX Studio generates a function skeleton in the Code Editor, ready for implementation in the JavaScript language.

3. The document tree lists all JavaScript documents belonging to the current DX Studio document, and a developer views a document by double-clicking on it in the document tree view. Doing so will change the Code Editor panel to display the contents of the selected document. Each JavaScript document has its own scope in terms of programmatic scope (or variable scope). Furthermore, a script can be attached to three types of document elements or levels: the document, scenes, and scene objects. A document script handles application-level events such as application start and end events. A script attached to a scene handles scene-level events such as scene creation, frame loop code, and scene end events. Object-level scripts work at an object level

such as editing mesh vertex data and handling object creation and destruction events as well as mouse clicks and keyboard button presses. There is one script file for the document script, one script file for each scene, and one script file for each scene object. It has been mentioned that the script scoping rules apply on a per script file basis, and thus each variable exists within the scope of that file. The scoping rules work as follows:

- Variables declared inside functions or code segments, such as loops, have local and block scope, respectively; that is, such variables are valid only within that scope.

- Variables declared outside any function within a single JavaScript document have global scope for that document.

**NOTE**. The functions of one document can access and reference the variables and functions of another. A later section in this chapter demonstrates how to do this.

## 12.6.7    Testing and Compiling the Application

The Hello World sample application is now completed and ready for testing. Once tested, a developer can proceed to compile the document into a standalone executable that can be run on any computer with the DX Studio Player installed. The following steps detail how to test and compile a DX Studio document:

Step 1.  To debug (or test) the document directly from the editor, click the **Play** button on the DX Studio toolbar, or click **Tools | Preview** from the application menu, or press the **F12** keyboard shortcut on the keyboard. Doing this will launch the application in a separate window for testing. This option, however, does not compile the application into a standalone executable; rather, it allows the developer to test the application as though it were a compiled execution running independently.

Step 2.  To build an EXE file from the DX Studio document, select **Tools | Build EXE** from the application main menu. This displays the Build EXE window in which developers can specify build options for compiling the project into an executable; options include setting the EXE icon and the bitmap splash screen presented to the window as the application loads at startup (see Figure 12.21). To complete the build process, specify a destination path where the EXE file will be generated and click the **Build** button.

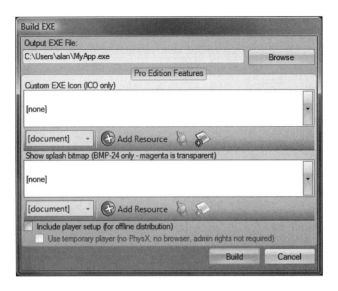

**| FIGURE 12.21**   Build EXE window. Courtesy of Chris Sterling, Worldweaver, Ltd.

## ■ 12.7   Moving Further with the DX Studio Editor

Building the Hello World sample application in the previous sections of this chapter has demonstrated both a variety of DX Studio features and the speed and ease with which an application was built in comparison to the long-winded hard coding methods found in previous chapters. Using a GUI editor and scripting window, a developer could drop a box into a 3D scene, apply a material and texture with the mouse, script an onMouseUp event, and click a build button. This is not to suggest, however, that there is any problem with the previous technologies, but only that productivity with them will be *increased* when a developer produces their own editor tools to complement them. This chapter should already have demonstrated what is possible using editor tools, and this section goes on to demonstrate what else can be implemented into an engine editor. Specifically, this section will consider the scene XML file and the XML editing tools, the animation sequence editor, document preferences and scene properties, and finally camera properties.

### 12.7.1   Scene XML and the XML Editor Window

The term "scene" in DX Studio corresponds exactly to the concept of a scene used throughout the rest of this book. A scene refers to a single coordinate space in which scene objects exist in relation to each other, each object having a position measured relative to the origin of that space, as well as a rotation and scaling value. Rotation measures the amount of turn in either degrees or radians from its starting orientation, and scale measures the amount of stretching or shrinking applied to the object relative to its starting scale (which is 1). Thus, a DX Studio document refers to a single application, and a document can contain one or more scenes, where each scene refers to a coordinate space containing none, one, or more scene objects. In addition to being a coordinate space, however, readers will remember that relationships between objects in the scene are expressed via a hierarchical scene graph, featuring a parent node at the top of the graph from which all other nodes descend. Transformations applied to one node will cascade downward through the tree until the bottommost node of the affected branches has been reached. In DX Studio, the scene graph is expressed in XML form in a scene-level resource file named "header.xml"; as users interactively add objects to and remove objects from the scene, DX Studio edits the XML file under the hood and on-the-fly to reflect the changes being made in the editor. For this reason, most users will not need to edit the scene XML file manually, but it can be a useful diagnostic tool for listing and parsing the contents and properties of a scene. Consider the sample XML scene file presented here, with comments afterward.

> **NOTE.** With a scene active in the editor, XML scene files can be viewed in one of two ways: (1) From the main menu, select **Tools | Edit XML Source**, or (2) in the Resources sheet, double-click the header.xml file in the resource list. The header.xml file is embedded and not an external scene-level resource, meaning that it will be compiled into the DX Studio application when the document is built. Developers will not need to distribute the XML file along with the application executable.

```
<?xml version="1.0" encoding="utf-8" standalone="yes"?>
<dxscene version="3.2.10" type="3d" width="800"
height="600" defaultscriptlanguage="javascript"
fwdzneg="yes" autoaspect="yes">
  <physics>
    <prop id="engine" type="string" value="physx" />
  </physics>
  <ambientlight r="90" g="90" b="90" />
  <object type="camera" id="camera_1">
    <init>
      <prop id="pos" type="vector" x="2.5" y="2.5" z="-8"
/>
      <prop id="rot" type="quaternion" x="0.08878729"
y="-0.1502539" z="0.0135499" w="0.9845592" />
      <prop id="ui.mouseLook" type="bool" state="yes" />
      <prop id="ui.keyboardMove" type="bool" state="yes"
/>
      <prop id="ui.keyboardMoveSpeed" type="float"
```

```
      value="10.0" />
        </init>
      </object>
      <object id="light_1" type="light">
        <init>
          <prop id="pos" type="vector" x="-1.5" y="3.0"
    z="-0.5" />
          <prop id="rot" type="quaternion" x="0.3662051"
    y="-0.268188" z="0.1110871" w="0.8840977" />
          <prop id="light.type" type="string" value="point"
    />
          <prop id="light.range" type="float" value="50" />
          <prop id="light.attenuation0" type="float"
    value="0" />
          <prop id="light.attenuation1" type="float"
    value="1" />
          <prop id="light.attenuation2" type="float"
    value="0" />
          <prop id="light.theta" type="float" value="30" />
          <prop id="light.phi" type="float" value="45" />
          <prop id="light.falloff" type="float" value="1" />
        </init>
      </object>
    </dxscene>
```

## Comments

- The document begins with the root scene node—dxscene. This node features two child scene nodes, each scene node being of type <object>. Thus, each <object> XML tag represents a unique object in the scene. In this case, the two scene objects are a camera and a light.

- For each object in the scene, the file contains a series of "prop" (property) tags. Each prop tag describes a unique property of the object. Each object has more properties than is defined in the XML here, but default values are applied to nonspecified properties. Notice how the camera object features tags for "pos" (position) and "rot" (rotation), the former specified as a 3D vector and the latter as a quaternion. Notice also how the light object features properties for attenuation, range, falloff, and type. (See Chapter 10 for more information on light properties).

  NOTE. DX Studio offers classes and functions for processing XML files, both the scene XML file and other external XML files. Thus, developers can add custom tags and information to the scene XML file. The following sidebar demonstrates a sample function in JavaScript for opening and parsing an XML file in DX Studio.

### ■ DX Studio—Parsing XML Files in JavaScript

DX Studio depends on XML files for storing and reading much of its game data. XML files are used for recording scene information, environment maps, particle systems, and more. Furthermore, it is also likely that developers will be eager to utilize the XML standard for storing and retrieving their own custom data as well as retrieving data stored by DX Studio. For this reason it is useful to be familiar with the DX Studio XML parsing classes, available in JavaScript. The following code sample features a function intended to parse a scene XML file:

```javascript
//Function for parsing a scene file

function loadFromXML(XMLFilename)
{
    var doc = system.xml.loadDocument(XMLFilename);
    var rootNode=doc.selectSingle("dxscene");

    if(rootNode != null)
    {
        //Cycle through objects
        var camerasNode=rootNode.
selectSingle("object");
        var childNode = camerasNode.firstChild;

        //Loop through child nodes
        while (childNode != null)
        {
            print(childNode.name);

            //Call recursive function here to
cycle through child nodes
        }
        childNode = null;
        camerasNode = null;
        rootNode = null;
    }

    doc= null;
}
```

## 12.7.2   Creating Animations via the Sequence Editor

The term "sequence" is used to describe a standard keyframe animation in DX Studio, and such animations are a sequence of nondeformable transformations smoothly applied to scene objects across a series of frames. Each key frame in the animation represents a crucial point of change, and as the animation is played back, DX Studio will interpolate between key frames to produce continuous motion. The term "nonde-formable" is used here to emphasize that the transformation applied to objects consists of the translation, rotation, and scaling of the complete object and not of its parts. The whole of a human body mesh, for example, can be rotated, moved. and scaled in 3D space, but not its arm in isolation unless the arm is a separate mesh distinct from the rest of the body mesh. Almost every numerical and boolean property of any number of scene objects can be animated in a single sequence, and furthermore scripted functions can be executed on each key frame of the sequence as they occur during playback. Sequences are created in DX Studio using the Edit Sequences window. This window can be accessed as follows: Select a scene object to be animated, and right-click the object using the mouse button. From the context menu, select Edit Sequences. The Edit Sequences window, shown in Figure 12.22, will appear.

1. Creating a new sequence begins by clicking the Add button. Users can then edit the name of the created sequence using the Rename button, and delete a sequence using the Delete button. The Duration box is used to specify the total duration of the animation in seconds. Auto Play is a boolean value determining whether the

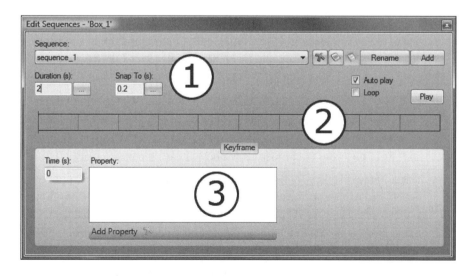

**I FIGURE 12.22**   Edit Sequences window. Courtesy of Chris Sterling, Worldweaver, Ltd.

animation should play automatically when the application is run, and Loop is a boolean determining whether the animation should loop indefinitely, repeating again and again.

2. The time line bar is a graphical representation of the key frame points across the duration of the animation, with playback beginning on the left side and moving linearly toward the right. Each vertical notch along the track refers to a key frame in the sequence, and any single key frame in the sequence can be selected using the mouse. The keyframe editing controls are shown in Figure 12.24.

3. The keyframe editing controls are used for editing the selected key frame in the time line bar above. Editing a key frame involves creating, editing, and removing the properties and values to be set for that frame. Users edit properties on key frames by clicking the Add Property button. A window appears in which users can select the properties to edit on that frame. Once properties are added, the Edit Sequences window presents editing controls for specifying the values of the added properties. See Figures 12.23 and 12.24.

---

### ■ Tutorial—Creating an Animation Sequence

This tutorial will extend upon the Hello World sample created earlier to animate the position of the box in 3D space over time using a sequence. It will also configure the sequence to call a scripted function on completion that will print an "Animation Completed" message to the window. The following instructions detail how to do this, resuming where the Hello World sample ended:

Step 1.   Select the box in the world view of the editor and right-click to show the object properties context menu. From this menu, select **Edit Sequences**.

Step 2.   In the Edit Sequences window, click the **Add** button to create a new sequence. Rename this sequence "Box Move Seq." Set the Duration to **4**.

Step 3.   Select the first key frame in the sequence to specify the starting position values for the box in the scene. To do this, click the **Add Property** button and select **pos** from the properties window. Leave the position at (0,0,0).

Step 4.   Select the middle key frame in the sequence and click the **Add Property** button. From the properties window, select **pos** again and set the X position to **20** so that during playback the box will be at X Pos 20 on the middle key frame. For the Tween In interpolation method, select **Linear** to ensure DX Studio interpolates smoothly between the first and middle key frames.

Step 5.   The final key frame will be the same as the first to ensure the box returns to its starting position when the animation completes playback.

**I FIGURE 12.23**   Adding keyframe properties. Courtesy of Chris Sterling, Worldweaver, Ltd.

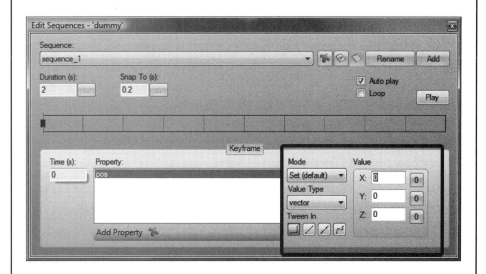

**I FIGURE 12.24**   Keyframe editing controls. Courtesy of Chris Sterling, Worldweaver, Ltd.

To set the final frame, a developer could repeat for the last frame the steps used to create the first. However, there is an alternative method that involves copying and pasting key frames. Select the first key frame in the sequence time line and right-click the mouse. In the menu that appears, select **Copy Key Frame**. Select the last key frame in the time line sequence and right-click the mouse. Select **Paste Key Frame** and ensure the Tween In method for the final frame is set to **Linear** to ensure a smooth method of interpolation between the middle and final key frames of the animation.

Step 6.   In addition to specifying a position value for the final frame of the animation, it is also necessary to call a JavaScript function to print a message to the window when playback of the animation completes. To do that, right-click the last key frame in the time line sequence and select **Edit Script at this Time**. The scripting window appears (see Figure 12.25). From the Events list in the scripting window, double-click the **onShow** event. This event will be called when the final key-frame frame is reached during playback. Inside the body of this event, insert the following code to print a message to the window:

```
print("Animation completed");
```

Step 7.   To test this work, close the Edit Sequences window and click the **Preview** button in the DX Studio toolbar. See Figure 12.26.

**| FIGURE 12.25**    Animation scripting. Courtesy of Chris Sterling, Worldweaver, Ltd.

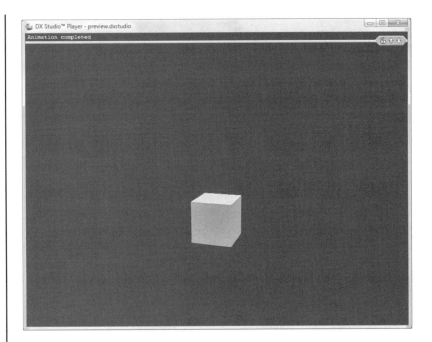

**I FIGURE 12.26**   Animation application. Courtesy of Chris Sterling, Worldweaver, Ltd.

## Document Preferences

It was stated earlier that the term "document" is used by DX Studio to refer to the project or application as a whole. The document Properties window therefore specifies how the document is to run, or more accurately, how the document is to be presented to the gamer by the DX Studio Player at run time. Using the document properties window, a developer can specify the resolution of the document, whether it should run full-screen or in windowed mode, whether the FPS rate should be capped at a maximum, and more. The document Properties window can be accessed via many routes, the most common perhaps being via the DX Studio application menu item Tools | Preferences. This window is shown in Figure 12.27.

The document Properties window shows properties for several elements in the document. It shows one general set of properties that relate to editor preferences and the rest for run-time preferences: one for the document, and one for each scene in the document. Using document properties, a developer can specify the following:

- **Min and Max Version**

  The min and max version settings determine the minimum and maximum version numbers of the player with which the document is compatible. Running the document on the end user system therefore requires that a player

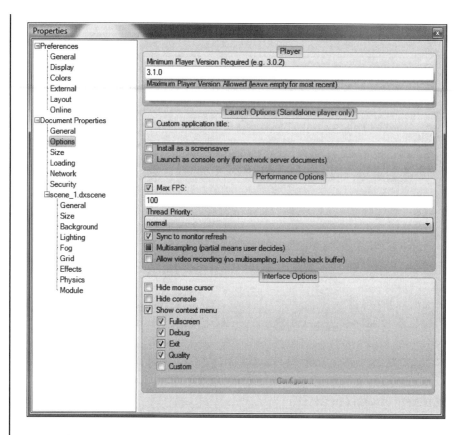

**I FIGURE 12.27**    Document properties and preferences. Courtesy of Chris Sterling,
Worldweaver, Ltd.

version between and inclusive of the min and max versions is installed on
the computer. By default, DX Studio sets the minimum value to the version
of the player used at the time the document was created, and leaves the
maximum value blank to indicate that all subsequent versions are supported.

- **Application Title**

  The application title refers to the text that will appear in the application
  button on the Windows start bar when the application is run, and also the
  text in the windows title bar if the application is run in windowed mode.
  If left blank, DX Studio will use its own default text.

- **Max FPS**

  The maximum FPS (frames per second) setting can be used to cap the total
  number of frames per second allowed by a DX Studio application when run.

- **Hide Mouse Cursor**

  Boolean value indicating whether the mouse cursor should be visible when the application is run. True shows the cursor, and false hides the cursor.

- **Hide Console**

  The console refers to the region at the top of the window in which debug messages are printed by the JavaScript print statement. By default the console is enabled for debug use but can be disabled for final release versions of an application.

- **Fullscreen**

  Boolean indicating whether the application should be run in full-screen mode. If true, the application runs full screen; if false, the application runs in windowed mode. An application can be toggled between full-screen and windowed modes at run time with a call to the following JavaScript method:

  ```
  system.fullScreenToggle();
  ```

- **Debug**

  Boolean value indicating whether the interactive debugger should be enabled or disabled. The interactive debugger allows users to view the value of JavaScript objects and to run JavaScript statements while an application is running. More information on the interactive debugger is given later. Most release applications will have this setting disabled since it is used mainly for debugging purposes.

### 12.7.3    Camera Properties

Each and every 3D scene in a DX Studio document has one or more cameras, and the camera represents the vantage point from which the scene will be rendered when shown at run time. In DX Studio, a camera is recognized as an object in the scene; thus, it has a position and orientation within the 3D coordinate space of the scene (scaling a camera has no effect). When a camera is selected in the scene, its properties are shown in the Object Properties pane at the right side of the window. Camera objects feature a set of properties specific to cameras. Consider Figure 12.28. These properties are explained as follows:

- **Allow Mouse Look**

  Boolean value indicating whether the pitch and yaw of the camera should be locked to the movement of the mouse when the right mouse button is pressed.

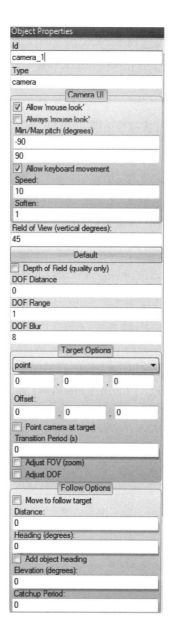

**| FIGURE 12.28**    Camera settings. Courtesy of Chris Sterling, Worldweaver, Ltd.

Rotations in 3D space can be described in terms of pitch, yaw, and roll. Rotation about the X axis is termed pitch, about the Y axis is yaw, and about the Z axis is roll. If true, the camera pitch and yaw will be locked to the mouse movement when the rightmost mouse button is pressed. Sliding the mouse either left or right rotates the yaw, and up and down rotates the pitch.

- **Always Mouse Look**

  Boolean value that works in collaboration with Allow Mouse Look. When both settings are true, the camera pitch and yaw is locked to mouse movement regardless of mouse button presses.

- **Allow Keyboard Movement**

  Boolean value that specifies whether the camera is translated using the arrow keys on the keyboard. Up and down move the camera forward and backward, respectively, and left and right strafe the camera from side to side along its local X axis.

- **Speed**

  Integer value that determines the speed at which the camera moves when translated by pressing the arrow keys on the keyboard. This option works in collaboration with Allow Keyboard Movement.

- **Soften**

  Integer value that works in collaboration with both Allow Keyboard Movement and Speed, and specifies the rate at which the camera decelerates when the keyboard arrow keys are released.

- **Target**

  Specifies the look at target of the camera and can be left blank when no look at target is required, or can indicate either a specified position in 3D space or a specified object in the scene to act as the target. When the target is set, the camera will always turn to face the target position wherever it is moved in the scene.

- **Move To Follow Target**

  Applies only if the camera has a target. This option specifies whether the camera should follow the target object as and when the object moves, maintaining the same relative distance from the target.

## ■  12.8   Coding Tips and Tricks

Thus far this chapter has considered how to create a sample application featuring a 3D scene with a textured and animated cube. It also explored more of the nuances of DX Studio in detailing the XML structure of scenes, the properties of cameras—such as position, field of view, and targets—and also the properties of DX Studio documents—such as resolution and cursor visibility. This section examines further the possibilities and benefits scripting brings to a game engine by detailing some JavaScript tips and tricks as it pertains to DX Studio. It considers: (1) how to create a mesh object that accepts multiple textures; (2) how to create JavaScript function libraries in external files that can be referenced by DX Studio applications; (3) how to execute strings as JavaScript commands at run time; (4) how to use the System object to control the execution and properties of an application at run time; (5) how to call a function from an external DLL file (see Chapter 2 for more information on creating DLLs); and (6) how to use the integrated run-time debugger to trace and correct errors in DX Studio documents.

## 12.8.1    Meshes with Multiple Textures

Section 12.6.5 demonstrated how to use the Material Editor to apply a texture to the diffuse channel of a material and then to apply that material to a cube in the 3D scene. Applying a material to a cube in this way ensures that the surface of the cube is mapped with the default material in the Material Editor, though each face of the cube is mapped with the same material. This section uses both the Material Editor and a JavaScript function to apply different materials to each unique face of the cube; thus a total of six textures are needed, one for each face. The following step-by-step guide details how to do this:

Step 1.  Create a total of six textures, one for each face, and load them into the DX Studio Editor as linked resources. To do that, access the Resources sheet via the **Resources** button at the bottom left of the editor window. Right-click on the Resources sheet and from the context menu, select **Add Resource Link**. Select the six textures to add.

Step 2.  Once six textures have been added to the scene, a material for each texture should be created. Select the cube mesh in the scene and right-click to access the Object Properties context menu. From this menu, select **Edit Materials** to display the Material Editor.

Step 3.  Remove *all* materials in the Material list box, including the default material. Then use the **Add** button to create a total of six materials, one for each face of the cube. Name each material appropriately ("left," "back," front," "right," "up," and "down").

Step 4.  For each material, set the Ambient and Diffuse color components to white. Then use the Default Maps tab to add a unique texture to the texture map channel for all six materials. Thus, each material should have an ambient and diffuse color of white and a unique texture map. Click the **Apply** button and then **OK** to exit the Material Editor. The cube in the World View editor might show all faces to be mapped with the same material. This is fine.

Step 5.  It is now time to script a JavaScript function inside the object onInit event of the cube mesh to programmatically assign a unique material to each face of the cube. The onInit event is called once as the object is created and added to the scene, when the scene is first shown at run time. To add this code, open the JavaScript code window by right-clicking the cube mesh in the scene, and from the context menu select **Edit Script**. This displays the JavaScript scripting window. From here, double-click the onInit event handler in the Events list. This function should be implemented as in the following code section. Once implemented, run the application; each cube face should feature a unique texture.

```
function onInit()
{
var faceArray = objects.cube.subgroups.Root.
faceGetArray();
faceArray[0].materialIndex=1;
faceArray[1].materialIndex=1;
faceArray[2].materialIndex=2;
faceArray[3].materialIndex=2;
faceArray[4].materialIndex=3;
faceArray[5].materialIndex=3;
faceArray[6].materialIndex=4;
faceArray[7].materialIndex=4;
faceArray[8].materialIndex=5;
faceArray[9].materialIndex=5;
faceArray[10].materialIndex=6;
faceArray[11].materialIndex=6;

objects.cube.subgroups.Root.faceSetArray(faceArray);

objects.cube.subgroups.Root.setMaterialMap(1, "front");
objects.cube.subgroups.Root.setMaterialMap(2, "left");
objects.cube.subgroups.Root.setMaterialMap(3, "right");
objects.cube.subgroups.Root.setMaterialMap(4, "back");
objects.cube.subgroups.Root.setMaterialMap(5, "up");
objects.cube.subgroups.Root.setMaterialMap(6, "down");
}
```

**Comments**

- The onInit function of the cube mesh is called once as the object is created when the scene begins. This function starts by retrieving a pointer to the array of mesh faces, faceArray. This array lists all triangular faces of the cube mesh, two triangles per square face. Thus, there are a total of 12 faces in the array since a cube has 6 square sides.

- For each unique side of the cube, a unique material ID is assigned, ranging from 1 to 6. These materials can be any numbers the developer chooses, but each side of the cube must have a unique number. All faces with the same number will be mapped with the same texture.

- Once each polygon (side) of the cube is assigned a unique material ID, a material map should be created. The purpose of the material map is to create an association between a material ID (as given to each unique cube side) and a named material in the Material Editor. The map associates a named material with an ID, and this association is used by DX Studio to determine the appropriate material to assign to any given face in the cube.

## 12.8.2    Scripting JavaScript Libraries and Including External Files

As DX Studio projects grow in both size and complexity, developers will likely seek to divide their code into classes and methods and will further want to separate those classes and methods into specific files based on their relationship to one another. For example, a developer might place file I/O functions in one file and XML parsing routines in another. Until now this chapter has considered only the creation and editing of JavaScript functions within the files DX Studio generates for the document, scenes, and objects, but developers can also create their own JavaScript files filled with reusable classed and functions, just as a C++ programmer can create their own headers and libraries. The following instructions detail how to do this:

Step 1.    Open the JavaScript code editor by accessing the DX Studio main menu and selecting **Edit | Edit Scene Script**.

Step 2.    In the document tree pane, create a new file by right-clicking to display a context menu. From this menu, select **Add Include File | New**. Assign the file a name and click **OK**. This creates a new JavaScript file and adds it to the project. The new file now appears in the document tree pane.

Step 3.    For testing purposes, create the following function in the new file:

```
function sayHello()
{
        print("hello");
}
```

Step 4.    To reference this file and to call its function from other JavaScript files and functions, it must be "included" in the calling file as a header. To do this, the following directive must be included at the top of the calling file. This statement equates to the C++ #include preprocessor directive:

```
//@"MyFile.js" - XML code
```

**NOTE.** The text "MyFile.js" should be replaced by the appropriate name of the file to include.

### 12.8.3   Dynamic Scripting—Executing Statements at Run Time

Thus far JavaScript as a scripting language has been used in more or less the same way as one would use C++ as a compiled language in that code is created and entered into the script editor prior to execution of the application. One of the benefits of using an interpreted scripting language such as JavaScript, however, is the ability to parse and execute string objects on-the-fly as though they were JavaScript statements written in the code editor. This means that an application can accept a JavaScript statement as a string and then execute that string immediately. This process is referred to as *dynamic scripting* because by using it the engine can be fed new classes, statements, and functions on-the-fly through string objects. The following code sample demonstrates a function that defines a JavaScript statement in a string and then proceeds to execute that string using the eval function:

```
var MyString = "function sayHello() {print(\"hello\");}
sayHello();";

//Execute string here
eval(MyString);
```

### 12.8.4   Working with the System Object

Almost every aspect of a DX Studio application can be customized and controlled through scripting. DX Studio exposes its function set and properties through a series of classes and functions that are instantiated automatically by DX Studio and can be called and accessed from JavaScript statements to program a DX Studio document. DX Studio encapsulates each element of a document into a unique class with its own appropriate properties, methods, and events. The Scene class encapsulates a scene, and a document features as many instances of this class as there are scenes in the editor. The Scene class features properties and methods for editing and controlling scenes at run time, including methods such as soundAdd for adding scene-level sound resources and meshAdd for adding scene-level mesh resources. Furthermore, the objects of a scene—such as cameras, meshes, and boxes—can also be accessed as *properties* of the Scene class, where the name of the property corresponds to the name of the object. Thus, the following code controls the visibility of the box mesh from the sample Hello World application:

```
//Hides box object
scenes.scene_1.box.visible=false;
```

The System object is another of the core DX Studio objects and encapsulates both the document overall and the window in which it runs. Using the System object, programmers can control the document at run time, terminating the application, toggling the screen mode, restarting the document, and even dynamically adding and removing scenes. This section now considers the System object in further detail by focusing on its core feature set and listing some of its most important functions and properties, providing examples of usage where appropriate.

> **NOTE**. The following class declaration for the System class is given as though it were a C++ class, but the intention is to demonstrate only the member properties and methods belonging to this class, as well as their arguments and return values.

```
class system
{
public:
//properties
//background color of document (default: black)
Color backgroundCol;

//True means the console panel will be hidden
bool consoleHide;

//True allows user to exit application with Esc keypress.
Default: True.
bool ExitWithEscape;

//Integer value indicating the current frame rate (frames
per second: FPS).
int fps;

//Indicates whether application is running in full-screen
mode
bool fullScreenMode;

//Specifies an interval on which JavaScript garbage
collection
//will be performed. Garbage collection refers to the
releasing of
//redundant objects in memory
int garbageCollectPeriod;

//Boolean indicating whether the application window has
input focus.
Bool hasFocus;

//Indicates the maximum FPS, if a maximum is set.
```

```
int maxFPS;

//Script object that provides access to global variables
in the document.
Script* Script;

//Number of milliseconds that have elapsed since the
application started
float ticks;

//Number of milliseconds that have elapsed since the last
frame
float timerDelta;

//Version number of the current player
int version;

//Pointer to a window object representing the application
window
Window* window;

//methods
int callDLL(string Filename, string Functionname);
void consoleClear();
bool downloadFile(string URL, string Dest);
void exit();
void fullScreenToggle();
void garbageCollect();
string generateGUID();
layer* layerGetArray();
void restart();
bool saveScreenCapture(string Filename, string Format,
string postPrefix);
bool sceneAdd(string SceneID, string Filename, bool
inBackground);
scene* sceneGetArray();
void sceneReload(string SceneID);
bool sceneRemove(string SceneID);
};
```

### Common Tasks with the System Object

Tasks that can be performed with the System object include accessing global variables, calling functions from DLLS, adding and removing scenes at run time, and saving screenshots, all of which are now discussed in detail.

**Accessing Global Variables**

It has been mentioned that each script file contains the variables and functions inside in the sense that neither its variables nor its functions can be accessed from another script. It is, however, likely that an application will want to create global variables; that is, variables that can be accessed and edited in any script file throughout an application. Such variables should be declared outside the scope of any function and within the document-level script file. These variables can then be accessed via the System object. The following code demonstrates the convention for declaring and accessing global variables using the script property of the System object:

```
//Document script file
//----------------------------------------------
var myVariable = "hello";
//----------------------------------------------


//Other script file
//----------------------------------------------
//print global variable

print(system.script.myVariable);
//----------------------------------------------
```

**Calling Functions from DLLs**

Chapter 2 demonstrated how to create dynamic link library files (DLLs) using both Code::Blocks and Visual C++. DLL files are similar to executables insofar as they are both compiled and contain functions and variables. But executables are distinguished from DLLs by their ability to run on a standalone basis. DLLs in contrast remain inanimate until a calling process, such as an EXE, initiates them. The DX Studio System object offers the callDLL method to invoke a specified function of a DLL. The following code demonstrates how to do this for a sample DLL featuring a PrintMessage function. This function accepts one string argument that is to be printed in a pop-up message box:

```
system.script.callDLL("MyLibrary.dll", "PrintMessage",
"MyMessage");
```

NOTE. The argument list for the callDLL function takes the form of:

```
<DLL Path>, <Function Name>, <Parameter List...>.
```

**Adding and Removing Scenes at Run Time**

A DX Studio scene refers to a unified coordinate space, either 2D or 3D, in which objects exist. The DX Studio Editor offers the ability to export complete scenes (including their contents to its own proprietary file format, a .dxscene file). The .dxscene file contains the settings of a single scene: the associated script files, scene objects, lighting information, and more. In short, it contains all information required to describe a scene on a standalone basis. The DX Studio System object offers a function for adding scenes to the document and then loading and playing them, all at run time. The following step-by-step guide demonstrates how to export a scene, and then load that scene to a document and remove that scene from a document at run time, using the system object methods sceneAdd and sceneRemove:

Step 1.   Use the DX Studio Editor to create a scene in the document. Once created, use the editor tabs to switch the editor view away from the scene and back to the document overview menu.

Step 2.   Select the **Scene** menu item from the Scenes list view at the bottom right-hand side of the window. Right-click the mouse and from the context menu, select **Export**. Assign the scene a name and click **Save** to export the scene to a .dxscene file.

Step 3.   Once saved, the scene can be removed from the DX Studio document. To import and then remove the scene at run time, consider the following code:

```
//Loads a scene with ID of "Scene_1" from file on
disk.
system.sceneAdd("Scene_1", "c:\MyScene.dxscene",
false);

//Scene can be assigned to layer:
Layers.layer1.scene = scenes.Scene_1;

//Scene can be removed
system.removeScene("Scene_1");
```

**Saving Screenshots**

Often it can be useful both for gamers (especially beta testers) and for developers to export a screenshot from the application window to an image file on disk. The screenshot saved to the file includes everything that was shown in the window at the time the screenshot was taken. The DX Studio System object offers the method save-ScreenCapture to both capture a screenshot and save it to a specified file on disk. The following code demonstrates how to do this:

```
//Captures screen-shot and saves image as a PNG file
system.saveScreenCapture("MyImg.png", "png");
```

**NOTE.** In addition to the System object, the DX Studio class library includes the following classes. More information on each class can be found at the DX Studio reference guide. Also, the DX Studio Editor offers Code Complete and Class Browser features. "Code Complete" refers to the context-sensitive feature that monitors the keystrokes of the developer in the code editor in order to correct invalid statements or to complete unfinished statements. The Class Browser features allow developers to graphically explore the methods and properties of a class in a tree view or list from the code window. The following collection of class names lists some of the common classes used in DX Studio scripts for manipulating scenes, documents, objects, and the application window.

| | | |
|---|---|---|
| alert | keys | SequenceInstance |
| alertMask | Layer | SequenceQueue |
| anyVarType | Material | SOAPMethod |
| Array | Math | SOAPParameter |
| Background | Module | SOAPProxy |
| Bitmap | network | SOAPResponse |
| bool | NetworkSet | sound |
| ByteData | object | sounds |
| Color | Object | string |
| Control | objects | Subgroup |
| Data | Particle | system |
| DataSource | ParticleDef | Texture |
| Effect | print | UtilMath |
| Event | printMask | Vector |
| Events | Resources | VectorMath |
| Face | Rotation | Vertex |
| File | RotationMath | Wiimote |
| float | Scene | Window |
| HitInfo | scenes | XmlDocument |
| int | Script | XmlNode |
| Keyframe | Sequence | |

## 12.8.5    Working with the Interactive Debugger

The process of debugging an application involves finding and removing run-time errors that cause the application to behave in unexpected and unpredictable ways. The standard debugging convention when building compiled applications, such as C++ applications, is to first create the code, then to compile and run that code while watching and tracing for errors as they arise. This is to determine *where* and *when* the error occurred in order to ascertain its cause. This convention also holds for the DX Studio debugging tool, but this tool offers additional features that allow developers not only to watch the value of properties as they change at run time but also to execute scripted statements on-the-fly so as to observe their effect on the application without having to recompile. The following step-by-step guide explains how to access and use the interactive debugging tool:

Step 1.   The first step to using the interactive debugger is to ensure it is enabled, since it can and often will be disabled when building and distributing release applications; that is, final applications distributed to the end user. This is to prevent gamers from viewing the application source code and from running scripted statements to change the behavior of the game. The interactive debugger can be both enabled and disabled using from the document Preferences menu. This setting can be accessed from the Editor main menu by selecting either **Edit | Scene Preferences** or **Edit | Document Preferences**.

Step 2.   The Preferences menu displays many settings for both the Editor and the active document and scenes. The interactive debugger options are found on the **Document Properties | Options** page. To enable the interactive debugger, the following *two* check boxes must be checked: **Show Context Menu** and **Debug**. The debugger can be disabled by removing the check from *either* box. Close the Preferences window to confirm the settings.

Step 3.   The debugger is now ready to use. Run the DX Studio document by clicking the **Preview** button. Once running, initiate the debugger by right-clicking to access the application context menu, and from there select the option **Debug**. This displays the Debug window.

---

### ■  Debugging Window

The Debug window (see Figure 12.29) is used for debugging DX Studio applications and is accessed at run time from the application context menu. The debugger can be used to view the source code of an application, to view each and every member of a scene, and to observe when and where these values change during execution; it can also be used to run JavaScript statements.

1. The Scripts list box lists all script files belonging to the application. A DX Studio document has one script file at the document level, one script file per scene, and one script file for each object in the scene that has custom scripting. A document might also feature additional scripts that are included into other files via the include directive.

2. The Variables list box lists both the name and current value of all global variables for the script file selected in the Scripts list.

3. The Source box lists all JavaScript source code for the file selected in the Scripts file list.

4. The Execute Script Now edit box at the bottom of the window allows users to enter and run JavaScript statements on-the-fly. Statements written here are executed within the scope of the document script.

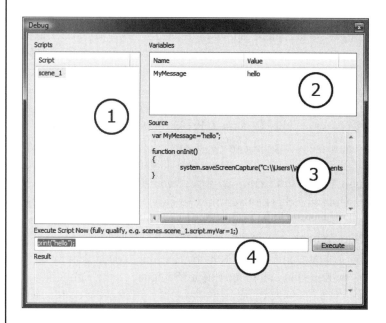

**FIGURE 12.29**    Debug window. Courtesy of Chris Sterling, Worldweaver, Ltd.

## 12.9    Using JavaScript in C++ Applications with Mozilla SpiderMonkey

Game engine tools such as the map editors, material editors, and integrated scripting features found in DX Studio save developers both time and money, and thereby increase productivity. They are time-saving because by using map editors developers are saved from investing time in editing large text files and instead they can build maps by making edits and changes in a GUI, and by using integrated scripting developers are saved from having to recompile an application each and every time a change is made in code. By saving time, developers also save money, since the time saved by engine tools can be invested for other lucrative purposes. Thus, engine tools are valuable for game development, and this section concentrates further on the issue of scripting. It does this by moving away from DX Studio entirely and focusing on how scripting features can be integrated into the reader's own engine in C++. Specifically, it focuses on the Mozilla SpiderMonkey JavaScript engine, which can be integrated into C++ applications, allowing them to read, parse, and execute JavaScript files at run time. In short, an application that uses SpiderMonkey can:

- Parse and call one or more JavaScript functions or statements from a string at run time.

- Provide a JavaScript interface to its own internal classes and methods that can be called from JavaScript files.

> **NOTE.** The DX Studio engine itself is based on C++ and uses the SpiderMonkey engine to provide its JavaScript support.

## 12.9.1   Downloading, Installing, and Configuring Mozilla SpiderMonkey

To build a JavaScript-enabled application on Windows using Mozilla SpiderMonkey, a developer must first download, install, and configure the Mozilla SpiderMonkey Build Tools. Once downloaded, the SpiderMonkey engine source code must be downloaded from the Mozilla Developer website and then built into a compiled library appropriate for linking. The following tutorial details how to do this, but readers should also consult the latest Mozilla development information found at the following URL if build problems are encountered: http://www.mozilla.org/js/spidermonkey/.

Step 1.  Navigate a web browser to the Mozilla SpiderMonkey development URL: https://developer.mozilla.org/en/Windows_Build_Prerequisites. From there, download the latest MozillaBuild Tools as a Windows installer. At the time of writing, this package is MozillaBuild 1.4 and can be downloaded from:

http://ftp.mozilla.org/pub/mozilla.org/mozilla/libraries/win32/ MozillaBuildSetup-1.4.exe. See Figures 12.30 and 12.31.

Step 2.  Once downloaded, run the MozillaBuild installer to install the Build Tools to the local computer. These tools do not contain the SpiderMonkey engine source code but are *required* to build that code. See Figure 12.32.

Step 3.  Once installed, open a command prompt window by running the Windows command **cmd** or by accessing the command prompt application from the Windows Start menu. In a command prompt window, navigate to the folder in which MozillaBuild was installed and run the appropriate batch file for the version of C++ installed on the computer: start-msvc8.bat for Visual Studio 2005 and start-msvc9.bat for Visual Studio 2008 or above. The result will look something like Figure 12.33

**┃ FIGURE 12.30**    Downloading the SpiderMonkey source.

**┃ FIGURE 12.31**    Downloading MozillaBuild.

Mozilla Build Setup: Installing
Extract: tar.dll
Show details
Cancel
Nullsoft Install System v2.33
< Back
Close

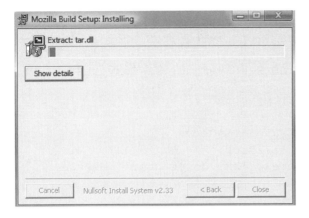

**FIGURE 12.32** MozillaBuild installer.

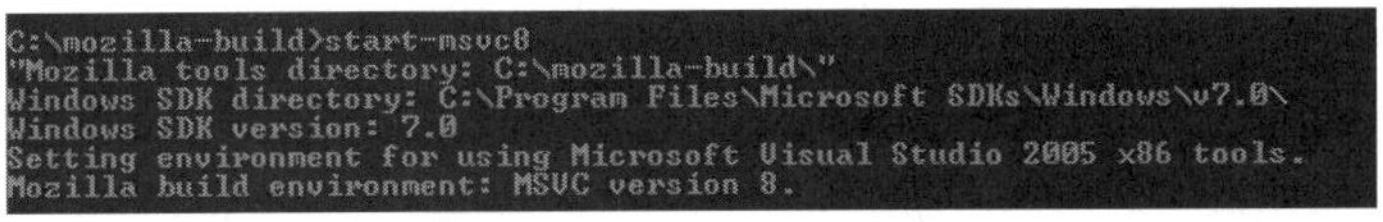

C:\mozilla-build>start-msvc8
"Mozilla tools directory: C:\mozilla-build\"
Windows SDK directory: C:\Program Files\Microsoft SDKs\Windows\v7.0\
Windows SDK version: 7.0
Setting environment for using Microsoft Visual Studio 2005 x86 tools.
Mozilla build environment: MSVC version 8.

**FIGURE 12.33** MozillaBuild ouput.

Step 4. Once the MozillaBuild Tools are configured, download the latest SpiderMonkey source from: http://ftp.mozilla.org/pub/mozilla.org/js/js-1.8.0-rc1.tar.gz. Check the following URL to ensure this is the latest package: https://developer.mozilla.org/En/SpiderMonkey/Build_Documentation.

Step 5. Extract the contents of this package to a folder on the local hard disk. Then open a command prompt, navigate to the source folder (src), and run the following command to build the SpiderMonkey source:

```
make -f Makefile.ref
```

Step 6. After compilation, a series of files are generated, including object files and executables. Applications intending to utilize the JavaScript library should link to the libraries generated and include the jsapi.h header file. To create a test build application with the SpiderMonkey library, the Mozilla website provides the following sample application:

```
#include "jsapi.h"

/* The class of the global object. */
static JSClass global_class = {
```

```
    "global", JSCLASS_GLOBAL_FLAGS,
    JS_PropertyStub, JS_PropertyStub, JS_PropertyStub,
JS_PropertyStub,
    JS_EnumerateStub, JS_ResolveStub, JS_ConvertStub,
JS_FinalizeStub,
    JSCLASS_NO_OPTIONAL_MEMBERS
};

/* The error reporter callback. */
void reportError(JSContext *cx, const char *message,
JSErrorReport *report)
{
    fprintf(stderr, "%s:%u:%s\n",
            report->filename ? report->filename : "<no
filename>",
            (unsigned int) report->lineno,
            message);
}

int main(int argc, const char *argv[])
{
    /* JS variables. */
    JSRuntime *rt;
    JSContext *cx;
    JSObject  *global;

    /* Create a JS runtime. */
    rt = JS_NewRuntime(8L * 1024L * 1024L);
    if (rt == NULL)
        return 1;

    /* Create a context. */
    cx = JS_NewContext(rt, 8192);
    if (cx == NULL)
        return 1;
    JS_SetOptions(cx, JSOPTION_VAROBJFIX);
    JS_SetVersion(cx, JSVERSION_LATEST);
    JS_SetErrorReporter(cx, reportError);

    /* Create the global object. */
    global = JS_NewObject(cx, &global_class, NULL, NULL);
    if (global == NULL)
        return 1;

    /* Populate the global object with the standard
```

```
globals,
      like Object and Array. */
   if (!JS_InitStandardClasses(cx, global))
      return 1;

   /* Your application code here. This may include JSAPI
calls
      to create your own custom JS objects and run
scripts. */

   /* Cleanup. */
   JS_DestroyContext(cx);
   JS_DestroyRuntime(rt);
   JS_ShutDown();
   return 0;
}
```

Step 7.   Further documentation on the use of SpiderMonkey can be found at: https://
          developer.mozilla.org/en/docs/JavaScript_C_Engine_Embedder's_Guide.

> **NOTE.** Readers might also be interested in another popular JavaScript
> alternative to SpiderMonkey called V8, developed and maintained by
> Google. More information on this library can be found at http://code.
> google.com/p/v8/.

## ■ 12.10   Chapter Summary

This chapter has covered extensive ground in considering the importance of engine
tools and integrated scripting for the productiveness of game developers, the benefits
offered by map editors, material editors, and scripting editors using a fully featured
game engine called DX Studio, and an introduction to integrating the JavaScript
scripting language into C++ applications with the Mozilla SpiderMonkey engine.

# Game Engines, Tools, and Libraries

This book has considered a variety of game engines, SDKs, and development tools. This appendix now summarizes each of those libraries and tools, as well as others, and discusses where to find them and the kinds of licenses under which they are available. Each tool discussed here may belong to any of the following categories:

- **Graphics SDK**

  Graphics SDKs like SDL (Simple Directmedia Layer) and OGRE (Object-Oriented Graphics Rendering Engine) are largely concerned with presenting real-time graphics to the game window, whether 2D or 3D graphics. As this book has hopefully shown, such APIs offer tools and classes designed specifically for loading images from files on disk and into system (or other hardware) memory as resources, ready for display or animation in the game window.

- **Audio SDK**

  Audio SDKs (such as SDL_Audio, FMOD, and BASS) are libraries featuring classes and tools used by developers to play audio (music and sound effects) via the audio hardware to the speakers where it is heard by gamers.

- **Physics SDK**

  Engines with GUI editors such as DX Studio and Adobe Director® offer to game developers a whole subset of game-editing and level-designing features to create comprehensive game worlds in which exist buildings, NPCs, and all kinds of other objects and phenomena, many of which can be found in the real world, the physical world. The purpose of a physics SDK is to offer developers a mathematical framework of functions and classes designed to simulate real-life physics so game objects and game worlds may behave like real-world counterparts. Thus, its purpose is to do all the computational hard work for you; that is, to do the physics part automatically.

- **Network SDK**

  Games described as multiplayer (such as Unreal Tournament, Quake, or World of Warcraft®) are those that bring together into a single online social space thousands of gamers from many disparate regions around the globe, each of them meeting up with others to play their games both competitively (e.g., death-match) or cooperatively (e.g., team death-match). Network SDKs include some of the libraries and tools that make it possible for game developers to create games that "talk to one another" across the Internet; that is, games that establish mutual socket connections and through these transmit data to and from another to synchronize multiplayer facilities.

- **Artificial Intelligence SDK**

  Artificial intelligence (AI) refers to the processes (the set of functions and algorithms) that make computers think for themselves, or appear to think for themselves. Through AI, computers can play chess, control NPCs, navigate NPCs intelligently through levels avoiding obstacles and traveling the shortest route between any two points in a map, engage players in combat in real-time and turn-based strategy games, etc. A cross-platform AI SDK, then, offers to developers the "thinking," calculating, and cognitive apparatus (functions, classes, and tool sets) to implement AI into their cross-platform games in order to make their games think, reason, and respond.

- **Input SDK**

  Cross-platform input SDKs (like OIS used by OGRE) boast a set of platform-independent functions and classes that allow developers to read user input from input peripherals such as keyboards, mice, and joysticks.

- **Scripting SDK**

  Game engines like DX Studio, graphics engines like OGRE, or Shockwave® games made in Director make use of scripting facilities; that is, developers use a scripting language (Lua, Python, or JavaScript) for each game to code and edit its behavior without needing to recompile the entire source code from scratch. Thus, scripting SDKs offer the bridging tools (the functions and classes) to bridge the gap between binary executable and script in a file.

- **Game Engine**

  Game engines constitute the main focus of this book. In short, a game engine represents the foundation on which a game can be built; it is the core that makes a game possible. Though much of this book has been concerned with developing an engine from scratch, it also pauses to consider third-party engines, some of which are considered throughout this book and others which are mentioned only here.

- **GUI SDK**

  The term "GUI" (graphics user interface) refers to the widgets, gadgets, and gizmos (like buttons, list views, edit boxes, and other interface components) found on game menus such as main menus and game save menus. A GUI SDK, then, offers a set of easy to use tools and classes for creating in-game GUIs for games.

- **Distribution SDK**

  Generally, contemporary game developers distribute their games to users primarily through one of two methods: (1) as a published CD/DVD sitting in a box on a shelf in a computer game store or at an online retailer, or (2) as a self-published online download (either directly from the developer's website or through an online gaming portal like Reflexive® Arcade or Big Fish Games®). But in either case, the game typically installs itself to the user's computer via an automated installer. This appendix examines some means of creating game installers using a distribution SDK.

## ■ Graphics SDKs

- **OpenGL**

  *Description:* OpenGL (Open Graphics Library) is a cross-language, cross-platform SDK for fast-paced (hardware-accelerated) 2D and 3D computer graphics. The library has over 250 different function calls to draw complex three-dimensional graphics and scenes, from simple primitives to complex animated geometry. OpenGL was developed by Silicon Graphics Inc. (SGI) in 1992 and is widely used in CAD, virtual reality, scientific visualization, information visualization, flight simulation, and video games.

  *Platforms Supported:* Windows, Linux, and Mac

  *Website:* http://www.opengl.org/

  *License:* Free for commercial and noncommercial use.

- **PTK**

  *Description:* "PTK is a multi-platform 2D game engine with 3D capabilities built around OpenGL or Direct 3D accelerated hardware, however, it is also possible to create 3D multi-platform games with OpenGL. [...] PTK can be used by a wide variety of users: from the most experienced programmers to the newbie aspiring game programmers." (from website)

  *Platforms Supported:* Mac and Windows

  *Website:* http://www.phelios.com/ptk/

  *License:* Free only for noncommercial use; more license details available at their website.

- **ClanLib**

  *Description:* Freely available, high-level and cross-platform, ClanLib is an OpenGL-powered open source SDK for creating cross-platform (Windows, Linux, and Mac) 2D games using the C++ language. ClanLib boasts a variety of features, some of which are: XML/DOM support; 2D collision detection; network library; sound mixer supporting WAV format, tracker formats (mod/s3m/xm/), and ogg-vorbis; and high-level 2D graphics API supporting OpenGL and SDL as render targets.

*Platforms Supported:* Windows, Mac, and Linux

*Website:* http://www.clanlib.org/

*License:* BSD-style; free for commercial and noncommercial use. See website for more information.

## ■ Audio SDKs

- **FMOD**

  *Description:* FMOD is a cross-platform commercial audio library made by Firelight Technologies that plays audio files in the following formats: AIFF, ASF, ASX, DLS, FLAC, FSB, IT, M3U, MID, MOD, MP2, MP3, OGG, PLS, RAW, S3M, VAG, WAV, WAX, WMA, XM, and XMA.

  *Platforms Supported:* Windows, Mac, Linux, Nintendo GameCube, Wii, Solaris, Xbox, Xbox 360, PlayStation2, PlayStation Portable, and PlayStation 3

  *Website:* http://www.fmod.org/

  *License:* Free only for noncommercial use; more license details available at their website.

- **BASS**

  *Description:* Commercial cross-platform audio SDK by Un4seen Developments supporting audio files in the following file formats: WAV, AIFF, MP3, MP2, MP1, OGG, XM, IT, S3M, MOD, MTM, and UMX.

  *Platforms Supported:* Windows and Mac

  *Website:* http://www.un4seen.com/

  *License:* Free only for noncommercial use; more license details available at their website.

- **irrKlang**

  *Description:* Commercial cross-platform audio SDK by Ambiera supporting audio files in the following file formats: WAV, MP3, OGG, XM, IT, S3D, and MOD.

  *Platforms Supported:* Windows, Linux, and Mac

  *Website:* http://ambiera.com/irrklang/

  *License:* Free only for noncommercial use; more license details available at their website.

- **Audiere**

  *Description:* Free, open source, and cross-platform audio SDK supporting audio files in the following file formats: WAV, AIFF, MP3, MP2, MP1, OGG, XM, IT, S3M, MOD, MTM, and UMX.

  *Platforms Supported:* Windows, Mac, and Linux

  *Website:* http://audiere.sourceforge.net/

  *License:* LGPL; free for commercial and noncommercial use.

- **OpenAL**

  *Description:* Generally free, open source, and cross-platform audio SDK.

  *Platforms Supported:* Windows, Mac, Linux, BSD, Solaris, IRIX, Xbox, and Xbox 360

  *Website:* http://www.openal.org/

  *License:* LGPL; free for commercial and noncommercial use.

## ■ Physics SDKs

- **ODE**

  *Description:* ODE (Open Dynamics Engine) is a free, open source, and cross-platform physics SDK for simulating both rigid body physics and collision detection. It has powered many games, including BloodRayne 2, Call of Juarez, and S.T.A.L.K.E.R.

  *Platforms Supported:* Linux, Windows, and Mac

  *Website:* http://www.ode.org/

  *License:* BSD-style; free for commercial and noncommercial use.

- **Newton™ Game Dynamics**

  *Description:* Newton Game Dynamics is a cross-platform physics SDK which "is an integrated solution for real time simulation of physics environments. The API provides scene management, collision detection, dynamic behavior and yet it is small, fast, stable and easy to use." (from website)

  *Platforms Supported:* Windows, Mac, and Linux

  *Website:* http://www.newtondynamics.com/

  *License:* Free with restrictions; see website for further details.

- **True Axis Physics**

  *Description:* True Axis is a cross-platform physics SDK featuring collision detection, scene management, joints and rigid body dynamics, and contact force computation.

*Platforms Supported:* Windows and Linux

*Website:* http://www.trueaxis.com/

*License:* Free only for noncommercial use; more license details available at their website.

- **OPAL**

  *Description:* Open Physics Abstraction Layer is a free, open ource, and cross-platform physics SDK featuring linear and angular motion damping, collision detection, sensors, joints, and more.

  *Platforms Supported:* Windows, Mac, and Linux

  *Website:* http://opal.sourceforge.net/

  *License:* LGPL; free for commercial and noncommercial use.

- **Bullet**

  *Description:* Bullet is a free, open source, and cross-platform physics SDK featuring both Soft and Rigid body physics, collision detection, sensors, joints, and more.

  *Platforms Supported:* Mac, Windows, Linux, and PlayStation 3

  *Website:* http://www.continuousphysics.com/Bullet/

  *License:* zlib, free for commercial and noncommercial use.

- **PhysX**

  *Description:* PhysX is a commercial, cross-platform physics SDK featuring Soft and Rigid body physics, and support for hardware accelerated physics calculations. It used by many games including Unreal.

  *Platforms Supported:* Mac, Windows, Linux, and consoles

  *Website:* http://www.ageia.com/

  *License:* Free only for noncommercial use; more license details available at their website.

## ■ Network SDKs

- **RakNet**

  *Description:* "RakNet is a networking API that is a wrapper for reliable UDP and higher level functionality on Windows, Linux, and Unix. It allows any application to communicate with other applications on the same computer, over a LAN, or over the internet. Although it could be used for any networked application, it was developed specifically for rapid development of online games and the addition of multiplayer to single player games." (from website)

*Platforms Supported:* Windows and Linux

*Website:* http://freshmeat.net/projects/raknet

*License:* Free with restrictions; more license details available at their website.

- **HawkNL**™

   *Description:* HawkNL is a free, cross-platform, open source, game-oriented network API designed largely as a wrapper over Berkeley/Unix Sockets and Winsock. NL also provides other features including: support for many groups of sockets, socket statistics, high accuracy timer, CRC functions, macros to read and write data to packets with endian conversion, and support for multiple network transports.

   *Platforms Supported:* Windows, Linux, Mac, IRIX, AIX, BSD, and Solaris

   *Website:* http://www.hawksoft.com/hawknl/

   *License:* LGPL; free for commercial and noncommercial use.

- **SDL_net**

   *Description:* A free, open source, cross-platform SDL networking extension library for the SDL library.

   *Platforms Supported:* Linux, Windows, BeOS, Mac OS, Mac OS X, FreeBSD, NetBSD, OpenBSD, BSD/OS, Solaris, IRIX, and QNX

   *Website:* http://www.libsdl.org/projects/SDL_net/

   *License:* LGPL; free for commercial and noncommercial use.

## ■ Artificial Intelligence SDKs

- **Boost Graph Library**

   *Description:* Boost is a series of open source, cross-platform, and peer-reviewed C++ libraries, including the graph library used by many for path finding and other AI game development purposes.

   *Platforms Supported:* Windows, Linux, Mac, and consoles

   *Website:* http://boost.org/libs/graph/doc/table_of_contents.html

   *License:* Free; more license details available at their website.

- **OpenSteer**

   *Description:* "OpenSteer is a C++ library to help construct steering behaviors for autonomous characters in games and animation. In addition to the library, OpenSteer provides an OpenGL-based application called OpenSteerDemo which displays predefined demonstrations of steering behaviors. The user can quickly prototype, visualize, annotate and debug new steering behaviors by writing a plug-in for OpenSteerDemo." (from website)

*Platforms Supported:* Linux, Windows, BeOS, Mac OS, Mac OS X, FreeBSD, NetBSD, OpenBSD, BSD/OS, Solaris, IRIX, and QNX

*Website:* http://opensteer.sourceforge.net/

*License:* MIT; free for commercial and noncommercial use.

- **FANN**

  *Description:* FANN (Fast Artificial Neural Network Library) is an open source, cross-platform AI library, which "implements multilayer artificial neural networks in C with support for both fully connected and sparsely connected networks." (from website)

  *Platforms Supported:* Windows, Mac, and Linux

  *Website:* http://leenissen.dk/fann/

  *License:* LGPL; free for commercial and noncommercial use.

- **Garfixia AI Repository**

  *Description:* A free, cross-platform, and open source collection of common AI functions, classes, and algorithms.

  *Platforms Supported:* Linux, Windows, BeOS, Mac OS, Mac OS X, FreeBSD, NetBSD, OpenBSD, BSD/OS, Solaris, IRIX, and QNX

  *Website:* http://www.dossier-andreas.net/ai/index.html

  *License:* Free only for noncommercial use; more license details available at their website.

## ■ Input SDKs

- **LibGII**

  *Description:* A free, cross-platform, and open source input management library featuring functions and classes to read user input from peripheral input devices, including mouse, keyboard, joysticks, and others.

  *Platforms Supported:* Linux, Windows, Mac OS, Mac OS X, FreeBSD, and OpenBSD

  *Website:* http://www.ggi-project.org/packages/libgii.html

  *License:* MIT; free for commercial and noncommercial use.

- **OpenInput**

  *Description:* "OpenInput as a free, open source, cross platform, and portable input handling library written in C. The library can take input from several devices like mice, joysticks and keyboards, and presents it to the user using a simple, platform independent and easy-to-use API." (from website)

*Platforms Supported:* Windows and Linux

*Website:* http://home.gna.org/openinput/

*License:* LGPL; free for commercial and noncommercial use.

## ■ Scripting SDKs

- **SpiderMonkey**

  *Description:* Originally created by Brendan Eich at Netscape Communications, the SpiderMonkey JavaScript engine is now released as open source software by the Mozilla Foundation. It powers the JavaScript functionality of both the browser Mozilla Firefox and the DX Studio engine.

  *Platforms Supported:* Windows, Linux, Mac

  *Website:* http://www.mozilla.org/js/spidermonkey/

  *License:* MPL/GPL/LGPL

- **V8**

  *Description:* V8 was developed in association with Google and is the Javascript engine powering the Google Chrome Web browser. It can be downloaded as a separate library and used to power game applications.

  *Platforms Supported:* Windows, Linux, and Mac

  *Website:* http://code.google.com/p/v8/

  *License:* BSD

- **Lua**

  *Description:* Created in 1993 by Roberto Ierusalimschy, Lua (pronounced Loo-ah) is a free, cross-platform, and open source imperative procedural scripting language, used by many games including World of Warcraft, SimCity™ 4, Crysis™, and Supreme Commander®; and also used by Novashell as well as other game engines and game editors.

  *Platforms Supported:* Windows, Linux, Mac, Brew®, Symbian, and PocketPC

  *Website:* http://www.lua.org/

  *License:* MIT; free for commercial and noncommercial use.

- **Python**

  *Description:* "Python is a dynamic object-oriented programming language that can be used for many kinds of software development. It offers strong support for integration with other languages and tools, comes with extensive standard libraries, and can be learned in a few days. Many Python programmers report substantial productivity gains and feel the language encourages the development of higher quality, more maintainable code." (from website)

*Platforms Supported:* Windows, Mac, Linux, Amiga, Palm® handhelds, and Nokia mobile phones

*Website:* http://www.python.org/

*License:* Free for commercial and noncommercial use.

- **Ruby**

  *Description:* Ruby is a free, open source, cross-platform, object-oriented scripting language.

  *Platforms Supported:* Windows, Linux, and Mac

  *Website:* http://www.ruby-lang.org/

  *License:* Free for commercial and noncommercial use.

- **Squirrel**

  *Description:* Squirrel is a free, open source, cross-platform, object-oriented scripting language, some of whose features include dynamic typing, exception handling, classes and inheritance, tail recursion, and automatic memory management.

  *Platforms Supported:* Windows, Mac, and Linux

  *Website:* http://squirrel-lang.org/

  *License:* Free for commercial and noncommercial use.

- **AngelCode**

  *Description:* AngelCode is a free, open source, cross-platform, object-oriented scripting language.

  *Platforms Supported:* Windows, Linux, Mac OS X, XBox, XBox 360, PS2, PSP, PS3, Dreamcast, Nintendo DS, and Windows Mobile

  *Website:* http://www.angelcode.com/angelscript/

  *License:* Free for commercial and noncommercial use.

- **GameMonkey**

  *Description:* "GameMonkey is a embedded scripting language that is intended for use in game and tool applications. GameMonkey is however suitable for use in any project requiring simple scripting support. GameMonkey borrows concepts from Lua (www.lua.org), but uses syntax similar to C, making it more accessible to game programmers. GameMonkey also natively supports multithreading and the concept of states." (from website)

*Platforms Supported:* Windows, Mac, and Linux

*Website:* http://www.somedude.net/gamemonkey/

*License:* MIT license; free for commercial and noncommercial use.

## ■ Game Engines

- **Torque**

  *Description:* Torque is a commercial game engine, complete with level editor, sound, input, graphics renderer, and more.

  *Platforms Supported:* Windows, Mac, and Linux

  *Website:* http://www.garagegames.com/

  *License:* Commercial.

- **Irrlicht**

  *Description:* Irrlicht Engine is a free, open source real-time 3D engine written in C++. Cross-platform (using Direct3D®, OpenGL, and its own software renderer), Irrlicht has a huge active community where you can find enhancements and extras such as terrain renderers, portal renderers, exporters, world layers, tutorials, editors, language bindings for Java, Perl, Ruby, Basic, Python, Lua, and so on.

  *Platforms Supported:* Windows, Mac, and Linux

  *Website:* http://irrlicht.sourceforge.net/

  *License:* zlib; free for commercial and noncommercial use.

- **Game Editor**

  *Description:* Game Editor is aimed at those new to game programming.

  *Platforms Supported:* Windows, Mac, and Linux

  *Website:* http://game-editor.com/

  *License:* Commercial.

- **C4 Engine**

  *Description:* Cross-platform real-time 3D engine.

  *Platforms Supported:* Windows and Mac

  *Website:* http://www.terathon.com/c4engine/

  *License:* Commercial.

- **Gamestudio**

  *Description:* 3D and 2D game engine. This engine has been used to power a selection of commercial games, including 3D Hunting, Great Clips Racing, and 3D Driving Academy.

*Platforms Supported:* Windows

*Website:* http://www.3dgamestudio.com/

*License:* Commercial.

- **Panda3D**

  *Description:* Panda3D is a free, cross-platform, and open source 3D engine coded in C++ and supporting the Python scripting language. Panda3D has been used on a selection of commercial projects, including A Vampyre Story and Ghost Pirates of Vooju Island.

  *Platforms Supported:* Windows, Mac, and Linux

  *Website:* http://www.panda3d.org

  *License:* Free.

- **Esenthel Engine**

  *Description:* Esenthel Engine is a commercial game engine available for Windows PC.

  *Platforms Supported:* Windows

  *Website:* http://www.esenthel.com

  *License:* Commercial.

- **Unity 3D**

  *Description:* Unity 3D is a cross-platform, commercial 3D engine complete with a map editor and other engine tools.

  *Platforms Supported:* Windows and iPhone

  *Website:* http://unity3d.com/

  *License:* Commercial.

- **ShiVa 3D**

  *Description:* Shiva 3D is a cross-platform, commercial 3D engine complete with a map editor and other engine tools.

  *Platforms Supported:* Windows, iPhone, and Android™

  *Website:* http://www.stonetrip.com/

  *License:* Commercial.

- **FPS Creator**

  *Description:* FPS Creator is a commercial engine for the Windows platform dedicated to the creation of first-person shooter games.

  *Platforms Supported:* Windows

  *Website:* http://www.fpscreator.com/

  *License:* Commercial.

- **LÖVE**

  *Description:* **LÖVE** is a free, open source, and cross-platform engine for creating 2D games.

  *Platforms Supported:* Windows, Linux, and Mac

  *Website:* http://love2d.org/

  *License:* Free.

- **Haaf's Game Engine**

  *Description:* Haaf's Game Engine is a free, open source, and cross-platform engine for creating 2D games.

  *Platforms Supported:* Windows, Linux, and Mac

  *Website:* http://hge.relishgames.com/

  *License:* Free.

## ■ GUI SDKs

- **OpenGUI**

  *Description:* OpenGUI is an open source, cross-platform, and freely available C++ GUI framework for games and other cross-platform applications.

  *Platforms Supported:* Windows, Mac, and Linux

  *Website:* http://opengui.rightbracket.com/index.php

  *License:* BSD; free for commercial and noncommercial use.

## ■ Distribution SDKs

- **NSIS**

  *Description:* NSIS (Nullsoft Scriptable Install System) is an open source library designed to create Windows installation packages for developers aiming to distribute their games to an audience.

  *Platforms Supported:* Windows

  *Website:* http://nsis.sourceforge.net/

  *License:* Free for commercial and noncommercial use; see website for more details.

- **Inno Setup**

  *Description:* Created in 1997, Inno Setup is a freely available library used to create Windows installation packages.

*Platforms Supported:* Windows

*Website:* http://www.jrsoftware.org/isinfo.php

*License:* Free for commercial and noncommercial use; see website for more details.

---

### ■ Inno Setup Tutorial

**Downloading, Installing, and Creating an Installer**

Inno Setup is a freely available library used by many game developers for creating an installation package (installation wizard) that installs their game to the local machine; that is, transfers the game files from a compressed archive on a CD or downloaded package to the local machine in a form that can execute successfully. The following step-by-step guide highlights how to download, install, and use Inno Setup to create installers for your own games:

Step 1.  Beginning from the Windows desktop, navigate a web browser to the Inno Setup homepage at http://www.jrsoftware.org/isinfo.php.

Step 2.  At the Inno Setup homepage, select the **Downloads** link in the page margin to display the downloads page. There, download from the web to the local machine both the latest Inno Setup release and the Inno Setup QuickStart Pack, downloading *and* installing each package to the local computer.

Step 3.  From the Windows Start menu, launch the newly installed Inno Setup IS Tool (script editor to create installation packages). Then from the IS Tool main menu, select **File | New** to create a new installation project (a project soon to be compiled into a completed installer, ready to run).

Step 4.  Enter the following script into the editor pane:

```
        [Setup]
        ; This is a comment. The setup section
describes the basic properties
        ; of the installer; such as program title,
version number, default
        ; installation (destination) directory
AppName=My Program
AppVerName=My Program version 1.4
DefaultDirName={pf}\My Program
DefaultGroupName=My Program
```

```
OutputDir=C:\Ouput

[Files]
; Here list all files to be compiled into
installation package; files to be
; installed to the system by the installer at run-
time
Source: c:\mystestpic.jpg; DestDir: {app}
```

Step 5.  Then from the Inno Setup main menu, click **Project | Compile Project** to generate a self-executing installation package. The installer is now compiled and ready to run.

```
//! Keyboard scan codes
enum KeyCode
{
        KC_UNASSIGNED  = 0x00,
        KC_ESCAPE      = 0x01,
        KC_1           = 0x02,
        KC_2           = 0x03,
        KC_3           = 0x04,
        KC_4           = 0x05,
        KC_5           = 0x06,
        KC_6           = 0x07,
        KC_7           = 0x08,
        KC_8           = 0x09,
        KC_9           = 0x0A,
        KC_0           = 0x0B,
        KC_MINUS       = 0x0C,    // - on main keyboard
        KC_EQUALS      = 0x0D,
        KC_BACK        = 0x0E,    // backspace
        KC_TAB         = 0x0F,
        KC_Q           = 0x10,
        KC_W           = 0x11,
        KC_E           = 0x12,
        KC_R           = 0x13,
        KC_T           = 0x14,
        KC_Y           = 0x15,
        KC_U           = 0x16,
        KC_I           = 0x17,
        KC_O           = 0x18,
        KC_P           = 0x19,
        KC_LBRACKET    = 0x1A,
        KC_RBRACKET    = 0x1B,
        KC_RETURN      = 0x1C,    // Enter on main
keyboard
        KC_LCONTROL    = 0x1D,
        KC_A           = 0x1E,
```

```
KC_S            = 0x1F,
KC_D            = 0x20,
KC_F            = 0x21,
KC_G            = 0x22,
KC_H            = 0x23,
KC_J            = 0x24,
KC_K            = 0x25,
KC_L            = 0x26,
KC_SEMICOLON    = 0x27,
KC_APOSTROPHE   = 0x28,
KC_GRAVE        = 0x29,      // accent
KC_LSHIFT       = 0x2A,
KC_BACKSLASH    = 0x2B,
KC_Z            = 0x2C,
KC_X            = 0x2D,
KC_C            = 0x2E,
KC_V            = 0x2F,
KC_B            = 0x30,
KC_N            = 0x31,
KC_M            = 0x32,
KC_COMMA        = 0x33,
KC_PERIOD       = 0x34,      // . on main keyboard
KC_SLASH        = 0x35,      // / on main keyboard
KC_RSHIFT       = 0x36,
KC_MULTIPLY     = 0x37,      // * on numeric keypad
KC_LMENU        = 0x38,      // left Alt
KC_SPACE        = 0x39,
KC_CAPITAL      = 0x3A,
KC_F1           = 0x3B,
KC_F2           = 0x3C,
KC_F3           = 0x3D,
KC_F4           = 0x3E,
KC_F5           = 0x3F,
KC_F6           = 0x40,
KC_F7           = 0x41,
KC_F8           = 0x42,
KC_F9           = 0x43,
KC_F10          = 0x44,
KC_NUMLOCK      = 0x45,
KC_SCROLL       = 0x46,      // Scroll Lock
KC_NUMPAD7      = 0x47,
KC_NUMPAD8      = 0x48,
KC_NUMPAD9      = 0x49,
KC_SUBTRACT     = 0x4A,      // - on numeric keypad
KC_NUMPAD4      = 0x4B,
```

```
        KC_NUMPAD5      = 0x4C,
        KC_NUMPAD6      = 0x4D,
        KC_ADD          = 0x4E,     // + on numeric keypad
        KC_NUMPAD1      = 0x4F,
        KC_NUMPAD2      = 0x50,
        KC_NUMPAD3      = 0x51,
        KC_NUMPAD0      = 0x52,
        KC_DECIMAL      = 0x53,     // . on numeric keypad
        KC_OEM_102      = 0x56,     // < > | on UK/Germany
keyboards
        KC_F11          = 0x57,
        KC_F12          = 0x58,
        KC_F13          = 0x64,     //           (NEC PC98)
        KC_F14          = 0x65,     //           (NEC PC98)
        KC_F15          = 0x66,     //           (NEC PC98)
        KC_KANA         = 0x70,     // (Japanese keyboard)
        KC_ABNT_C1      = 0x73,     // / ? on Portuguese
(Brazilian) keyboards
        KC_CONVERT      = 0x79,     // (Japanese keyboard)
        KC_NOCONVERT    = 0x7B,     // (Japanese keyboard)
        KC_YEN          = 0x7D,     // (Japanese keyboard)
        KC_ABNT_C2      = 0x7E,
        KC_NUMPADEQUALS = 0x8D ,
        KC_PREVTRACK    = 0x90,
        KC_AT           = 0x91,     //           (NEC PC98)
        KC_COLON        = 0x92,     //           (NEC PC98)
        KC_UNDERLINE    = 0x93,     //           (NEC PC98)
        KC_KANJI        = 0x94,     // (Japanese keyboard)
        KC_STOP         = 0x95,     //           (NEC PC98)
        KC_AX           = 0x96,     //         (Japan AX)
        KC_UNLABELED    = 0x97,     //           (J3100)
        KC_NEXTTRACK    = 0x99,     // Next Track
        KC_NUMPADENTER  = 0x9C,     // Enter on numeric
keypad
        KC_RCONTROL     = 0x9D,
        KC_MUTE         = 0xA0,     // Mute
        KC_CALCULATOR   = 0xA1,     // Calculator
        KC_PLAYPAUSE    = 0xA2,     // Play / Pause
        KC_MEDIASTOP    = 0xA4,     // Media Stop
        KC_VOLUMEDOWN   = 0xAE,     // Volume -
        KC_VOLUMEUP     = 0xB0,     // Volume +
        KC_WEBHOME      = 0xB2,     // Web home
        KC_NUMPADCOMMA  = 0xB3,     // , on numeric keypad
(NEC PC98)
        KC_DIVIDE       = 0xB5,     // / on numeric keypad
```

```
        KC_SYSRQ        = 0xB7,
        KC_RMENU        = 0xB8,     // right Alt
        KC_PAUSE        = 0xC5,     // Pause
        KC_HOME         = 0xC7,     // Home on arrow
keypad
        KC_UP           = 0xC8,     // UpArrow on arrow
keypad
        KC_PGUP         = 0xC9,     // PgUp on arrow
keypad
        KC_LEFT         = 0xCB,     // LeftArrow on arrow
keypad
        KC_RIGHT        = 0xCD,     // RightArrow on arrow
keypad
        KC_END          = 0xCF,     // End on arrow keypad
        KC_DOWN         = 0xD0,     // DownArrow on arrow
keypad
        KC_PGDOWN       = 0xD1,     // PgDn on arrow
keypad
        KC_INSERT       = 0xD2,     // Insert on arrow
keypad
        KC_DELETE       = 0xD3,     // Delete on arrow
keypad
        KC_LWIN         = 0xDB,     // Left Windows key
        KC_RWIN         = 0xDC,     // Right Windows key
        KC_APPS         = 0xDD,     // AppMenu key
        KC_POWER        = 0xDE,     // System Power
        KC_SLEEP        = 0xDF,     // System Sleep
        KC_WAKE         = 0xE3,     // System Wake
        KC_WEBSEARCH    = 0xE5,     // Web Search
        KC_WEBFAVORITES = 0xE6,     // Web Favorites
        KC_WEBREFRESH   = 0xE7,     // Web Refresh
        KC_WEBSTOP      = 0xE8,     // Web Stop
        KC_WEBFORWARD   = 0xE9,     // Web Forward
        KC_WEBBACK      = 0xEA,     // Web Back
        KC_MYCOMPUTER   = 0xEB,     // My Computer
        KC_MAIL         = 0xEC,     // Mail
        KC_MEDIASELECT  = 0xED      // Media Select
    };
```

# DX Texture Format Constants

```
typedef enum DXGI_FORMAT
{
    DXGI_FORMAT_UNKNOWN = 0,
    DXGI_FORMAT_R32G32B32A32_TYPELESS = 1,
    DXGI_FORMAT_R32G32B32A32_FLOAT = 2,
    DXGI_FORMAT_R32G32B32A32_UINT = 3,
    DXGI_FORMAT_R32G32B32A32_SINT = 4,
    DXGI_FORMAT_R32G32B32_TYPELESS = 5,
    DXGI_FORMAT_R32G32B32_FLOAT = 6,
    DXGI_FORMAT_R32G32B32_UINT = 7,
    DXGI_FORMAT_R32G32B32_SINT = 8,
    DXGI_FORMAT_R16G16B16A16_TYPELESS = 9,
    DXGI_FORMAT_R16G16B16A16_FLOAT = 10,
    DXGI_FORMAT_R16G16B16A16_UNORM = 11,
    DXGI_FORMAT_R16G16B16A16_UINT = 12,
    DXGI_FORMAT_R16G16B16A16_SNORM = 13,
    DXGI_FORMAT_R16G16B16A16_SINT = 14,
    DXGI_FORMAT_R32G32_TYPELESS = 15,
    DXGI_FORMAT_R32G32_FLOAT = 16,
    DXGI_FORMAT_R32G32_UINT = 17,
    DXGI_FORMAT_R32G32_SINT = 18,
    DXGI_FORMAT_R32G8X24_TYPELESS = 19,
    DXGI_FORMAT_D32_FLOAT_S8X24_UINT = 20,
    DXGI_FORMAT_R32_FLOAT_X8X24_TYPELESS = 21,
    DXGI_FORMAT_X32_TYPELESS_G8X24_UINT = 22,
    DXGI_FORMAT_R10G10B10A2_TYPELESS = 23,
    DXGI_FORMAT_R10G10B10A2_UNORM = 24,
    DXGI_FORMAT_R10G10B10A2_UINT = 25,
    DXGI_FORMAT_R11G11B10_FLOAT = 26,
    DXGI_FORMAT_R8G8B8A8_TYPELESS = 27,
    DXGI_FORMAT_R8G8B8A8_UNORM = 28,
    DXGI_FORMAT_R8G8B8A8_UNORM_SRGB = 29,
    DXGI_FORMAT_R8G8B8A8_UINT = 30,
    DXGI_FORMAT_R8G8B8A8_SNORM = 31,
    DXGI_FORMAT_R8G8B8A8_SINT = 32,
```

```
DXGI_FORMAT_R16G16_TYPELESS = 33,
DXGI_FORMAT_R16G16_FLOAT = 34,
DXGI_FORMAT_R16G16_UNORM = 35,
DXGI_FORMAT_R16G16_UINT = 36,
DXGI_FORMAT_R16G16_SNORM = 37,
DXGI_FORMAT_R16G16_SINT = 38,
DXGI_FORMAT_R32_TYPELESS = 39,
DXGI_FORMAT_D32_FLOAT = 40,
DXGI_FORMAT_R32_FLOAT = 41,
DXGI_FORMAT_R32_UINT = 42,
DXGI_FORMAT_R32_SINT = 43,
DXGI_FORMAT_R24G8_TYPELESS = 44,
DXGI_FORMAT_D24_UNORM_S8_UINT = 45,
DXGI_FORMAT_R24_UNORM_X8_TYPELESS = 46,
DXGI_FORMAT_X24_TYPELESS_G8_UINT = 47,
DXGI_FORMAT_R8G8_TYPELESS = 48,
DXGI_FORMAT_R8G8_UNORM = 49,
DXGI_FORMAT_R8G8_UINT = 50,
DXGI_FORMAT_R8G8_SNORM = 51,
DXGI_FORMAT_R8G8_SINT = 52,
DXGI_FORMAT_R16_TYPELESS = 53,
DXGI_FORMAT_R16_FLOAT = 54,
DXGI_FORMAT_D16_UNORM = 55,
DXGI_FORMAT_R16_UNORM = 56,
DXGI_FORMAT_R16_UINT = 57,
DXGI_FORMAT_R16_SNORM = 58,
DXGI_FORMAT_R16_SINT = 59,
DXGI_FORMAT_R8_TYPELESS = 60,
DXGI_FORMAT_R8_UNORM = 61,
DXGI_FORMAT_R8_UINT = 62,
DXGI_FORMAT_R8_SNORM = 63,
DXGI_FORMAT_R8_SINT = 64,
DXGI_FORMAT_A8_UNORM = 65,
DXGI_FORMAT_R1_UNORM = 66,
DXGI_FORMAT_R9G9B9E5_SHAREDEXP = 67,
DXGI_FORMAT_R8G8_B8G8_UNORM = 68,
DXGI_FORMAT_G8R8_G8B8_UNORM = 69,
DXGI_FORMAT_BC1_TYPELESS = 70,
DXGI_FORMAT_BC1_UNORM = 71,
DXGI_FORMAT_BC1_UNORM_SRGB = 72,
DXGI_FORMAT_BC2_TYPELESS = 73,
DXGI_FORMAT_BC2_UNORM = 74,
DXGI_FORMAT_BC2_UNORM_SRGB = 75,
DXGI_FORMAT_BC3_TYPELESS = 76,
DXGI_FORMAT_BC3_UNORM = 77,
```

```
                    DXGI_FORMAT_BC3_UNORM_SRGB = 78,
                    DXGI_FORMAT_BC4_TYPELESS = 79,
                    DXGI_FORMAT_BC4_UNORM = 80,
                    DXGI_FORMAT_BC4_SNORM = 81,
                    DXGI_FORMAT_BC5_TYPELESS = 82,
                    DXGI_FORMAT_BC5_UNORM = 83,
                    DXGI_FORMAT_BC5_SNORM = 84,
                    DXGI_FORMAT_B5G6R5_UNORM = 85,
                    DXGI_FORMAT_B5G5R5A1_UNORM = 86,
                    DXGI_FORMAT_B8G8R8A8_UNORM = 87,
                    DXGI_FORMAT_B8G8R8X8_UNORM = 88,
                    DXGI_FORMAT_R10G10B10_XR_BIAS_A2_UNORM = 89,
                    DXGI_FORMAT_B8G8R8A8_TYPELESS = 90,
                    DXGI_FORMAT_B8G8R8A8_UNORM_SRGB = 91,
                    DXGI_FORMAT_B8G8R8X8_TYPELESS = 92,
                    DXGI_FORMAT_B8G8R8X8_UNORM_SRGB = 93,
                    DXGI_FORMAT_BC6H_TYPELESS = 94,
                    DXGI_FORMAT_BC6H_UF16 = 95,
                    DXGI_FORMAT_BC6H_SF16 = 96,
                    DXGI_FORMAT_BC7_TYPELESS = 97,
                    DXGI_FORMAT_BC7_UNORM = 98,
                    DXGI_FORMAT_BC7_UNORM_SRGB = 99,
                    DXGI_FORMAT_FORCE_UINT = 0xffffffffUL,
              } DXGI_FORMAT, *LPDXGI_FORMAT;
```

# D | Windows Messages

WM_NULL = 0x00
WM_CREATE = 0x01
WM_DESTROY = 0x02
WM_MOVE = 0x03
WM_SIZE = 0x05
WM_ACTIVATE = 0x06
WM_SETFOCUS = 0x07
WM_KILLFOCUS = 0x08
WM_ENABLE = 0x0A
WM_SETREDRAW = 0x0B
WM_SETTEXT = 0x0C
WM_GETTEXT = 0x0D
WM_GETTEXTLENGTH = 0x0E
WM_PAINT = 0x0F
WM_CLOSE = 0x10
WM_QUERYENDSESSION = 0x11
WM_QUIT = 0x12
WM_QUERYOPEN = 0x13
WM_ERASEBKGND = 0x14
WM_SYSCOLORCHANGE = 0x15
WM_ENDSESSION = 0x16
WM_SYSTEMERROR = 0x17
WM_SHOWWINDOW = 0x18
WM_CTLCOLOR = 0x19
WM_WININICHANGE = 0x1A
WM_SETTINGCHANGE = 0x1A
WM_DEVMODECHANGE = 0x1B
WM_ACTIVATEAPP = 0x1C
WM_FONTCHANGE = 0x1D
WM_TIMECHANGE = 0x1E
WM_CANCELMODE = 0x1F

WM_SETCURSOR = 0x20
WM_MOUSEACTIVATE = 0x21
WM_CHILDACTIVATE = 0x22
WM_QUEUESYNC = 0x23
WM_GETMINMAXINFO = 0x24
WM_PAINTICON = 0x26
WM_ICONERASEBKGND = 0x27
WM_NEXTDLGCTL = 0x28
WM_SPOOLERSTATUS = 0x2A
WM_DRAWITEM = 0x2B
WM_MEASUREITEM = 0x2C
WM_DELETEITEM = 0x2D
WM_VKEYTOITEM = 0x2E
WM_CHARTOITEM = 0x2F

WM_SETFONT = 0x30
WM_GETFONT = 0x31
WM_SETHOTKEY = 0x32
WM_GETHOTKEY = 0x33
WM_QUERYDRAGICON = 0x37
WM_COMPAREITEM = 0x39
WM_COMPACTING = 0x41
WM_WINDOWPOSCHANGING = 0x46
WM_WINDOWPOSCHANGED = 0x47
WM_POWER = 0x48
WM_COPYDATA = 0x4A
WM_CANCELJOURNAL = 0x4B
WM_NOTIFY = 0x4E
WM_INPUTLANGCHANGEREQUEST = 0x50
WM_INPUTLANGCHANGE = 0x51
WM_TCARD = 0x52
WM_HELP = 0x53
WM_USERCHANGED = 0x54
WM_NOTIFYFORMAT = 0x55
WM_CONTEXTMENU = 0x7B
WM_STYLECHANGING = 0x7C
WM_STYLECHANGED = 0x7D
WM_DISPLAYCHANGE = 0x7E
WM_GETICON = 0x7F
WM_SETICON = 0x80

WM_NCCREATE = 0x81
WM_NCDESTROY = 0x82
WM_NCCALCSIZE = 0x83
WM_NCHITTEST = 0x84
WM_NCPAINT = 0x85
WM_NCACTIVATE = 0x86
WM_GETDLGCODE = 0x87
WM_NCMOUSEMOVE = 0xA0
WM_NCLBUTTONDOWN = 0xA1
WM_NCLBUTTONUP = 0xA2
WM_NCLBUTTONDBLCLK = 0xA3
WM_NCRBUTTONDOWN = 0xA4
WM_NCRBUTTONUP = 0xA5
WM_NCRBUTTONDBLCLK = 0xA6
WM_NCMBUTTONDOWN = 0xA7
WM_NCMBUTTONUP = 0xA8
WM_NCMBUTTONDBLCLK = 0xA9

WM_KEYFIRST = 0x100
WM_KEYDOWN = 0x100
WM_KEYUP = 0x101
WM_CHAR = 0x102
WM_DEADCHAR = 0x103
WM_SYSKEYDOWN = 0x104
WM_SYSKEYUP = 0x105
WM_SYSCHAR = 0x106
WM_SYSDEADCHAR = 0x107
WM_KEYLAST = 0x108

WM_IME_STARTCOMPOSITION = 0x10D
WM_IME_ENDCOMPOSITION = 0x10E
WM_IME_COMPOSITION = 0x10F
WM_IME_KEYLAST = 0x10F

WM_INITDIALOG = 0x110
WM_COMMAND = 0x111
WM_SYSCOMMAND = 0x112
WM_TIMER = 0x113
WM_HSCROLL = 0x114
WM_VSCROLL = 0x115

WM_INITMENU = 0x116
WM_INITMENUPOPUP = 0x117
WM_MENUSELECT = 0x11F
WM_MENUCHAR = 0x120
WM_ENTERIDLE = 0x121

WM_CTLCOLORMSGBOX = 0x132
WM_CTLCOLOREDIT = 0x133
WM_CTLCOLORLISTBOX = 0x134
WM_CTLCOLORBTN = 0x135
WM_CTLCOLORDLG = 0x136
WM_CTLCOLORSCROLLBAR = 0x137
WM_CTLCOLORSTATIC = 0x138

WM_MOUSEFIRST = 0x200
WM_MOUSEMOVE = 0x200
WM_LBUTTONDOWN = 0x201
WM_LBUTTONUP = 0x202
WM_LBUTTONDBLCLK = 0x203
WM_RBUTTONDOWN = 0x204
WM_RBUTTONUP = 0x205
WM_RBUTTONDBLCLK = 0x206
WM_MBUTTONDOWN = 0x207
WM_MBUTTONUP = 0x208
WM_MBUTTONDBLCLK = 0x209
WM_MOUSEWHEEL = 0x20A
WM_MOUSEHWHEEL = 0x20E

WM_PARENTNOTIFY = 0x210
WM_ENTERMENULOOP = 0x211
WM_EXITMENULOOP = 0x212
WM_NEXTMENU = 0x213
WM_SIZING = 0x214
WM_CAPTURECHANGED = 0x215
WM_MOVING = 0x216
WM_POWERBROADCAST = 0x218
WM_DEVICECHANGE = 0x219

WM_MDICREATE = 0x220
WM_MDIDESTROY = 0x221

WM_MDIACTIVATE = 0x222
WM_MDIRESTORE = 0x223
WM_MDINEXT = 0x224
WM_MDIMAXIMIZE = 0x225
WM_MDITILE = 0x226
WM_MDICASCADE = 0x227
WM_MDIICONARRANGE = 0x228
WM_MDIGETACTIVE = 0x229
WM_MDISETMENU = 0x230
WM_ENTERSIZEMOVE = 0x231
WM_EXITSIZEMOVE = 0x232
WM_DROPFILES = 0x233
WM_MDIREFRESHMENU = 0x234

WM_IME_SETCONTEXT = 0x281
WM_IME_NOTIFY = 0x282
WM_IME_CONTROL = 0x283
WM_IME_COMPOSITIONFULL = 0x284
WM_IME_SELECT = 0x285
WM_IME_CHAR = 0x286
WM_IME_KEYDOWN = 0x290
WM_IME_KEYUP = 0x291

WM_MOUSEHOVER = 0x2A1
WM_NCMOUSELEAVE = 0x2A2
WM_MOUSELEAVE = 0x2A3

WM_CUT = 0x300
WM_COPY = 0x301
WM_PASTE = 0x302
WM_CLEAR = 0x303
WM_UNDO = 0x304

WM_RENDERFORMAT = 0x305
WM_RENDERALLFORMATS = 0x306
WM_DESTROYCLIPBOARD = 0x307
WM_DRAWCLIPBOARD = 0x308
WM_PAINTCLIPBOARD = 0x309
WM_VSCROLLCLIPBOARD = 0x30A
WM_SIZECLIPBOARD = 0x30B

WM_ASKCBFORMATNAME = 0x30C
WM_CHANGECBCHAIN = 0x30D
WM_HSCROLLCLIPBOARD = 0x30E
WM_QUERYNEWPALETTE = 0x30F
WM_PALETTEISCHANGING = 0x310
WM_PALETTECHANGED = 0x311

WM_HOTKEY = 0x312
WM_PRINT = 0x317
WM_PRINTCLIENT = 0x318

WM_HANDHELDFIRST = 0x358
WM_HANDHELDLAST = 0x35F
WM_PENWINFIRST = 0x380
WM_PENWINLAST = 0x38F
WM_COALESCE_FIRST = 0x390
WM_COALESCE_LAST = 0x39F
WM_DDE_FIRST = 0x3E0
WM_DDE_INITIATE = 0x3E0
WM_DDE_TERMINATE = 0x3E1
WM_DDE_ADVISE = 0x3E2
WM_DDE_UNADVISE = 0x3E3
WM_DDE_ACK = 0x3E4
WM_DDE_DATA = 0x3E5
WM_DDE_REQUEST = 0x3E6
WM_DDE_POKE = 0x3E7
WM_DDE_EXECUTE = 0x3E8
WM_DDE_LAST = 0x3E8

WM_USER = 0x400
WM_APP = 0x8000

**BSD License**

# MIT License

The MIT License

Copyright © <year> <copyright holders>

Permission is hereby granted, free of charge, to any person obtaining a copy
of this software and associated documentation files (the "Software"), to deal
in the Software without restriction, including without limitation the rights
to use, copy, modify, merge, publish, distribute, sublicense, and/or sell
copies of the Software, and to permit persons to whom the Software is
furnished to do so, subject to the following conditions:

The above copyright notice and this permission notice shall be included in
all copies or substantial portions of the Software.

THE SOFTWARE IS PROVIDED "AS IS", WITHOUT WARRANTY OF ANY
KIND, EXPRESS OR IMPLIED, INCLUDING BUT NOT LIMITED TO THE
WARRANTIES OF MERCHANTABILITY, FITNESS FOR A PARTICULAR
PURPOSE AND NONINFRINGEMENT. IN NO EVENT SHALL THE AUTHORS
OR COPYRIGHT HOLDERS BE LIABLE FOR ANY CLAIM, DAMAGES OR
OTHER
LIABILITY, WHETHER IN AN ACTION OF CONTRACT, TORT OR OTHERWISE,
ARISING FROM, OUT OF OR IN CONNECTION WITH THE SOFTWARE OR
THE USE OR OTHER DEALINGS IN THE SOFTWARE.

# The zlib/libpng License

Copyright © <year> <copyright holders>

This software is provided 'as-is', without any express or implied warranty. In no event will the authors be held liable for any damages arising from the use of this software.

Permission is granted to anyone to use this software for any purpose,
including commercial applications, and to alter it and redistribute it
freely, subject to the following restrictions:

1. The origin of this software must not be misrepresented; you must not claim that you wrote the original software. If you use this software in a product, an acknowledgment in the product documentation would be appreciated but is not required.
2. Altered source versions must be plainly marked as such, and must not be misrepresented as being the original software.
3. This notice may not be removed or altered from any source distribution.

# Index